WOUNDS THAT DO NOT BIND

Wounds That Do Not Bind

Victim-Based Perspectives on the Death Penalty

Editors

James R. Acker

David R. Karp

Assistant Editor

Jarrett B. Warshaw

Carolina Academic Press

Durham, North Carolina

Library of Congress Cataloging-in-Publication Data

Wounds that do not bind : victim-based perspectives on
the death penalty / [edited] by James R. Acker and David
Reed Karp.

   p. cm.

  ISBN 1-59460-080-5

  1. Capital punishment. 2. Victims of crimes. I. Acker,
James R., 1951- II. Karp, David R., 1964-

  HV8694.W68 2005

  364.66'0973--dc22   2005023058

CAROLINA ACADEMIC PRESS

700 Kent Street
Durham, North Carolina 27701
Telephone (919) 489-7486
Fax (919) 493-5668
www.cap-press.com

Printed in the United States of America

To Jenny, Elizabeth, and Anna
—JA

To Bill, Aimee Lee, and Pam
—DK

We dedicate this book and all its proceeds to the families of homicide victims and the victims' advocates who support them.

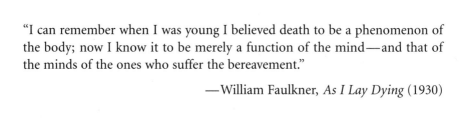

"I can remember when I was young I believed death to be a phenomenon of the body; now I know it to be merely a function of the mind—and that of the minds of the ones who suffer the bereavement."

—William Faulkner, *As I Lay Dying* (1930)

CONTENTS

WOUNDS THAT DO NOT BIND

Introduction

James R. Acker and
David R. Karp

Victims and the Death Penalty

Criminal homicide exacts incalculable harm. Individual lives are cruelly extinguished. Surviving family members—the co-victims of this devastating crime—are left without warning to cope with their loved one's violent death. Shock waves of horror, grief, and anger sweep through communities, accompanied by a profound sense of collective vulnerability. Murder, the most aggravated form of criminal homicide, evokes the law's severest punishment.

Thirty-six states and the federal government presently authorize capital punishment for murder.[1] In the remaining states the maximum punishment is life imprisonment without parole. Even in death penalty jurisdictions, capital punishment is reserved for a narrowly defined category of criminal homicide: aggravated murder (Acker and Lanier 1993a, 1993b; Bonczar and Snell 2004:2–3). The number of death sentences annually imposed and carried out in this country pales in comparison to the intentional criminal homicides committed each year (see Table 1).

Although the death penalty is statistically rare in response to criminal homicide, its symbolism and political significance makes it a central rhetorical plank in discussions about victims' rights. And because thousands upon

---

1. At this writing, twelve states and the District of Columbia provide by statute that life imprisonment (or life imprisonment without parole) is the maximum punishment for murder (Death Penalty Information Center 2005). Judicial decisions in two other states, Kansas (*State v. Marsh* 2004) and New York (*People v. LaValle* 2004), have invalidated death penalty legislation, leaving life imprisonment as the maximum authorized punishment. The U.S. Supreme Court has agreed to review the state court decision striking Kansas's death penalty law and is likely to issue a ruling in 2006 (*Kansas v. Marsh* 2005).

3

Table 1. Murders and Non-Negligent Manslaughters, Death Sentences Imposed, and Executions in the United States: 1990–2003

Year	Murders and Non-Negligent Manslaughters	Death Sentences Imposed	Executions
1990	23,440	251	23
1991	24,700	267	14
1992	23,760	286	31
1993	24,530	289	38
1994	23,330	314	31
1995	21,610	318	56
1996	19,650	320	45
1997	18,210	276	74
1998	16,970	302	68
1999	15,520	276	98
2000	15,590	232	85
2001	15,980	164	66
2002	14,054	168	71
2003	14,408	144	65

(Sources: Bonczar and Snell 2003:1, 2004:1, 14; Federal Bureau of Investigation 2002: Table 2.10, 2003: Table 2.10; Maguire and Pastore 2004:534)

thousands of family members each year are directly affected by decisions about whether capital punishment will be sought, imposed, and carried out in individual cases, the death penalty's personal toll on murder co-victims is substantial. Among the many justifications offered in support of capital punishment is its presumed value in providing redress to society in the name of murder victims and offering some measure of solace to victims' survivors. Yet we know surprisingly little about many important related issues, including the extent to which co-victims are involved in and how they are affected by prosecutors' decisions about whether to pursue a capital sentence; the significance of presenting victim impact evidence in capital trials; the stresses imposed on survivors by the criminal justice system in murder cases, from police investigations through the lengthy process of trials, appeals, and clemency decisions; how co-victims prepare for and what they experience following an execution; how co-victims' needs, feelings, and attitudes change over time; and a host of others. The purpose of this volume is to explore victim-based perspectives on capital punishment.

Terms like "justice" and "closure" are frequently advanced to cement the connection between capital punishment, murder victims, and victims' survivors (Gross and Matheson 2003; Zimring 2003:58–63). Anecdotal accounts about co-victims' feelings, needs, and priorities in the wake of murder are plentiful yet contradictory. These discordant expressions underscore the vast chasm between what many people assume—and perhaps want to believe—and what we actually know about how the death penalty and the death penalty process affect murder victims' surviving family members.

For example, victims were the focal point of media accounts when serial killer Michael Ross was executed in Connecticut in May 2005—marking the first death sentence carried out in that state in forty-five years. Ross insisted on waiving appeals that remained available to him, explaining that he "wanted to spare the families of his victims … further torment" (Tuohy 2005:A1). Newspaper stories featured the biographies of the eight young women Ross was known to have murdered, along with moving remembrances offered by families and friends (Tuohy and Griffin 2005). Following Ross's execution, Governor M. Jodi Rell declared, "I hope that there is at least some measure of relief and closure for [the slain victims'] families" (ibid.). Meanwhile, the chief state's attorney admonished, "And so I say today, it's time to forget about Michael Ross, but we should never forget about his victims and we should always remember and embrace their families" (Associated Press 2005a). One victim's father thanked jurors and the state "for finally giving us the justice that our children are due" (ibid.). Another co-victim remarked, "I thought I would feel closure, but I felt anger just watching him lay [sic] there and just sleep after what he did to these women" (Yardley 2005:B1).[2]

Co-victims are united by the grievous event of a loved one's murder, but they are not a monolithic group. Their thoughts and reactions regarding capital punishment vary markedly. Some report achieving "closure," or at least a measure of relief, in the knowledge that their loved one's killer has been executed (see Miller 2004; Ratcliffe 2005; Weber 2005). Others emphatically reject that closure is possible following the murder of a spouse or relative and even "bristle at the word" (Korosec 2005:A1). The widow of one murder victim exclaimed, "Closure is something that society's come up with to make them feel better … It'll never be over" (Petersen 2004:A1). Following the execution of her daughter's murderer, another co-victim commented, "There will be no closure while I live" (Associated Press 2005b). A mother whose daughter was slain explained, "There's a hole there that doesn't close … I don't think I'm going to get closure … maybe peace" (Associated Press 2003).

---

2. The same co-victim also volunteered, "but I'm sure I will feel some closure soon" (Tuohy 2005:A1).

Although a majority of Americans report being in favor of the death penalty (Bohm 2003), for most citizens the issue remains mercifully theoretical. But murder co-victims have involuntarily been thrust into a position where the question has become intensely personal. Many passionately support capital punishment for the murder of their loved ones. One co-victim, when allowed to confront her daughter's murderer in court, told him, "I want them to put you to death as soon as possible ... You deserve to burn in hell for all eternity" (Finz 2005:A1). For some, executions bring "[t]he satisfaction ... [of] knowing justice is done" (Shurley 2004:15). Others express relief about their own and others' safety. "'I'll be sleeping a little better at night,' said [the daughter of a murder victim following the offender's execution]. 'I know there will be no chance of me ever running into him ever, ever'" (Miller 2004:B1; see also Hallifax 2003).

Still other murder victims' survivors repudiate capital punishment altogether (King 2003; Pelke 2003). They do so for various reasons—some to honor the values and memories of their slain loved one (Hallifax 2003), others in part to avoid lengthy and disruptive legal proceedings (Schieber and Schieber 2004), and still others because of personal opposition to the death penalty. Following their son's murder, one couple explained, "We don't condone killing by anybody or the state, for any reason" (Green 2003:B1). In another case, a murder victim's widow stated, "My kids learned that another killing, even if it is by the state, doesn't help and that it does not bring my husband, Carlos, their nano, back" (Terrell 2005:A5).

Questions about the significance of capital punishment to murder victims' survivors, and the impact of the death penalty and related legal procedures on co-victims and their recovery process, far outstrip the answers. Individuals and their reactions clearly differ. There is much that we do not understand. Criminal justice system responses and legal and administrative policies are too important to be established on oversimplified and potentially erroneous assumptions about what co-victims experience and need in the wake of murder.

Pathways to this Collection

The co-victims who share their stories in the collection are brave souls who demonstrate that the death penalty is not merely a "hot topic" for school debate teams, but touches many lives deeply and irreversibly. As editors of this volume, we consider ourselves to be social scientists and remain committed to a careful consideration of all available evidence and perspectives. But we are also two persons who are concerned about the death penalty and its various consequences, especially on victims' families. Therefore, it makes sense for us to share how we each become interested in editing this book.

David Karp's Path

My history of this project traces back to four events. The first was the murder of my wife's friend Wendy Cheek in 1985. Twenty years later, the offender, Robert Fairbank, remains on death row in California. Some part of me is always aware of the grief experienced by Wendy's sister and parents.

The second event was a hike in the Adirondack Mountains of New York with a friend and local judge. We spent much of it discussing the constitutionality of capital punishment and my interest in restorative justice. I told him that I knew of cases where family members of homicide victims had met with offenders in order to get questions answered and convey the depth of their pain—as a step in their healing journey. While we enjoyed climbing up the steep banks beside a waterfall, we pondered if the death penalty is invoked in the name of victims, and whether executions preclude at least some victims from an important opportunity for recovery.

I took these questions with me to a professional meeting in 2002 in Myrtle Beach, North Carolina. I was there to conduct a workshop on a New York City probation program that included both restorative justice and treatment components. But I dined with experts in victims' services and asked them about the concerns of victims' families in capital cases. What I learned was that the research was slim, but the needs were great. That the victims' community had been ignored by death penalty scholars. That the lengthy criminal justice process in capital cases was grueling for victims' families. That many detested the word "closure" and believed it misrepresented the path of recovery. That the victims' community was internally conflicted about the death penalty.

Finally, I had lunch with Jim Acker and Charlie Lanier, both death penalty scholars at the University at Albany School of Criminal Justice, and David Kaczynski, brother of Ted Kaczynski (widely known as the Unabomber). Because of the Justice Department's handling of the Kaczynski case, David ultimately became the director of New Yorkers Against the Death Penalty. At lunch, I learned that David had been reaching out to victims' families and was hoping to sponsor a forum where family members could share their views about the death penalty. And I learned about an organization of victims' families who were opposed to the death penalty—Murder Victims Families for Reconciliation. Jim and I committed to creating a forum to discuss these issues, and enlisted the support of Anne Seymour, a victims' advocate and co-director of the Washington, D.C., organization Justice Solutions.

Jim Acker's Path

My engagement with the death penalty began on exclusively intellectual ground when *Furman v. Georgia* (1972)—the landmark Supreme Court decision that temporarily halted capital punishment in this country—was assigned reading in one of my law-school classes. To this day, I remain enthralled by the rich lessons of history, government, ethics, sociology, and jurisprudence that spill from this epochal ruling. Just a heartbeat after entering the legal profession, or so it now seems, I was appointed to represent a man accused of capital murder in North Carolina at a time when the gas chamber was a staple of the criminal justice process. The responsibility of defending a person whose life was in jeopardy by virtue of this charge abruptly changed my perspective on capital punishment. I had moved from books to the front lines.

Practicing law reinforces, if it does not inculcate, an insular view of the world—one dominated by the advocate's duty to advance a client's cause. As a defense attorney, I focused narrowly on the interests of those accused and convicted of crimes and on closely connected procedural safeguards. In a sense, it was my job to deny responsibility for criminal victimization on my clients' behalf, and to minimize culpability when guilt could not be negated. "Victims' rights" sounded decidedly out of place in this worldview, more closely resembling a threat than an aspiration.

When I left law practice for academia, my interest in capital punishment continued, but the issues gradually assumed a subtler and more variegated hue. I have explored many questions relating to the death penalty and encountered numerous others while speaking about the topic. I have consistently disclaimed the ability to respond meaningfully to one interrogatory—a question that often (but not inevitably) is delivered more in the form of a challenge: "How would you feel if a member of your family was murdered?" I hope to the very core of my being that I am never in a position to answer that inquiry. I also know that others have tragically been forced to go there. And although I cannot appreciate the depths of what they experience and feel, I know intuitively that whatever punishment might befall an offender, society's response to criminal homicide cannot in good conscience ignore their plight.

Similar thoughts were on others' minds. As David has described, they were voiced one day over a lunch that we shared with Charlie Lanier and David Kaczynski. Sensing the complexity of the issues, we agreed that bringing people together to talk about them should be our starting point. We knew that academic perspectives would be important, but considered the insights of homicide co-victims to be indispensable. David Karp continued the conversation with Anne Seymour, whose energies fortified us tenfold. When Beau Breslin joined our planning group, we were on our way to developing what we hoped would be a groundbreaking and productive conference.

The Skidmore Conference

A conference held in September 2003 on the campus of Skidmore College addressed "The Impact of the Death Penalty on Victims' Families" and served as a bridge between the questions explored there and this volume. The conference, co-sponsored by Skidmore College, the University at Albany School of Criminal Justice, and Justice Solutions, Inc. (a nonprofit organization devoted to crime victims and co-founded by conference participant and contributor to this volume, Anne Seymour), was unprecedented—at least to our knowledge—in its mission and composition. It brought together over the span of three days a national representation of approximately forty co-victims, victim advocates, and academics from multiple disciplines to share their insights, perspectives, and knowledge about murder co-victimization and the death penalty. The dialogue began with a candid and free-flowing session among co-victims; it concluded with a plenary session that summarized what had been learned during the conference and aimed to capitalize on the groundwork that had been laid. Many of the contributors to this volume attended the conference.

Widely diverse views were expressed at the conference about matters that were both acutely practical (such as the logistics of cleaning blood from a murder scene and how best to keep open communication channels with a prosecutor's office) and loftily conceptual (embracing healing, justice, pathos, and spiritualism). Some consensus emerged as well. Participants were largely joined regarding the significance of the questions being addressed and in recognizing that much remained to be accomplished. Those sentiments gave rise to this volume.

A Précis

In keeping with the tradition of the Skidmore conference, we regard this book as a beginning. Its chapters offer no final answers about what co-victims experience, feel, and most urgently need when a loved one is murdered, nor about how capital punishment and the criminal justice process generally figure into that mix. Indeed, the chapters strongly suggest that the pursuit of final answers would be both futile and counterproductive; that to a considerable extent each co-victim of criminal homicide is destined to find his or her own way on a journey with no clear road map or destination. Yet we are confident that the book's contributors advance questions and offer perspectives that brightly illuminate matters of importance to individual co-victims, criminal justice and related service providers, academic researchers, and legal and social policymakers. We hope that this collection will stimulate discussion and research about murder co-victimization and capital punishment and help promote just and meaningful individual and societal responses.

The book is divided into four parts, although the subjects addressed in the different sections are not so easily compartmentalized. Part I presents "Personal Accounts: The Experiences of Co-Victims of Murder and Other Crimes." The chapters in this section are gripping and tragic. All were authored by individuals touched directly by criminal violence—people whose children (Linda White, Stanley and Phyllis Rosenbluth, Roberta Roper, and Marsha Kimble), father (Shane Wagner), or brothers (Charisse Coleman, Dan Levey) were murdered, or, in Gary Wright's case, who nearly died in a life-shattering explosion orchestrated by the brother of his co-author, David Kaczynski. These chapters take readers into worlds where none should have to go. The authors eloquently and poignantly share with us their victimization experiences, their interactions with the criminal justice system, and their thoughts about reclaiming broken lives, deciphering the meaning of justice, and supporting or opposing capital punishment. They demonstrate that stereotypes and generalizations regarding them and their attitudes about the death penalty are unjustifiable and frequently injurious.

Collectively, they attest to the truism that murder co-victims are a remarkably diverse lot. Some favor the death penalty, but many do not. Their stories reflect a case that resulted in a death sentence, but the offender still lives on death row; cases where the offenders have been executed; another where the offender, previously sitting on death row, was given clemency by a state governor. In one account, the defendants were not eligible for the death penalty because they were too young; in another the defendant received a lesser sentence through a plea agreement. One author tells us that the jury chose life sentences in lieu of capital punishment; and in another case a capital prosecution was terminated in lieu of a negotiated guilty plea and sentence of life imprisonment without parole, motivated largely by the offender's mental illness. Some contributors experienced the intense media frenzy associated with celebrated cases, such as the Unabomber and Oklahoma City bomber Timothy McVeigh. One author chose to meet with the offender as part of her recovery process; another sought such a meeting, but was denied permission. One became close friends with the offender's brother.

Part II offers "Legal Perspectives" relating to murder, victimization, and the death penalty. The four chapters in this section examine the legal identity and rights of victims of crime. They focus on decisions made by actors within the legal system—prosecutors, courts, and governors—that relate directly to the capital punishment of murderers. James Acker and Jeanna Mastrocinque describe the legal evolution of crime victims' status and question whether the death penalty, which represents a social policy response to murder, is well suited to redress the needs of individual co-victims. Wayne Logan probes the legal relevance of murder co-victims' opinions to capital charging and sentencing decisions and analyzes the Supreme Court's changing justifications in rulings addressing the admissibility of victim impact evidence in capital trials. The chapters by Charles Lanier and Beau Breslin, and Austin Sarat, dwell particularly on Governor George Ryan's decision immediately before leaving office to commute to life imprisonment the sentences of all prisoners on Illinois's death row. The authors closely examine the justifications for Governor Ryan's actions and the ramifications of the blanket commutations for the murder victims' surviving family members.

Legal perspectives give way to "Research Perspectives" in Part III of the book. Margaret Vandiver leads off by highlighting the urgent need for researchers to marshal systematic evidence bearing on several compelling unanswered questions concerning the impact of the death penalty and the capital punishment process on murder victims' family members. The remaining chapters explore two broad questions. Some authors (David Karp and Jarrett Warshaw, and Theodore Eisenberg, Stephen Garvey and Martin Wells) focus on the responsiveness of jurors charged with making sentencing decisions in capital trials to testimony about the characteristics of murder victims and the hardships endured by surviving family members. Other authors (Mark Reed and Brenda Blackwell, and Judith Kay) shed light on murder co-victims' post-crime needs and how official procedures and outcomes can exacerbate or be responsive to the survivors' plight. The chapter by Mark Umbreit and colleagues reports on the experiences of surviving family members who participated in unique face-to-face, carefully mediated meetings with their loved ones' murderers shortly before the offenders were executed.

Part IV of the book explores "Policy Implications: Capital Punishment, Criminal Justice Practices, and Victim Services." Peter Loge scrutinizes the rhetoric used in discussions involving capital punishment and victims' rights and offers strategies for bridging gulfs between interest groups and stakeholders—which, he argues, would redound to the benefit of murder co-victims. Michael Radelet and Dawn Stanley describe a unique college class offered at the University of Colorado, which saw undergraduate students and families unite to identify unsolved homicides and create support and informational networks for the co-victims of unsolved murders. Tammy Krause urges criminal defense teams to place increased reliance on victim outreach specialists to work directly with murder victims' families and prosecutors to identify, and—to the extent consistent with their roles as legal advocates—mediate mutually agreeable case resolutions. Carroll Ann Ellis, Karin Ho, and Anne Seymour combine their decades of experience as victim advocates to recommend key policies and action steps that should be implemented to serve the best interests of co-victims of criminal homicide.

We do not presume that definitive answers emerge in the following pages to the daunting litany of questions encompassing murder victims and capital punishment. At the same time, we believe that the experiences recounted, the questions posed, the arguments made, and the research results reported in the ensuing chapters significantly enhance our insights concerning victim-based perspectives on the death penalty. It is our hope that readers will gain a deeper understanding of the issues confronting murder victims' family members, including the specific relevance and consequences of capital punishment to individual survivors and as a legal and social policy tool. Ultimately, we anticipate the day when the needs of murder victims' survivors can be more perfectly harmonized with the procedures and imperatives of social justice.

References

Acker, James R. and Charles S. Lanier. 1993a. "The Dimensions of Capital Murder." *Criminal Law Bulletin* 29:379–417.

_____. 1993b. "Aggravating Circumstances and Capital Punishment Law: Rhetoric or Real Reforms?" *Criminal Law Bulletin* 29:467–501.

Associated Press. 2005a. "Man Called 'Destroyer of Children' Is Executed." (May 18). Available at http://web.lexis-nexis.com/universe/document?_m=369016e03e60774 e112 (consulted 15 June 2005).

Associated Press. 2005b. "Quotes About Connecticut's Execution of Michael Ross" (May 13). Available at http://web.lexis-nexis.com/universe/document?_m= 0bd781936455d9d2490 (consulted 15 June 2005).

Associated Press. 2003. "Clemency Hearing Brings Back Memories for Victims' Families." (July 7). Available at http://web.lexis-nexis.com/universe/document?_m= 369016e03e60774e112 (consulted 15 June 2005).

Bohm, Robert M. 2003. "American Death Penalty Opinion: Past, Present, and Future." Pp. 27–54 in *America's Experiment With Capital Punishment: Reflections on the Past, Present, and Future of the Ultimate Penal Sanction*, 2d ed., edited by James R. Acker, Robert M. Bohm, and Charles S. Lanier. Durham, NC: Carolina Academic Press.

Bonczar, Thomas P. and Tracy L. Snell. 2004. *Bulletin: Capital Punishment, 2003*. U.S. Department of Justice, Bureau of Justice Statistics.

_____. 2003. *Bulletin: Capital Punishment, 2002.* U.S. Department of Justice, Bureau of Justice Statistics.

Death Penalty Information Center. 2005. "State by State Information." Available at http://www.deathpenaltyinfo.org/state/ (consulted 16 June 2005).

Federal Bureau of Investigation. 2003. "Uniform Crime Reports: Crime in the United States—2003." Available at http://www.fbi.gov/ucr/03cius.htm (consulted 16 June 2005).

_____. 2002. "Uniform Crime Reports: Crime in the United States—2002." Available at http://www.fbi.gov/ucr/02cius.htm (consulted 16 June 2005).

Finz, Stacy. 2005. "Families Pour Out Anguish and Rage; Before Judge Sentences Him, Peterson Silently Faces Former In-laws." *San Francisco Chronicle,* 17 March 2005, A1.

Furman v. Georgia. 1972. 408 U.S. 238.

Green, Frank. 2003. "Views Vary on Death Penalty: Some Murder Victims' Kin Reject Capital Punishment; Others Endorse the Sanction." *Richmond Times Dispatch,* 22 December 2003, B1.

Gross, Samuel R. and Daniel J. Matheson. 2003. "What They Say at the End: Capital Victims' Families and the Press." *Cornell Law Review.* 88:486–516.

Hallifax, Jackie. 2003. "Victims of Death Row Inmates Support, Oppose Executions." Associated Press (July 1). Available at http://web.lexis-nexis.com/universe/document?_m=2995dd2309d402441e4 (consulted 15 June 2005).

Kansas v. Marsh. 2005. 125 S. Ct. 2517.

King, Rachel. 2003. *Don't Kill in Our Names: Families of Murder Victims Speak Out Against the Death Penalty.* New Brunswick, NJ: Rutgers University Press.

Korosec, Thomas. 2005. "Oklahoma City Bombing: 10 Years Later." *The Houston Chronicle,* 19 April 2005, A1.

Maguire, Kathleen and Ann L. Pastore (eds.). 2004. *Sourcebook of Criminal Justice Statistics—2002.* Washington, DC: U.S. Department of Justice, Bureau of Justice Statistics.

Miller, S. A. (2004). "Oken Executed After Appeals Denied." *The Washington Times,* 18 June 2004, B1.

Pelke, Bill. 2003. *Journey of Hope ... From Violence to Healing.* Xlibris Corporation.

People v. LaValle. 2004. 817 N.E.2d 341 (N.Y.).

Petersen, Bo. 2004. "Victim's Family Awaits Killer's Death." *The Post and Courier* (Charleston, S.C.), 15 March 2004, A1.

Ratcliffe, Heather. 2005. "Police Detective Sees Killer 'Get what he had coming.'" *St. Louis Post-Dispatch,* 17 March 2005, B1.

Schieber, Sylvester J. and Vicki A. Schieber. 2004. "Justice Not Served." *The Washington Post,* 13 June 2004, B8.

Shurley, Traci. 2004. "Mother Pushes to Watch Killer Die." *Arkansas Democrat-Gazette,* 4 January 2004, 15.

State v. Marsh. 2004. 102 P.3d 445 (Kan.).

Terrell, Steve. 2005. "Slain Lawyer's Widow Opposes Death Penalty." *The Santa Fe New Mexican,* 1 February 2005, A5.

Tuohy, Lynne. 2005. "Execution Concludes Decades of Legal Limbo for Families; Ross Saga Ends." *Hartford Courant,* 13 May 2005, A1.

Tuohy, Lynne and Alaine Griffin. 2005. "Eight Lives Cut Short: Families, Friends Share Their Memories of the Young Women Killed by Michael Ross Two Decades Ago." *Hartford Courant*, 23 January 2005, A1.

Weber, Harry R. 2005. "Georgia Execution Brings Closure for Murdered Teen's Family." *Associated Press State and Local Wire* (Jan. 26). Available at http://web.lexis-nexis.com/universe/document?_m=2995dd2309d402441e4(consulted 15 June 2005).

Yardley, William. 2005. "Execution in Connecticut." *New York Times*, 14 May 2005, B1.

Zimring, Franklin E. 2003. *The Contradictions of American Capital Punishment*. New York: Oxford University Press.

PART I

Personal Accounts: The Experiences of Co-Victims of Murder, Other Crime Victims, and Victim Advocates

CHAPTER 1

MATTERS OF LIFE OR DEATH

Charisse Coleman

At a little before 1:00 a.m., closing time on a Friday night in August 1995, three last-minute customers walked into the Thrifty Liquor Store in Shreveport, Louisiana, where my older brother, Russell, worked as a stock clerk. Russell sat on the turnstile near the entrance, waiting for his co-worker behind the cash register to toss him the keys he'd need to lock up. Three guys walked around the store, not seeming to look for anything in particular, not in a hurry to leave. Then the tall, skinny one asked Frank, the clerk who was bagging up the day's trash, which beer was cheaper, the Bull or the Old Milwaukee? The short, stocky guy he'd come in with stood at the counter, buying a bag of chips and a Sprite. The third—just a kid, too young even to be in a liquor store—hovered around, not saying or buying anything.

Russell perched on the turnstile, his back to the counter, still waiting for the keys. Frank walked to the back of the store in search of garbage bags. Collette, the cashier, looked down at her register, punching in the sale of the Sprite and chips, just as the short guy stepped away from the counter, saying he'd left his money out in the car. No one saw a thing. Just the sound of three gunshots, and then Russell lay bleeding to death on the rug in front of the entrance to the store.

No one knows why Bobby Lee Hampton, the short, stocky "customer," decided to launch the robbery with a murder that night. Maybe not even Bobby knows. After shooting Russell in the back, Hampton threatened several times to kill Frank—if he moved, if he got up off the floor where Bobby had put him, if he couldn't break into the manager's locked cubicle, if he couldn't get into the strong box in the cubicle and hand over the cash inside. Then, after the register drawers and the manager's office had been ransacked, Hampton was the first to head for the door, though he issued a command to his accomplices before he left: "Take care of the other two," he said.

Charisse Coleman (left) with brothers Cameron, Russell, and mother Barbara, 1983.

Had Bobby's cousin (the lanky, bargain-hunting robber), or that cousin's half brother (the sixteen-year-old robber) followed his orders, it's likely three dead bodies would have lain on the floor of Thrifty Liquor instead of only one—no eyewitness identifications, no arrests, and no trial. But they declined. Within a couple of weeks, all three had been arrested. And nearly two years later, in late May of 1997, a sequestered Caddo Parish jury convicted Bobby Lee Hampton of first-degree murder.

Hugo Holland, the prosecutor in the case, had told my family long before we came to trial that, in the event of a first-degree conviction, Hampton had a good chance of getting a death sentence. Hugo wanted Hampton on death row; but he said if our family was unanimous in wanting him to seek a life sentence instead, he would. "But if there's any disagreement among you," he let us know, "then I'll be trying to get that jury to vote for execution."

I am opposed to the death penalty. Before Russell's murder, my mother would probably have said she opposed it, too. But now, everything in her clamored for the death of her son's killer, even as she understood that nothing could bring Russell back or make up his loss to her. It's not that she rethought the moral, political, or societal implications of executions after Russell died and then realigned her position. She didn't care if no one was ever again executed anywhere on earth, as long as the chance remained that Bobby Hampton might be. When she thought about Hampton's being in prison for the rest of his life, she could not bear the idea of him free to walk around, think, feel, read letters from home, watch TV, eat, or even *exist,* no matter how reduced that existence might be.

I'd seen my mother suffer the private indignation of being divided against herself: wanting Hampton to die, not wanting to be a person who would want such a thing, wanting it anyway. She surprised me a little when the possibility of a plea bargain arose. Hampton's defense wondered if we would be willing to accept a sentence of life imprisonment with no eligibility for probation or parole. Mama said yes. She knew the risks of trial and feared the emotional cost, besides. She said she'd accept those terms rather than face the remote but unendurable chance of a jury's granting Hampton an acquittal. But no one could convince Bobby Hampton to take the deal, and so we'd gone to trial.

Like me, my younger brother, Cameron, was not in favor of executions (though before we came to trial, he would change his mind about that); but we agreed that we should follow Mama's lead in the decision. I don't know why it felt right to defer to her, but it did. The sum total of my immediate family now numbers exactly two: my mother and Cameron. Our tiny band was about as battered and sad and weak and angry as we'd ever have occasion to be. Maybe it was passivity or fatigue or cowardice on my part, but I just couldn't see arguing with my bereft mother over the one thing she believed would be the answer to her agony, even if I had the deepest doubts about the truth of that. I had lost a brother. She had lost her firstborn child. Maybe the strength of my claim in the decision just seemed weaker than hers. And why try to reason with her (or, God forbid, argue) about beliefs, when the prosecutor was going to go after the death penalty, anyway, once he knew we were divided over the issue.

My concession to my mother aside, I do not believe that personal feelings of vengeance should dictate our public policy, our laws, or the standards by which we govern our society, especially those which then lead to our killing citizens. That hunger for retribution is understandable and real and powerful and even important. What is equally important is how we, both individually and as a society, are going to address those longings when they take hold.

What I've found, from my own experience, and from time spent among many other families of murder victims, is that the world generally tries to yank victims' families around in one of two opposing directions. Most often, we are expected to keep our sense of injury and rage whipped into a constant call for retribution (putting many families who do *not* seek the execution of their loved one's killer "in the wrong"), as if the only decent way to honor loss is to take another life, to create more brokenhearted families, more fatherless children (it is mostly men who are executed), and to further assault communities already ravaged by violence, poverty, racism, and other problems. The pressures on victims' families to demand this dubious and macabre tribute to their loved ones can be tremendous, and not least of all from some of the victims' rights groups themselves. (Need I point out that if the death penalty were not an option, then all of this pressure and manipulation of people already torn apart by personal tragedy would instantly disappear?)

The other extreme, of course, is the pressure to eradicate any strong feelings as quickly as possible. Our cultural fixation with looking on the bright side, and sugaring up the bitter acid in all the lemons life sends our way, verges on hysterical, if not outright pathological. Grieving families are leaned on in ways small and large, subtle and overt, to hurry up and *get better*. We are often coerced—smoothly, and under the guise of concern—by friends, family, clergy, even support groups, to quickly turn the rage and devastation we feel into forgiveness. What would happen if we changed our message to families shattered by violence from: "Here, let us help you get over this," to: "We are here with you. We offer our presence for the duration of your pain and anger. We honor the strength and truth of those feelings. We are here to help to keep you from losing yourself in sorrow, and we will be here when you are able to step more fully into yourself as the weight of sorrow begins to lift."

What if the town criers for retribution and punishment changed the question from: "Don't you want to kill the guy who did this to you?" to: "How can we heal this family, this community?" (A community, by the way, that often includes the killer's family.)

And of course, I can't help wondering: How is the State any different from your garden-variety murderer if it shows no more conscience, creativity, imagination, or intelligence than to simply mow down whatever obstacle to order it has identified, even if that "obstacle" should happen to be a human being? Why should we follow Bobby Hampton's model for creative problem solving? Shouldn't the State seek to conduct itself more nobly than the worst of its own citizens, instead of embracing the crude tactics of thugs? And what to make of the obvious hypocrisy in declaring that killing is wrong, and to prove just how seriously we believe that, we're going to kill people who kill people? "Do as I say, not as I do," never has struck me as a terribly effective style of governance, certainly not a deterrence. Indeed, a study published in *The New York Times* in September 2000 showed that, during the last twenty years, the murder rate in states that have capital punishment has been 48 to 101 percent higher than in states without the death penalty.

But Russell had been murdered in Louisiana, and Louisiana is a death-penalty state. My family was fortunate to have a prosecutor who would actually have taken our wishes into account, if only they'd been in accord. Since they weren't, the penalty itself came into play as the jury took up the job of deciding Hampton's sentence.

The first-degree murder conviction had triggered the trial's penalty phase— time for the jury to hear testimony meant to assist them in deciding Hampton's punishment: life imprisonment without benefit of probation or parole, or death by lethal injection. Mama, Cameron, and I would be the first to testify for the prosecution. We gave what are known as "victim impact statements," though the term is something of a misnomer. Much to our relief, we were not required to compose an actual statement and deliver it from the witness stand. Instead, Hugo let us know that he would be asking each of us a short series of questions; we had only to respond. Normally, he said, a family selects one representative among them to testify. Our request that we should all have a turn to speak was apparently a bit unorthodox, but Hugo had willingly divided the material into thirds, letting each of us establish a small portion of the testimony he wanted the jury to hear.

Why did I choose to testify? Why not at least honor my opposition to capital punishment by staying silent, by not participating in a process that could lead to an outcome I found insupportable? It's a fair question, and not one I can necessarily answer to anyone's satisfaction, least of all my own. What I can say is that, along with the opportunity to speak my love and sorrow in the public forum of the murder trial, and my decision to embrace that opportunity, came an agreement to enter a sort of devil's compact.

How else to describe the intensity of the dilemma? Part of the dictionary definition of "testify" is "to bear witness." If my bearing witness to my love for Russell brought another human being closer to death, then it felt like a terribly selfish thing to do. Yet I desperately wanted to speak. It would be the only chance I had to say even one small, true thing about Russell, my love for him, our loss. The formality of court proceedings would take the act of speaking to the level of public ritual, participated in and acted out, not only by me, but by friends and witnesses, by people the community regarded as authorities, and by a representation of the community itself—those twelve people sitting in the jury box.

If Russell had been a soldier, maybe we would have had uniforms and "Taps" and a folded flag to say: *The world beyond your family makes note of what another member of society has taken from you.* If we'd been more devout, maybe our religion would have given us something to enact. But neither of those scenarios held for me and my family, and no other offer had come along to have our experience recognized, treated seriously, publicly, and with respect. However imperfect the setup, I couldn't resist the pull of that ritual, even one created by the criminal justice system and played out in a worn, cheerless room of dirt-brown walls and speckled linoleum floors. Here, in a Louisiana courtroom, we would be able to speak in our own voices, and attention would be paid.

Yet I could not escape the obvious: to the extent that I spoke with any eloquence at all, to the degree that the jury felt closer to Russell, closer to our suffering, they might be moved, however slightly, nearer to a choice I found repellent and wrong. I could keep silent and preserve the integrity of my beliefs (which felt remote and abstract compared to the desire to declare my love for my slain brother), or I could swallow my discomfort and take the stand. The fact that my desire to bear witness overpowered some of my deepest beliefs about right and wrong only added to the confusion and suffering of being a murdered man's sister. There is so much that feels wrong about losing someone you love to murder, so much, somehow, that makes you feel *in* the wrong. My decision to speak just became another stone weight tossed onto the pile of wrongness that had been accumulating since the moment of Russell's death.

In Louisiana, since there are no definitive guidelines for what is admissible in victim impact statements, each judge must decide the scope of that testimony according to their own interpretation of legal precedent. One by one, then, out of each other's hearing, and out of hearing of the jury, Hugo led us through the questions he'd planned so the judge could rule on what we would be allowed to say.

The parameters proved very narrow. Cameron could not testify about the income he'd lost when his depression in the wake of Russell's murder crippled his ability to function in his job. He wasn't allowed to mention depression at all, in fact. Similarly, the judge ruled that Hugo could not elicit my testimony describing months of insomnia (as long as I thought of him, Russell existed, but as soon as I surrendered consciousness, he died all over again; sleep, then, became a betrayal, an abandonment, something to trade for keeping Russell "alive"). Since sleeplessness could not be mentioned, the disruption to my work and general well-being that resulted from being awake all night and sleeping away the daylight hours would also go unremarked. My mother would not be telling the jury about the debilitation of a sorrowful fury that had no outlet, or of her often diminished ability to concentrate (an avid reader, eighteen months after the murder she found herself still unable to start, much less finish, a book). We were not permitted to tell of the friendships that had evaporated overnight, or of the friends who had drifted more gradually away, steered by the duration of our unassailable grief and their own queasiness and fear, as if the violence that had befallen us might somehow be contagious. My family and I would not be speaking of the blank and wordless stares we'd endured from some of our co-workers and neighbors when they learned what had happened to Russell, news that apparently had the ability to disconnect the common citizen's usual reflexes of simple courtesy.

These homely narrations of what, besides Russell, had been taken from us when Bobby Hampton fired his gun gave the most accurate sense of the "impact" we lived with every day. Our moment-to-moment existence, steeped in the acid of violent loss, had been corroded by sorrow and outrage; nearly two years after the murder, weakness still often reigned where before we had known strength; ease remained elusive, and effort, even to accomplish the most quotidian routines of life, had become the demoralizing norm. Almost worse than the diminishments themselves, none of us could predict when the effects would fade—or even trust that, eventually, they would.

Apparently, though, this is not the sort of portrait the criminal justice system, at least in the state of Louisiana, seeks to put before the jury when it asks for victim impact statements. It's still not clear to me, actually, just what purpose a victim's family's appearance in court is supposed to serve. Perhaps it is just that: an appearance. In a crime where the victim himself is so resoundingly absent, this is the closest a jury will get to having an actual person to connect with, to envision, to imagine being destroyed by the murderer's gun. At any rate, in the end, my mother, Cameron, and I were able to give the jury only the sketchiest portrait of our family, a few details about Russell as a person, and the basic fact of our affection for him. And we were, each of us, given the chance to declare the obvious: that we missed him.

The prosecutor then brought forward witnesses to document Hampton's long history of felony convictions and violent behavior—assaults, attempted robberies, the fighting in (and the attempted escape from) juvenile jail—a history that ran unabated from his early teens to the day of the Thrifty murder and robbery when he was 26. Corrections officers testified about Hampton's less-than-stellar disciplinary record during his eighteen-month incarceration while awaiting trial, and about finding gang recruiting material in his cell.

And then a slight, demure woman took the stand. Dressed in a crisp, spring suit of navy blue trimmed in white, her brown hair curling softly around her shoulders and framing her thin face, Joyce Gorecki raised her hand and swore in a soft, firm voice to tell the truth. In the summer of 1995, a few nights before the Thrifty Liquor Store robbery and murder, Joyce had been the night-shift manager at a twenty-four-hour Kroger when Hampton and his cousin turned up with ski masks and guns. Hampton grabbed Joyce by the hair and smashed her face into the cigarette display, demanding the combination to the store's safe. But Joyce didn't know. It was only her fourth night as manager, and no one had told her how to open the safe. Hampton, enraged that the only cash available lay in the register drawers Joyce had been counting up, pistol whipped her until one eye puffed shut and yanked her so hard by the hair that he tore a hank from her scalp. She'd seen the strands threaded through his fingers as she lay curled in a ball on the floor while he kicked her in the ribs.

Joyce's quiet dignity as she spoke stood in stark contrast to the violence she described. At last, she recalled, when she thought that Hampton and his helper had left the store and that it was safe to call for help, she pulled herself up from the floor. When she got to her feet, however, she found herself staring into the muzzle of Hampton's gun. "And I thought: If he's going to shoot me in the head, I don't want to see it coming. So I turned around, and the only thing I focused on was my little grandson's face. I thought, if he's going to take me out, I'm not going to be taken out on a bad note; I'm going to focus on an innocent little face."

I saw a man on the jury glare long and hard at Hampton; one of the women flicked away a tear; another man stared down into his hands, shaking his head slowly side to side.

Myself, I felt a shock of gratitude and admiration. Admiration, obviously, for Joyce Gorecki's courage in telling a roomful of strangers about the most horrifying moments of her life; for the simplicity of her telling, a simplicity that made whatever she said cut to the bone. The gratitude, though, came as a surprise. Russell's murder was still—not impossible to believe, exactly, but impossible, somehow, to comprehend. No matter how many times I heard the facts of what had happened, no matter how clearly constructed the narrative, my mind refused to absorb the sense of what it knew.

Sitting for days in a courtroom, mere yards from the man responsible for the shooting, had not fused the facts into any clearer, more graspable shape. Hampton's impassive bearing, if anything, made the reality of what he'd done even more remote and bizarre. He gave off no heat, no electric charge of a violence barely contained sparked blue around him as he sat, leaning his round cheek into one hand, listening as if the issue of his own life and death did not lay at the center of everything taking place before him. But Joyce Gorecki's story, with its occasional tremble and quiet relentlessness, achieved what nothing else so far had: I could look at the man who had destroyed my brother's life and, for a moment, feel the force of comprehension at last—a palpable connection between the man, his action, the result. I don't know that what happened to Russell has ever again felt so real.

The defense, when it came their turn, gave evidence of Bobby's family life—his fatherless upbringing, his ill mother; the difficulties that a large, impoverished family had had keeping Bobby, as a youngster, from being taken in by the toughs around the neighborhood—older guys who were into drugs and gangs. A brother and a sister told faintly humorous stories of Bobby as a child. The jury heard about Hampton's having earned a G.E.D. since the robbery, and of his recent, voluntary participation in a program at the jail that enabled him to talk to young people, to convey the message: "Don't do like me and get in a gang and go wrong with your life."

I tried, as always, to listen, not with the ears of a sister whose brother had been murdered, but with the ears of a stranger, new to all this information, impartial in my regard. An impossible task, perhaps, but throughout the trial, that was my obsessive focus as I tried to imagine: *What is the jury making of all this?* I couldn't help noting that all the cheerful anecdotes Bobby's siblings told about him predated his incarceration at the age of 13 (a sentence that lasted to the age of 21), and that, more than once, they'd had to admit to all the years they hadn't seen him or known him much at all because he'd been away, locked up in juvenile jail. The stories themselves seemed pale, hapless things, so far back in the nearly irrelevant past, so weak compared to Joyce Gorecki's battered body and her fear—a fear that had made twenty pounds drop from her already slight frame over the twenty-one months since Bobby's attack.

The guileless, eager testimony of Hampton's two sisters and one brother made me squirm. I wanted to put a stop to it, to tell them that this pathetic display could only make things worse, that they were in danger of exciting a kind of hard bitterness in the jury, who might take exception to being asked to summon sympathy for a guy who, without provocation, had fired his gun into the back of an innocent man; to being asked for this sympathetic consideration on the basis of a thin, stale nostalgia for a kid who'd long ago ceased to exist. Of course, I may have been the only person in the courtroom, besides the defense attorneys and Hampton himself (and assuming the impartiality of the judge and jury), who wasn't rooting for the penalty phase to end in a sentence of execution.

Still, I'd be lying if I said I cared much what became of Hampton. My preference for a life sentence (as long as it truly *was* a life sentence, with no opportunity for release under any circumstances) had nothing to do with Hampton himself. In his relatively short tenure on the planet, Bobby Lee Hampton seemed to have amply demonstrated his commitment to a life of chronic, casual savagery—from the day he had (at the age of 12) helped two boys use a stick to sodomize another, late one night in a cemetery, to the day fourteen years later when he'd murdered my brother. Hampton's record, both the official one and the word-on-the-street kind (according to a veteran homicide detective who'd investigated Hampton for years), was one of unrelenting violence.

Given all I knew, and given the sheer, gratuitous brutality of how he'd killed Russell, I had a hard time summoning much in the way of sympathy for Hampton, whatever his future held. If he'd keeled over dead in his cell one morning, I doubt it would have given me a moment's discomfort or pause; it might even have been a relief. So the idea of Bobby Hampton's suddenly ceasing to exist did not trouble me. But only if his nonexistence had been accomplished without the State of Louisiana's assistance, without my participation or complicity.

And, thanks to my having accepted the State's invitation to take the stand and speak my own brief portion to the jury, my little bit of complicity was assured, should that same jury then opt to kill him. For reasons almost too numerous to name, I do not believe the government has the right to enact the premeditated murder of one of its citizens, regardless of what offense that citizen has committed. While losing my brother to a cold-blooded killer has, more than ever, made me aware of the almost universal longing for retribution (a craving that leads us, here in America, to persist in a form of punishment that almost every other industrialized nation on earth has long since abandoned), my belief that executions are wrong has not changed.

Though I, too, have deeply imagined an almost sensual satisfaction at the thought of extinguishing the life that has taken my brother's away, I have tried to keep my fantasies and feelings distinct from what I believe is the right thing to do. Isn't that what it means, really, to be a conscious, responsible, adult person? To have developed the ability to recognize impulses, wishes, even overwhelming urges, and then make considered decisions about whether to act on them? Whether it's a matter of not eating so much cake that you make yourself sick, or refraining from having sex with every person you find attractive, choosing to counter destructive impulses so intense that they masquerade as *needs* strikes me as being at the root of maturity and good citizenship. (One might even say it helps to forge character, but the concept of developing character (or of even having one) is not terribly fashionable in a time when the much shallower and more easily manufactured (and marketed) substitution of "personality" is so popular.)

I am not talking, here, about some Calvinistic cult of denying oneself for denial's sake, or some poisonous mistrust of pleasure. It's not about being ascetic or repressed or even sinful. It's about having, and making, choices that determine the kind of person you want to be in the world, and, by extension, what kind of world it's going to *be*, since we're all here, populating each other's lives, making each other's world. That's why we send the Bobby Hamptons among us away to live forever outside of our community—even Hampton's defense told the jury that he'd clearly demonstrated his unfitness to live among us. We have a right to keep the peace. I just don't think that peace justifies killing our most disruptive members, or that killing them, in fact, engenders the peacefulness we seek.

Before Russell was killed, my opposition to the death penalty stood firmly on a foundation of reasoned pragmatism and my own sense of social justice:

all the usual arguments about its being more costly than a life sentence; its being a perfect (and lethal) vehicle for expressing the racism that still exists in our society; that only poor people wind up on death row (rich people can afford better defense attorneys); that executing criminals completely negates the idea that people can change or be better in any way than the worst thing they've ever done; and how it totally extinguishes the possibility of reconciliation, or restitution, or the murderer making a positive contribution (from prison) to the community he's harmed.

Last, but perhaps most simply and profoundly: mistakes, as with any system enacted by human beings, are unavoidable. With capital punishment, we commit ourselves to a "solution" that is irredeemable when it goes wrong—we explicitly or tacitly endorse the military concept of "collateral damage," where the loss of innocent life is considered an acceptable price for the eradication of other, guiltier, beings. Perhaps I am just squeamish, but the execution of even one innocent person has always seemed too high a price to pay in order to assuage whatever emotional or political need demands our keeping the practice alive. Surely we can find something to toss into the maw of vengeance other than the bodies of the wrongly convicted, or even the guilty.

After Russell's murder, all these arguments continued to sustain my objections, but my sense of capital punishment's fundamental barbarism grew deeper and more personal. When Russell died and I emerged from the deepest levels of shock and sadness, it began to occur to me that I had an enormous decision to make. It further struck me that this decision might well be the only one I'd get to make about any of this, really. I hadn't chosen for Russell to die in such a fashion; nothing I could have done would have prevented it. And certainly nothing I could do would change the fact of it, not even giving my blessing to the execution of his killer. The decision that settled before me posed itself in these terms: *Who will I become, and who will I refuse to let myself be, now that my brother has been murdered in this way?*

I had been tempted by the seductive sway of bitterness; I had listened, entranced, to sinister whisperings urging me to feed an unending appetite for revenge, had felt the vertigo of longing to take a dive straight into a chronic and deep mistrust of the world, all the people in it, myself. I ached to simply grow calloused. Hard-heartedness would at least have been some armor against the pain, and I found that there was nothing like murder to make me feel I'd earned my right to a toughened cynicism. I mean, really: why bother keeping faith, keeping integrity, planning a future, *making a life* when there was such evil and chaos in the world that a mere stranger might come along and blow it all to pieces?

Oftentimes, I found, I would just as soon hug the mat and slide into unconsciousness. But I am sensuous and selfish—I love being in the world with its smells and visual bombardment and all the textures there are to rub up against my skin. I like feeling hopeful and expecting the best from people and from real and imagined possibilities; and even though people often prove disappointing and circumstances unyielding to my desires, I cannot seem to shake these habits of expectation whenever a new situation presents itself. Also, I am a plot junkie—I want to know how people's stories, my own included, will eventually turn out, if only for the satisfying pleasure of being appalled, or right in my own predictions, or taken totally by surprise by unanticipated developments. "To live is so startling that it leaves little time for anything else," as Emily Dickinson put it. And so, the first answer I could muster to the question of who I would now become, given the impact of murder in my life, took the shape of refusal: *I will not let Hampton take me down, too.* He took too much the night he took Russell. I wasn't going to add my psychic death to the body count.

I swore it to myself, to friends, to trusted advisors; I made the vow with fierce solemnity, and it scared me to do so. I was afraid of breaking it. I didn't know how to keep it. I didn't know how to tackle what seemed to be the task of cracking myself open wide and growing somehow so large that this terrible thing could not get and keep the upper hand in my life, tyrannizing my feelings and shaping my days, maiming my spirit. It is one thing to survive tragedy. Most of us do, in whatever fashion, go on. But how to latch onto the audacity and means to thrive? How to resume cultivating faith, extending generosity, forgiving myself and others for our gravely flawed humanity? These are the ongoing challenges. For everyone, really, not just the survivors of the myriad forms of personal tragedy that can fall into a life. It's just that certain kinds of blows tend to make you wonder if you'll ever walk straight again, or if you should resign yourself to being punch-drunk ever after.

* * *

At the end of the day, the jury left the courtroom to begin deliberations. All of us—my family, Cameron's girlfriend JoAnn, and the friends who had come from all over the South for the trial—wandered the courthouse lobby and Hugo's office in limbo. Should we go out to eat? Order dinner in? We'd been told that even a quick decision would take at least a couple of hours. The smokers in our bunch headed outside for a cigarette. We decided we'd all meet up on the fifth floor in the prosecutors' offices and make a plan together there. I bought a Diet Coke from a vending machine and rode the elevator up with JoAnn.

Waiting around for the rest of our group, feeling pretty certain we shouldn't risk leaving the building, and wondering if there were any takeout menus around we could order from, JoAnn and I discovered that Hugo's secretary had laid out chips, dip, veggies, and other snacks. Just as we'd started to help ourselves, Bruce Dorris, another prosecutor on the case, hustled through, his suit coat flapping as he nearly trotted towards Hugo's office. "Let's wrap this up," he said to me and JoAnn. "We have a verdict." JoAnn and I laughed, thinking he was teasing us for eating so heartily on the D.A.'s dime. "I mean it," he said, and disappeared around a corner. JoAnn and I gaped at each other. The corn chips and onion dip did a woozy somersault in my stomach. "We'd better get your mom," JoAnn said to me. I nodded. Forty-five minutes. The jury had been out for only forty-five minutes.

Moments later, there we sat: Hugo and Bruce at the prosecution's end of the table. Me, Mama, Cameron and JoAnn, my Aunt Bobbie and Uncle Henry, my mother's friends from Texas and Arkansas and Alabama, two of Bobby's sisters, one of his brothers, several folks from the prosecutor's office, and Hugo's daddy scattered around in the spectators' benches. The defense team had reassembled at their end of the table, and, of course, Bobby Lee Hampton, convicted murderer, sat among them. For the last time, we took our places in the bitterly cold courtroom—the dapper clerk, the kindly faced blond bailiff who'd slipped us the skinny on where the jury went out to dinner each night (so that we would avoid that restaurant), the plump and pleasant court reporter, the twelve jurors in their established seats.

I knew they were bringing back a death penalty. They had to be. All the way back to the courtroom, rounding up our group, riding the elevator, walking the halls, sliding into the wooden pew next to my mother, this certainty had been settling itself around my shoulders like a heavy cloak. In order to hand down a death sentence, the jurors had to be in unanimous agreement. If even one of them had misgivings, the sentence would automatically default to life imprisonment. If they'd had to wrangle, I thought, if they'd had to hash out their doubts and persuade one another, we would not be heading back so soon. Forty-five minutes is not enough time for twelve people to debate and resolve disagreements of any real importance.

When the clerk read aloud that Bobby Lee Hampton was to be executed, I felt a muffling sense of anti-climax, the way sounds reach your ears underwater, discernible but also removed. I sat, unable to feel much. My fundamental opposition to the death penalty mingled with my awed respect for the enormity of the jury's decision. The emotion that I could see flickering through the fissures in the jury's composure, my scrutiny of Bobby Hampton, my glancing sidelong at Cameron and Mama to gauge their responses, perhaps even the heavy, simple disbelief that it was all over, stalled the engine of my own feelings.

Looking at Cameron and Mama, I saw their grave, controlled faces. No gleam of satisfaction played across their features or lit their eyes, though I knew this sentence of death was what they most desired. I understood their dispassionate expressions as a combination of dignity, respect for the jury and Hampton's family, and deep fatigue. For all the vengeance that had often driven their urge to see Hampton executed, in the moment of securing that destiny for him, no malice or triumph surfaced in either of them. They seemed to accept their due as mourners and as victims—they received it quietly, as snow settles on field and covers over the gouges in the land. The decision could never be adequate, for them it could only be right, and though "right" is thin consolation for what can never be restored, maybe in that moment of accepting the jury's sentence, it allowed them to feel complete.

The young forewoman confirmed, through her tears, that execution was indeed the jury's decision. The defense requested an individual poll of the jurors. Twelve times over, the clerk read that the decision called for the death of Bobby Lee Hampton and asked each juror by name, "Is this your verdict?" Some spoke up clear and strong, "Yes, it is." Others replied in weaker, more clouded voices.

As the call and response of the verdict rolled out its rhythmic furl, I discovered that my dismay mingled with a tremendous satisfaction. This upset and confused me. I felt no satisfaction that, in eight to ten years Bobby Hampton would be unceremoniously injected with the drugs that would kill him. I would just as soon have been free to focus on making repairs to my damaged faith, on searching out whatever peace could be made with what was done to Russell—to all of us—and the long shadow cast by Hampton's execution only encumbers the effort. But I couldn't help being gratified by what the jury seemed to say: that what was done to Russell appalled them—appalled them enough to warrant the strongest response legally available. Twelve strangers, seven women and five men ranging in age from early twenties to mid-sixties, mostly white, a couple black, had listened for three days to a mass of information and made one of the most burdensome decisions a person can make: that another person should die. In fact, they had pondered ending Bobby Hampton's life more deeply and with much greater conscience than Bobby ever gave to ending Russell's. I was moved, unsettled, and grateful.

The forewoman was now red-eyed and sobbing. The beautiful caramel-skinned woman with the large, pretty eyes quietly dabbed away tears. Even a couple of the men were crying.

And how did Bobby take it? Chin high, disbelieving half-smile on his face, shaking his head back and forth in wonder as though at some obvious and ridiculous mistake, he turned to look over his shoulder at his stunned, grief-stricken sisters and brother, and mouthed a large and silent, "Be strong, be strong." I couldn't bring myself to look directly at any of Bobby's family. It seemed like an intrusion on their grief, for one thing, and I would have been mortified to have a stray glance of mine mistaken for a look of triumph. But in my peripheral vision, I could see their devastated shock. It occurs to me now that they were just then feeling something similar to what I had felt almost two years before, when I'd heard the news of Russell's execution, already carried out.

Regret, misery, loss, devastation, death, brutality and tragedy, all extending further and further out, radiating from this hub of violent energy that has been Bobby Lee Hampton's life. And now, with the sentence of death upon him, the destruction and misery have left their indelible mark on his loved ones instead of only upon the nameless strangers he has attacked over the years. I am pained for them. Whatever Bobby has done, to them he is still brother, son, family—and for them, this is a cruel conclusion. Though, really, Bobby was lost to them years ago, when he stopped being that grinning, prank-loving eight-year-old they testified about, that kid who helped out old folks in the neighborhood and loved to make his five brothers and sisters laugh, and always had some teasing joke to pull. They lost him the night he stood in a dark cemetery, helping to beat and hold down a naked boy while letting another boy take up a stick. It seemed to me they loved a remembered child. I don't know what they let themselves know about the vicious, cold man that child grew up to be, or how they reconcile the contradictions within him.

It occurred to me, sitting in the courtroom that last day, having heard the sentence and watched Bobby attempting to infuse his brother and sisters with fortitude, if not hope, that in an odd way, he was at a new beginning. I could imagine his feeling sustained by a sense of purpose, which would be to overturn, however possible, the decision that had just been made. I remember thinking, "He's got a lot of work to do." Mama, Cameron, and JoAnn would all fly back to Cincinnati. I would fly home to New York. The family friends would scatter back across the southern states from which they'd come, and Hugo and his team would plunge into the next trial. Bobby would, after a few days, be transported to the swampy isolation of Angola prison, keen, I would guess, not to put the trial behind him so much as to pick it apart for any possible flaw that might release him from this sentence of death.

I had been warned by families of other murder victims not to expect too much from the trial, whatever its outcome. The message had been: don't expect "closure." All of us had laughed, sometimes a little bitterly, at the media's mantra-like repetition of the word, their passionate insistence on this supposed panacea for victims everywhere. Mostly, we wondered what the hell it could possibly mean. We understood that murder, rather than being a finite event, slams down into your life with meteoric force, that the ripples and rings that hurtle outward from that center would last as long as we did. Maybe that's why we hear so little, overall, from the people murder leaves behind, at least compared to the glut of stories about the killers themselves. For the families, it's never really over. And that's a hard thing to be told; it's hard to take, especially for anyone who wants to believe that every poison has an antidote, every wildness can be tamed, every broken thing can be fixed—and isn't that most of us?

Bobby Lee Hampton's trial and conviction, his sentence to death, did not bring closure. It brought, simply, an outcome. An outcome which, to my deep discredit, I cannot find it in myself to mourn, except in the abstract. My opposition to the death penalty remains. But my sympathy for Hampton himself still refuses to take shape. When I pray for Bobby Hampton, which I try to remember to do, I pray for his heart to be touched with grave remorse and anguish over what he's done, I pray that something in him opens itself to taking up even a small measure of responsibility for the destruction he has caused. When I think of Hampton but pray for myself, I pray that my own heart might someday be moved to feel pity for his fate at the hands of the State of Louisiana. Perhaps, when the actual day of execution draws near, the resurrection of agony for all that's transpired will pierce my heart and let such compassion for my brother's killer seep in.

CHAPTER 2

FEELINGS FROM THE HEART

Dan Levey

This chapter is presented from the point of view of crime victims. It offers readers a sense of the impact of losing a loved one to a homicide. It also presents some of the challenges that surviving family members (who are considered by law to be victims in most states) may face, and describes the feelings and emotions some victims feel, when the perpetrator is sentenced to death. Victims many times face conflicting feelings about the death penalty, or they may feel strongly one way or another. Valid and passionate arguments exist on both sides of the issue. Capital punishment can be a very divisive and emotional topic for murder-victim survivors, and there are few black-and-white answers.

It is important to make clear that although I intend to put forth some victims' feelings toward the death penalty, survivors should not be labeled as "pro" or "con" concerning capital punishment. They deserve to be treated with fairness, respect, and dignity by all who work with them. In my work as a victim advocate I have handled several death penalty-eligible cases. I have also attended an execution with the victim's family. While talking with the victim's family prior to the execution I learned that they were not looking forward to attending but they knew it was something their grandfather (the victim) would have wanted them to do. I worked on one case where the defendant received the death penalty and the victims were elated. I also worked on a case where the death penalty was handed down and the victims were upset because it was their wish that the offender stay in prison for the duration of his natural life.

One thing that is clear to me, in working with many victims over the years: they are often in an intense emotional state following the murder. Hearing opinions on the death penalty that differ from their own can be extremely painful to victims.

Dan Levey (left) with sister Robin and brother Howard, late 1970's.

My Story

In the early morning hours of Sunday, November 3, 1996, my life as I knew it changed forever. In this respect I was like so many other victims of violent crime who receive telephone calls or a knock on the door with news that fundamentally alters their existence. My sister-in-law called and told me that my brother Howard had been shot in Arizona. Howard was waiting for his buddies to show up for their weekly Sunday morning basketball game. My brother was well educated, a husband, a father of two (he had a nine-year-old daughter and a sixteen-year-old son), a son, a brother, and a friend to many. We later learned that Howard was shot by two gang members at point-blank range, thrown out of his car where he was sitting, and left to die. The perpetrators saw him sitting in his vehicle and never thought for a second about who was behind the wheel; they only wanted his car. Why would someone who did not even know Howard take his life for such a trivial reason? Unfortunately, our family is left with no answers to our questions.

I learned firsthand the harsh reality of what it is like to lose a loved one to murder. My family and I at least know that the people who were responsible are being held accountable for their actions in prison. Because of my work with violent-crime victims, I know that the outcome of the criminal proceedings is important to many victims, for several reasons. First, and perhaps most obvious, is that it holds perpetrators accountable for the heinous crimes they committed against victims and their loved ones. A second, and maybe more subtle reason, is that it allows a certain amount of "judicial closure"; although appeals may linger for many years, at least the perpetrator is incarcerated during that time. Third, it allows victims to begin to construct a "new sense of normal" in their lives in the aftermath of their victimization. Most of my experience is in dealing with victims' families who have lost someone to murder. Accordingly, my perspective has been shaped by talking with victims with whom I have personally worked and with other victims whom I have met and whose view I have heard.

My brother's case was filed as a death-penalty case, and the shooter decided that rather than face the death penalty he would plead guilty to first-degree murder. However, my family and I only knew it as a capital case for many months. We had mixed emotions about going for the death penalty. On the one hand, we knew we would have to go through a trial and, in the event of a conviction and death sentence, the long appeals process and considerable time it would take to carry out the execution. On the other hand, we felt that death was the sentence he deserved and that the crime met the threshold "legal elements" of capital murder and could properly be charged as a "death penalty" case. The decision by the prosecutor not to pursue the death penalty and have the defendant plead to first-degree murder was a difficult one for my family, but one that was satisfactory considering we were given the opportunity to provide input to the prosecutor's office on what we thought should happen. Although we could not dictate what should happen, the prosecutor's office, to its credit, sought our input. According to the Arizona Victims Bill of Rights, victims have the right to "confer with the prosecution, after the crime against the victim has been charged, before trial, or before any disposition of the case and to be informed of the disposition."

To understand homicide, we must gain some sense of what a survivor or a victim of a homicide goes through. As my friend, colleague, and fellow survivor (whose sibling was murdered) Carrie Freitag, says so eloquently about murder in her book *Aftermath: In the Wake of Murder* (2003, pp. 1–2):

> Every death brings to its survivors the one nonnegotiable moment that hurts forever. After that one moment, there is no returning home. Just as the dead have crossed a point of no return, those left behind to live must cross a similar point when that first wave of grief divides everything we know into a before and an after. The waves of grief that follow remind us as dependably as the redawning of the sun that we cannot have what we miss the most. In an instant, life as we once knew it disappeared, and the future becomes a struggle between moving on and hanging on. Survivors are left to contend with this struggle and find a balance that allows them to emerge from their

most painful and vulnerable moments with newfound strength and reasons for living. Although the struggle with grief is part of every death, murder is darker than death, and so is the road to surviving and healing. Murder devours innocent lives with a cruelty that is absent of reason, values, and compassion. Murder breaks all the sacred rules, knows no fairness, and can never be compensated for or undone. It provokes fear and rage and tempts us to battle it on its terms instead of our own. Murder drives even the most loving and compassionate people to the edge of that fine line that separates our respect for life from our violent potentials. The aftermath of murder takes us straight through hell, where we stand eye to eye with the evil that hides behind human faces, and what we do in the face of the evil defines us for what lies ahead. The aftermath of murder is nothing less than a full-blown emotional and spiritual struggle.

Personal Stories

Dick Adams

Dick Adams's life changed when a repeat offender shot and killed his only son, Richard, execution-style, during a robbery on December 23, 1983. Richard, 21, had graduated from college in May 1982. He was employed by Pillsbury Corporation, and worked at one of their restaurants in Winston Salem, North Carolina. Richard was counting receipts that December night when he was murdered by John Sterling Gardner. This bright, articulate young man was murdered by someone who had already been convicted of armed robbery and had served two years in prison before being paroled. Gardner ultimately was convicted of killing three people, including Richard Adams. He was tried in September 1984 and executed in October 1992.

Prior to the murder of his son, if someone had asked Dick Adams his position on the death penalty, he would have responded, "I have no position on it." However, after Richard's murder, he vowed to his son that "justice will be served." In the course of enduring and learning about the criminal justice system, he became a strong advocate for the death penalty. Dick Adams buried his son on a Sunday, the day after Christmas, and went to the district attorney's office the following morning. He asked the DA what his options were. He was told, "Mr. Adams, let's establish an understanding here—this crime was not committed against your son, but against the state, and I will handle it." Adams responded, "The state did not bury a son, the state does not cry or grieve, or have emotional stress." He promised the DA that he was going to see a lot of him. The DA's office did not offer him even a cup of coffee or any assistance at all.

Adams witnessed the execution of his son's murderer. When reporters asked him if he had experienced a sense of closure, he said, "There is no such thing as closure for homicide survivors." After the execution, the family felt some relief in knowing that John Gardner will never murder again, and they did not have to think about the appeals process. Reporters also asked Adams if he felt the death penalty was a deterrent. He responded, "When he murders his next victim, give me a call." Adams explains, "The death penalty makes a statement that life is valuable. Not having the death penalty would encourage more murder and mayhem." He believes the death penalty is a deterrent to crime and says "the bedrock of our society is our criminal justice system." He believes that "among all great societies that preceded us, the one thing they had in common was that citizens arrived at a place where pleasure and greed overwhelmed them to the point they refused to discipline themselves." Adams hopes that America is not on the road to a similar demise.

Bud Welch

Bud Welch became an outspoken opponent of the death penalty after coming to terms with his daughter Julie's death in the Oklahoma City bombing perpetrated by Timothy McVeigh. He has testified before the U.S. Congress and many state legislative committees, made numerous radio and television appearances, and met frequently with the McVeigh's father. He is a member of Murder Victims Families for Reconciliation and serves on the board of directors of the Oklahoma City National Memorial Foundation.

Born seven weeks premature, Julie Marie Welch was given a 10 percent chance of survival. Her early difficulties, though, did not cause any permanent physical defects. In seventh grade Julie met a non-English-speaking Mexican girl who quickly became bilingual, which made Julie long to speak a foreign language. She mastered Latin, German, Spanish, and French in Catholic high school and spent eleven months of her junior year studying in Spain. She returned there during her Marquette University undergraduate days. In August 1994 she began work as an interpreter for the Social Security Administration in Oklahoma City. On the morning of April 19, 1995, Julie had walked to the waiting room to meet a client when the bomb detonated.

I spoke to Bud Welch about his feelings concerning the death penalty. He said:

> I was opposed to the death penalty all my life, until my daughter Julie Marie was killed in the Oklahoma City bombing. For many months after the bombing I could have killed Timothy McVeigh myself. Temporary insanity is real, and I have lived it. You can't think of enough adjectives to describe the rage, revenge, and hate I felt. But after time, I was able to examine my conscience, and I realized that if McVeigh was put to death, it wouldn't help me in the healing process. People talk about executions bringing closure. But how can there be closure when my little girl is never coming back? I finally realized that the death penalty is all about revenge and hate, and revenge and hate are why Julie Marie and 167 others are dead.

"Revenge and hate are the reason for the bombing," he further explained, because it was "in retaliation for the incident at Waco." His hatred drove Welch's one-and-a-half-packs-a-day smoking habit to a three-packs-a-day obsession. His social drinking turned excessive. "What I found out was, if I drank enough at night, I could sleep," he recalled, though he paid the price in hangovers that lasted well into the next day. Furthermore:

> I had suppressed my feelings about the death penalty in the immediate aftermath of the bombing; but then one day I was watching TV and saw Bill McVeigh on TV. Timothy's father's pain has to be incredible. As best I can tell, he did everything right. He raised his kids as Catholics. I think the U.S. military screwed up Timothy McVeigh. There are some people who are not fit for military service. I think Tim was one. He couldn't separate the trained killer instinct he had been taught during his years with the military from civilian life when he got out. I can't imagine what it must be like for Bill McVeigh. I'm not sure I could survive if my son had participated in causing death like that.

Welch believes that Timothy McVeigh was suicidal. "No person who isn't [suicidal] drives a truck from Kansas loaded with 4,000 pounds of explosives just a few feet from his head!" Bill McVeigh's former neighbor helped arrange a meeting between him and Welch in September 1998, three years after the bombing. At that meeting, Welch told the McVeighs that they were all in this together for the rest of their lives. Then he cried all the way back home to Buffalo, where two friends waited for him. "I couldn't stop sobbing," he says. "I drove 85 miles per hour because I needed to get to people I knew. When I pulled up at the house, I was still crying."

Welch has strong feelings about the death penalty:

We shouldn't be killing people because of a popularity poll. In this country, we take on the easy ones, we kill the easy ones. That's all we kill are the easy ones. We put about one percent of the murderers on death row in this country, and those are mainly poor people. They're all poor. There are 159 people on death row in Oklahoma today. Not one of those, not a single one, paid for their own defense....

Prior to the execution of Timothy McVeigh, Welch said, "When we take him out of his cage to kill him, all we'll end up with is a staged, political event."

Sharon Tewksbury

Sharon Tewksbury's husband, Monte, was brutally murdered in Ohio on April 18, 1983. In January of that year Monte had come back from a trip to the convenience store two blocks from their home and announced to Sharon and their children that the store was looking for help, and he thought he might apply. Monte was such a giver and caretaker all his life, and he always worried about money, so even though he was a seventeen-year employee of Procter & Gamble, he was always moonlighting. He usually worked in area hospitals as a phlebotomist, but this time he said he just wanted something easy, a "no-brainer." Over very strong objections from his daughter Kim and Sharon, he applied for, and got, the job.

Three months later he was dead from a knife wound to the right side of his chest. The stabbing cut his diaphragm and severed his liver. The result is called exsanguination—he drowned in his own blood. Sharon Tewksbury tells me that Monte did what anyone who knew him would expect him to do: he made his way to the pay phone on the outside of the building and called her. He breathlessly told his wife that he was hurt, needed help, and that she should get there as quickly as she could. Kim, 19, was in school at the University of Dayton, but David, 15, and Matthew, 12, were at home, asleep. Tewksbury called for the police and an ambulance, then screamed for the boys to wake up and get their neighbor to come and stay with them. She went to the store and found Monte lying on the dirty floor, with a gaping wound in his right side, conscious, but in great pain. If nothing else, she says, "At least I was able to say good-bye ... a chance most survivors never get...., an opportunity his children did not have."

Once at the hospital, early reports told Tewksbury that her husband wasn't going to make it. Two hours later, the doctors came to tell her what she already knew. Monte was gone, and Sharon remembers thinking, "We would never again feel his warm embrace around our fragile lives.... We would never again be the way we were." At that same time, the three men who murdered him were being arrested.

Tewksbury shared with me a part of the victim impact statement she submitted to the judge at the trial of the man who murdered her husband. She was not allowed to give this statement in open court.

> Monte was a giver in a world of takers, and on April 18, three of this world's takers senselessly and brutally took his life. Monte's life was truly unique. He had a flair for sensitivity and warmth, for gentleness and affection; he excelled at congeniality and friendship. He was a champion of commitment and dedication. He was a bestower of cheer. He was a master of the artistry of love. Monte had the ability to relate, to communicate, to touch our lives and help us to feel special. He sought to love without restraint, without imposing conditions, without demands or obligations. He sought not only to share God's love himself, but enabled others to share God's love in their own wonderfully creative and personal ways—in ways that rose above and beyond the typical. He was able to meet people where they were and to love them authentically, purely, and divinely. He not only loved us when we were beautiful, he loved us most when we were at our worst. And it is this loving that is our greatest loss.

Tewksbury told me that she wrote extensively in a journal over the next several years. She wrote about how hard it was to stop thinking of Monte as a flesh-and-blood person and allow him to become a memory in her mind and heart. "I knew if I didn't let go, I would never make it, I would never heal ... and I had three children to raise. It was the most painful thing I had to do." She also wrote about events that happened several months before Monte was murdered. One day when they were driving in the car, Monte asked her to listen to a song by Roger Whittaker called "For I Loved You." He said that if anything ever happened to him, to have the song sung at his funeral. Then he became detached and distant, sad and melancholy.

The nightmare and trauma of losing her husband, Tewksbury says, "will last forever." Her and her family's journey through the criminal justice system lasted nineteen years. "How naive I was to think that it would all be over after two appeals. There were years of appeals, requests for clemency, and struggles against appeals-court judges whose desire to abolish the death penalty overruled their responsibility as officers of the court to uphold the law."

At one point, John Byrd, the man who murdered Monte, sent Sharon Tewksbury a threatening letter telling her he didn't like her speaking to the media about him, and that he could take care of all of them because he knew people on the outside who would do it for him. Most of the letter could not be repeated publicly. Tewksbury says she cannot count the number of appeals and requests for clemency, but she and her family were there for every one of them—and they made sure that the judges knew it and that the parole-board members heard their statements in person. During this entire time, Tewksbury says,

> My children and I have not spoken out for or against the death penalty. My concern has always been for justice and truth in sentencing. John Byrd was tried, convicted, and sentenced by a jury of his peers in August 1983. *Why* did it take nineteen years to have that sentence carried out? I have come to understand that the rights of those who do violence in this country are much greater than any survivor, and I hope people will understand that this serves to revictimize victims over and over again. I have no problem with people being against the death penalty but, in my experience, these people believe that their cause is so righteous that they are justified in doing anything to get their goals accomplished. That would include distortion of facts, outright lies, and attacks against the victim's family. That would include *using* families and their cases to make their point, and I am outraged over the fact that they know very little about these cases, take the word of others without researching the facts, and in general, really don't care about anything but their cause. I have no patience, tolerance, or respect for people like this. What I usually say to them is that if they want to abolish the death penalty … [they should] go to Washington, find congressmen and women to support them, write a bill, and change the law … *but do not use me or others like me to make it happen.* I am tired of being victimized, and I tell them that if they weren't there at the trials, if they didn't read every word of every transcript and know the case inside out, then they have no business using us in this manner. There is a right and wrong way to do things, and there is no cause worthy enough to pursue at the expense of other innocent people.

> On the day of execution, most of our family was at the office of Hamilton County Prosecutor Mike Allen, awaiting a phone call from my youngest son, Matthew, letting us know that the execution was over. Matthew decided at the last minute to go, and we as a family decided that there would be no media following him to the death house. We didn't want this to be about John Byrd. We wanted it to be about Monte. Matthew was only 12 when his father was murdered. He and his brother and sister were very fearful of John Byrd and his threats.

Matthew went into the death house that day as a twelve-year-old ... and he came out as a young man ... no longer afraid. It was his desire to see this through for his Dad ... and he did ... but very privately. Family, friends, co-workers and so many others came to my home to be with us and to share stories about Monte. They came just like they did nineteen years ago, not knowing what to do or say ... just compelled to be there. We made plans to have a huge celebration of Monte's life, which would take place in April 2002. We wanted to give other survivors another more positive way of handling their grief and loss by celebrating life, not death. So we talked about music, food, balloons, pictures, stories (everything that Monte loved) and invited many, many people who were there for us from the beginning through to what I call not the end, not closure, but another transition.

Tewksbury agreed to share with me some of what she read at her final statement given in a press conference after the execution of John Byrd. It best summarizes her long journey through murder, grief, and the criminal justice system, and she hopes it serves as an inspiration to others like her to persevere and come out on the other side as whole, productive, happy people:

The sentence for the brutal, senseless murder of Monte Tewksbury has, after nineteen long years, finally been carried out. There is no elation, no joy, no feeling of revenge ... just a feeling of relief and the realization that the violence done to Monte will no longer threaten his wife and children. My strongest emotion, now and for the last nineteen years, has been deep, overwhelming grief. With great determination, Monte's children and I have pushed forward and learned to live our lives in the most positive way possible in order to honor the memory of a man who taught us all the meaning of unconditional love. Because of who he is, I believe Monte is at a place where he could speak of forgiveness and mercy to the man who took his life. I cannot. But my strong faith allows me to acknowledge that the God who created us all has the love, mercy, and power to grant forgiveness to any of us who ask. In my heart I truly hope that Monte's murderer asked, ... but in my heart, I truly believe he did not. This family will never be healed, but will always be healing. We have chosen to do it in the most positive way possible, ... to give others like us a way to find love and joy in their lives once again, ... and to pray that those who have *not* been forced to go to this dark, evil place.... ..never have to find themselves there. I do not celebrate death today, I celebrate life, ... the life of a sweet, innocent man who was loved and respected by so many in this community. For all who hear me now, ... I tell you to go home, hug your wives, husbands, children, and all those you love ... because sometimes tomorrow never comes. Celebrate life.... It is the most important gift you have ever been given."

Renny Cushing

Renny Cushing's father, Robert, was killed by two shotgun blasts fired through the screen door of the family's New Hampshire home on June 1, 1988. Cushing relates:

My father answered a knock at the front door. When he opened it, a couple of shotgun blasts went off, ripped his chest apart, and he died in front of my mother. But all my mother saw was the blast; she had no idea who had done it. We buried my father and spent a long summer trying to figure out who was responsible. After about twelve weeks, we got a call that a local cop had turned himself in and had been arrested. Then we found out that it was the cop who lived next door to my parents. After my father was murdered, we had taken some comfort in knowing that there was a police officer next door. Little did we know that that source of comfort had actually been the source of pain.

This man had had a long history of violence. He had a whole host of bad actions while he was on the police force. In 1975 he pulled over a woman named Gladys who was on her way to church with a friend. They were both in their eighties. Gladys was roughed up and charged with resisting arrest. I found out about this because Gladys lived two doors down from my parents; she was Aunt Gladys to us in the neighborhood when I was growing up. My brother and I initiated a petition to try to get the local town fathers to look into what had happened. They ended up saying that it was Gladys's word against the cop's. So nothing came of it.

By 1988 this cop, Robert McLaughlin, had moved in next door to my parents in an apartment house, and, as we later learned, he had decided he was going to kill a Cushing. He knew we had initiated the petition, and I had had other encounters with him over the years. I did a lot of political work in opposition to the Seabrook Atomic Plant, and he was present at demonstrations and avowed that my brothers and I didn't have much respect for law enforcement. But then we forgot about him, we forgot his name, so we didn't realize that he had moved in next door. He later confessed that he talked over with his wife how he was going to kill a Cushing and together they came up with a disguise and concocted a plan. Eventually they were both convicted of first-degree murder and sent to prison.

"I get sick when death-penalty advocates self-righteously prescribe execution to treat the wounds we live with after homicide," Renny Cushing says. "Those who hold out an event—execution—as the solution to pain have no understanding of healing. Healing is a process, not an event." A former two-term member of the New Hampshire House of Representatives, Cushing sponsored legislation to abolish the death penalty in 1998. The former director of Murder Victims Families for Reconciliation, he tells this story:

> A man came up to me after my father was murdered and said, "I hope they fry those people. I hope they fry them so you and your family can get some peace." I know that man meant to comfort me, but it was the most horrible thing he could possibly have said. Before my father's murder I had evolved a set of values that included a respect for life and an opposition to the death penalty. For me to change my beliefs because my father was murdered would only give more power to his killers, for they would then take not only his life but also his main legacy to me: the values he instilled. The same is true for society. If we let murderers turn us to murder, we give them too much power. They succeed in bringing us to their way of thinking and acting, and we become what we say we abhor.

Cushing says the death penalty "doesn't bring anybody back. I suppose we could have justice if you could exchange the life of the murderer for the life of the one in the grave. But you can't. I don't presume to prescribe a way to heal for other people. I just know for myself that healing does not come from murdering people."

For Renny Cushing, reconciliation means coming to accept. He says:

> I reconcile myself to the fact that I am a survivor of a murder victim, and then proceed to figure out how I can lead a full life with that reality. When I met the son of the man who murdered my father—we met outside the courthouse one day—I told him that we both lost our fathers on June 1. Just as I'm forever marked, so is he. Just as I felt isolated, I could see clearly the isolation that comes from people knowing that you're the family member of a murderer. And I knew that to kill somebody else not only wouldn't honor my father's life; it would create another grieving family. I think people don't actually

want vengeance. They would like to end their own pain. Sometimes they think it's a zero-sum game: if they can make someone else feel pain, theirs will go away. I just don't think it works that way. My pain would not be lessened by having the son of my father's murderer lose his father through execution.

Mark Milke

Mark Milke's son Christopher, 4, was murdered by Milke's ex-wife in 1989. Debra Jean Milke committed the murder with the help of her roommate, James Lynn Styers, and another man, Roger Mark Scott. The two men took the little boy out into the Arizona desert, shot him, and buried him in a hastily scratched out grave. He was told he was going to see Santa Claus at a local mall. Debra Milke had promised the two men a share of a $5,000 life-insurance policy. She was convicted of first-degree murder and condemned to death on January 8, 1991. Styers and Scott, also convicted of first-degree murder, have been on death row since February 14, 1990, and April 22, 1991, respectively.

This murder is one of Arizona's most horrific crimes and resulted in Debra Milke being the only woman on Arizona's death row. Mark Milke feels it was a "just sentence" for his ex-wife (although he admits that at some level he does feel a little bit of love for his ex-wife and that "a piece of me will always be with her"), and he believes it is cruel to make family and friends wait twenty-plus years to see an execution carried out. "We need to limit the appeals," he says. Mark does report that he has turned his tragedy into advocacy for victims and still awaits the day when the sentence is carried out.

Concluding Thoughts

These stories reveal that victims have strong, valid, and understandable arguments for and against the death penalty, and that their emotions run the gamut. I deeply believe that survivors are entitled to their own personal feelings about the death penalty. After all, they have paid the price that underlies their feelings. I believe that the death penalty produces conflict that is imposed on society by murderers, not survivors. What I mean by this, is the survivors are not in this conflict for anything they did but it was the actions of the murderer that put this conflict upon them. One thing is certain: survivors should not be pigeonholed as deserving or non-deserving, or admirable or non-admirable, based on their opinions and feelings about an issue that our society as a whole cannot agree upon. When the death penalty spotlight shines on survivors, they risk getting ridiculed by either anti-death-penalty advocates or pro-death-penalty advocates. For survivors, it is a no-win situation.

Whatever a survivor's opinion might be on the death penalty, that individual needs and deserves support and validation as much as any other survivor. As one can imagine, it is difficult for survivors to hear opinions that differ from their own regarding what should happen to the person who murdered their loved one. It is also difficult to endure the media scrutiny that sometimes takes place in death penalty cases. Unlike in some societies, where the justice system helps carry out the survivors' chosen penalty, in the United States, survivors have little or no control over capital punishment. Unfortunately, survivors sometimes become engaged in the death-penalty debate without choice, and they may not be emotionally prepared for this.

An important lesson can be learned about pushing survivors to comment on the death penalty. Sometimes murder victims' families are asked how they feel about capital punishment, only to be verbally attacked if their opinion differs from the person asking the question. The survivors might be told that their opinion is not valid or beyond understanding. If pushed too far, it is easy for them to become defensive and lose their composure. Instead of recognizing that the death penalty is an emotionally loaded issue for survivors, many extremists on both sides of the argument become even more harsh and judgmental about the issue. When soliciting survivors' views about the death penalty, caution and respect are in order. It is fine if survivors want to talk about capital punishment, but they should be allowed to do so on their own terms, and they should not be sought out to be spokespersons on the issue.

The only certainty is that murder victim survivors, whether they are for or against the death penalty, have a right to their opinions without being harassed. Verbal attacks by death penalty extremists on either side of the debate are not worth the breath they take to deliver. If critics were really interested in what survivors think and feel about the death penalty, they would simply listen and reserve their own thoughts for a later date. Seeking out murder victim survivors in order to argue with them or to try to pressure them to be spokespersons on the issue is not appropriate. If survivors want to discuss death penalty issues, they will bring it up and come forward to advocate their position (Freitag, 2003).

Although survivors of homicide have varying feelings about the death penalty, it still seems certain that they have far more in common with each other than they have differences. All who lose a loved one to murder share the incredible pain and grief that follows. Survivors are forever bonded by this tragic fact. Although we all grieve differently, we all have grieved profoundly following the murder of a loved one. Homicide grief involves grasping at opportunities to connect, to share, and to care. We might otherwise have left these opportunities for tomorrow, but now everything has changed. We have become ever mindful that there may be no tomorrow.

In closing, I can only say that it has been my honor to meet and talk with the survivors who contributed to this chapter. They truly gave a piece of themselves in spite of losing their loved ones in such a cruel and heinous way—they have honored their loved ones by sharing their feelings.

Reference

Freitag, Carrie M. 2003. *Aftermath: In the Wake of Murder.* Ellicott City, MD: Chevron Publishing Corp.

CHAPTER 3

A Tiger by the Tail: The Mother of a Murder Victim Grapples with the Death Penalty

Linda L. White

I have been grappling with the issue of the death penalty for quite some time. In some ways I have struggled with the question all my adult life. I had no strong motivation to settle on a position, however, until my daughter was murdered. That began the struggle in earnest, and it precipitated my desire to find out more about this aspect of our culture. I wanted to learn more about the death penalty in order to base my position on more than my visceral reaction to my daughter's murder. This desire to learn more didn't happen immediately, though, and that's the story I want to tell. But first, I will recount the experience of those few days in which my husband, John, and I gradually came to know that someone had killed our daughter.

My Daughter's Disappearance

Cathy was missing for five days prior to our finding out what had actually happened to her. At the beginning of those five days we tried hard not to admit to ourselves that the worst had happened. After all, murder isn't the first thing that enters your mind—it's too horrible—and several circumstances combined to keep us from facing the truth. We knew that Cathy was pregnant and engaged to be married, but, up to that point, there had been no talk of any plans for the upcoming ceremony. This knowledge, coupled with a call that

White family, Christmas 1985. Mother Sally, Linda, husband John, father Dick, daughter Cathy, and son John Michael.

we received the night she disappeared, enabled us to delay the situation's inevitable harsh reality.

The call was from one of the boys who had killed her. He proceeded to tell Cathy's brother Steve, who received the call at the home that he shared with Cathy and her daughter Ami, that she needed some time away and not to look for her. Based on that conversation, we attempted to calm ourselves with the idea that she was undergoing some difficult soul-searching in regard to her impending marriage and pregnancy. We thought perhaps that either she or her fiancé had developed some second thoughts about the marriage and that she needed time to herself to make some decisions. Naturally, we thought her chosen method of just disappearing was irresponsible, but better to believe her irresponsible than harmed.

Even though we continued to try very hard to convince ourselves that what the caller said was true, we didn't really believe it. I recall a conversation John and I had that evening in which I told him that the feeling in the pit of my stomach wasn't anger, but fear—the same fear that had been there for most of the day. Cathy's five-year-old daughter Ami had called around 8:00 that morning, saying that she had awakened and found she was in the house alone. Ami said her mother had never returned home from dinner with a friend the night before, and her uncle must have gone off to work very early in the morning without realizing that he was leaving her alone upstairs in the house.

I dressed hurriedly and got to the house as quickly as I could—it was almost thirty minutes away from my home. When I arrived I called my son Steve to ask him what he knew about Cathy's departure the night before and her apparent failure to return. He agreed to call all her friends in order to see what he could find out. After feeding Ami breakfast and dropping her off at preschool, I drove to my mother's house to celebrate her birthday, realizing that it would provide at least a degree of distraction; I didn't want to disappoint my mom after promising to spend her birthday with her. I still find it ironic that November 18, my mom's birthday, is also the date of Cathy's death, so I never really think of it that way. Instead, I consider the day we were visited by the police officer confirming her death as the actual day of her death, November 22, 1986. Though it helped a little to play games with my mom, helping make her birthday more special for her, the entire day was quite stressful. Steve called one friend after another and found out nothing that was reassuring for us.

Sometime around 6:00 that evening Steve received the call that Cathy had just gone away to think about some problems she was having. Even though it didn't really ring true, we made an effort to continue believing it through the next couple of days—until the night of November 20, when we received another call, this one from the police in Greenville, Texas, a small town outside of Dallas. They had picked up two fifteen-year-old boys in Cathy's car and were holding them in custody. One of them, a boy named Gary, had been recognized by the officer as someone who was supposed to be in a youth facility in the Houston area, so he brought him in and ran a check on the registration of the car. It was the registration that led him to contact the authorities near us. They also found Steve's calling card on the floor of the car and then called him.

Steve explained why we had not reported Cathy missing or her car stolen so far, which the officer understood. At that point, however, the officer suggested that we needed to call the local Harris County authorities and do both. At this time I finally called Cathy's fiancé, Willis, while Steve called the police. Willis told me that there had been no trouble whatsoever in their relationship, but that he had been so busy that week that he had not talked to her in a few days. He didn't think it strange they hadn't spoken because it happened from time to time due to their demanding schedules. Willis was an emergency-room physician on twelve-hour shifts, and Cathy divided her time between her daughter, a part-time job, and a computer training school she attended. After I explained to him what had happened, he came over and spent the rest of the evening with us as we tried to gather courage from one another, knowing at some level that this was not going to end well at all.

I spent as much time as possible trying to distract Ami during that time. It helped me as well to spend as much time as I did with those I considered my closest friends, since I had really needed them that week. My main coping strategy in any crisis is to enlist the help of friends, especially those who would listen to me and offer unconditional strength and support. Because of this need to distract Ami and gain strength from friends, I followed through on previous plans to attend a Saturday morning event with some friends. Although I was so stressed out by this time that I could not enjoy myself, it did occupy my time and keep Ami from asking too many questions that I couldn't answer. We were gone most of the day and were not there, unfortunately, when the officer arrived to give us the news of our daughter's death.

Immediately after Steve reported Cathy missing and her car stolen, two officers were dispatched from the Harris County Sheriff's Department to Greenville, to question the two boys in custody. Within a few hours of their arrival there, at least one of the boys had confessed to raping and killing Cathy in the early morning hours of Tuesday, November 18. But it would not be until Saturday, November 22 that a police officer would visit us to tell us the horrendous truth. After the written confession from one of the boys, the police sent two more officers to Greenville to bring back the boys in separate cars, giving them no time for further collaboration. Gary, the one who had thus far not offered more than an oral confession, was taken to the area where they had left Cathy to provide identification of the body, the location of the gun used to kill her, and to connect him to the crime. Only after locating and identifying both Cathy and the gun did the sheriff's office send someone to our house to notify us. Sadly, my poor husband was there alone when it happened.

The Dreaded News Arrives

The doorbell rang around 1:00 that afternoon, according to my husband. He answered the door and, seeing the police officer, said, "Oh, no." The officer promptly said, "Yes, I'm afraid so." He came in and only stayed about 30 minutes, just long enough to see some pictures of Cathy and thus be comfortable calling in the identification so that we would not have to do it. He also waited until John placed calls to our oldest son and to a close friend of ours he knew I would want there when I returned to the tragic news. The news quickly traveled to many of our friends, and by the time I returned several hours later, there were so many cars in our driveway that I knew before I drove up that our Cathy was gone. I waited in the car for John to come out and tell me what happened—I knew he would come out when Ami ran into the house and signaled my return. I just couldn't hear the words in front of a bunch of people, even though they were people I loved. I remember his telling me like it was yesterday. Some things never get easier, and those words—"It is the worst you can imagine"—are still difficult to ponder today.

We made it through the first few days with the help of family and friends. There is no way to express to them, even today, how much they meant to me. Those early days and several months to follow were marked by a feeling of emptiness deep down inside. I remember the sadness, certainly, but the emptiness was like a hole opened up in the middle of my soul. That would become the principal dimension of grief I would experience for about two years, and the primary one I still recall, all these years later.

In addition to the compassion and support offered by my friends, two things were especially helpful for me in those early days following Cathy's death. And both were quite pivotal in my journey the next few years, including the grappling I have done over the issue of the death penalty. One of them was going to a homicide survivors' support group for about a year, and the other was reading bereavement literature. They worked together for several months, but then they began to diverge in my mind and send me differing messages. I wasn't sure what was going on for a while, but a conversation with my husband on the way home from one of the meetings provided a clue. John said to me, "Where do they get the energy for all that anger and bitterness?" His question surprised me because I was wondering the same thing without being conscious of it. I had to admit that I didn't know either, and for the first time, I realized why I had become so uncomfortable going to the meetings after receiving so much help there initially.

In the early days following Cathy's death, attending the meetings of other families of homicide victims had been beneficial in several ways. These people knew the pain we were experiencing for they had been down the same road we were on, and they listened to us with compassion. They knew that the criminal justice system is not really designed for the comfort of victims' family members; it is designed to deal with the perpetrators. Its personnel often do not understand how some of their procedures are demeaning and detrimental to us, and how often we feel that justice simply is not done. They made clear immediately that they would be there to help us through the process of trials and the inevitable postponements of trials. It was a refuge for me, and I was profoundly grateful. I heard their protestations of how wrong it was that the age of the boys would prevent their getting the death penalty, and even got caught up in that frenzy for a short time. This was enormously therapeutic for me. That is, in the beginning.

The Journey toward Healing

I had been working on healing—by reading about it as well as by talking to a therapist. I was actively grieving, knowing that this would benefit Ami, who was living with us and depending on us for emotional support. We had sought the advice of a child psychologist the minute we knew that Cathy had been killed. I knew that, if the worst had happened and we had to tell a five-year-old that her mommy was dead, I would have no idea how to do it appropriately. So John and I had already discussed calling someone the night before the officer came to the door. The psychologist's advice to us was to model appropriate behavior and provide Ami with as much security and stability as we were able to provide under the circumstances. If she didn't see what grief looked like, she wouldn't know how to interpret her own feelings, and thus wouldn't know how to express them.[1]

Due to my own emphasis on healing and the support I was receiving in that area, I was feeling ill at ease with the high level of bitterness that I continued to observe at the support meetings. That it was understandable was obvious to me, but it also seemed that many people were not moving forward in their lives, whatever that meant to me in that first year. The main difficulty I saw, however, was that the level of anger seemed to permeate their lives, and I wondered if that was inevitable for a homicide survivor. I didn't want my life to always be about this anger and bitterness, and it bothered me that it might. I realized that I might need to leave the support group in order to heal and find a way to live the rest of my life.

I have looked back on that experience many times, trying to articulate what I saw and felt that compelled me to withdraw after finding so much support there for months. It is still difficult to put into words, but I need to, not only to do justice to the group, but also to enable victims' assistance personnel to see what might be a problem for some survivors. My experience is not the same as everyone else's, but it is still an important point of view, I think. It is essential to value the experiences of all victims and to see, also, that we need to focus on what victims need as well as what they want, especially in those early days following a crime. As I have studied more over the years about grief and all its dimensions, I have wondered many times how kind it is—and how ethical it is—not to encourage some degree of moving on toward healing in

---

1. I learned years later that a five-year-old needs a great deal of help in coping because children this age are often at risk for later emotional instability, even when the appropriate coping assistance is provided. I therefore was doubly glad that we had sought professional advice.

homicide survivors. This encouragement obviously has to be offered with respect and subtlety, but I believe it needs to be initiated in some way to prevent some of what I have seen over the years.

First of all, there was a great deal of talk about the unfairness of the system and how it favored criminals. I had heard this many times before, but I wasn't absolutely sure that it was true. Another thing that bothered me was the parole blocking. At many meetings, we signed petitions to block the paroles of people we didn't know anything about except that they had committed murder. I began to question this practice: Was it necessary to know more than that? Were there mitigating circumstances? Is it good moral practice to blindly sign a petition that hurts another human being without knowing more? I wondered if there could be another way to facilitate this support group, to be more focused on healing but also address the needs of those who were new to the group and who required help getting through the criminal justice system. I thought of some models of self-help groups that divided themselves into newcomers and long-time members. I often wondered if that approach might not be more beneficial to those who remained in the group for a long time.

I remember one meeting in particular where a counselor or psychologist came and talked to us about grief and its many dimensions and layers. I found it enormously interesting and beneficial. Afterwards, however, at the coffee bar, members were very critical of the presentation, saying that no one could possibly understand the nature of their grief unless they had experienced the murder of a loved one too. All that the speaker had offered was totally rejected as unrelated to them and their experiences. I believed then, and still do, that this reaction was a form of denial. They were "stuck" in the early stages of their grief, and seemed to need to stay there in order to find any meaning in their lives at all; so they rejected any suggestion that they would move beyond anger at some point. Denial can be very protective in the early period of one's grief, and most of us go through some degree of denial. I know that I did in those early days and weeks, primarily in my inability to fully experience the reality of Cathy's death and the ensuing pain. It is not necessarily adaptive, however, for the denial to last forever.

I have realized over the years that there are those who can no longer find any meaning in the world after the murder of a loved one, especially a son or daughter. The psychological literature has a lot to say about this search for meaning that many of us endure, and how it can serve to make us new people in some ways.[2] I have found this lesson to be true for me; the search for

---

2. See Davis, Nolen-Hoeksema, and Larson 1998; De Vries, Lana, and Falck 1994; Nerken 1993; Edmonds and Hooker 1992; Schwartzberg and Janoff-Bulman 1991; Gray 1988; Thompson and Janigian 1988; Maniacek 1982; Craig 1977.

meaning has been an integral part of my life. That search has led me down a very different path, however, from the one found by many homicide survivors. I am still not certain why, at that time, it felt so wrong to try to bring about something good by doing something hurtful to others (blocking paroles), especially when such a good case could be made for murderers not deserving any consideration. I understand this sentiment better now, but I didn't then and for a long time afterward.

A New Awareness

It began to dawn on me why such negativity seemed wrong when I took a course on death and dying some time later. I had returned to college almost a year after Cathy's death, wanting to find meaning in doing grief counseling and educating others about grief and loss. I reasoned that both grief counseling and helping educate others had been truly beneficial for me, and I wanted to offer the same to others. I especially wanted to educate others about grief so that they would not remain as ignorant of so many issues as I had for most of my life, such as how to communicate with those who had lost a loved one. I had been so ignorant of just that one issue. It seemed obscene that one must endure the death of a child in order to know how to speak to others about their losses and provide understanding and patience in the face of the unspeakable. I wanted to offer people that insight without their having to go through what I had been through.

In one of our reading assignments for the class, there was some material listing "Factors Favoring Violence" (DeSpelder and Strickland 1987:384). Eight factors were identified, but the one that jumped out at me was the first one: "Anything that physically or psychologically separates the potential killer from the victim." I knew that when I was willing to sign those petitions it was because I had separated myself from the inmates psychologically—they were "fundamentally different from [me]" (ibid.). They were not really human beings, deserving of any respect. After all, they had killed people! When I blindly accepted the fact that the system favored criminals over victims, I was acting on this notion of separateness. When I began to be uncomfortable with the idea of acceptance without any critical inquiry, I was beginning my journey away from that idea of total separation. It would be a long journey, and I would have a number of stops along the way.

The first of these stops was about three years after Cathy's death, when I was presented with an opportunity to find out more about the death penalty. Until that time, my perceptions had been primarily emotional ones, and my support for the death penalty had waxed and waned depending on whom I had talked to last. Numerous people I had encountered had assumed that my support for the death penalty would be strong and unwavering, which had bothered me. I wondered why this was such a simple matter for some people but not for me. I thought it was time I took a more critical look at the issue, rather than simply accepting what I had heard from others, especially others in the victims' group I had attended.

Interestingly, the opportunity to do this exact research came in another class I took while working toward my bachelor's degree. In this class—Perspectives on the Present—we studied a number of political, historical, and philosophical issues affecting our world, many of them fraught with controversy. Among the books we could choose to review was *The Death Penalty in America*, Hugo Adam Bedau's (1964) anthology of arguments for and against the death penalty. Here was my chance to explore the topic adequately, I thought, since the book contained a line of reasoning for both sides of the debate. It also included, at the end, some stories of real people who had been charged with and convicted of capital crimes. Those accounts were especially powerful examples of why the death penalty was such a wrong-headed idea.

I took that course in the fall of 1989, a time of great change in the world, including the tearing down of the Berlin Wall in Germany and the beginning of the dismantling of the Soviet empire as we then knew it. It was also a time of great change for me in terms of breaking down some walls of my own. After reading all the arguments for and against the death penalty, I realized that the only arguments I could call rational and reasonable, given my knowledge of the social sciences (including scientific methods of inquiry), were those against the death penalty. What really surprised me, though, was the fact that I found most of the arguments supporting the death penalty either somewhat appalling, or especially lacking in the values that are important to me as a compassionate and caring human being. I found the positions put forth by some of the Christians in the volume to be especially galling; "blood-thirsty" is the term that first comes to mind.

Opposition to the Death Penalty

I realize that I have a tendency, perhaps, to weigh matters more carefully than some in my position are prone to do. Such a deliberative approach can be considered a virtue in some circles and an impediment to action in others, but I cannot ignore the volumes of evidence against the death penalty as an appropriate response to violent crime. In addition to that first book I read, I have tackled a host of others over the ensuing years (e.g., *The Contradictions of American Capital Punishment*, 2003; *Who Owns Death: Capital Punishment, the American Conscience, and the End of Executions*, 2002; *When the State Kills*, 2001; *Just Revenge: Costs and Consequences of the Death Penalty*, 1997; *Against the Death Penalty: Christian and Secular Arguments Against Capital Punishment*, 1997; *Dead Man Walking*, 1993). Anyone who opposes the death penalty will likely do such reading for a variety of reasons. I am no different from most in that regard. When I look at the issues of deterrence, fairness of application, costs of the death penalty versus alternatives, public support, and execution of the innocent, the death penalty just doesn't seem effective public policy to me. I will elaborate briefly on those issues, as they were the reasons I came to oppose capital punishment initially, and I have offered to share that journey faithfully and completely. The following five paragraphs appeared previously in *Crime Victims Report*, March/April 2000, under the title "A Reasoned Opposition to the Death Penalty," and still represent the greater part of my thinking on the above issues, so I have chosen to include them here.

> One of these areas of focus is the idea of deterrence, one of the original rationales for the death penalty. According to what I've read, I don't believe anyone but the most ardent proponents of the death penalty still believe that it is a deterrent at all—there is a mountain of evidence to suggest that it is not. In fact, many researchers have found the opposite to be true: that the application of the death penalty seems to have a "brutalizing effect," if only for a short while. By this, they mean that murder rates tend to go up for a short time immediately following an execution, especially a highly publicized one. Thus, rather than preventing violence, the death penalty adds to the level of violence in our communities (Costanzo 1997; Hanks 1997).[3]
>
> Another argument in favor of the death penalty is that it is cheaper than supporting offenders for the remainder of their lives in prison. This is a popular misconception, and one that politicians and the media choose not to dispel. The entire structure that has to be maintained in order to continue the death penalty is enormously expensive, from beginning to end. This includes the appellate process to attempt to guarantee the proper due process of each person convicted of a capital crime, but is not limited to it. The investigation, jury selection, trial, and security measures maintained within the founda-

---

3. See Bedau 1997:152–155 for an analysis of this research [not in original article].

tions supporting the death penalty are all extremely expensive, many times more so than life without parole. Some have suggested ending the death penalty and spending the money saved on victims' assistance programs. In a similar vein, there is a sentence called "life without parole plus restitution," in which the offender works to earn money placed in a fund for his victim's family (ibid).

An additional argument used by proponents of the death penalty is that the public supports the death penalty overwhelmingly, and most polls do support this statement, at least on the surface. When those polled are given only the two choices of support or rejection of the death penalty for those convicted of murder, they tend by about 75 percent to favor the death penalty, at least in theory. When called upon, however, to assess the death penalty for most murderers eligible for the death penalty, juries tend not to do so. Only in about a third of the cases where it applies do juries call for the death penalty for the convicted murderer. Also, when offered the choice of life without parole or life without parole plus restitution, the 75 percent support for death penalty drops below 44 and 32 percent, respectively. So much for the overwhelming public support for the death penalty (ibid).

A really vital area that opponents of the death penalty point to is whether the death penalty is fairly applied. Since the majority of the population of death row are poor and of color, the answer for opponents is that it is not. Proponents seem able to dismiss these two facts, even deny them, but the facts stubbornly remain if one wants to take an honest look at them. There are few if any wealthy people on death row, for they have the funds to seek experienced and competent representation from day one—this is simply not true of the majority of poorer Americans. And though there are numerous attempts to deny the racism omnipresent within our justice system, that bias exists and persists to this day. Only the most intentionally blind among us can ignore it. The reasons for the overrepresentation of African-Americans within the system are complex, but a great deal of it has to do with systemic racism at all levels of the judicial process. Disregarding these two sources of bias in our system is a blot on our national pride and calls our stand on human rights issues into question in the eyes of the rest of the world. Our stand in this area is already suspect since we remain the only nation in the western world still retaining the death penalty (ibid).

Probably the most important issue for opponents of the death penalty is that there are many incidences of the innocent being executed for crimes they did not commit, as well as many others found innocent just in time to prevent this horrible miscarriage of justice. Very often, these people were not saved by the system itself but by the superhuman efforts of a few special people (ibid). Errors in arrests and convictions take place every day—the system is run by human beings and it could not be otherwise—but errors can be found and overturned when there is no chance of death having occurred. When the alleged offender has been executed, there is no such chance. How can we ignore this issue so thoroughly as well? (White 2000:1–13)

These are the five issues that originally brought me to a position of opposition to the death penalty. The area I haven't mentioned yet, however, is the victims' issue. And I will, in due time. First, however, I want to explain how those initial seeds of discontent, planted in those two courses, gradually began growing within me, because the next leg of my journey was a pivotal one. Though the discomfort was developing, often without my ability to understand fully its origins, it didn't bear fruit for some time. It took another murder for that to happen—a murder halfway across the nation.

My Perspectives on Violence and the Criminal Justice System: Ensuing Changes

I had finished both my bachelor's and master's degree and was teaching in a community college. A young woman in South Carolina had been in the news and had become the focus of discussion one afternoon. Susan Smith had originally reported that a black man had hijacked her car and kidnapped her two toddler sons who were sleeping in their car seats at the time. A week to ten days of searching had produced no results and the authorities apparently became suspicious and began to question her more thoroughly. It had been disclosed in the media the night before our class meeting that Susan Smith's children were not abducted as she had reported to the police initially, but had instead been killed by her. Some of the students in my class couldn't wait to discuss it and wanted to tell me how they would punish her for having killed her two sons. The methods were varied and inventive, and all quite punitive—the students almost seemed to be competing with one another for how much they could make her suffer. One very kind young man, a good student I had really enjoyed during the semester, told us in very deliberate terms how he would tie her in a car and drive it into the water and watch her die the same way that she had killed her sons. The expression on his face spoke volumes. I stood there in horror as this proceeded, slowly shaking my head at the display of raw violence I was witnessing, and realizing that few, if any, of them would ever associate their behavior with violence. On that day, violence and its alternatives became the major focus of my work.

Following this experience, I began to think about my previous experiences in terms of violence. I realized that I was eventually repelled by the parole blocking and negative remarks about the criminal justice system because both represented responding to violence with more violence. Were these responses justified? Were they accurate? I simply didn't know, and it wasn't ethical for me to respond that way without more information and a degree of critical thinking. Others may see it differently, and I respect their right to do so, but I needed to know if what I did in my daughter's memory was actually going to reduce the level of violence in our society or have the opposite effect. It wasn't morally acceptable for me to act out of stereotypical thinking or ignorance; I had to know more and I began to look for a way to educate myself about the issues. Strangely, it was at a church meeting that I found my first source.

I had gone to a meeting of our local presbytery—an assemblage of some 110 Presbyterian churches in the Houston area where I live—and was browsing the tables of literature published by the Presbyterian Church of the USA. I saw a title, *Restorative Justice: Toward Nonviolence* (Mackey 1992), and was attracted by the subtitle of the book, as I certainly had no idea what restorative justice was at that point. I took home a copy of the publication, and a whole world opened up to me—a world that is still a big part of my life today, especially in terms of philosophy of justice. I immediately learned that I had some very stereotypical ideas about our criminal justice system; those ideas had colored my judgments for many years. I was open to the material in the book, however, due to some vague sense that much of what we did within the system was returning violence for violence. It had seemed to me that we should be able to come up with something better than that, but I certainly didn't have a clue what that might be.

The next two books I read were Howard Zehr's *Changing Lenses: A New Focus for Crime and Justice* (1990) and Gerald Austin McHugh's *Christian Faith and Criminal Justice: Toward a Christian Response to Crime and Punishment* (1978). Although both of these books have overtones of a Christian faith perspective, they also contain a great deal of rational discourse about the manner in which we dispense justice in America. They were ultimately mind-altering books for me, as they continued my education into restorative justice— a way of envisioning crime differently. Zehr's book provided the background I needed to understand fully this re-visioning of crime into harms and violations of people and relationships (Zehr 1990 and 2002). Those operating out of a restorative justice perspective will seek, above all, to find ways to address the harms without creating further harms. This is restorative justice's greatest strength, from my perspective, for I see such great harm caused by the manner in which we dispense punishment today. I was able to turn away from this reality for many years, but I am unable to do so today. An in-depth exploration of restorative justice is beyond the scope of this work,[4] but I can say, with complete honesty, that the principles of restorative justice have changed the way I view our system today, including the administration of the death penalty.

McHugh's book gives a history of the prison system in America, along with how the church in its various manifestations has contributed to some of the difficulties evident in today's prisons. Above all, McHugh calls upon American Christians to look more closely at prison issues and leave stereotypes behind. He encourages them to consider volunteering to serve in some manner inside a prison, in order to see for themselves what goes on there. Since prisoners often see themselves as just as worthless as the public does, he suggests that any attempt to see inmates as human and reach out to them on that basis can have significant effects. The following words leaped out from the page when I read them:

> Such a reaching out could take many concrete forms—visits to prison, support before parole boards or in court, contact with a convict's wife and family, *volunteering to teach inside prisons* [my emphasis], offering jobs to prisoners who are released, etc. The important element is not so much the specific action taken as the genuine concern which it signifies (McHugh 1978:153).

Teaching in Prison

I knew that Sam Houston State University, where I was teaching part-time, offered classes in the prison system, and I inquired whether our department needed another teacher in this program. One of my colleagues suggested I teach my favorite subject, Death and Dying, in prison. He informed me that there was often a need for a philosophy course as part of the curriculum we

---

4. I hope anyone at all interested will read one of the numerous works on restorative justice, for it is widely misunderstood, especially by homicide survivors. I would suggest *The Little Book of Restorative Justice* by Howard Zehr (2002), for both its breadth and brevity.

offered, but none had been offered in quite some time; Death and Dying, as a philosophy course within our university, could fulfill that need.

In 1997 I taught one class at each of two prisons, both near Huntsville, the home of the Texas Department of Criminal Justice, and my life has never been the same. What I saw there took me further down the road to the values I hold today. I presented to the students I taught there the face of a woman who had endured the murder of her daughter but had come out the other side without hatred for them as criminals. I admit they found this particularly astounding, and I hoped they would reflect on what my actions offered in terms of modeling different behavior from what they normally saw. I treated them with respect and, on the whole, got it back tenfold. I expected to see human beings and that's what I saw; people often live up to our best, or worst, expectations of them. I had a good model for the manner in which I taught and how I treated the students; my department head, who had taught in the same prisons for years, had spoken of his experiences in class when I was his student.

My experiences over the years of teaching in prison have affected me profoundly. I am often glad that I live at least an hour away from the units in which I taught, because it usually took some time for decompression when I left the prison following class. It is both exhilarating and depressing to do the job of prison education, at least from my perspective. I frequently had moments when I believed I saw into the soul of another wounded human being, someone who may have wounded another as well, admittedly, out of ignorance, desperation, impulsiveness, and pain. It wasn't always rosy, let me hasten to add. There were difficult times also. I remember one class in which two inmates were very disrespectful, although this was rare. One of the other students who knew me from previous classes stayed after class to beg me not to let them drive me away from teaching in prison, as the majority of the men truly appreciated who I was and what I tried to do. Furthermore, prison is a sad and depressing place, when you consider that we keep human beings in cages there, regardless of how much it might be necessary for a time. And though I imagine that most correctional officers are appropriate in their behavior toward the inmates, I saw a number who were sadistic, I'm sorry to say.

The most healing thing I have done since my daughter's death is the work I've completed in prison, both teaching and participating in victim-offender encounters as part of a program called Bridges to Life. Recently I heard someone who works in the system say, with sarcasm, that she had never met a guilty person in the system. My encounters in prison have been quite the opposite— I only had one inmate ever tell me that he was innocent of the crime for which he had been convicted—and I know from subsequent events that I taught at least one innocent man. I have heard other homicide survivors say the same things I say: the stereotypes leave you with a high degree of anger, but the realities of those we lock up for long periods of time can bring some measure of healing, if one allows it to happen. This is one realization that would be beneficial to homicide survivors—embracing the reality, not the stereotype—for stereotypes feed prejudice.

As I said previously in differing ways, I am strongly in favor of criminal justice reform across the board, including the ultimate punishment. The strongest reasons for my opposition to the death penalty today are societal, however, rather than the offenders or the issues that changed my opinion originally. My original experiences are simply the background that, I think, will help others understand my current views about this controversial issue, which have evolved over the last fifteen years. While I completely understand the frequent response of homicide survivors to consider the death of the person responsible as the only fitting punishment they will accept, I simply do not see in this reaction what most of them see. I am especially opposed to the death penalty, because for me, capital punishment 1) is not what victims need, and 2) is not worthy of us as a nation.

My Current Position on the Death Penalty

These are highly emotional issues, and not easy to depict in rational terms. The death penalty has enormous symbolic value for many victims and their families. I recall a recent local case in which the jury did not give the defendant the death penalty, contrary to the fervent hopes of the family of the victim. In the press conference after the sentence was pronounced, a representative of the family said that they had been slapped in the face, or some words to that effect. I confess to remembering the tone much more accurately than the precise words used: they were affronted that he had *only* received a life sentence of forty years before he could be considered for parole. I also recall my own reaction to these words, having spent time in several Texas prisons over the years. Forty years in a Texas prison is in some ways a worse sentence than execution, and certainly not the light sentence the victim's family believed the defendant had been given.

When homicide survivors believe that only a death sentence is true justice, it sets them up for such incredible disappointment if it doesn't come about, as frequently happens. Very few homicide cases are tried as capital crimes to begin with, and even in capital trials many offenders do not receive the ultimate punishment. What does this say to most homicide survivors, some 98 percent of them? Your loved one just wasn't worthy of the ultimate punishment? If the offender does receive the death sentence the family wants so badly, what then? Years and years go by before it is carried out. Shorten the process of appeal, some say, and I do understand this impatience with the appellate process. I see this response as dangerous, however, considering the number of people who've been exonerated in recent years, some of them many years after the original sentence was given.

When the death penalty is finally carried out, many survivors find the execution wasn't all they hoped—it was too easy for him, they often say. I'm sure it looks easy, considering the sterile manner in which capital punishment is carried out today in most jurisdictions. Some victims' family members find it has helped them have a reason to live, to see this person punished—but then it falls far short of their expectations. Where do they go with those feelings that the offender's execution didn't provide what they needed? Where do they go with their grief and anger now? I recall reading in a local paper following the execution of someone who had killed several people in a psychotic episode, "We can finally go on with our lives!" It had been some fifteen years since the conviction and sentence, and the family had been living at least partly in limbo, waiting for the justice they deserved. I thought that was one of the saddest statements I had ever heard. This is the primary reason I am so grateful today that the defendants in my daughter's case, because of their age, were not eligible for the death penalty. I cannot imagine having lived for many years awaiting what I perceived to be justice for her.

One of the sad facts about losing a loved one to murder is that there is both a loss and a crime. It is very easy to get wrapped up in the crime element and not deal with the loss aspect of it, as most of us know. If you have been waiting for the state to take action to provide you with some kind of "closure" so you can move forward with your life, you may be very disappointed following the execution. While many people have swallowed the myth of closure, most of us know that there is no real closure—it is an empty promise. And there is nothing that the state can do to bring about what homicide survivors really need— healing— for healing is an inside job. It takes a long time, and it takes a lot of work on the part of the survivors. Certainly, the manner in which the state treats victims can either promote or inhibit the healing that is so badly needed, but the healing itself is a product of the active engagement with the grief process by the victims themselves. The state could provide much greater support for victims in several areas if it had the funding, and that financial assistance might be provided if the death penalty didn't consume such huge amounts of our financial resources.

Victims are currently able to seek assistance in some of those areas I refer to—funeral expenses, counseling, and lost time at work—but these compensation funds are very limited and have been co-opted in some states for purposes other than those originally intended. My family and I were able to obtain help with Cathy's funeral expenses but not the high cost of years of counseling for her daughter. I am familiar with at least one family who didn't even know about compensation funds until the deadline had passed for application. Since many victims' families are within the working class, these funds could really help with the monetary costs associated with the crime and enable the family to have enough energy left to deal with its emotional and psychological consequences, which are devastating enough on their own.

Another issue often overlooked regarding the death penalty is that it often focuses our attention on the defendant, rather than on the plight of the victims involved. When I initially present the death penalty in my Death and Dying class, I write the names of three victims of the Oklahoma City bombing on the board and ask who knows who these people are. No one has ever recognized the names, sad to say. When I add the name of Timothy McVeigh, there is instant recognition, of course. Then I tell the class who the others are. Next I write the name of Bill McVeigh, Timothy's father. I say that he is also a victim, which is why I add his name to the list. The families of those who receive the ultimate sentence are victims as well, for they endure the long wait until the execution and then are added to the list of the grieving. After living as a bereaved parent for more than eighteen years, I cannot imagine being willing to sanction killing another person. When we execute someone, we simply enlarge the circle of grief. I can never again ignore this fact. It is a sad fact of our culture that so many people can.

In addition to the death penalty not being particularly good for victims, I see it as not being worthy of our society. That is not to say that I don't hear of crimes that I find so heinous as to be filled with exactly the same indignation and revulsion as anyone else. Some crimes are beyond the pale in their horror. I like to believe, though, that we don't need to imitate what we abhor in others in order to register our total condemnation of those acts. For me, it will always be about who *we* are as opposed to what the crime is. Must I demand a life for my daughter's life? Is that the only way I would appreciate that society values her life—if another was sacrificed in her name? Is it appropriate for us to take a life in order to show value for another one? Must we continue to extend the circle of death and grief in order to say that murder—and with it, death and grief—is simply not a value we can accept? My answer to all these questions is an unqualified "no." I can no longer distance myself so far from other human beings that these actions on our part are acceptable— even if those human beings have committed inhuman acts. Somewhere, sometime, the violence has to stop—and I am content to have it stop with me.

I have met with one of the young men who killed my daughter through a program we have in Texas for mediated dialogues between victims and offenders. This meeting was a profoundly liberating experience for me and for my daughter Ami,[5] who engaged in the dialogue also. I found in the young man a badly mistreated human being who was enormously remorseful for the crime he took part in. He never offered his abusive childhood as an excuse for his actions, I am pleased to say; he knows as well as I do that it isn't an excuse. He offered the details of his horrid upbringing only because I asked for them. It helped me, however, to understand how he came to be there that night and a little about why my daughter was no longer alive. It helped me to understand a little about how it all happened—and that kind of information, I hope, can help prevent others from going down the same paths, if we use what we learn to reform our system.

He also shared with us what Cathy's last words were, which was a wonderful gift after all those years. I doubt that I could have fully appreciated them earlier, though, for they were words of forgiveness for the two boys. Right before she turned her head away so they could shoot her in the back of the head she looked up and said, "I forgive you, and God will forgive you too." Hearing this from him and seeing the shame he felt about it, knowing that they had killed her anyway, had a tremendous impact on me. It gave me a sense of something special. I cannot call it closure, since I do not believe in that at all, but it is a sense of reconciliation of sorts about the manner in which she died. It is truly hard to come to grips with the last moments of your loved one's life and how he or she died—for me this has always been the most challenging issue. Meeting with him gave me some degree of peace with that aspect of it, almost as if she gave us a message in those last moments, a legacy of who she was and what she wanted to leave behind. And it made me realize that my work over the last nineteen years was exactly the memorial she deserved.

References

Bedau, Hugo A. (ed.). 1997. *The Death Penalty in America: Current Controversies*. New York: Oxford University Press.

_____. 1964. *The Death Penalty in America: An Anthology*. New York: Doubleday.

Braun, Mildred J. and Dale H. Berg. 1994. "Meaning Reconstruction in the Experience of Parental Bereavement." *Death Studies* 18:105–29.

Costanzo, Mark. 1997. *Just Revenge: Costs and Consequences of the Death Penalty*. New York: St. Martin's Press.

Craig, Yvonne. 1977. "The Bereavement of Parents and Their Search for Meaning." *British Journal of Social Work* 7:41–54.

---

5. Ami grew up in our home and became our legal daughter when she was 11 years old, at her request.

Davis, Christopher G., Susan Nolen-Hoeksema, and Judith Larson. 1998. "Making Sense of Loss and Benefiting from the Experience: Two Construals of Meaning." *Journal of Personality & Social Psychology* 75:561–74.

De Vries, Brian, Rose D. Lana, and Vilma T. Falck. 1994. "Parental Bereavement over the Life Course: A Theoretical Intersection and Empirical Review." *Omega: Journal of Death & Dying* 29:47–69.

DeSpelder, Lynne A. and Albert L. Strickland. 1987. *The Last Dance: Encountering Death and Dying (2nd ed.)*. Mountain View, CA: Mayfield.

Edmonds, Sarah and Karen Hooker. 1992. "Perceived Changes in Life Meaning Following Bereavement." *Omega: Journal of Death & Dying* 25:307–18.

Gray, Ross E. 1988. "Meaning of Death: Implications for Bereavement Theory." *Death Studies* 12:309–17.

Hanks, Gardner C. 1997. *Against the Death Penalty: Christian and Secular Arguments Against Capital Punishment*. Scottsdale. PA: Herald Press.

Lifton, Robert J. and Greg Mitchell. 2002. *Who Owns Death: Capital Punishment, the American Conscience, and the End of Executions*. New York: Harper Collins.

Mackey, Virginia. 1997. *Restorative Justice: Toward Nonviolence*. Discussion paper on Crime and Justice, Presbyterian Justice Program, Presbyterian Church USA.

Maniacek, Mary A. 1982. "Logotherapy: A Grief Counseling Process." *International Forum for Logotherapy* 5:85–91.

McHugh, Gerald A. 1978. *Christian Faith and Criminal Justice: Toward a Christian Response to Crime and Punishment*. New York: Paulist Press.

Nerken, Ira R. 1993. "Grief and the Reflective self: Toward a Clearer Model of Loss Resolution and Growth." *Death Studies* 17:1–26.

Prejean, Helen. 1993. *Dead Man Walking: An Eyewitness Account of the Death Penalty in the United States*. New York: Random House.

Sarat, Austin. 2001. *When the State Kills: Capital Punishment and the American Condition*. Princeton: Princeton University Press.

Schwartzberg, Steven S., and Ronnie Janoff-Bulman. 1991. "Grief and the Search for Meaning: Exploring the Assumptive Worlds of Bereaved College Students." *Journal of Social & Clinical Psychology* 10: 270–88.

Thompson, Suzanne C. and Aris S. Janigian. 1988. "Life Schemes: A Framework for Understanding the Search for Meaning." *Journal of Clinical & Social Psychology* 7: 260–80.

White, Linda. 2000. "A Reasoned Opposition to the Death Penalty." *Crime Victims Report*, March/April 2000, 1–13.

Zehr, Howard. 2002. *The Little Book of Restorative Justice*. Intercourse, PA: Good Books.

———. 1990. *Changing Lenses: A New Focus for Crime and Justice*. Scottsdale, PA: Herald Press.

Zimring, Franklin E. 2003. *The Contradictions of American Capital Punishment*. New York: Oxford University Press.

CHAPTER 4

THE DEATH SENTENCE:
FOR CRIMINALS OR VICTIMS?

Shane Wagner

This chapter will focus on the question: Who is the death sentence for, the criminal or the victim? I will describe the murder of my father along with the investigation, trial, and subsequent clemency process that occurred in Illinois under former Governor George Ryan. This chapter also explores topics including what life is like on death row, the services provided by victim assistance programs, and the effects of the lengthy death sentence process on victims' families.

On July 9, 1997, I had called my dad at his pawnshop to see how he was doing; it had been several weeks since I had talked to him because of the busy summer baseball schedule. During a typical summer, I would have visited with him often because he loved to watch his grandchildren play. He frequently helped me coach, and I would ask his advice about how to handle difficult baseball situations. We would also go to major-league baseball games together, and he would reminisce about how baseball was played when he was a kid. His grandchildren loved listening to his stories and loved going to games with him.

I had called him to ask him if he could meet me for coffee, one of our favorite things to do. He did not answer the phone—which was not unusual, as he frequently went out for coffee during the day. So I went back to installing the in-car video system in my partner's squad car. I had worked as a police officer for about two years. My father was a retired police officer, and I had always wanted to follow in his footsteps. He would always ask how the job was going.

When I graduated from the police academy I invited him to attend the graduation ceremony; he was so happy to be there. The night was even more special when the master of ceremonies asked for the president of the class to say a few words. I stood up and told the audience how special this was for me to follow in my father's path of life. He was completely unaware of what I was

Shane Wagner with father Dale, 1989.

doing. I had not told him that I was the class president because I wanted it to be a surprise. The surprise did not stop there because I also was given the academic achievement award for the class. It was a special night for us, and I could tell that he had to choke back tears of joy.

Not too long after I made this phone call, the dispatcher requested that I telephone my sister at home. It was not unusual for people to contact me through the dispatcher, so I went inside the police station to call her. As I waited for Cheryl to pick up the phone, I wondered why she might be calling; maybe it was to let me know about a family get-together? When she answered, I asked her what she wanted. She said, "He's dead." As you can imagine, I was completely shocked and confused. There was complete silence on both ends of the phone. I had to ask who she was talking about, to which she replied, "Someone shot him." It was obvious that she was very upset. I could hear the inflection in her voice as if she were trying not to cry.

Still unsure who she was talking about, I began to get that sinking feeling in my stomach. I started to wonder if it might be my brother. Not really wanting to ask the question again, I muttered the words, "Who is dead?" As she started to sob I could feel the uneasiness in my stomach getting worse. Terrible thoughts were flying through my head. I could only think of how terrible it must have been for my brother to have been shot to death. How painful it was, what he might have been thinking. The lump in my throat started to swell and tears began to run down my face, when all of a sudden she said,

"Dad's dead." After first thinking that my brother had been killed, and then finding out it was my dad, I felt like I was on an emotional roller coaster.

A long period of silence ensued as we gathered our emotions. When I asked her what had happened, her voice cracked, and all she could tell me was that he had been shot in the pawnshop. When I inquired who had given her the news, she replied, "The police department called to let me know." She said that she did not get the caller's name. Still sobbing, she asked me to call the police department in Mt. Vernon, Illinois, to find out what had happened. She thought that I might be able to learn more because I was a police officer. I told her that I would go there in person to talk with the detectives and see what I could find out.

Before hanging up the phone I asked my sister if anyone had called the rest of the family, and in particular our grandma. Cheryl told me that the police department had called Grandma and explained that my father had been in an accident. They had been afraid to tell her what had really happened because of her age. Cheryl told me she was going to Grandma's house to tell her the truth.

As I gathered my things, I could not help but think of the fun times I had had with my dad. Days spent fishing and hunting with him drifted through my mind as I thought about the loss of my best friend. When I was a child, I had always wanted to be just like my dad. I wanted to be a policeman just like him, I wanted to serve in the military just like him, and of course I wanted to be a great dad just like him.

While driving home, I realized it would not be easy to tell my family what had happened. I started to think about how I could tell my wife and children that he was dead. I could feel that frog starting to form again in my throat as I opened the door to my house. My wife, Kim, could tell that something was wrong and asked if I was OK. Tears began rolling down my face as I started to tell them what had happened. It was a dreadful feeling, like someone had kicked me in the stomach.

After sobbing for some time, I was able to gain some composure. I drove to the Mt. Vernon Police Department to talk to one of the detectives. They were very reluctant to give out information on the case, but they were able to confirm that my dad was dead. His bloodied body had been discovered by a traveler passing through, just looking to sell some items.

The Investigation

The investigation was led by the Mt. Vernon Police Department. The Illinois State Police, the Bureau of Alcohol, Tobacco and Firearms (ATF), and a few other agencies assisted with the investigation. It took close to three days for these groups to process the crime scene, and they secured an unbelievable amount of evidence. In addition to my dad's body, the investigators were able to recover bullet fragments, blood, palm- and fingerprints, bloody shoe prints, and glass fragments. They also collected the last few pawn and sales receipts, the cash register, and a golf club believed to have been used to break the glass in the showcases. A list of missing jewelry taken during the robbery/murder also was compiled.

A bullet had penetrated a door and lodged in a VCR. Another bullet fragment was recovered from a piece of window trim, and yet another fragment was recovered from the floor. The investigators used several laser devices to determine bullet trajectory. One laser device was placed into the bullet hole in the VCR and turned on. Another was situated to determine a bullet's entry and exit path through a chunk of the service counter. The use of lasers enabled the detectives to determine where the perpetrator stood when the shots were fired and to estimate the height at which the gun was held. These calculations helped them to get a better understanding of the suspect's possible height and positioning.

A large amount of blood was at the scene, including sections of blood-soaked carpet. Droplets of blood and blood splatter were used to formulate theories about where the crime started and how it occurred. Luminol, a chemical substance capable of revealing blood not detected by the naked eye, was used to retrieve bloody footprints leading from my father's body to other areas of the pawnshop, and finally outside. These footprints were used to determine the size and type of shoe worn by the offender.

The last few sales receipts and pawn tickets revealed the names of individuals who were in the pawnshop close to the time of the crime. Investigators were able to locate and interview those people. The cash-register tape reflected that the last known sale occurred at approximately 4:10 p.m. The cash register also had a small blood smear on it, which investigators speculated was there because the perpetrators could not open the cash drawer so they tried to force my father to open it.

As soon as they finished processing the scene, the ATF wanted to get a complete inventory of the firearms from the store because it appeared that some had been taken in the robbery. This would prove to be a very important part of the investigation because the defendant and two accomplices were caught with some of the stolen firearms in their possession. Firearms stolen during the robbery and murder of my father were discovered during a raid on a known drug house. Police personnel involved in the raid ran the firearms through the National Crime Information Center and found that the firearms were connected to a murder. One of the suspects present during the raid admitted in the course of an interview to possessing a .38 revolver. This gun was unique not only because it belonged to my dad, but also because the hammer on the weapon was broken off, which made it easily identifiable. The detectives also were able to secure palm prints from the suspects, one of which matched the palm print left on the glass display case in the pawn shop. This evidence was crucial because it linked this suspect to the crime scene.

When the investigators were notified of this breakthrough, they conducted several interviews of this suspect. When he could not explain away the fact that he was in possession of a stolen firearm involved in a murder, he decided to cooperate with the investigation. He told police bits and pieces of the events that occurred the day of the murder. He also told them about others involved in the crime.

Accordingly, the investigation quickly centered on the defendant and his accomplices. Not surprisingly, the defendant was not about to admit to anything, but the police had statements from his accomplices that placed him at the murder scene. The police also had a statement from a woman indicating that she had seen the defendant and his accomplices entering the pawnshop as she was leaving. Unfortunately, she was unable to identify the suspects in a lineup. In a piece of great police work, the detectives had the witness herself placed in a lineup, and one of the defendant's accomplices picked her out as the lady who was leaving as they entered the shop.

As a result of interviews conducted with the defendant and his accomplices, the detectives were able to piece together the crime. They were further able to recover glass fragments from the pawnshop display cases in the getaway car and several pieces of jewelry stolen from my father's store. Some of the jewelry had been pawned the day following the crime by one of the accomplices, which clearly linked him to the case. Other items stolen during the robbery were recovered from the defendant's girlfriend, who later testified that the defendant had given her the pawnshop goods the night of the robbery/murder.

The Trial

After the grand jury indicted the defendant on first-degree murder and armed robbery charges, the case was set for the trial. As I sat in the courtroom waiting for the trial to begin, I wondered how I would feel when the defendant was brought in. Would I be angry? Would I look him in the eye? Would he look into my eyes? Would I be able to look at his family? And, in turn, would he look at my family, the co-victims?

As people started to file into the courtroom it became evident that the room would be divided: one side for the prosecution and one side for the defense. I looked at the defendant's family members as they entered, first his mother, and then a woman who I believed to be his sister. I was shocked that only two people from his family were present during the trial. In addition to family members, a number of people from the press were there to cover the courtroom proceedings.

From the testimony of the defendant's accomplices, I learned that they had planned the crime the day before they carried it out. On the day of the robbery, the defendant and his accomplices drove from Decatur to Mt. Vernon in hopes of scoring from my father's shop. They drove directly to the pawnshop, and the defendant and one of his accomplices went inside. What followed were acts of sheer brutality committed by the defendant.

Apparently, the defendant did not get what he wanted from my dad and proceeded to make him suffer. When my dad attempted to defend himself he was viciously attacked and murdered. According to the coroner's testimony, the cause of death was multiple gunshot wounds to the head, face, arm, and torso. Two gunshot wounds—one to the arm and another to the shoulder area—most likely occurred first, but neither would have been fatal (*People v. Hicks* 2000:18).

Even after the defendant shot my dad twice he could have made the choice to take what he wanted and leave. However, he decided that was not enough and he had to finish the despicable deed. As my dad begged for his life, saying, "Please don't kill me," the defendant shot him a third time. The bullet entered his body in the corner of the left eye next to the bridge of his nose and exited behind the right ear, breaking his jaw. This undoubtedly was an extremely painful injury, but the coroner explained that this wound would not immediately have been fatal; it would have caused blindness and disorientation.

The defendant again had the opportunity to leave with the robbery proceeds, but he could not resist completing the evil acts that he had begun. As if committing an execution, the defendant shot my dad in the head. The fourth and final bullet entered the right temple area and exited through the left side of his head. The coroner testified this wound would have been fatal almost immediately.

Some of the most incriminating evidence presented during the trial included the notes recovered from the defendant while he was incarcerated at the Menard Correctional Center during the trial. In these notes, the defendant asked fellow inmates to fabricate testimony for the trial. He could not explain why he attempted to have others fabricate testimony on his behalf. In fact, he could only say that he was merely trying to level the playing field because the trial appeared to be going in favor of the prosecution.

On September 27, 2000, the jury found the defendant guilty of armed robbery and first-degree murder. One of the most painful moments of the trial came following the guilty verdict, when I was asked to prepare a victim impact statement.

The fond memories of my dad surfaced as I had to write how his loss would affect me and the other survivors. The thought of the loss of my best friend brought tears to my eyes, as I knew that I would forever be unable to hear his voice or seek his advice again. Thinking of how my children would miss being around him and how he would miss out on watching them grow up made the lump in my throat swell. Thoughts of how life had been when I was a child crossed my mind.

I found myself staring at the computer screen, wondering just how I would fill all that white space. Tears were streaming down my face as I wrote the words of how he would be missed. Having to read it was equally difficult. I looked the defendant right in the eye, but he would not look at me. I told him that I would forgive him, but that forgiveness is separate from punishment. I looked at the jury and asked them not to misinterpret my forgiveness because I believed that the defendant should be punished. I told the defendant and the jury that the surviving family will forever be changed because of this despicable act and how we have forever lost those moments we cherish with my father and our friend.

As I sit here writing, I find myself daydreaming about my father and how we loved to spend time with each other. The wonderful memories that I have of him far outweigh the memories I have of the murder, yet those awful memories always seem to overtake the high-quality ones.

After I read the victim impact statement, the judge gave the jurors their instructions and had them retire to the jury room to decide what punishment the defendant would receive. Late in the evening, after several hours of stressful waiting, the state's attorney informed us that a decision had been made. As I walked into the courtroom I looked at the jury and noticed that some were in tears. The jury found that there were no mitigating factors to preclude the imposition of the death sentence, and the court sentenced the defendant to death (*People v. Hicks* 2000:35).

I was somewhat shocked to see that the defendant's family was not there for the whole trial, only showing up two or three days. As I recall, only the defendant's mother was present during the sentencing phase of the trial. When the sentence was given, neither the defendant nor his mother showed any sign of emotion.

From the time the crime occurred through the conclusion of the trial was absolutely the most stressful time of my life. Fortunately, the support my family received throughout the investigation, trial, and to this day was and is remarkable. We were treated with honor and dignity by the police department, the state's attorney's office, the victim assistance advocate, and all other agencies involved.

The State's Attorney's Office made sure that we were informed about every aspect of the trial, even asking if it would be OK to show the jury autopsy photos of my father. The victim's advocate introduced us to programs, described more fully later in this chapter, that were available through her office. Furthermore, she was present every step of the way, making sure we had a quiet place to sit while the trial was in recess, making sure that our questions were answered, and providing comfort throughout the most difficult times of the trial.

Life on Death Row

Currently, thirty-eight states authorize capital punishment, and nearly 3,500 prisoners are awaiting execution in the United States. California has the largest death row, with well over 600 inmates. In marked contrast are the death rows in New Mexico and Wyoming, each of which houses just two inmates. New Hampshire's death row remains empty (Fins 2004).

Life on death row has become a long journey for most inmates today. Although the outcome for many condemned prisoners ultimately is death, as they await the fulfillment of their sentence life is fairly easy. For most, life consists of being locked in their six-by-ten foot cell twenty-four hours a day, except for one hour, which is typically used for exercise. Because of their status, death-row inmates normally do not participate in heavy labor activities. Cell temperatures are regulated, and these inmates are segregated from the general population (Buehl 1998).

For the most part, death-row inmates present fewer behavioral problems and are less disruptive than other prisoners. However, it is also true that they have little opportunity to misbehave. Whenever they are moved, each inmate is searched by guards and scanned with a metal detector (Abu-Jamal, Vest, and Conniff 1995). They are served three meals per day in their cells (White 2004). Death-row inmates typically are allowed to shower three times weekly. A no-contact policy prevails during visitation. Condemned prisoners characteristically are limited to two hours per week for visits (Buehl 1998), and visits are conducted in a closed room, with the inmate handcuffed and kept isolated by a shatterproof glass partition. Communications typically occur with the use of a phone set (Abu-Jamal et al.1995).

Many escape the looming outcome of the death penalty only by way of common diversions such as television or radio (ibid.). These items are normally approved because they serve as a behavior-control device. Prisons generally function to control and suppress human beings, and these purposes are at the forefront for death-row inmates (Buehl 1998).

As the inmate waits, so must the victim's family. Years of appeals, the possibility for clemency, and stays of execution extend the time the victims' families must experience the emotional roller coaster of a death-penalty case. Some death-row inmates await their execution for more than twenty years. These inmates take advantage of the judicial system so they can delay their trial, conviction, and execution date. Most hope that their state's governor or pardon board will give them a stay of execution or clemency.

Yet while these inmates wait safely in their cells for their execution, co-victims are faced with fear of retaliation from offenders' associates. Additionally, we wait for the emptiness to go away, but it never does. We also wonder why it takes so long to carry out the sentence that was given to the wrongdoer. Society would be better served if these sentences were carried out more quickly. It is a constant aggravation to think that, for years, our hard-earned tax dollars are used to support the offender who committed horrific acts against our loved ones. Moreover, the possibility that the offender might be granted a stay of execution or clemency adds even more frustration to our grief.

Clemency in Illinois

Just when my family had started to put this painful experience behind us, former Governor Ryan decided he would exercise his clemency powers. Clemency is defined as mercy or leniency and usually describes acts of the U.S. president or a governor when pardoning a convicted criminal or commuting a sentence (Garner 1999). Clemency generally includes five varieties of leniency: amnesty, pardon, commutation, remission of fines, and reprieve (Kobil 1991).

Illinois has had four constitutions since it became a state in 1818. The first Illinois Constitution's clemency provision gave the governor the power to grant pardons and reprieves after conviction. The only exception to this rule was in cases of impeachment (Illinois Constitution 1818). The Constitutions of 1848 and 1870 perpetuated the governor's clemency powers, with the latter providing: "The governor shall have power to grant reprieves, commutations and pardons, after conviction, for all offenses, subject to such regulations as may be provided by law relative to the manner of applying therefor" (Illinois Constitution 1870, Art. V, Sec. 13).

The present Constitution, approved in 1970, gives the governor the power to grant reprieves, commutations, and pardons, after conviction, for all offenses on such terms as he considers proper. This provision gives the governor the power to commute anyone's sentence, including prisoners on death row (Illinois Constitution 1970).

Following invalidation of its capital-punishment law in the wake of *Furman v. Georgia* (1972), Illinois reinstated the death penalty in 1974. However, the first post-*Furman* execution did not occur in the state until 1990 (Bienen 1998). Illinois's capital punishment statute is similar to laws in other states; it is broad in scope and has an inclusive set of aggravating factors. Only persons who have committed aggravated murder are eligible for the death penalty (Holthusen 2004).

While Governor Ryan was in office he did not agree with the Illinois General Assembly about the death penalty. He alleged that the capital punishment system in Illinois was riddled with flaws. Because more people had been exonerated than were executed under the law since the death penalty had been reinstated, he believed the fairness of the system should be examined (Armstrong and Mills 2000).

Based on his grave concerns about Illinois's capital punishment system, he declared a moratorium on executions in January 2000. In addition to the moratorium, he appointed a special commission to make a comprehensive study of the Illinois capital punishment system (Blackerby 2003). The commission was instructed to make recommendations to the governor about the fairness and accuracy of Illinois's administration of the death penalty (Rupcich 2003).

Following two years of research, the commission issued a report suggesting eighty-five changes designed to enhance fairness and prevent wrongful executions (Blackerby 2003). The general assembly did not respond to the commission's proposals as Governor Ryan had hoped, and tension between the executive and legislative branches mounted. The governor announced that he was considering a blanket commutation that would extend to all death-sentenced prisoners and reiterated his hope that the general assembly would consider implementing the reforms the commission had recommended (Mills 2002).

As the commission was studying the capital punishment system, Ryan organized a clemency board to begin reviewing the cases of prisoners on death row. In October 2002 the Illinois Prisoner Review Board was to hold 120 clemency hearings. The public hearing schedule included only death-sentenced inmates who had signed clemency petitions. Several family members of victims were allowed to express their feelings to the board. After the hearings, the board was to make recommendations to the governor, and he would decide how to proceed (Holthusen 2004).

Prior to announcing his decision regarding clemency for the condemned prisoners, Ryan depicted himself as leaning toward not granting blanket commutations. While meeting with several family members at the governor's mansion in Springfield, he assured victims' families that he was not going to grant mass clemency and that he would consider each case individually.

On January 11, 2003, over the objections of prosecutors, political figures, and the families of hundreds of murder victims, Governor Ryan issued four pardons to death-sentenced prisoners and commuted the capital sentences of all other death-row inmates to life imprisonment (Pierre 2003). Ryan clearly disregarded the prisoner review board's recommendations. This board, created by the governor himself, recommended that only ten inmates be granted clemency and that no pardons be granted. Furthermore, with just days left in his term, Ryan could not have reviewed each case individually, because that process would have taken years to complete. His actions most certainly angered victims' family members.

Personally, I was furious. It felt as if the offender was going to win his freedom even after he had committed a terrible act. I think I would have been more receptive to clemency if the governor had taken the time to review each case. I was additionally angered by the fact that he waited until the last few hours of his scandalous administration to mail me a form letter informing me of his decision. Justice most certainly was slighted.

Although I cannot deny that the capital punishment system needs reform in Illinois, it was unjust to group guilty inmates with those few who may have been mistakenly found guilty; surely some fraction of those inmates on death row received sentences they deserved. Although the Illinois Constitution confers the clemency power to the highest officer in the state with hopes that he will not abuse it, Governor Ryan may have done just that.

Inspired by opposition to Ryan's blanket clemency decision, the Illinois House later approved a proposal to open up the secretive clemency process and cripple a governor's ability to grant mass clemency. Under the bill, recommendations made by the prisoner review board to the governor on any petition seeking pardon, reprieve, or commutation would be made public. This reform would help create public accountability and make it harder for a governor to ignore the prisoner review board's recommendations. I am upset that Governor Ryan was able to issue a blanket clemency to Illinois's death-row inmates, but somewhat relieved that legislators are taking action to prevent this from happening again.

Crime Victim Services

Historically, the primary goal of the criminal justice system has been to identify, prosecute, and punish offenders rather than address the needs of their victims. However, for the past four decades, the trend has been to afford crime victims an increasing role within the justice system. Today, all states have adopted victims' rights statutes, which were enacted at the behest of crime-victim survivors and their advocates to help empower victims in previously powerless situations (Baird and McGinn 2004:448).

In the past, victims were not entitled to support from the criminal justice system. As a result, they felt revictimized by the system that was designed to help them. The offenders' rights were constitutionally protected, and they had a personal advocate in the defense attorney. Yet the prosecuting attorney did not play the same role for the victim; the prosecutor instead is an advocate for the state (ibid., 449).

As victims and co-victims expressed their concerns, researchers began to examine the psychological impact of crime on victims and their survivors, as well as their exclusion from the prosecutorial process. This research led to proposals designed to respond to victims' needs. In 1990 Congress enacted the Victims Rights and Restitution Act, granting victims the right to be notified about and attend court proceedings, and to be kept aware of the status of offenders' convictions, sentencing, imprisonment, and release (Baird and McGinn 2004).

Illinois offers services to victims and witnesses through the state's Crime Victims Services division. Available services include the Crime Victim Compensation Program, the Automated Victim Notification System, the Statewide Victim Assistance Program, and the Violent Crime Victim Assistance Program.

The Crime Victim Compensation Act was enacted in 1973, with the goal of helping to reduce the financial burdens of crime imposed on victims and their families. The Crime Victim Compensation Program can provide innocent victims up to $27,000 for expenses resulting from a violent crime.

One of the most valuable services available is the Automated Victim Notification System. This system allows crime victims across the state to obtain information about case or custody status of offenders twenty-four hours a day, via a toll-free number, e-mail, or the Web. The Automated Victim Notification System has been implemented on a statewide basis through the Illinois Department of Corrections, Illinois Prisoner Review Board, Department of Human Services, county circuit clerk offices, and county jails.

The Statewide Victim Assistance Program provides services to crime victims and witnesses involving cases prosecuted by the attorney general's office. This program also is available through state's attorneys' offices. Its services include victim and witness notification, prosecution assistance, and crime victim compensation.

The Violent Crime Victim Assistance (VCVA) Program provides grants to victim and witness assistance programs within the state. The mission of the

VCVA is to develop services that promote victims' rights, needs, and interests. The bureau assisting with the Crime Victim Compensation Act's implementation also is committed to educating the public about victims' services. Fines collected from offenders who have committed violent crimes are deposited in the VCVA fund.

With the evolution of the victims' rights movement, prosecutors' offices bear principal responsibility for creating and implementing programs and services to provide victims with information and the opportunity to participate in the criminal justice process (Baird and McGinn 2004). These services are very important to victims' families. Grieving the loss of a loved one is one of the most difficult of all personal experiences. When a loved one's loss is due to murder, the experience is even more difficult. The effects of the criminal act and the death penalty process are everlasting.

Fortunately, we have been able to use all of these services. My younger brother and sister were given a substantial amount of financial support from the Crime Victim Compensation Program. Additionally, the Automated Victim Notification System works extremely well. We are notified in advance whenever the inmate is about to be moved. Updates in case status are also communicated through the system.

Death penalty cases are more burdensome on victims' loved ones than other criminal cases. Years of appeals and the constant possibility of a commutation to life in prison for the offender haunt the victim's loved ones, feelings I know all too well.

Moreover, if the clemency process is abused, as it was in Illinois, the consequences are even more difficult for survivors. In Illinois, survivors not only had to go through the normal death penalty process, but they also were betrayed by the very system designed to protect them. This type of betrayal infuriates victims' families and adds additional strain to what already is a stress-filled process.

Fortunately, states have realized that victims of violent crimes and their survivors need assistance. This realization has fostered services such as those noted earlier. Unfortunately, little research exists on the impact of the death penalty process on victims' surviving family members and loved ones.

Conclusion

As I write this chapter, it is difficult to hold back tears of sorrow as the horrible memories of that fateful day bounce around in my head. The despicable acts of the defendant forever took away my dad, my best friend. He took away the individual who molded me into the person that I am today. My children no longer have a grandpa to watch them play ball or teach them how to hunt or fish.

Even though the court gave the defendant just punishment, former Governor Ryan decided that the entire judicial system was flawed and commuted all of the death sentences imposed under Illinois law to life in prison. There is no doubt that the capital punishment system needs to be reformed. Although the governor may have had lofty intentions, he did not improve the criminal justice system by unraveling years of work by prosecutors. Moreover, while life on death row seems hard, it certainly is not what most people think. Due to their unique status, most death-row inmates live better than other offenders confined within the general prison population.

Thus the question still remains: is a death sentence for the criminal or the victim? It can fairly be observed that a death sentence has been given to the victim long before the trial ever starts. The death sentence for the offender directly results from the criminal acts he has chosen to commit. As for the victim's survivors, I believe most are able to withstand the pressure and stress of the lengthy process.

Fortunately, there was a victim advocate in place to help with even the smallest details for my family and me. The constant care and emotional support of the advocate was immeasurable. Our advocate kept us informed during this whole ordeal and made sure that we had the best accommodations available during the trial. She would always drop whatever she was working on to care for us. When I spoke to the Prisoner Review Board about Governor Ryan issuing a blanket clemency, she was there to render support every step of the way. To this day she continues to check with us to see how we are doing. These advocates serve a vital role in the well-being of victims and their survivors.

Whether I am at work or play, everything reminds me of my dad. Sometimes it is as if I can reach out and touch him, only to come to the realization that he is gone forever. When he was murdered he left the family no large inheritance, but what he did leave was a priceless legacy.

References

Abu-Jamal, Mumia; Vest, Jason; and Conniff, Ruth. 1995. "Live from Death Row." *Progressive* 59:18–24.

Armstrong, Ken and Mills, Steve. 2000. "Ryan Suspends Death Penalty." *Chicago Tribune,* 31 January 2000, 1.

Baird, Charles, F. and McGinn, Elizabeth, E. 2004. "Re-Victimizing the Victim: How Prosecutorial and Judicial Discretion Are Being Exercised to Silence Victims Who Oppose Capital Punishment." *Stanford Law & Policy Review* 15:447–73.

Bienen, Leigh, B. 1998. "The Quality of Justice in Capital Cases: Illinois as a Case Study." *Law and Contemporary Problems* 61:193–97.

Blackerby, Jean, C. 2003. "Life after Death Row: Preventing Wrongful Capital Convictions and Restoring Innocence after Exoneration." *Vanderbilt Law Review* 56:1179–226.

Buehl, Roger. 2004. "Life on Death Row" *The New Abolitionist*. http://www.nodeath-penalty.org/newab006/rogerBuehl.html (14 September 2004).

Fins, Deborah. 2004. "Death Row U.S.A." The Criminal Justice Project of the NAACP Legal Defense and Educational Fund, Inc. http://www.deathpenaltyinfo.org/article.php?scid=9&did=145 (September 1, 2004).

Furman v. Georgia. 1972. 408 U.S. 238.

Garner, Bryan, A. (ed.). 1999. *Black's Law Dictionary*. Eagan, MN: West Group.

Holthusen, Kelly. 2004. "How to argue for your life in fifteen minutes or less: An analysis of Illinois Governor Ryan's clemency review boards." *New England Journal on Crime and Civil Confinement* 1: 105–30.

Illinois Constitution of 1818, Article III, Section 5.

Illinois Constitution of 1848, Article IV, Section 8.

Illinois Constitution of 1870, Article V, Section 13.

Illinois Constitution of 1970, Article V, Section 12.

Kobil, Daniel, T. 1991. "The Quality of Mercy Strained: Wresting the Pardoning Power from the King." Jurist. http://jurist.law.pitt.edu/kobil.htm (3 August 2004).

Mills, Steve. 2002. "A Late Plea on Clemency Hearings." *Chicago Tribune*, 15 October 2002, A1.

Pierre, Robert, E. 2003. "Illinois Governor Pardons 4 on Death Row: The Outgoing Official Said Innocent Inmates Were Beaten into Confession." *Philadelphia Inquirer*, 12 January 2003, A5.

People v. Hicks, 98 CF 22, 18 (2000).

People v. Hicks, 98 CF 22, 35 (2000).

Rupcich, Joseph, N. 2003. "Abusing a Limitless Power: Executive Clemency in Illinois." *Southern Illinois University Law Journal* 28:1–15.

White, Quenton. 2004. "Life on Death Row." Tennessee Department of Corrections. http://www.state.tn.us/correction/newsreleases/lifeondeathrow.html (19 August 2004).

CHAPTER 5

BUILDING A BRIDGE

David Kaczynski and
Gary Wright

Introduction

The case of Theodore Kaczynski, better known as the Unabomber, is one of the highest profile and longest running cases in American history. For over seventeen years, beginning in 1978, the Unabomber strategically placed and mailed explosive devices that were designed to maim and kill people. Mr. Kaczynski was directly responsible for the death of three people and the injury of twenty-three others. While these victims were the primary targets of his attacks, an exponentially larger group was also seriously affected by his actions, including the victims' families, friends, co-workers and, in some cases, entire communities.

In this chapter David Kaczynski, the brother of Ted Kaczynski who turned him in to authorities, and Gary Wright, a victim of one of Theodore Kaczynski's devices, share their personal experiences with the complicated, confusing and sometimes painful journey associated with the death penalty and the healing and forgiveness process.

Gary

February 20, 1987, was very uncharacteristic for a winter day in Utah. The sun was shining, and at 10:30 in the morning it was fairly warm. I was driving back to my office with the sunroof of my car open after completing some early morning business appointments. I was listening to music as I pulled my car into the rear parking lot of CAAMS, Inc., a family-owned computer sales and service company that I had co-founded.

As I drove into the parking stall, I noticed what appeared to be a block of wood about thirteen inches long and four inches square, with four nails pro-

David Kaczynski and Gary Wright, 2005.

truding from it. It was sitting in a spot where someone might run over it, and I thought, I had better move it, so it doesn't damage a tire. After I parked the car and began to walk over to throw what appeared to be a piece of scrap wood into the garbage dumpster, I noticed that one of the protruding nails was slightly bent, and they all appeared to be made of chrome. The way they reflected the sunlight struck me as a little odd, but at the time I didn't think anything of it. The object appeared to be two 2" x 4" pieces of wood that were nailed together, and I thought, "This looks like it must have come from a construction site." As I bent down to pick it up, I placed my fingers on the end of the longer of the two pieces, and as I moved it something happened that was very wrong.

In a millisecond, I felt a "click" and I heard something that sounded like the scream of a jet fighter flying overhead. When I looked around, I realized that somehow I had moved over twenty feet and I was jumping up and down as if I were on a pogo stick. I looked up and could see the overhead electrical and telephone wires that were attached to the building and they were moving in a wave pattern while pieces of red tape and debris fell around me like confetti. For some reason everything was moving in slow motion, and it sounded like I was swimming under water because I could barely hear anything. As I was jumping and moving around the parking lot, I slowly began to recognize that I was yelling for help. In that moment, I thought someone had shot me with a shot gun, and my mind raced with the idea that I may not make it through whatever had just happened. At that point, I heard a very deep voice inside my head that I did not recognize say, "You will be all right." I wasn't sure if it was my own subconscious speaking to me or something else, but I did begin to feel a little more at ease, and my thoughts became crystal clear.

I looked down at my clothes and could see the remnants of my pants. My shoes had white burn marks on them, and I couldn't figure out why my voice sounded so strange. I saw blood beginning to seep through my white dress shirt, and I could see what looked like needles threaded through the cloth. They turned out to be wood fragments. As the bomb exploded it burst into thousands of needle-like projectiles. Many of these were impaled in and around my neck making it difficult to move. The surgeon I met at the hospital later told me that I looked like a porcupine.

At this point the rear door of my office opened and members of my family and other co-workers rushed outside to see what had happened. From the looks on their faces, I knew that it must be bad. My father had been a Utah highway patrolman, and one of my brothers was involved with the local ski patrol. They took a quick look at my injuries and then walked me into my office and laid me on the floor until an ambulance arrived to transport me to the hospital. Once I arrived, the doctors and surgeons discovered that the ulnar nerve in my left arm had been severed. They performed plastic surgery on my face, tried to repair the damaged nerve, and removed pieces of shrapnel from my body. From the trajectory path of some of the nails it was evident that I would probably have lost part of my eyesight if I had not been wearing sun glasses.

When the FBI spoke to me about who they suspected in this crime, I was more than surprised. I have always read a lot of the newspapers and magazines, but up to this point I had never heard of the person called the "Unabomber."

David

Since he had quit his job as an assistant professor at the University of California at Berkeley in the late 1960s, my brother Ted had been living in an isolated cabin along the continental divide in Montana. At one point he'd written to me with some pride that he'd lived for a whole year, kept his accounts, and managed to survive on just twelve cents a day. He had no running water, no electricity, and no telephone, so most of our communication was through the mail.

One day my wife Linda said to me, "David, I think your brother is sick." I guess I didn't have her objectivity. My first response was, "Well, you know, this is the way Ted is. This is the way he thinks." And she said, "David, read this letter. People who are healthy do not think this way." It was at that point that we took some of Ted's letters to a psychiatrist and began to explore whether there was anything we could do to try to find out what was wrong, to see if there was anything we could do to help him or intervene for his benefit in some way.

Some years later, in the late summer of 1995, Linda sat me down and said, "Dave, don't get angry with me, but—I've been kind of burdened with this— did it ever occur to you, as even a remote possibility, that your brother Ted might be the Unabomber?" During this time there was a flurry of newspaper articles about how the Unabomber had sent his manifesto to the press, demanding that it be published. The newspapers were debating whether it should be published or not. It had also been revealed that law enforcement officials thought the Unabomber had come from Chicago, since that was where the first bombs had gone off. There were also connections with the University of California at Berkeley, since two devices had been set off there. Linda thought, "Gee, Ted grew up in Chicago and later taught at Berkeley, and now there's this anti-technology manifesto." She knew, through me, that my brother had a long-standing preoccupation with the problems associated with technology.

At that point, I was really dismissive. I said, "You don't know him. I know him. He's not capable of this." But I promised to read the manifesto if it were ever published.

Several weeks later, I read that manifesto, and I was determined to find something that disqualified it as Ted's writing. Unfortunately, I couldn't. I still thought there was only a slim chance that he'd written it. I told Linda, "Well, maybe there's one chance in a thousand." In fact, I went to the library and read everything I could, hoping to find something that would eliminate Ted. I looked at the police sketch and felt that it didn't particularly look like Ted. The description was of someone three inches taller, ten years younger, a different hair color. I thought this was good. It wasn't a match. On the other hand, through my research I had learned that there was an association with Salt Lake City. I knew Ted had spent a summer working there. So that was another piece of the puzzle: the realization that I could connect him with each of the three places.

Linda and I spent about three weeks combing through the manifesto and bunches of my brother's old letters, and it seemed as if through that process (not that I found the proverbial smoking gun or anything) I could almost hear my brother's voice in the manifesto.

I remember waking up on a particular morning and feeling a crushing sense of depression. My first thought was, "Gee, that's the worst nightmare I've ever had." But then as the cobwebs melted away, I realized it wasn't a nightmare. I was literally considering the possibility that my own brother might be a serial bomber, killer of three people and the most wanted criminal in America. I walked to the breakfast table where Linda was already seated, eating some cornflakes. I sat down, looked up at her and said, "You know, Hon, I think there might be a fifty-fifty chance that Ted wrote the manifesto." It was the first time I'd acknowledged such a strong possibility that Ted might be the person responsible.

Gary

When a bomb explodes and razor sharp pieces of metal and debris are moving at over 20,000 feet per second, the physical wounds inflicted vary in degree from superficial abrasions and burns to deep lacerations and potentially the loss of limbs or life. Much of how badly a person is injured is sheer luck and depends entirely on where the deadly shrapnel enters the body.

The physical injuries that I received were spread across my entire body and are consistent with what you would expect to find when a bomb explodes. I required three separate surgeries to reconstruct nerves and to move and graft tendons in my left arm and hand. I had extensive plastic surgery to my face, and hundreds of metal and wood fragments were removed from areas throughout my body. To this day, over eighteen years since the explosion, I still remove pieces of shrapnel that continue to rise from below the surface of my skin.

As difficult as it was recovering from these physical injuries, the emotional and psychological challenges were tougher. For a minute sit back and imagine what it is like to constantly wonder what would make a stranger want to kill you, to continually search your memory for any small indiscretion or act that could trigger this kind of hostility, and to be overwhelmed with the feelings of rage and the heartache of knowing that you will never again be the same person.

The complex series of emotions that I felt after the bombing ranged from happiness for being alive to anger, frustration, and fear that the stranger responsible for my injuries might strike back at me or my family again. My days were fragmented at best, and my ability to cope with the issues of injury, family pressure, law enforcement, and media drained my patience and severely stressed my emotional capabilities. I spiraled down like a leaf in the wind with no bottom in sight. I became irritated and angry at the slightest things and started to close off the people that were closest to me. As the pressure increased, I began to shut down, withdraw, and internalize my feelings about the event. I only wanted to deal with how I was feeling and didn't really care about how others were coping with the changes in their lives.

I struggled with these feelings for between six and seven years, looking for answers as to why I felt so strange and unsettled. I had generally been a very happy and optimistic person with a great outlook on life, but during the first two years after the bombing, I found that my patience and capacity to cope with issues had dwindled to the point that I was becoming unbearable. At times I was happy, and then suddenly I was so angry it was unbelievable. It was during this time that I made the decision that I would find a way to feel whole again. After speaking with several counselors and determining that they weren't quite sure about why I was having the feelings I was experiencing, I decided to look for answers on my own. I started to read books, pamphlets, and any other material that might be related to healing after a violent event. I soon discovered that the path each person must pass down as he or she progresses through the healing process is as unique as each of the people on that road of discovery. Without a road map or guidance, each is free to move in any chosen direction. Some may progress rapidly while others might struggle and become mired in emotional turmoil.

This was also the beginning of a seven-year drought where the Unabomber didn't send or place any devices. That is probably a result of the now famous sketch of a person in a hooded sweatshirt and sunglasses that was drawn from information provided by my secretary, who witnessed Ted place the bomb at my business.

David

I can never forget the day I told Linda that I thought there was a fifty-fifty chance that Ted might have committed these crimes. We were both very upset. We were consumed with it. The word "Unabomber" seemed too frightening to say out loud. Is he or isn't he? What does this mean? What does this ask of us? We talked about "it" on into the night. As we lay there in bed, sleeplessly, I tried to connect my brother as I remembered him with a person who might be capable of such horrific crimes. Instead, I'm having memories that have an opposite tone. I'm remembering things from many years back: fond memories, camping trips, playing softball together on an informal team one year.

I told Linda one story that really had an effect on her. When I was two and a half years old, our family moved from the Back-of-the-Yards neighborhood of Chicago out to the suburbs. It was our first house and my first back yard as a little boy. I can recall that during that first summer I'd push my way out through the screen door and play around in the backyard. However, I had trouble getting back inside the house since at two and a half I was so short I couldn't reach the doorknob. But one day Ted, who was about ten years old at the time, came out of the house and began fiddling with something at the back door. I remember I walked up close to him, thinking, "What's Teddy doing?" Always a very ingenious person, he'd taken a little spool of thread from our mom's sewing kit, a hammer and a nail from our dad's tool kit, and he nailed the bare spool onto the wooden screen door so that it made a makeshift door handle that I could reach.

So, I'm reliving this memory forty-two years later, wondering if my brother's the Unabomber. As I lay there, I hear a little sound coming from Linda. The room was dim but there was a little light shining through the shade from the street lamp outside. I looked over and I could see that her face was just flowing with tears.

That was a very important moment for me because it might have been the first time that Linda really saw the full human dimensions of this tragedy; in fact, the first moment that she saw Ted as a human being. Up until then, he had been the weird brother-in-law, the mentally ill guy, the hermit in Montana, now perhaps, even the Unabomber. But on hearing this story, Linda understood what a deep bond I had with Ted, and that this was really tearing me apart. And I suppose, as well, that no matter what happened, no matter how twisted Ted may have become, that nice little ten-year-old boy who cared about his baby brother was part of who he was. It was part of his history. It would always be there. And this was just an enormous tragedy for our family.

But remembering that Ted was human didn't make our dilemma any easier. Actually, it intensified it. We were facing a situation where any choice we made could lead to someone's death. What would it be like to wake up one day and realize that somebody else had been killed and that we had been in a position to prevent it and failed to do anything? We'd have the blood of some innocent person on our hands. How do you live with that for the rest of your life? On the other hand, how do you live with turning in a brother who ends up being executed? How do you face your mother, an elderly woman who's worried for years about her son because of his estrangement from the family and his emotional problems? When you see in her eyes that she knows he's being executed because you turned him in? Those weren't pleasant thoughts.

I think it's important to note that our decision to go to the authorities was a couple's decision. Often, we think that there's got to be one heroic conscience that makes a moral decision. But from that moment on, we were really together in this. Linda had been a philosophy professor at a small college in upstate New York for eighteen years. Among the courses she taught were courses in ethics. She has always been a very principled person.

I was working as a counselor in a youth shelter for runaway and homeless kids. I had often advised kids, "Even if you don't fully trust the school principal or the police, you've got to find some adult that you do trust if it's a matter of protecting someone's health and safety. You've got to do the right thing. You won't regret it." Well, it's easy to give advice and set standards for other people. But here I was confronted with a situation where I would have to live up to this advice or live with the realization that I'd just been saying those words to make myself feel good.

There was still a lot that had to be wrestled with. But there was a clear sense that we couldn't just sit by and hope for the best, or say that it wasn't our job, that no one should expect a family member to turn in a family member. At least if we took some action, we weren't helpless. We'd do something to stop the bombs. And then, perhaps, if we communicated to the authorities that Ted was mentally ill, it might save his life. But we had to take on that first responsibility first.

At that time, and really for a couple of years after, I was deeply conflicted about the decision. This was my brother. Brothers are supposed to protect brothers. I love Ted. I know that he had loved me. I remember at one of our first meetings with the FBI, one of the agents showed me a map of rural Montana and asked me to point out the place on the map where my brother lived. I remember walking to the map and putting my finger gingerly down on the spot where Ted's cabin was located and feeling ... how painful that was for me.

We had wanted to spare Mom from this for as long as possible. Even when we approached the FBI, we didn't feel certain that Ted was responsible. We hoped that they would find some way to rule him out as a suspect. But eventually I got the call I'd been dreading. An agent we'd been working closely with said, "David, we've done everything possible to rule out your brother as a suspect, but unfortunately he's moved to the top of our suspect list. We're now at a point in the investigation where we need to speak with your mom. Do you think you could arrange an interview for us?"

I remember going to her apartment. It was on a Saturday morning. She opened the door and I saw her face change. Obviously, my anguish must have been written all over me. She said, "David, something's wrong! You've got to tell me. What is it?" I said, "Yeah, Mom. I think you better sit down."

Her first reaction was a mother's reaction, perhaps a mother's intuition. "It's Ted! Is it something about Ted?" I said, "Mom, as far as I know, he's in good health. But I do have something very troubling to tell you." She sat down in this little La-Z-Boy chair, where I always picture her reading or watching television. I was much too agitated to sit down myself. I was kind of pacing the room, trying to find some way to deliver the news painlessly. But there was no way to do that. Before long, I'm crying a little bit. Mom is just sitting there in that chair. Not saying a word. Looking at me, with this fixed look of horror on her face. At that moment I realized that not many relationships are tested in quite this cruel way. How could I be certain that she'd even love me after I told her that I had reported my suspicions about Ted to the FBI? I got to the end of what I had to say and I said, "Mom, I think there might be a chance that Ted is involved. Mom, I've even taken the step of calling the FBI, and they're currently investigating him."

I'll always remember what Mom did next. It was just an extraordinary gesture. She got up out of her chair. She is a very small woman. I'm a little over six feet tall and she's a little under five feet tall. She walked up to me, reached up her arms around my neck, drew me down and put a kiss on my cheek. The first thing she said was, "David, I can't imagine what you've been going through."

It was amazing to me that in this most terrible moment, her first concern was for my feelings. And then she said probably the most comforting words I could have heard. She said, "David, I know that you love Ted. I know you wouldn't have done this unless you felt that you had to." In many ways, she's truly a hero of this story. Probably at that moment half the weight of the world came off my shoulders. I realized that I hadn't lost my mother's love and that she, Linda, and I were now in this together.

After telling me this, Mom said, "You know, David, I just can't imagine … I mean, Ted loves animals. He's never been violent. I just don't think he's capable of doing these sorts of things. Maybe it's a good thing that you've contacted the authorities. They're going to investigate. They're going to find out that he's innocent. All of this will go away like a bad dream." I think she felt that very strongly at the outset.

I don't know what happened to Ted. I mean, I can read the diagnoses. I can have them carefully explained to me. It doesn't exhaust the question that we always ask: "Why? Why? Why?"

Gary

As with any act of violence, people would continually ask me, "How are you ever going to get over this? Can you forgive the person who did this to you?" In the beginning I did not have the answers to these questions, nor did I understand the enormity associated with the healing process that would allow me to answer them. I struggled for about six years trying to bring closure to an event for which I didn't have a face, a name, or a reason to associate my injuries. I wavered in my ability to accept what had happened, and I wasn't entirely sure of how I was supposed to get over the restless feelings I had.

One event in particular stands out in my mind. I was driving down the street on a day similar to when I was first injured, and I had a thought that was so crystal clear it actually surprised me. It went something like this: If Christ was tortured, nailed to a cross, crucified, and he could still forgive a criminal and the people who were killing him, how could I hold myself above forgiving the person who had terrorized and attacked me? That single question slapped me in the face with a dose of reality and honestly allowed me to begin to forgive this person, even though I had no idea who he was.

I believe that forgiveness is a very complicated word because it can take on many forms and have a different meaning to each person. For many people, saying that they forgive someone is an act of saying that what you did was acceptable. I don't believe in this concept. I prefer to believe that it means letting go. Not unconditionally accepting an act of hatred or violence, not forgetting the event or a family member who is no longer with you, but allowing you to love and honor yourself and those around you. Accepting that while your life is forever changed you will permit yourself to live and experience it again.

I learned of the arrest of Theodore Kaczynski on my 35th birthday while working at my office. One of my co-workers said he had just read of the capture of a reclusive man in a remote area of Montana. I immediately looked for myself to verify the information and was still skeptical. Having had a prior false notification of a person being held in custody, I was afraid to accept that they had truly found the man responsible for changing the course of my life. Several hours later, I received a telephone call from the head of the Unabomber task force. He indicated that the physical evidence was very good and that shortly they would be formally charging him with the crimes.

I watched the news that night, and for the first time saw video of the arrest and was able to place a name and face to my assailant. The emotions were overwhelming and I began to cry, realizing I had spent nine years of my life dealing with an unknown enemy who had tried to kill me. I also realized that this was the beginning of another chapter of my story and that I might be involved in a death penalty case.

David

When Ted was arrested, they found, in addition to a carbon copy of the manifesto and other incriminating evidence, a live bomb under his bed, apparently waiting to be mailed to somebody. So there was no question that he was responsible, or that he probably would have struck again. I just look back and thank God that Linda and I had the insight and the courage to do what we did. We were able to stop it.

Gary

Soon after I knew who was responsible for my injuries, I began to realize that the perpetrator's family had also been traumatized by this event. I had only ever seen David or his mom in brief television or news clips, and the way that they approached this tragedy was so admirable. They had always demonstrated almost a reverence toward victims and their families even though they themselves were experiencing a great deal of their own pain. I thought to myself that there isn't a lot of difference between a victim's and a perpetrator's family when it comes to an act of violence, and I felt a great deal of compassion for the Kaczynskis.

David

After my brother's arrest, there was a period of time where the Justice Department began signaling its intention to seek the death penalty for Ted. I was feeling pretty sorry for myself, and I remember Linda, maybe having heard that one time too many, saying to me, "You know, David, there are other people in a lot of pain over this." My first reaction was to say, "No, my pain is special. You know, I turned in my brother. It's not only pain and loss, it's guilt." And she said, "David, there are people who've lost body parts. There are people who've lost their dearest loved one. There's a lot more pain here than just your own."

My wife and I are Buddhists, and part of our practice involves a morning sitting meditation. On the day following that conversation, Linda set three candles up on the altar in our meditation room. I didn't have to ask what the candles were for. They represented the three people my brother had killed. I think that was my first real awakening to the realization that there was another "side" to this tragedy, and that there was a kind of connection I had with those people on the other side.

It was almost by chance that I got to speak to Gary at all. Linda and I had asked a friend of ours to do some research and find addresses for the victims so that we could write to them. We wanted to communicate how badly we felt about the terrible harm that Ted had caused. We also hoped they would realize that when we asked the government to spare Ted's life, it didn't mean we were treating his crimes lightly. We didn't have Gary's address at that point. We ended up getting only his phone number. I remember thinking maybe I should give this guy a call, then thinking in the next second, no maybe I better not. I hoped that some contact with a victim might be possible—that as human beings we might be able to talk, share perspectives, and maybe help each other. But I was afraid, too, that I could just as easily be greeted with a blast of anger. I was feeling very sad and vulnerable. Now I just feel very fortunate that it was Gary.

When I finally made the decision to place the call, I took a big gulp and dialed Gary's phone number and tried to think of what I was going to say. When the phone picked up on the other end, a voice said, "You have reached the Wright house at the wrong time." It was an answering machine, and I wasn't prepared for that. I left an awkward message explaining who I was and said that I'd like to talk if he'd be open to that. I said I'd call back later.

I guess Gary was a little prepared and it didn't strike him completely out of the blue when I called again. When I finally spoke with him it was just amazing. I was braced for perhaps a blast of anger and instead I just got real warmth. He said that he understood that my brother was ill and that he thought it took a lot of courage and guts to do what we had done. He also said that he appreciated it. He told me that I should never blame myself for what my brother had done. And I shouldn't blame myself if the worst happens from our point of view and Ted were executed. He said, "If you ever want to talk about this ... I've been dealing with the trauma of this for a number of years. Just give me a call."

Here was a guy just about killed, who then deals for years with uncertainty and worry, wondering if the killer's going to come back to finish the job. Finally, nine or ten years later, he gets a call from the brother of the person who did this, and he takes the call. He almost takes me under his wing, and says, "David, this is just the beginning for you. I've been dealing with this for nine years. You know, it can get better." So, as this very public process was playing out, I had this resource. Someone I could talk to on the "other side" to say, "You're a good guy, Dave, and I feel for you." I can't tell you how much that meant to me, and to Linda, and to Mom.

Gary

I received a telephone call from a friend of David and Linda's in late October 1996. The friend said that David would like to call me on behalf of his family. Although I was somewhat surprised to hear the request, I thought I would probably do the same thing if I were in his position, and I told her that would be fine.

I was washing dishes one night shortly before Thanksgiving when David called. He introduced himself and said that he wanted to apologize on behalf of his family for what his brother had done. I could tell that he was uncomfortable, and I did my best to make him feel at ease. I told him that while I sincerely appreciated and accepted the apology, he and his family could not bear the burden of his brother's actions. I said that as painful as it was, he needed to let it go and move forward with his life, and that if he ever needed to talk he could call me at any time. David said he didn't expect me to be so kind, thanked me for the invitation, and indicated that he would take me up on the offer. About two weeks later he called again, beginning what was the first of many telephone conversations.

When I tell people that David and I are friends, the response I get most often is, "You're kidding." For a while, I didn't understand why. And then it hit me: "Why wouldn't they think that?" The typical stereotype portrayed in movies and books states that the victim's and the perpetrator's families must hate each other, that there is an invisible line drawn through the center of a courtroom that cannot be crossed, and that a single act defines the value system of an entire family. If logic is applied, we know this is not true.

Ted's case was ultimately pled out and a jury trial was unnecessary. The sentencing hearing itself was very tough, with a lot of emotion and pain that was expressed. It was probably one of the most poignant points of my life. I was allowed to speak directly to Ted. I had the option to sit next to the prosecution, to face the judge at a podium, or to sit in the witness box. I chose to sit in the witness box and face a man I had never met who had tried to kill me. I read a rather lengthy statement and during my presentation, there was one defining moment that changed the course of the entire proceeding. It was when I said, "Ted, I do not hate you. I learned to forgive and heal a long time ago. Without this ability I would have become kindling for your cause." You have no idea how powerful that statement was. For the first time, I found a chink in the armor of the man responsible for causing so much damage and pain to so many people. He did not know how to handle this statement, and I watched him sit straight up, stop what he was doing and look right back at me. In his eyes, I saw something I will never forget. It was a look of shock and not knowing how to handle the situation. It was then that I realized that the balance of power had been transferred to me.

Many people have asked, how did you get past this. I tell them that I had to make a change in the way I looked at life and appreciate what I have been blessed with, that I found new ways to stretch my belief system because for too long I had looked in the mirror at a face that was grieving. I learned to simplify and appreciate the truly wonderful things in life that I would miss if I weren't able to move forward down a path of forgiveness. I also told them that in working toward forgiveness I realized that the implementation of the death penalty in this case would not help me to heal.

David

After the trial, I received a call from a law enforcement chaplain. She said that there was a victim's family that had requested a meeting with Mom and me, and wondered if we'd be open to that. I asked Mom and she said, "Well, I think we should go."

We were taken to a room in the courthouse. As we walked into the room, we saw three women there. One was the widow of somebody my brother had killed. One was her sister. And the third was her husband's sister. We walked in and kind of said, "We're sorry, we're sorry," and we began to cry. We always realized that no matter how much we said that we were sorry, or how sincerely, it wouldn't undo the harm that was done.

The widow spoke for the family and said that they'd wanted to take this opportunity to thank us. That they knew what we had done must have been very difficult. She also said that she wanted us to know that all they had ever really wanted was for the violence to stop. I think they were telling us that they hadn't needed the death penalty for their sense of justice or closure. That was very, very meaningful to us.

On the other hand, here is my mom. She's facing three women whose lives have been just shattered by her son. I think she felt a deep need to communicate to them that her son was not a monster, but a very, very sick person. So she began talking to them about schizophrenia, trying to make them understand. But you know, it's not with our brains that we understand such things. I don't think they were ready yet for what Mom was trying to tell them. She was seated in a chair, and I was standing behind her, with my hands on the back of the chair. As I looked over her head, I saw that the faces of the women didn't look pleased. Maybe they thought Mom was making excuses for Ted. In fact, the widow said suddenly, "He knew what he was doing." It was a very intense moment. The room was suddenly frozen in silence. What had been an attempt to reach out in compassion, with the very best of intentions, looked like it was blocked. We'd come so far, but now there was this gulf of pain and loss separating us. You could sort of see to the other side, but there was no bridge to the other side.

Mom, at that moment, kind of instinctively dropped her head and said, "I wish he had killed me instead of your husband." All she had really wanted to accomplish in life was to be a good mother, to nurture her children so that they would be happy, maybe so that they'd leave the world a better place for having been there. Yet here, at least with her eldest son, the result was a disaster. In her mind, I don't think she had anything to live for at that moment. But as I'm looking over her head, I happened to be looking at the widow and I could see that she's just stricken by what Mom had said. In fact, she got out of her chair and knelt down beside my mom's chair. She put her hand on my mom's shoulder, touched her lightly, and said, "Oh, Mrs. Kaczynski, don't do this to yourself. You're not responsible. Don't ever think that you're responsible." That was amazing for my mother to hear.

That experience was so powerful for me. I remember leaving the room that day probably a very different person. Thinking about the dignity that was present there at that moment; the honesty and the good intentions; the empathy that comes from acknowledging another person's loss. I really felt what a fine thing the human heart is, that the human soul is. That there is this core of decency that really redeems us. I mean, it really is the only thing we have to cling to when the worst happens. It was so much in evidence in the room that evening. It made me proud to be human.

Gary

There is no rational reason why I am standing here today. It just wasn't my time to go and I beat the laws of physics. For some reason, I was able to pick up that device in the only way possible that allowed every major piece of shrapnel to miss my body.

It is my sincere belief that there is an incredible amount of compassion and understanding that can be provided through a connection with a person from the perpetrator's family. David and I call this "Building a Bridge" because the bridge connects two families that are looking across a great abyss and feel isolated from one other and helpless or uncomfortable to offer any assistance or consolation.

My conversations with David and his family allowed me to humanize the event and understand things that I otherwise would never have known. They helped me realize that a perpetrator does not represent the morals, values, or dreams of an entire family and that there can be extenuating circumstances that are never presented in the courtroom. That many very good and upstanding people who have pride, integrity, and incredible values, unnecessarily wear their family's name with a sense of dishonor because of the actions of a single individual.

While I know that it is not possible for everyone to connect in the way that David and I have, it may be possible to have an intermediary ask questions of the perpetrator's family that may bring some comfort and understanding to the event. To ask questions that otherwise might have gone unanswered and could have provided some relief to the victims, their families, and friends.

I am thankful that David made that phone call in October 1996. Because he did, we have been able to support each other through some very difficult times. We have learned a great deal about each other, our families, and the healing process. We jointly speak on the subjects of the death penalty, the difficulties of healing, and the act of forgiveness. Most importantly, we have been blessed with the gift of friendship.

Being a survivor of violence can teach a person so many lessons about life and those around us. I learned that when something terrible happens, in the beginning when things are fresh, there are times for anger, grief, depression, confusion, and the need for retribution. Later, when our mind and human spirit begin to heal, there is also a time for forgiveness and compassion. In some ways, I think I have been blessed to have had each of these experiences because it has forced me to question my beliefs and actions toward others. It has also made me realize that even though this world shows us a side of humanity that is full of violence and rage, there is also a side of us that is able to let go and move forward.

This has been especially true regarding my thoughts on the death penalty. I know without a doubt that if Ted Kaczynski had been executed, it would not have helped me or decreased the amount of time that was necessary for me to heal. In fact, I think it would have extended that period of time and that I would always have felt a severe loss for David and his family. It is something that I would have felt terrible about each time someone mentioned the case. My father has always said, "There are things much worse in this world than death." I believe one of those things is the necessity of a perpetrator to live with and think about his actions. It is so much more difficult to do this than just close your eyes and go to sleep. Besides, if we put another to death, it isn't the person we execute who suffers, it's his family.

My son, a wise sixteen-year-old who studies Kung Fu, gave me a note from a book written by a martial artist that says, "It is compassion rather than the principle of justice which can guard us against being unjust to our fellow man." This is an Eastern principle that has been around for thousands of years, and I think much of the world could benefit from its wisdom, especially when applied to the principles of the death penalty. I have always felt that the human mind is the most powerful force in the universe and that true healing always comes from within.

David

If we think about what justice consists of, it's got to be more than retribution. I think if there's been one very disturbing trend in the past ten or fifteen years it is the equation of justice with retribution: the notion that there is no meaning to the word justice beyond imposing retribution—the harsher the better, it seems. What we've got to do is to take back the ideal of justice from the impulse of vengeance. We've got to recover the principle of human dignity. We've got to recover from hatred and all the various forms of denial that go with it. We've got to say, "Look, we're all in this together. We are all human beings."

I don't think vengeance has a place in a system of justice. I think justice, for me, is that which draws out our humanity and our essential human dignity. In my view, there can't be justice without wisdom, and there can't be real wisdom without compassion. If you recognize that it's a human being there, that there is a kind of human presence there, you respond to those people in a very different way, at a deeper level. You can and should hold them accountable. You can grieve for their loss of humanity. You may even feel impelled to help them, although they've done something terrible. The notion that we're going to beat down people, who probably got in this situation because they were damaged to begin with, is contrary to my understanding of justice. For me, justice is born out of the heart. It's a deep human dimension. It's ultimately that which connects us all. And I think to say, "Well, certain people are disposable, or certain people we just need to get rid of," violates that principle of justice, the inclusiveness of a community of justice and a community of conscience.

I think it's a real tragedy that my brother, with his promise, with some of the sensitivity that I know he had, surrendered to his demons and left the world a far worse place, a poorer place for having been there. I think it was the delusions, the confusion, the fear—all of the things that came with his isolation and his mental illness—that distorted his understanding of his place in the world. I think he felt ultimately very disconnected. It's really the sense of connection that heals us, that creates justice, that creates community. And Ted was so isolated he lost his sense of being connected to others.

CHAPTER 6

ACCIDENTAL DEATH IS FATE,
MURDER IS PURE EVIL

Stanley and Phyllis Rosenbluth

Death comes to us and to those we love in many different ways. We die of old age. We die of illness. We are killed in accidents. We are killed by the forces of nature. We even self-inflict death. But murder!

So when my mother died of a heart attack in her late fifties, I thought I knew what pain and sorrow were. When my dad died several years later due to complications with Parkinson's Disease, I thought I knew what pain and sorrow were. When my brother—my only sibling—died of a cancer I thought I knew what pain and sorrow were. Then when my only other blood relation, my niece, was killed in an auto accident, I thought surely I knew what pain and sorrow were. I did not.

When my beloved oldest son Richard and his wife Becky were murdered, I truly learned the depth of pain and sorrow. Then I knew. We stood at the gravesite on the day of the funeral, and through teary eyes we watched two coffins being lowered into the ground. Two coffins! One would have been beyond our threshold of terror. But two?

Who were Richard and Becky? Let us tell you who they were, not as victims of murder, but as two children who were part of our small, loving family.

Richard was a beautiful infant—5 lbs., 2 oz. when he was born, the smallest in the nursery. He had lots of dark hair (which a nurse slicked into a Rudolph Valentino look) and dark blue eyes. He grew up so quickly. The Valentino hairdo was replaced with an abundance of brown curls, and the dark blue eyes brightened into cornflower blue. At five months he pulled himself up and stood and spoke words! He parroted words we spoke to him and constantly amazed all of us with his abilities. Early in school he excelled. By high school we knew (and were told) that his IQ was exceptional. He was a

Rosenbluth family, 1987. Stanley, Phyllis, Richard and Becky.

boy scout, played Little League (a star pitcher), was a paper delivery boy, was a member of the volunteer fire department as a part of the emergency medical team and rescue squad, worked in the local pizza shop, and even pumped gas at a local gas station.

In addition to all this, he displayed an unusual talent for music with a rare ear for perfect pitch. Music became his first love. There were lessons—first piano and then percussion. He was accepted as a student by the percussionist with the Washington National Symphony, then went on to music college. As parents, we would have preferred another interest, but we respected his desires to pursue a music career. Eventually, Rock and Roll did not prove to be financially wise, and with great sadness, he gave up his dream. It was then that he met Becky and they married. No more '60s music and lifestyle.

Looking for a career move, Dad helped by opening a door for a job opportunity with one of his accounts, Richard preferred no favors. He started at the bottom and eventually rose to manager at the Tidewater branch of this company.

Becky was a loving and supportive wife—and the daughter we always wanted. We did not know her as a baby but had the joy and love of knowing her as a young adult and wife of Richard. Her sun-filled smile, radiant red hair, and her beauty were second only to her cheerful personality. She filled us with happiness, love, and much caring.

Becky and Richard were so in love, so happy, so inseparable with so much to live for, and on their way to a successful life together. They represented the American dream: happily married, with a small house, two cars, a dog, and so much love. The only other joy they wanted was a baby—but it wasn't to be, and we all talked about an alternative to fulfilling this great desire. That, too, was not to be—ever.

Our family, as we knew and loved it, was small but close. Stan, an only child, Phyllis with no living siblings, so no aunts or uncles. Barry, our much-loved youngest son, is married to Diane, an only child. They have two children, Kyle and Julia. So our little family of eight was shattered, and we are now only six. Our second son Barry is now an only child, too. Kyle and Julia will no longer have an aunt and uncle to dote on them, nor will they ever have cousins. Our family has been decimated. When a family member (or two) is murdered, it's like dropping a stone in a pond and watching the circles grow from this act. That is what our lives have become. Just one circle of misery after another.

Murder Is Evil— The Side Effects Are Pure Hell

In 1993, Mark Sheppard and Andre Graham murdered our son Richard and daughter-in-law Becky. Breaking into their home a few days after Thanksgiving, Sheppard and Graham—who had known their victims from supplying them with drugs—shot our Richard and Becky to death, stole personal belongings from the home, and took their cars as well. We later learned that Sheppard killed Richard, and then he took aim at Becky to add to the damage Graham had inflicted upon her; Sheppard supposedly didn't like the way Graham shot her, so he did it himself. Richard was 40 and Becky was 35.

Eleven years later we still dare not go back to that day. We live with our heartbreak, we have managed to keep our tears private, and we have learned something else: We are not alone. Speaking to others who have had similar experiences, in addition to educating those who have not, has become our mission. It has also become the force that somehow keeps us sane.

There can never be an excuse for murder; there is *no* excuse! There is not one person among us who hasn't become so enraged at some incident—whether great or small—that a violent reaction hasn't crossed our mind. But what stops us from acting out? Is it the same thought mechanism that halts us from running through red traffic lights? Or, is it what inhibits us from smashing into the rear end of some obnoxious driver's car? What stops us? Fear? We think not. Timidity? No. Knowing right from wrong? Bingo! We know right from wrong, as we consciously make the choice to do what is right. We are not animals driven by the "might makes right" credo.

Those who cannot or choose not to make this choice are evil. That is, evil is the taking of an innocent life, it is someone who is a murderer, and it is a person who can't choose to spare life instead of destroying it. They also cannot and do not choose to ever be changed. Incarcerating these evil people will not change their mindsets. Up until the final moment, these people are free to make a choice before murdering another human being—they alone make that choice. They chose murder, and that is evil. Once they cross the line they can't go back.

Imprisoned murderers can earn the equivalency of a high-school education or even a college degree. They can become accredited optometrists, podiatrists, or lawyers, and they can find "God" as well as become "model prisoners." But they are still murderers because they crossed that line between law-abiding, civilized citizens and murderers. They are evil. They cannot hide behind a degree, religious calling, or perfect behavior. Evil is evil is evil.

In today's world of sophisticated forensics with DNA testing, those convicted should be guilty. These are no longer the days of "hang 'em high." You cannot reverse a murderer's way of reasoning right from wrong. You cannot put them back into society, for they do not fit—like a square peg into a round opening. Their way of approaching the world is already formed psychologically. You cannot reform them.

After killing Richard and Becky, the murderers tried to sell the couple's cars to a used-car dealership. Once there, they attempted to steal license plates, too—an act that was discussed during their respective trials. While the police were staking out Richard's stolen vehicle, they saw Graham, with Sheppard holding a can of gasoline to set fire to the car. When Graham was first arrested, he called his girlfriend from the jail phone. Right in front of the sheriff, he told her to get that "thing" in the closet and "get rid of it." The sheriff, taking heed of Graham's suspicious comments, reported the conversation, which led to the police finding the murder weapon. Before Sheppard was apprehended, he had shot a friend of his by mistake. He took his friend to a hospital, where the doctor removed the bullet. Having heard of the murders on TV, the doctor kept the bullet, in case Sheppard was the assailant. It turned out that it did match the one that killed Richard. Evil runs so deep in their veins, there's no way Graham or Sheppard could ever change. They went from one crime to another; destructive behavior and thinking is an inherent part of who they were.

It took six long painful years for justice to be meted out in our case. Six years, believe it or not, was a short time considering that most victims' families suffer anywhere from ten to fifteen, even twenty years. The wheels of justice turn slowly. The accused often seek many, many appeals while the victim's family just relives and relives the horror of the crime. The state tried Graham and Sheppard separately, seeking the death penalty in each case. Both were found guilty, but only Sheppard got the death penalty. Graham was sentenced to life, with an additional $1,000 fine—we were so outraged. How could the justice system save this man's life? However, justice was served later when Graham was tried for a previous murder he committed with the same gun that he used to shoot Becky. In that case he was found guilty and sentenced to die. Three trials and six years of appeals were difficult to endure.

For us there were no appeals, no visitation rights except to gravesites, and no phone calls—all of which are comforts afforded to prisoners. We only have our precious memories. Whether the accused is sentenced to life without parole or death, our lives will never be the same. But inmates, unlike us, can attempt to shorten their sentences, see their family, and even call their loved ones on the phone. Our only visit was from the police officers who came to tell us our children were dead. Little did we know on Thanksgiving that the next day would also be the last phone conversation we'd ever have with them. And then the murders imprisoned us, for all we could do was be patient with the justice system. We told the police and prosecutors that we weren't going to pressure them for information. We'd just wait for them to contact us when they could tell us as much as they could about the status of the case.

Does anyone know or care to know that the favored term "closure" is so wrong and so offensive, even though it's most often used when talking about victims' families? There is no closure, nor can there ever be any. "Acceptance" or "finality" might be a better word, but that comes only after shock, fear, funerals, grieving, tears, heartbreak, police, trials, and then appeals, appeals, and appeals. It is only then that "acceptance" or "finality" begins to settle within us. However, all of the above events take place while crushed hearts are mourning the intentional death of a loved one (or, as in our case, two loved ones). You never fully heal after suffering the wounds that we have. But we've come to recognize the full weight of what those two murderers did, and this is the acceptance or finality.

And while talking about foolish words, too many doctors, lawyers, police department personnel, clergy, psychologists, and victim service people are quick to tell us they are sorry for our "loss." We did not "lose" our beautiful children. We have "lost" gloves, our way on a road trip, a bet, and our place in a novel; but our children were taken from us. They were murdered, not "lost." How wonderful if we could go to the Lost and Found department somewhere and find our children. How ideal that would be.

Richard and Becky were professionals, and they had established a life for themselves in Richmond. Working his way up in the business world, Richard went from sweeping floors to being an officer manager for Coffee Butler (they set up coffee machines in business offices). Becky, Richard's wife of six years, was an office assistant for an air conditioning and heating company. They had come to see us and the rest of the family for Thanksgiving only a few days before their murders. Richard hadn't looked well because he was taking medicine for an illness. He and Becky left as they had to go to work the next day. We called them a day after they got home and everything was fine. But the next day, when we wanted to make sure Richard had made a doctor's appointment for himself, our call went unanswered. Still no answer the next day. We called both Richard and Becky's employers to see if they were busy at work, but neither of them was in the office. Same thing the next day, too. Something was wrong. We couldn't put our finger on it at the time, yet we knew things were not right.

They were not!!!

Sure enough, at 2:00 p.m. the doorbell rang—and our nightmare began: funerals, trials, appeals, and finally executions.

* * *

Asked if we chose to witness the executions, we faced great apprehension and much soul-searching. In the end we opted to be witnesses—not for any reason of revenge. You must understand that we (and all victim survivors) will fight as hard and as passionately for an innocent person to be kept out of prison as we would to put a guilty person behind bars. We opted to witness the execution because it was the final act we could perform for our children.

The executions echoed the trials: an opening of barely healed scars. We pained as we waited. There were two executions in our case; they occurred within a year of each other. In both cases, we agonized until the very last minute, waiting to hear if the executions would be stayed by the governor. The governor did not take any action, and the convicts were put to death as scheduled.

Each execution was gut-wrenching for us. We came away with three final feelings:

1. The process was too gentle—unlike the several bullets Sheppard fired into Richard's head.
2. It was now between "him" and "his" Maker.
3. Now, another mother will mourn her son's death, though it was her son's choice to commit murder and have her mourn.

We did not rejoice in nor mourn the deaths of the killers. They chose their destiny. We did not choose ours. We just found a deep relief in knowing that they could never commit this horrific crime against another family. And for that we felt some peace.

So now all we have left in our lives is visiting Richard's and Becky's graves, with us deep in despair, with tears welling in our eyes, dear beloved Richard and Becky. We loved them so much and miss them even more, knowing we will never see them, touch them, or delight in them ever again. It is our fervent mission to prevent other families from ever going through this horror and pain.

Do Not Cry For Us

A poem by Phyllis Rosenbluth

Do not cry for us, it eases not our pain.
Our children were murdered, they both were slain.
We do not mourn nor do we care—
The fate of those who stole our children so dear.
Quote not of scripture or punishment fair—
Not to these wounded parents doomed to despair.
So an "eye for an eye" or "thou shalt not kill"
It's with his maker now ... it is His will;
Whatever the choice for this murderer's fate—
Incarceration or execution our pain will not abate.

CHAPTER 7

FINDING HOPE:
ONE FAMILY'S JOURNEY

Roberta Roper

I am honored to be contributing my personal experience as the mother of a murdered daughter to this collection of experiences and dialogue regarding the impact of the death penalty on crime victims' families. Few of us as contributors would ever have thought to be involved in such a project. Each of the chapters reflects unique experiences with none being more valid, superior or inferior to another. Perhaps our stories help, in some small way, to explain the journeys of crime victims' families, the choices they make to become survivors, and pay tribute to the loved ones taken from them.

In expressing my personal views on capital punishment and its effects on victims' families, I am painfully aware of the perceptions and consequences it may create for the public, for other victim survivors, and for victim advocates who read my words. Until now, I have carefully avoided any discussion of or a position on the death penalty, either for myself or for the organization I represented. I understood those consequences. It has been my experience that any discussion of the death penalty, whether pro or con, is highly volatile and detracts from and inhibits progress in the area of crime victims' rights and services, very important work to which I am committed.

Sadly, there is an all-too-common assumption that to be a "strong" victim advocate and supporter and to be "tough" on crime, one must pursue the maximum penalty (death) in every case for those who are convicted of first-degree murder. Anything less than that is often viewed as being "soft" on crime, "coddling criminals" or betraying other survivors of murdered loved ones. I believe that such views, though far from accurate, may be convenient for the public and exploitive for politicians, mix myth with reality, and deter us from focusing on the true needs of crime victims and their families.

Likewise, I would never wish to imply or appear to speak for any other survivor of a murdered loved one. I respect and support all those courageous families who have been forced to confront the most horrendous criminal acts of others, bear those consequences for the rest of their lives, and somehow muster the courage and dignity to live with hope and productivity. I respect each individual's beliefs regarding the death penalty. The journeys each of us have made are ones that no parent, spouse, sibling, or friend should have to travel.

I speak only for myself, the mother of a murdered daughter, and a veteran victim advocate and service provider of more than twenty-three years. It is my hope that in sharing our personal experiences and views, we, the families of murdered loved ones, can contribute to the greater good of society. Most of all, it is my fervent hope and passion that we will attain a new awakening in America that focuses on a system of justice that is more balanced and fair—one that includes the compassionate and just treatment of victims and survivors of criminal violence.

While "who we are" can never explain why our families have suffered the murder of a loved one, it is a reminder that helps us appreciate the fact that crimes are inflicted every day upon good, ordinary people who did nothing to deserve criminal victimization. In a sense, crime is the "true equalizer." No one deserves to endure the cruel effects of another person's chosen criminal behavior. Nevertheless, far too many good, law-abiding citizens are forced to bear unspeakable crimes while their families are left to struggle with the consequences of those crimes and their shattered lives. Sadly, too many of our fellow citizens mistakenly believe that crime happens to "other people"—people who have made the wrong choices or engaged in risky behavior. While many people may have brief moments of empathy, others untouched by crime tend to dismiss crime's consequences as "someone else's problem." Public identification is often followed by feelings of helplessness or fear. Sometimes the public's worst conclusion is to blame the victim. That conclusion protects their own vulnerability, enabling them to ignore the problems and move on with their lives.

Life's Defining Moments:
Before and After April 3, 1982

Certain events become defining moments in our lives. The terrorist attacks on our nation on September 11, 2001, and the Oklahoma City bombing had powerful collective impacts on our society that continue today. Similarly, my family had our lives "re-defined" by no less powerful, though random criminal actions of two strangers who forever changed our lives. More than twenty-three years ago, on April 3, 1982, Jack Ronald Jones and Jerry Lee Beatty took the promising young life of our daughter, Stephanie, and nearly destroyed us as a family. Their choices and the criminal justice process that would follow, divided our lives into "before" and "after" periods that would forever leave a giant hole in each of our lives.

Before April 3, 1982, my husband, Vince, and I would have described our lives as all but perfect. As parents of five children, we had strived to be the best parents we were capable of being. Our efforts were beginning to bear fruit. As a military family who had lived throughout the world (Vince was a career Naval officer), we were finally able to put down roots in a safe community for our children. After a tour of duty in London, England, we returned to Maryland and bought five acres in a lovely rural area in Southern Prince George's County called Croom. Beginning in 1974, the whole family became involved in clearing the land and building the permanent new home we would complete and move into on Flag Day, June 1975. I was able to pursue the art that I loved by teaching at a parochial school. We felt extraordinarily blessed.

Stephanie, our first born child, had just turned 22 and was preparing to graduate magna cum laude from Frostburg State University. She was beautiful, intelligent, and a gifted artist. She was one of those extraordinary human beings with the gift to lead and inspire without creating envy—the kind of person people knew and loved or simply did not know—the child every parent prays for. She was a role model for her siblings: Sharon, 18, Brian, almost 17, Dan, almost 15, and Peter, almost 10. We would tease her and say that she wasn't *normal* because she hadn't prepared us for her *normal* sister and brothers! If I had to describe Stephanie in a single word, it would be "sunshine." She was the essence of goodness and joy in a sometimes-dark world. She was also my best friend.

The last weeks of March 1982 found Stephanie preparing for her senior art show. The challenges of those hectic weeks before graduation prompted her to come home for the last weekend in March, and in her words, "to re-charge my batteries." On Friday, April 2, she brought home two drawings that would never be completed. Later when I read the last entry in her journal, I would understand her fears and dreams of that period—that in the race to complete projects on schedule, her work might not be her best, and her dream was to be valued as a serious artist.

On that Friday evening, Stephanie (Steffi) shared a family meal with us that would be the last moments we would have with her on this earth. She and her best friend, Lisa, were meeting former high school classmates who were attending college in Washington, D.C. Afterward, she planned to spend the

Roper family, winter 1981. Top row, son Brian, Roberta, son Peter, and husband Vince. Bottom row, daughter Sharon, son Daniel and daughter Stephanie.

night at Lisa's home. I expected her home late the next morning so we could pick up frames and art supplies she had ordered. She was then going to join the family for the funeral of a beloved uncle in New Jersey. Before she left, I went through the usual "mom litany" about safety. Steffi reminded me that she knew how to take care of herself, never took risks, but that she had no intention of living life imprisoned by fear.

Ironically, a month before we had discussed the experience of a young Washington, D.C., woman who was abducted, robbed, and raped as she returned home from work. Steffi again reminded me that she had taken a rape awareness clinic at school and knew how to handle car emergencies. (Of course, this was prior to the extensive use of mobile phones!) I acknowledged my confidence in her, but ended by saying that I couldn't live if anything happened to her. She left with my parting words to have "a good time."

The Beginning of Our Nightmare

"Cruelty, like every other vice, requires no motive outside of itself; it only requires opportunity." —George Elliot

Saturday, April 3 began in light rain, and Stephanie didn't come home. I called Lisa's home, spoke with her mom, and my heart clinched in fear as she told me that Stephanie had decided not to spend the night because of all the errands we had planned. I could barely speak, abruptly ended the conversation saying that I had to call the police immediately. I knew that something terribly wrong had happened. If she could, Steffi would have found a way to call us.

My frantic call to the local police was my first encounter with law enforcement and the criminal justice system. It was not a good experience. I could barely convince the officer to listen to my plea—after all, Steffi had only been missing for hours. In the end he agreed to come to our home to take a report. My husband and children tried to comfort me, but I was seized with panic. I felt like I had been disemboweled without anesthesia. An officer arrived, reluctantly took the report, and complained about what kids did to their parents. He described Stephanie as probably "just another runaway."

Our daughter Sharon and son Brian met Lisa and her family in their neighborhood, discovering the family car Stephanie was driving that evening. Pulled off to the side of the country road, the car was found locked, and inside was a tote bag carrying Stephanie's clothes.

Stephanie had spent the last summers of high school and early years of college serving as a counselor and lifeguard at the local elementary school safety patrol camp. Consequently, reports of her missing quickly reached police officers who knew her, and they were soon on the scene. A search team of new police recruits was mobilized, and a door-to-door investigation ended with no clues as to Stephanie's whereabouts. The next morning, our parish community, Holy Rosary Catholic Church, and Stephanie's friends received the news of her disappearance, and in shock and fear, prayed for her safe recovery. In desperation, my husband and I sought the involvement of the media through TV interviews and announcements, had a missing person poster displayed, and offered a reward for information leading to her safe return. And nothing happened. Each new day dawned with the physical and emotional challenges of simply getting out of bed, caring for our children, and going through the motions of our daily routines.

One of the most difficult and painful first calls had to be made to my parents. They were awaiting our arrival in New Jersey for our uncle's funeral. The shock of the news about their first grandchild sent both of them to a hospital for emergency treatment and left them with lasting health problems.

In the meantime, the police sent a team to Frostburg State University to interview Stephanie's housemates, teachers, and friends. They grilled us about a possible crisis in her life, about boyfriends, even suggesting that she had intentionally run away. We were asked to keep a log of all calls. With few exceptions, it appeared that no one had seen or heard anything that might track the events leading to Stephanie's disappearance. We were inundated with calls from friends and family, with visits from neighbors bringing food and prayers, but only silence about Stephanie. Vince continued to go to work, our children went to school, and Holy Week began. Somehow, we managed to cling to our faith, to prayer, and to the rituals of our faith that would culminate with Easter Sunday.

Our youngest child Peter's tenth birthday was April 13. Previous party plans had been made so that his friends could celebrate during spring break. Despite everything, we decided that this celebration was too important for our son and for our family. Steffi had a very special relationship with her brother. She was twelve years old when he was born, and I often called her "Peter's other mother," relying on her maturity, caring attention and helpfulness. We reasoned that Steffi would want us to carry on with and for Peter.

Late on Easter Sunday evening, Vince was summoned to the police station, informed that our car could be released, and told that they expected breaking news and "it didn't look good." What no parent can ever prepare for was the call from the police at 2:00 a.m. on Monday, telling us that they had to visit us. Earlier, they had assured us that if there was news, they would deliver it to us in our home—not by phone. So we tried to prepare ourselves for their arrival and the news that no family wants to receive. The officers briefly explained that Stephanie's body had been found in a swampy area near the Patuxent River in St. Mary's County. They said that she had died from a gunshot wound to the head. I asked and they confirmed that she had been raped. They told us that one individual had been arrested, and that they hoped to make a second arrest later that morning. They promised to return with more information after they got some much-needed rest. Somehow, Vince had the presence of mind to urge them to do everything "by the book" and not to violate any of their rights as accused individuals. If they were responsible, we wanted them to be held accountable.

On Tuesday, April 12, seven ten-year-old boys arrived at our home to celebrate Peter's birthday with homemade pizza, birthday cake, and ice cream. Sadly, tragic news travels quickly, and a stream of friends, neighbors, parishioners, and strangers filled our home. One was Vic Pietkiewicz, the moderator of our church youth group. Vic came with clipboard in hand, announcing that he was in charge of the Stephanie Roper Family Assistance Committee, whose purpose was to support our family through the painful ordeal of a funeral and expected criminal trials. As the birthday party ended, a police officer friend, Corporal Patrick Grogan, sat comforting us in our family room.

The television was turned on, and the evening news began. In shocked horror, we listened and then began weeping and screaming as a reporter stood before an abandoned shack, described the path were Stephanie's body had been dragged and had been doused with gasoline and set afire—facts we were hearing for the first time. Much later, we would learn that her killers began dismembering her body in order to prevent identification. Evilness had entered our lives and taken a most precious gift—our sunshine.

The next days were consumed in a haze of planning a funeral. I kept thinking how wrong this all was … parents don't bury their children … why Stephanie … why our family? In shopping for our children, I'd find myself panicked and almost ill, seeing a young woman who resembled our Steffi. Yet the kindness of friends and strangers was overwhelming. Their frustration and anger were diverted into acts of love toward us. Family arrived from out of town, and April 17, Stephanie's funeral day, arrived. I prayed that God would give our family strength for this day and the days ahead. I begged our family and friends *to sing for Stephanie* at the mass of Christian burial, and to remember how she had lived her life … not how it had been taken from her. In truth, our hearts were broken—it seemed like our American dreams for our children had also died.

The Darkest Journey

"Our strength often increases in proportion to the obstacles imposed upon it. The lessons we learn in sadness and from loss are those that abide … sorrow clarifies the mind, steadies it, forces it to weigh things correctly … the soil moist with tears best feeds the seeds of truth."— Tyron Edwards, *The New Dictionary of Thoughts* (under "lessons learned")

Our journey through the criminal justice system began when Jack Ronald Jones, 26, and Jerry Lee Beatty, 17, were indicted for first-degree felony murder, rape, and kidnapping. Assigned for prosecution to the St. Mary's County State's Attorney's Office, and eligible for the death penalty, changes of venue quickly determined that trials would be held in Baltimore and Anne Arundel Counties. For me, there was no question that I had to attend every proceeding and learn even the cruel realities of what had happened to our beloved daughter. That meant that I would often travel to St. Mary's County to attend a hearing, only to discover that it had been postponed—and no one had told us.

Because we had never been involved in the criminal justice system, we became determined to learn and understand as much as possible before the trials began. Consequently, with the help of the newly formed Stephanie Roper Family Assistance Committee two public meetings were organized. The St. Mary's county prosecutor accepted the first invitation to describe the general process of a criminal trial. A second meeting had our local representatives of the Maryland Legislature who focused on the law and the legislative process. The public meetings were revealing and the first of many steps in our education about the system called justice. In my mind, a criminal trial was the search for truth. A courtroom, an almost sacred place, was where that search discovered the truth, and justice was imposed. Those beliefs would be crushed by our experience in the criminal trial.

I had learned that the 1982 Maryland General Assembly had approved legislation allowing for a court to consider crime's impact upon a victim before sentencing. The Victim Impact Statement law was being proclaimed as the first victims' right in Maryland. Vince and I obtained a copy of the bill, and as the naive citizens we were then, presented it to the prosecutor at our first meeting with him. We incorrectly assumed that as an attorney, he would understand and fully apply the law. When we asked the prosecutor if he had support services for crime victims' families, he laughed and said he was it! He went on to explain that defense attorneys frequently subpoenaed surviving family members of homicide victims, not because their testimony was needed but because that enabled the sequestration rule to be applied and excluded a family's presence in the courtroom. What he failed to explain was that we would also be excluded if and when we, as Stephanie's parents, testified for the State.

I have remembered those words many times over the past twenty-three years as a reflection of that era, and of a criminal justice system that appeared indifferent and uncaring to victims' concerns. Then, virtually the only right that crime victims had was to identify the perpetrator. That was "business as usual." Our journey and education continued.

Jones, the principal defendant, was indicted for first-degree felony murder, kidnapping, and first-degree rape, and brought to trial, beginning in late August 1982, in Baltimore County. Because so many friends wanted to support our family at the public trial, Vic Pietkiewicz and I agreed that it would be courteous to inform the clerk's office. As a result, the trial was assigned to the smallest courtroom and only a few people could be seated. All friends who were there conducted themselves with quiet dignity. If asked, they spoke only about their presence for Stephanie and support for our family. Nevertheless, press reports had the defense team describing us as "vigilantes" or a "lynch mob." I was characterized as an emotional mother who simply wanted revenge. This only added to our anguish. All we wanted was the opportunity to learn what had happened to our daughter and to honor her life by our quiet presence. Our presence was about love, not revenge.

The trial for Jack Jones would consume more than six weeks. After Vince and I testified as the State's first witnesses, the rule on witnesses was invoked, and we were banished from the courtroom. Our brief testimony related only to the last family meal we had shared with Stephanie, what she was wearing that evening, and the family vehicle she was driving. Nothing was essential or of an evidentiary nature. Did the prosecutor advocate for our presence in the courtroom? Did the judge question if our testimony or sequestration were necessary? The answer to both questions is no. It was devastating to accept that while the accused had the right to sit at counsel table, to attend bench conferences, and could even cross-examine us, we would be denied the right to observe the most important event of our lives.

While physically barred from the courtroom, I was determined to be a silent presence for Stephanie. I pressed myself to the courtroom door, attempting to see and hear anything. What I would hear were the thoughtless and painful remarks of strangers emerging from the courtroom saying: "What was she doing out at that time of night? What was she wearing? How many drinks did she have?" I turned to the police officers who stood with me and questioned the relevancy of those remarks. Had Stephanie been a prostitute, drunk, or homeless, she still would have had a right not to be violated. She fit none of those descriptions! My education about the process was growing. Clearly the goal of the defense was to make the best case for their client. When there is no defense, the task is to create reasonable doubt in the minds of the jurors. Stephanie was not only a rape victim, but one who had been forever silenced.

The trial progressed with little contact with the prosecutor. His focus was aggressive prosecution, not in communicating with us. Fortunately for us, the son of one of our legislative representatives was a third-year University of Baltimore law student who attended the trial whenever possible. Kurt Wolfgang became our link to understanding what was happening behind closed doors. He told us that the defense had succeeded in excluding any photos of Stephanie on the grounds that they were inflammatory. During a recess, Vince accidentally bumped into one of the defense attorneys as he attempted to navigate a crowded hallway. We were then summoned into the courtroom to hear this attorney ask for a mistrial because the father of Stephanie Roper had assaulted him! The trial judge chastised and warned us about our behavior when we had done nothing to deserve that. We had not even publicly shed a tear. It then became abundantly clear that this trial was not a search for truth and justice, but about winning the case!

In retrospect, the prosecutor would have probably described me as a nuisance. We were desperate to know what was happening. Finally as the guilt/innocence phase of the trial was ending for Jack Jones, I asked the prosecutor about the Victim Impact Statement. His reply was that after the lunch break, the sentencing phase of the trial would begin, and I would deliver the Victim Impact Statement. I neither fully understood what this meant nor was prepared to speak. I was reluctant to speak openly because some of our children would be observing the afternoon proceedings for the first time. We had not had the opportunity to discuss, prepare for, or agree upon what we would like the court to know. The prosecutor convinced me that my voice was essential. He said that the court knew nothing about Stephanie, or what these crimes against her had done to our family, to her friends, and to our community. So with great hesitancy, I was allowed to enter the courtroom and took the stand.

The defense immediately objected to anything I might say, on the grounds that it would be emotional, irrelevant, and probable cause for reversal on appeal. After a lengthy bench conference, the court agreed, and I was silenced. The now convicted defendant then took the stand, wept, and pleaded for mercy. He was followed by his father, his wife, his jailhouse minister (who said the defendant had found God), a former employer, and his child's teacher. All of them asked that the court give mercy and leniency to Jones, because a harsh punishment would cause lifelong anguish to his family. Yet we could not speak for Stephanie!

The sentencing phase concluded after the finding of guilt for first-degree felony murder, kidnapping, and rape. The jury began ten hours of deliberations while our family struggled to contain our weariness and fragile emotions. Desperate to make sense of this senseless crime, I approached the defense attorneys and challenged their behavior to us. I also asked permission to speak with Stephanie's killer. They denied my request, saying it wasn't a good time for their client.

In the early morning hours the court reconvened, and the jury announced its decision of a life sentence for Jones. (Later we would discover that the jury acted on the court's instruction, and truly believed that a life sentence meant life!) The court immediately imposed two life sentences plus twenty years to be served concurrently. Several things then happened. The prosecutor and virtually everyone present reacted to the sentence with stunned silence. Then a young man who had been an almost daily presence stood and said that on behalf of the family of one of the defense attorneys, he wished to express his apologies to the Roper family for this attorney's behavior throughout the trial! While this young man's words validated so much for us, we nevertheless left the courtroom feeling shocked and betrayed. Not because the defendant, Jack

Jones, was spared the ultimate penalty, but mostly because of how we had been treated throughout this process. We were appalled and angry at the ability of the defense to abuse the law at our expense. The court's multiple sentences meant that they would be served as one (concurrently), and that with diminution credits, the defendant would be eligible for parole in eleven and one-half years! While we never focused on a sentence of death, we naively believed that a life sentence, if not true *life*, meant more than fifteen years! No sentence would reverse what we had lost.

Weeks later, in an Anne Arundel County courtroom, Jerry Beatty pleaded guilty to the same charges as Jones and was handed an identical sentence. In 1985, prosecutors in Prince George's County filed charges for the crimes that began there. Though a trial began, both defendants pleaded guilty and received additional life sentences, to be served consecutive to their other sentences. In 1986 Jones attempted to gain entry into the Patuxent Institution, whose psychotherapeutic treatment program then routinely circumvented a court's sentence and granted early release to even the most serious criminal offenders. This information reached us through another inmate, and we were able to stop his admission. (Later reforms successfully altered release practices at Patuxent and returned accountability to the Department of Public Safety.)

Our family then began our grief journey in earnest. We came to truly appreciate that life is fragile and precious. If we were to become survivors and not lifelong victims, we would have to fight to rebuild our shattered lives. Vince and I now confronted the challenge of preserving our family and marriage. We also were determined to use our experience to somehow make a difference for future crime victims and their families. Like countless others of that time, we had discovered some very painful lessons. Unlike the two men who took Stephanie's life, we had no rights to be informed, to attend, or be heard in the criminal justice process. And the most difficult challenge was attempting to explain to our children that the criminal justice system we had taught them to trust and respect was responsible!

In the meantime, a dark abyss seemed to envelop us. It was as if each member of our family was struggling alone, pushing and pulling our way along a murky bottom of water, clinging to each other for hope, yet rejecting each other. We sought counseling for our family and found that the therapist was not prepared to counsel homicide survivors. In a sense, we became their teachers! We were convinced that unless we were able to find a productive channel for our grief and loss, we would not survive. For me, it was a personal realization that, without new meaning and purpose, I didn't want to live. And if we didn't survive, how could we help our children regain hope in their young lives. And if we failed, wouldn't evil surely win?

And so we began making choices. We acknowledged that Stephanie did not have a choice, but clearly we did. We could allow this tragedy to destroy us, or we could take action to benefit others and honor our beloved daughter. So by God's grace, fierce determination, persistence, and the support of many extraordinary people, we began a process of recreating ourselves to make the "broken pieces" of our former lives fit into something "new."

New Beginnings

"Have a purpose in life, and having it, throw into your work such strength of mind and muscle as God has given you."—Tyron Edwards, *The New Dictionary of Thoughts* (under "purpose")

The "something new" began after we had a few days to recover from the trial and the media onslaught that followed. A last meeting was scheduled for the Stephanie Roper Family Assistance Committee. Vince and I thanked the caring people who had supported us through the darkest days of our lives, and explained that we had to do something more. We announced our decision to begin lobbying efforts for victims' rights and services in Maryland. To our astonishment, volunteers came forward to help begin the formal organization of our grassroots efforts.

On a late October 1982 evening, Vic and Judy Pietkiewicz gathered a group of us around their kitchen table. Legal contacts were made, and the groundwork was laid for the creation and incorporation of two nonprofit organizations that would be under my direction. Vic would become the first chair of the board of directors, along with Kurt Wolfgang and me. Kurt volunteered to provide legal counsel and draft proposed legislation. A rally in our State capitol was planned, a petition of support was created (which gathered the signature of 93,000 citizens!), and many volunteers came forward. The generosity of a stranger provided an unfinished basement as the first office, and friends volunteered to staff the office of the Stephanie Roper Committee and Foundation, Inc. (SRC/SRF). Donations and bake sales provided our first fiscal resources. The Committee's focus would be advocacy for victims' rights and services, and the Foundation would provide free support services for crime victims and their families. The crimes against Stephanie were considered among the most heinous ever committed in our State. Consequently, the volunteer office staff was inundated with people wanting to help, "because they had to do more than just cry."

The rest, as they say, is history. The decisions of those early days laid the foundation for the missions, achievements, and services that continue today, more than twenty-three years after Stephanie's death. Though naive and originally uneducated about the criminal justice system or legislative process, we were determined to overcome those early weaknesses. We worked hard, maintained a dignified and positive attitude, persevered, and refused to accept defeat. Sometimes this work required us to *afflict the comfortable* attitudes of the public even as we *comforted the afflicted* crime victims and survivors that we served. It has been work inspired by the great American belief that each of us is government—individuals endowed not only with rights, but responsibilities to make our world a better place. We also have been inspired by the fellow victims and survivors we have served, people who have had everything they hold dear challenged or destroyed: their faith in God, their dependence on government, their trust in their fellow man, and their hope for tomorrow.

Volumes could be written about our experiences with the Maryland Legislature, the Judiciary, Supreme Court decisions, faith communities, the media, friends, and most of all, our children. Despite the challenges, our children have endured. They are survivors! We are very proud that each of them is a good person, living a happy, productive life.

In October 2002 Vince and I turned over the leadership of the SRC/F to Russell Butler, the legal counsel and lobbyist who succeeded Kurt Wolfgang, and the organization was merged into the Maryland Crime Victims' Resource Center, Inc. (MCVRC). While we will always be involved and passionate advocates for victims' issues, we wanted to reclaim a life that allows us more time for our family. Having begun as a grassroots, all-volunteer nonprofit organization, the MCVRC is today considered one of the most effective victim advocacy and service organizations in the nation. A professional staff provides criminal justice education; court accompaniment; individual and family therapeutic counseling; grief support groups; faith-based referrals; community education; crime prevention; policy advocacy; legal information and assistance; direct legal representation; referrals to other local, state, or national community services; and technical assistance for allied professionals and criminal justice agencies.

Our legislative achievements include the passage of more than seventy laws, the most significant being a Maryland Constitutional Amendment for crime victims' rights in 1994. We continue to be a part of the national effort supporting an amendment to the U.S. Constitution that formally began with a Rose Garden ceremony in 1996.

What we have *never* advocated for is the death penalty. The SRC/F and MCVRC have never taken a position on capital punishment. We explain that while our members hold views both in support of and opposition to capital punishment, we all share a strong belief in a sentence of life without parole (whose passage we successfully lobbied for in 1987). We continue to believe that life without the possibility of parole enables the State to prevent a convicted killer from murdering again without the excessive costs of capital proceedings; the endless pain and suffering imposed upon families who must endure repeated appeals, re-trials, and sentencing; and the possibility of error that an innocent person may be executed.

I did not support the death penalty for Stephanie's killers in 1982, nor do I today. Long ago however, I learned through very painful experiences and grief that the expression of my personal views (even when separated from the organization) came with enormous consequences. I have refused to be involved in any discussions about the death penalty because they detracted from and deterred the progress of meaningful victims' rights. How the justice system treats crime victims is separate and distinct from how it punishes their offenders. They should never be confused.

While I expressed my moral and practical opposition to the death penalty shortly after Stephanie's murder, I chose to support its repeal in Maryland only after I relinquished the organization's leadership. I believe that all life is sacred and for God alone to begin and end. By supporting State-sanctioned killing, I believe that I would be reduced to the abysmal level of our daughter's killers. That was not the moral lesson I wanted to teach our four surviving children then, nor is it the lesson I want to impart to our grandchildren today.

Like every family member whose loved one is taken by another person's criminal choice and actions, I was filled with grief, anger, rage, and incomprehension at the two men who snuffed out the promising life of our beautiful and precious Stephanie. The human side of my nature would not have had any difficulty in "pulling the switch" for her killers. Those are basic, human reactions that though frightening, are normal in the immediate aftermath of crime. The moral part of my nature, however, rebelled at lowering myself to that standard. The practical reasons for opposition seem very obvious to me. When life without parole is imposed upon a convicted killer, it means that! There are no automatic appeals, as in death penalty cases. There are no excessive costs, and years of new trials and sentencing for the victim's family. It is over! And, incarceration for life without parole is far less costly.

While individual beliefs deserve respect, most victims seek justice, not revenge! This means being true to one's convictions. Victims and their families deserve what every person accused or convicted of a crime is promised under our Constitution: equal justice under law.

For most of us, the word "closure" is offensive and inappropriate. For a family whose loved one has been taken from them without dignity, there is a giant hole in their lives that can never be filled. It is a false expectation to believe that State-sanctioned killing will fill that void. There is no closure. Stephanie believed that "one person can make a difference, and every person should try." Vince and I sought justice and resolution. We continue to choose life-affirming actions that pay tribute to Stephanie and strive to ensure victim justice for all crime victims and their families.

> "All that we can know about those we have loved and lost is that they would wish us to remember them with an intensified realization of their reality ... what is essential does not die but clarifies. The highest tribute to the dead is not grief but gratitude." —Thornton Wilder

CHAPTER 8

My Journey and the Riddle

Marsha Kimble

How many times have you thought about the death penalty, and on what level? The first time that I gave thought to the death penalty I was in high school, on a debate team. The debate was colorful and spirited, and at the same time shallow and empty: my focus was on who won and how many points my team scored—I was never thinking about death or life and what it really meant. My thoughts were strictly based on theory.

How many times do people ask how you feel about issues that you have never experienced firsthand? It is easy to express your views; however, living with that decision is a different matter.

I have learned on my journey in life that there are times when the answer or solution to an issue isn't clear—perceptions can be colored by religion, parental values, or popular opinion. Nor can the answer always be spontaneous, such as those gut feelings that we all have from time to time. For me, finding a solution is a process; not a simple learning process, but a searching of the soul, a journey. Life would be simple if answers were certain, but how empty.

Never in my wildest dreams did I think that I would be faced with deciding how I felt about whether a man should be sentenced to life imprisonment or death. It was easy for me to go back and forth in my opinion. I had not had to deal with the issue on a personal level. I had no vested interest. I had not studied the law. I thought life in prison meant just that. I did not know about plea agreements and sentencing guidelines. My opinions were based exclusively on emotion.

I did not know there would come a time in my life when I would have to give the death penalty serious, heart-wrenching thought. I never dreamed that capital punishment would affect my life so personally. I had no desire to engage in research and debate on the issue.

Marsha Kimble with daughter Frankie Merrell, 1992.

I never considered that one of my children would be murdered. Have you ever thought about such a prospect and what it entails? How it changes your life on a multitude of levels, forcing you to dig deep inside for answers to the unthinkable? Neither did I until April 19, 1995, when my life was forever changed.

My daughter, Frankie Merrell, worked for the Federal Employees Credit Union on the third floor of the Alfred P. Murrah Building in Oklahoma City. Frankie was twenty-three years old, married, and the mother of a two-year-old girl named Morgan.

Words seem trite in describing what follows. After hearing the explosion from my home in northwest Oklahoma City, I turned on the television. First, the sheer horror of seeing the building where my daughter worked reduced to a pile of rubble struck me, followed by the terrifying realization that my child might be seriously injured or dead. It was like someone had stabbed me in the chest. The phone rang constantly as the news quickly spread. I made arrangements for someone to come watch our granddaughter. I had to go find my child.

I had worked as a nurse for ten years, and I heard that a triage unit had been set up in the YMCA, across from the Murrah Federal Building. I hoped that my nursing experience might allow me access to those being found and treated. My husband and I jumped into the car and headed downtown. As we reached the main highway, the traffic was bumper to bumper. Cars were racing down the side of the road with their hazard lights flashing. The sound of sirens filled the air. Ten blocks from our destination we had to exit and park. Even at that distance, glass was everywhere and debris filled the air.

We neared the Murrah Federal Building and were stunned by the devastation. I looked up to the floor where my daughter worked. The Federal Employees Credit Union was a gaping hole with hanging rebar and concrete. My heart felt as if it would pound out of my chest: How could my daughter have survived such a blast?

As we started to question a police officer, people began running away from the building. We were told that we had to leave the area immediately due to the possibility of another bomb. We made our way to St. Anthony Hospital, where many of the victims were being treated. We waited in what appeared to be a gymnasium in the hospital. Volunteers placed victims' names on the walls along with information about where they were being cared for. We searched constantly for our daughter's name and called all the local hospitals in an effort to find her.

By late afternoon of April 19, the First Christian Church, several blocks north of the Murrah site, was selected as a place for families to gather to be informed about their loved one's fate. When we arrived at the church, we walked into a dining hall with rows of tables and twenty-five funeral directors. I was desperate to believe that my daughter was alive and expected only to fill out a missing person's report. I was outraged and called the funeral directors "vultures." They quickly took off their distinctive badges. This wasn't an airplane disaster where people pretty much know everyone is dead. I was not prepared for their presence.

Our family left the First Christian Church and returned to a church where the American Red Cross was stationed. The Red Cross had received a report that Frankie had been found and was alive in St. Anthony's Hospital. After going to the hospital in high hopes, we learned that it wasn't so. The emotional roller-coaster ride was too much and I fell to the floor, wailing and writhing on the ground in grief. The mental health folks were called and immediately sedated me. Public displays of grief that violated cultural behavioral protocols were labeled as abnormal.

The bombing immediately became a social spectacle of suffering as the media saturated a worldwide audience with the drama of rescue and recovery operations from April 19 until May 4, 1995. It became a time when the boundaries between public and private vanished; when people's "insides" were deemed public property (Linenthal 2001:2).

April 20. Our vigil continued. I remember lying on a cot watching television footage of the bombing in an attempt to get a glimpse of Frankie. Maybe she was one of the walking wounded. Across the room I noticed a telephoto lens pointed at my face. I bolted out of the church, running aimlessly. My son and husband caught me and pulled me to the ground. Later that day the media were sequestered, and family members could decide whether to talk with them or not. The next morning a picture of my husband trying to comfort me hit the front page of papers across the country. We decided the safest place to wait for further information was home.

The wait was agonizing, and it went on for four endless days and nights. On the fourth day, the authorities contacted us and asked for medical X-rays and dental records for identification purposes. Although we hoped for a miracle, we tried to prepare for the worst.

And the worst had happened. My daughter was blown from her teller's window and found by the elevator shaft on the first floor. We were told her body was located on the day of the explosion. We were notified of her death on April 23.

Onlookers followed the search for survivors, the grim recovery of bodies, the anguish of grieving family members, the public memorial services, and in some cases, even the televised funerals of those killed.

It is hard to explain to people about having a child, no matter how old, and being robbed of her life. It is the most hopeless and powerless feeling in the world. It used to be that when my children had a problem, I had an answer or solution. There was no answer or solution to this horror. There was nothing I could do to change things or bring her back. She was gone.

For many months after the bombing, I could barely put one foot in front of the other. My focus was not on Timothy McVeigh, the bomber, or on the judicial process, much less on how I felt about the death penalty. My focus was on my grandchild, who had begun to cry for her mommy. I also was deeply concerned about my son, Cody, who had lost his father — Tom Kight, my first husband — to cancer fourteen months before the bombing. I was bombarded by emotions, principally earth-shattering grief.

The grief industry descended on Oklahoma City immediately after the bombing. I was horrified by the overwhelming presence of the "death angels." I wanted and needed time alone with my family. I resented them hovering over me, dying for attention. Their good intentions were often greater than their clinical abilities, and they sometimes made things worse.

The widespread conviction that grief has "stages" wasn't working for me. In Lawrence Langer's words, violent mass death is "an event to be endured, not a trauma to be healed" (quoted in Linenthal 2001:96; see also Kleinman 1995:180). If I have learned anything from my struggles with the impact of violence, it is that there is rarely an "old" self to put back together.

Out of my pain, I decided to start a support group of families of lost loved ones and survivors of the bombing—Families and Survivors United. We spoke the same language, and we understood each other's pain. We confronted the judicial process on several issues concerning victims' rights. We met with charities and tried to make sure those in need received the financial assistance they deserved. We made a thank-you video for the rescue workers and distributed the copies nationwide. Our main goal was to help each other help ourselves. One of the worst things that individuals in such circumstances go through is the feeling of helplessness and hopelessness. Among our best accomplishments was to empower each other, to take control of our lives in some way, and to have a reason to get up and out of bed.

Near the first anniversary of the bombing, I was contacted by a Belgian television network that was doing a feature film on the issue of the death penalty. Representatives asked me if I would accompany crew members to McAlester, Oklahoma, where an execution was scheduled to take place. I agreed to go because I knew that at some point in time I would have to come to terms with how I felt about putting a person to death for the crime he or she committed. On our journey to McAlester, members of the Belgian television crew and I engaged in a debate about capital punishment, and I learned that the United States is the only western industrialized country that administers the death penalty.

As we approached the prison, it was beginning to get dark. It was eerie. We arrived at the guard station and were issued press passes. Then we were transported by a prison van to a section of the prison near the death chamber that had been set aside for the media. Approximately thirty people had gathered to protest the execution. They were holding candles and singing spiritual songs. I had a lump in my throat and fought back tears. I was already regretting my decision and feeling like a participant. While I vividly remember the events of the day, I can't remember the name of the prisoner who was executed. The whole experience was an exploration of my feelings in anticipation of the possibility that Timothy McVeigh could be sentenced to die. In a sense, it was a rehearsal.

As the television crew unloaded their gear, I noticed that there was a lot of activity inside of the building. The warden gave us instructions, and then we walked into the room where the media would report their stories on the execution. I expected a solemn atmosphere. What I experienced was something totally different. There were close to forty people in the room, including reporters, camera crews, and journalists. Tables were set up near the back of the room with all kinds of snack foods and desserts. There were desks with computers on the sides of the room, where reporters gave their accounting of their death watch. The room was full of laughter and chatter, and I felt confused by the environment in which I had put myself. Wasn't a man's life about to end? The atmosphere was more like a party.

As the clock ticked closer to the scheduled execution, the warden came in and explained what would be taking place within the next thirty minutes. Only one member of the media would witness the execution and would then report back to the media pool. Family members of the victim who witnessed the execution also would make their comments in the media room. Everyone was instructed to stay inside the building. Cameras outside the media center were strictly forbidden during this time.

I took a seat in the middle of the room and watched the clock. I thought about my daughter's murder and the man who had taken her life. I suppose I was trying to convince myself that taking a man's life for heinous crimes was justifiable. I also knew that if McVeigh or his accomplice Terry Nichols was sentenced to die, I would not watch the execution. I wanted no part of the drama that I was experiencing. It felt like a media circus, with no concern that a life was about to be taken, resulting in another family's grieving.

Shortly after the hour of the scheduled execution, the doors of the media center swung open. The warden made his statement to the press. Then a reporter, who seemed traumatized by what she had seen, reported her observations concerning the execution and answered questions from the press. The victim's family then made a statement. Their statement was brief. After years of waiting, justice had been served, they said. The press asked the family some follow-up questions. By that time I was numb. All I can remember is that I was anxious to leave.

The issue of the death penalty occupied my mind for several weeks following the execution. I felt confused. I knew that I hated McVeigh and Nichols, so why was I having so much trouble struggling with my feelings about the death penalty? It wasn't until I talked with reporter James B. Meadow, a staff writer with the *Rocky Mountain News*, that I started to scrape the iceberg of pain and rage that dwelt within me.

After being interviewed by ABC News, I sat and talked with Meadow about the death penalty. I confessed to him that I thought lethal injection was too easy. I told him that I would like to stand by McVeigh's cell whenever I wished.

I would bring a big stick with me and rake it across the bars and spit on him. I shared with this stranger a haunting moment of locking eyes with McVeigh in the courtroom and his nodding at me. I thought how peculiar that was. I've often wondered what he was thinking about when his eyes met mine. Meadow then asked me a very interesting question: "What do you want?" My hands shook. I inhaled deeply on my cigarette. My eyes filled with tears. "I don't know," I said. "I want something back. I want *her* back."

As the months went by I struggled to stay strong, trying to survive the undertow of marital troubles that had percolated into my life. I kept a journal. I tended to a flood of e-mail messages. I took walks in the mountains. I thought about the death penalty. I held tight to the teddy bear that my husband had given me, the bear I named "Justice." I meditated. I tried not to drink too much. I smoked like a freight train. I underlined passages in books such as Dale Salwak's *The Wonders of Solitude* (1995), a spiritual book on the journey to inner peace. One Sunday, I went to hear the Dalai Lama speak in Denver, Colorado. Frequently, I cried.

I attended every day of the McVeigh trial, gavel to gavel. McVeigh was found guilty and was sentenced to die. I attended nearly every day of the Nichols trial too, and he was given life without the possibility of parole. At Nichols's sentencing hearing I was allowed to give a victim impact statement. The following is part of my statement, taken from the court record.

> We live by laws in this country so that ideally, no one will ever have to know what it's like to be a victim of a violent crime. Crimes such as that which was committed against my family are intolerable in any society that calls itself not only free but civilized. The law recognizes as much and provides for punishment that will ensure, at least, that others will not suffer again at the same hands, even if it does not prevent recurrence at the hands of others.
>
> I do not know what your Honor's sentence will be. I do know for the families, survivors, and rescue workers, there is no time off for good behavior. For all the sorrow and the tears that we have shed, there is no parole. And our sentence from this tragedy is a life of only memories of those we love.

Following the trials of McVeigh and Nichols, I engaged in discussions and debates about the death penalty with family members and other people who had lost loved ones to murder. Due to anger associated with my loss, I would waver in my opinion and think it would not be such a bad idea to watch McVeigh take his last breath. I knew that the appeals process would drag on for years. I just wanted some peace. I just wanted him to go away.

Six years after the bombing, the execution of McVeigh was drawing near. I rallied for families of the victims to be included in every step of the judicial proceedings involving the execution. Watching should be their choice. My first thought was that I didn't want to witness McVeigh's death because I didn't want him to have the last word. I also remembered my experience at McAlester Prison. McVeigh had taken so much from me. I could not let him take any more. If I let this man drive me crazy, then I would empower him once again. I already had enough intrusive thoughts. Instead, I decided to write to McVeigh and asked him to meet with me. Here is my letter:

February 9, 2001

Timothy McVeigh
12076-064-D
P.O. Box 433
Terra Haute, IN 47808

Mr. McVeigh:

My name is Marsha Kight. I am the mother of Frankie Ann Merrell. Frankie died in the Alfred P. Murrah Federal Building on April 19, 1995.

That day, my life was changed forever. There have been many changes, not only for me but my entire family. One of the most difficult things we have had to cope with, however, is the fact that not only was Frankie taken from us, we have never figured out why it happened. Knowing "why" will not bring her back, and it will not give me "closure"—but it will help me.

I followed the trial carefully. I know what is in the court records. I know what the jurors said after the trial. They said that you were guilty. But that can't be 100 percent real to me until I have heard it from you personally.

I have harbored a dream for almost six years that one day I would be able to sit in a room with you and ask you questions that would help me to understand why Frankie had to die. When you asked that there be no more appeals in your case and an execution date was set, I knew that the possibility that I would ever get to talk to you had virtually vanished.

That is why I am writing to you today. I am hoping that, as you prepare for your final days, you will help me find some peace around Frankie's death. I am hoping that you will read this letter and know that these questions come from an anguished mother, not as someone who seeks vengeance. I am seeking only understanding.

Most of all, I want to understand you. I would like to know more about what happened in your life leading up to April 19. I hope that you will request the warden of the prison to allow me to visit with you to talk to you about these things in person, but if that is not possible, I hope you will answer me by mail. I am not seeking an apology, nor do I want to lash out at you. I just want to try to see things from your perspective, from your experience—or to find out if it is even possible for me to begin to understand.

I wonder how your childhood shaped your adulthood. I know that your mom left you, and as a mother, I could never imagine leaving my child. I know that must have hurt you. But I have known many children who have been hurt who did not grow up to hurt others. And nothing I've seen of your dad or your sister makes me think that they hurt you.

In my mind, I can see you as a member of our country's armed forces. You were a decorated soldier. At one point, you must have been a proud and patriotic American. When did that change? When did your love of country become hatred for your government? Was it something that happened while you were in the Middle East? Was it drugs? Did it have anything to do with how you were treated when you returned from service overseas? The court records indicate that you were influenced by reading *The Turner Diaries*, but were you disaffected before then or did that come later?

I wonder about your relationship with Terry Nichols. You reported to him when you were in boot camp, but how did that relationship change over time, and what is that relationship even now? Do you still view him as a commanding officer? Are you friends?

I've tried to imagine what might have been going through your mind as you sat on the hood of your car watching the Branch Davidian compound in Waco burn to the ground, knowing there were people in the complex. I've tried to imagine what thoughts were going through your mind as you bought the ingredients to build a bomb and rented a truck and drove to the Murrah Building on that April day. Most of all, I've wondered what your thoughts have been about since April 19, 1995.

Have you thought about the people who died or were injured? Have you thought about their families and friends? Can you imagine what it must be like for those of us who have been left behind? Are you sad about their deaths? Can you see them as innocent victims, not as representatives of a government you believed was evil?

If I were sitting across a table from you, I know I would find it difficult to think of all the questions I would like to ask, just as I find it difficult to even write them down. But I hope you can imagine how strong my need to know and understand is and always will be. I hope and pray that you will answer my questions. You are the only one who can, and your time is running out.

You have nothing to lose by helping me. I have everything to gain.

Sincerely,

Marsha Kight

I sent the same letter to the warden of the federal prison in Terre Haute, Indiana, where McVeigh was housed on death row. I requested victim-offender mediation. The Bureau of Prisons spokesman, Daniel Dunne, said the government would treat a request for victim-offender mediation seriously. The Bureau of Prisons has victim impact panels, in which victims tell inmates about the effects of their crimes. The panels are aimed at encouraging offenders to accept responsibility and change their behavior, and that's not likely to be the top priority of a condemned man, Dunne conceded. In any case, victim-offender mediation would require McVeigh's consent, and I was not hopeful of that. The mediation that I had hoped for did not take place. To this day I do not know if McVeigh was ever asked.

Some answers to my questions came, but not as a direct response to my letter. On March 28, 2001, I received a press release from Fox News written by Carolyn Thompson, an Associated Press writer:

A remorseless Timothy McVeigh calls the children killed in the Oklahoma City bombing "collateral damage," regretting only that their deaths detracted from his bid to avenge Waco and Ruby Ridge, according to a new book (*American Terrorist*). "I understand what they felt in Oklahoma City. I have no sympathy for them," McVeigh told the authors Lou Michel and Dan Herbeck, reporters for *The Buffalo News*.

Michel said McVeigh's only regret was that the children's deaths proved to be a public relations nightmare that undercut his cause. McVeigh said he was the sole architect of the plan, resorting to threats against Terry Nichols' family when his Army buddy hesitated before helping to load the explosives into the rental truck.

The emotional roller coaster began again for me and other family members of the Oklahoma City bombing when the execution date was announced. McVeigh was scheduled to die by lethal injection at the U.S. Penitentiary in Terre Haute on May 16. Just days away from McVeigh's execution, there was a delay for nearly a month. Attorney General John Ashcroft announced the delay after the FBI admitted that it had not turned over a foot-high pile of documents related to the case. I was stunned by the development and exhausted from the mental and emotional preparation. My mind began to race. How could the FBI make such a mistake? Could there be a new trial? As angry as I was, I did not want a cloud hanging over the judicial process. There should be no doubt given the fact that McVeigh was about to be executed.

As the days neared McVeigh's rescheduled execution, I tried to prepare myself emotionally and questioned my feelings about the death penalty. The roller coaster of emotions resurfaced, leaving me feeling restless, irritable, and overwhelmed by the media.

On Monday, June 11, 2001 at 7:14 on a warm, sunny morning, Timothy McVeigh was executed. I was sitting on a creek bank, hundreds of miles away, near my home in Arlington, Virginia. I had lived with the horror of losing a child for six years, one month, and twenty-three days. McVeigh, for all the pain and suffering he caused so many people, was executed by lethal injection. I wrote a poem to McVeigh while sitting on that creek bank. I thought about McVeigh's family and wondered what they were feeling. I thought about my daughter, Frankie. I thought about my son, Cody. I thought about my granddaughter, Morgan, and I thought about my ex-husband, Tom Kight. I thought about other victims' family members in Oklahoma. And I thought about my life and how it had changed in so many ways. Once again I cried as I crumpled the poem and walked away. McVeigh's time had run out. No more time for questions. No more time for McVeigh to reflect on his actions. He was the master of his fate, the captain of his soul.

Even now I carry disdain for McVeigh; it did not end with his execution. McVeigh's death did not bring my daughter back. No void was filled. Better he had lived for the rest of his life isolated with his thoughts instead of being allowed to "die" like a soldier for some cause. Better that our government be the one that stops the circle of violence by not invoking the death penalty than have someone like McVeigh gain support for his martyrdom. We gave McVeigh what he wanted.

Capital punishment must continue to play a role in our criminal justice system. Without the death penalty, the maximum sentence available for any crime, no matter how violent and pervasive, would be life imprisonment without the possibility of parole, which would be subject to plea bargaining. It is unthinkable that a crime such as McVeigh's could result in even the remotest possibility of a plea bargain culminating in the prospect of parole.

I conclude that death is the easy way out. I will live with the pain of the loss of my daughter for the rest of my life. When the lid of my casket is closed, only then will I have closure.

References

Kleinman, Arthur. 1995. *Writing at the Margin: Discourse Between Anthropology and Medicine.* Berkeley, CA: University of California Press.

Linenthal, Edward T. 2001. *The Unfinished Bombing: Oklahoma City in American Memory.* New York: Oxford University Press.

Salwak, Dale, ed. 1995. *The Wonders of Solitude (The Classic Wisdom Collection).* Novato, CA: New World Library.

PART II

LEGAL PERSPECTIVES

CHAPTER 9

Causing Death and Sustaining Life: The Law, Capital Punishment, and Criminal Homicide Victims' Survivors

*James R. Acker and
Jeanna Marie Mastrocinque*

One of the law's most vital functions is to safeguard citizens against harm. Yet legal protections are not foolproof. When they fail, and individuals suffer injury at others' hands, the law's responses vary. Some harms are too trivial to be legally cognizable. Others, such as harms inflicted during unforeseeable accidents, may be quite serious yet not entail legal consequences because it would be unfair or improvident to hold anyone accountable. When the law is invoked, some measures seek to make the injured party whole, while others promote social objectives—such as general deterrence, the rational distribution of economic risk, or rehabilitation—that involve the individual victim only indirectly, if at all. Within the category of civil wrongs, including breaches of contract and torts, injured parties typically must champion their own legal claims, and redress normally consists of monetary damages as compensation for the harm suffered. In contrast, crimes (by definition) represent harms committed against society at large, and are unique in occasioning punishment inflicted by and on behalf of the organized state. Paradoxically, individuals injured during the commission of crimes must look beyond the criminal courts for remediation. While an offender's punishment may be of primary significance to the injured party, neither the criminal justice process nor the sanction ultimately imposed is designed to vindicate the individual victim's interests.

In this chapter, we trace the history of the state's displacement of the individual as the "victim" in its criminal courts and explore the consequences of this divestiture for the parties who have directly suffered harm. We focus on the most serious form of personal injury, criminal homicide, where the deceased's family members assume the status of individual co-victims following a loved one's death. We begin by examining early English law, focusing on the evolution of homicide from a private injury that demanded retaliation or compensation, to a public harm resulting in state-administered punishment. We next recount how American law emulated this English tradition, which in time occasioned public dissatisfaction and spawned a "victims' rights movement" dedicated to securing greater recognition of the rights and interests of individual crime victims. We give particular attention to the results of this movement in the context of capital punishment, focusing on whether the death penalty can be expected to serve the needs of individual co-victims of criminal homicide in addition to functioning as an exemplary punishment.

Changing Legal Responses to Homicide: The Anglo-Saxon Tradition and Its Evolution

The seeds of modern English law were planted during the fifth century A.D. As Rome's influence eroded, England was invaded and inhabited by Teutonic tribes. The Jutes, Angles, Saxons, and other Germanic bands embedded customs and traditions throughout the land, some of which were codified in laws (called *dooms*) dating as far back as the sixth and seventh centuries (Johnson and Wolfe 2003:53). Early communities were small and loosely organized, and the laws were correspondingly primitive. Anglo-Saxon laws originally made no distinction between "crimes" and "torts" (Holdsworth 1936/1963:3–43). Consequently, the actor's intent or state of mind when causing harm were largely irrelevant, and strict liability principles applied. So extreme was this approach that it extended even to harms inflicted by animals and property that were not within the owner's immediate control. "Thus if Cedric in tripping over a branch knocked down Esgar's spear, which in falling punctured Edwin's left eye, Esgar was liable to pay Edwin a bot and his spear was accursed and had to be surrendered to some court, which would destroy it" (Lovell 1962:40).

Interpersonal conflicts were private affairs in early Anglo-Saxon communities and were resolved by the affected individuals, families, and clans (Plucknett 1956:463–65). Slayings frequently inspired violent retaliation in the form of blood feuds between the involved kin groups (Johnson and Wolfe 2003:52–53; Seipp 1996:63–64). Serious transgressions of this nature also could result in a declaration of outlawry which entitled or even obligated community members to pursue and kill the offending party (Pollock and Maitland 1895/1968:449). Over time, tribal chiefs assumed territorial ruling authority and eventually kingly status. Laws enacted during the reign of King Alfred (871–901 A.D.) attempted to mediate the cycles of interpersonal violence. Thus, the injured kin were prohibited from waging blood feud unless they first tried to exact monetary compensation—known as *wergild* in the case of homicide and *bot* for injuries short of death—from the wrongdoer and his family. In recognition of the debilitating consequences of such internal warfare on the community, and also to reinforce their ruling authority and generate revenue, later kings imposed further restrictions on blood feuds. They implemented complicated tariff systems that first encouraged and later required victims to seek pecuniary compensation from offenders for homicide and other harms before pursuing private vengeance (Gardner 1993:648–49; Holdsworth 1936/1963:43–51; Pollock and Maitland 1895/1968:449–51).

While enforcing measures to discourage violent retaliation and feuding, Anglo-Saxon laws gradually instituted more centralized mechanisms of social control and supplanted traditional claims for private compensation, a move that had dramatic implications for individual victims and their families. For example, in addition to payment of the *bot* or *wergild*, the party responsible for injuring another was required to pay a *wite* (resembling a fine) to the king. "In the *wite* we can see the germ of the idea that the wrong is not simply the affair of the injured individual—an idea which is the condition precedent to the growth of a criminal law" (Holdsworth 1936/1963:47). Indeed, a fundamental premise of the criminal law is that the primary harm is *social*, causing the interests of the community and ultimately the sovereign to take precedence over those of individual victims (Dressler 1995:1, 95–96; Dubber 2002:151–52). The principle thus became accepted that some wrongs transcended private parties and worked a breach of "the king's peace" (Hagan 1983:9; Holdsworth 1936/1963:458).

With that recognition, shortly following the Norman Conquest and certainly by the twelfth century and the reign of Henry II, the criminal law emerged with the distinctive purpose of punishing wrongdoers for committing serious harms. Willful homicide was defined as a crime punished by death, and "the kinsfolk of the slain los[t] their right to a *wer* and to compensation of any sort or kind" (Pollock and Maitland 1895/1968:459). Punishment became the exclusive dominion of the Crown and with that, individual victims lost both their unique standing and their entitlement to redress in connection with the prosecution of crimes (Frankel 1996:90; Gardner 1993:650–51; Henderson 1985:940–41).

The law's transformation from a system concerned with private vengeance and compensation to one focusing on punishment administered in the king's name was not immediate. Following the demise of Anglo-Saxon rule, after the Norman Conquest, victims in medieval England typically could choose between initiating discrete types of legal actions that entailed significantly different consequences for both themselves and the alleged wrongdoer. For example, between approximately the thirteenth and sixteenth centuries, homicide victims' survivors could bring an *appeal of felony* that, if successful, resulted in the offender's capital punishment by the Crown. Proceeding in this manner was not without risk. Defendants could dispute an allegation of wrongdoing by choosing trial by battle with the victim, which could be fatal to one of the parties. Appeals of felony, moreover, brought no compensation to the victim; the offender's property instead was forfeited to the king or a feudal lord. Victims who did not want to risk trial by battle alternatively could seek an *indictment of felony*, which if approved resulted in a jury trial for the accused. Indictments were brought in the king's name and convictions led to state-administered punishment. Victims received neither compensation nor restitution through such prosecutions (Seipp 1996).

In contrast, victims could seek compensation from offenders for most felonies by filing a *writ of trespass*. As a practical matter, it was not possible for victims to pursue punishment and compensation simultaneously. An offender's property and wealth would be confiscated by the king or lord, leaving none for the victim, following the successful prosecution of an appeal or indictment of felony. The statute of limitations would foreclose prosecution if the victim proceeded by writ of trespass. Moreover, the writ of trespass was unavailable in cases of homicide (Seipp 1996).

The criminal courts thus came to deny victims and their family members the satisfaction of either dispensing punishment or receiving compensation from the parties who had caused them injury. While ceasing directly to serve the interests of individual crime victims, these same courts continued to depend on victims, their relatives, or another private party to prosecute accused offenders. England lacked a Director of Public Prosecutions until well into the nineteenth century (Bessler 1994:515; Jacoby 1980:8–9). Although requiring interested private parties to initiate and prosecute criminal charges guaranteed victims a central role in managing trials, this practice caused both practical and emotional hardships. The cost of a criminal prosecution had to be borne by the party bringing it, until the latter part of the eighteenth century— a policy that represented a significant disincentive and burden for victims interested in seeking justice (Stephen 1883/1996:498–99; Wright 1991:7–8).

Criminal law and procedures in the American colonies largely mirrored the English common law with respect to victims of crime. However, inspired in part by Dutch and French influences, the office of public prosecutor gained hold in the colonies much earlier than in England. For example, Virginia established a system relying on county prosecuting attorneys in 1711, and Connecticut had provided for local public prosecution a few years earlier (Bessler 1994:515–17; Friedman 1993:29–30; McDonald 1979:20–24). Public prosecutors not only were commonplace in the United States, but quickly assumed political importance. The office of district attorney was widely established as an elected position by the time of the Civil War (Jacoby 1980:37–38). While public prosecutors removed the onus from victims to initiate, manage, and finance criminal trials, this innovation further served to disassociate victims from the criminal process. Indeed, crime victims had become so completely divorced from the justice system that the Supreme Court eventually recognized that "in American jurisprudence … a private citizen lacks a judicially cognizable interest in the prosecution or nonprosecution of another" (*Linda R.S. v. Richard D.* 1973:619).

Crime victims thus were formally reduced to serving as little more than witnesses in trials that were initiated at the discretion of elected prosecutors and designed to vindicate the public interest in punishing violations of the law. With their own interests minimized or ignored, many victims felt alienated and even "re-victimized" by the criminal justice process (Beck et al. 2003:386–87; Peerenboom 1993:66–68). Victims' issues eventually merged with related causes during the late 1960s and 1970s, including the struggle for the expansion of women's rights and concern about the country's surging crime rate (McCormack 2000). The result was renewed attention to the plight of crime victims and a series of legal reforms ushered in by the so-called "victims' rights movement."

The Victims' Rights Movement

Momentum promoting the interests of crime victims began building in the 1960s. California implemented a statewide victims' compensation program in 1965. On the national level, an influential 1967 commission appointed by President Johnson urged that greater consideration be given victims within the criminal justice process. The trend accelerated during the 1970s with the widespread enactment of legislation promising crime victims financial restitution, compensation, and medical and other assistance. The movement reached new heights in 1982, when President Reagan's Task Force on Victims of Crime issued a report containing scores of action recommendations. Many of the recommendations focused on guaranteeing victims greater involvement and participation in the criminal justice system (*President's Task Force on Victims of Crime: Final Report* 1982; Tobolowsky 1999:28–31). Congress implemented several of the suggested reforms and provided funding for others. Important legislation included the 1982 Federal Victim and Witness Protection Act; the Victims of Crime Act of 1984, which created the federal Office for Victims of Crime; and the Crime Victim Assistance Act (Donahoe 1999; McCormack 2000; Roland 1989).

States that had not already enacted their own measures rapidly followed Congress's lead. Using a combination of legislative and constitutional initiatives, the states armed crime victims with an array of new rights. The new rights included: "(a) notification of, and the right to attend, court proceedings, including bail hearings and parole hearings; (b) eligibility for compensation and restitution; (c) freedom from intimidation and harassment by the defendant; (d) fair and dignified treatment; (e) victim input at various stages of the criminal justice process; (f) information about the release or escape of defendants; (g) prompt return of victims' property; and (h) notice of all the rights in legislation" (Spungen 1998:205; see also Anderson and Woodard 1985; Byrne et al. 1999:278–79; Roland 1989). By 2000, victims' rights amendments had been incorporated into the constitutions of at least 32 states (Mosteller 2003:551 n. 50). An intense campaign to add a victims' rights amendment to the U.S. Constitution only ebbed in 2004 after a compromise agreement was reached regarding new federal crime victims' legislation.

One consequence of these laws has been to restore a measure of crime victims' special standing within the criminal justice system. No longer regarded simply as witnesses, victims now have rights to be notified about and participate in many aspects of criminal trials (Beloof 2003). Conceptually, the new victims' rights legislation has worked a "radical transformation" (Logan 1999:144) of the modern paradigm of State-dominated criminal trials. Although praised by many, the new model has not escaped criticism. While enforcement of the newly recognized rights is one issue, skeptics charge that crime victims have been used or exploited to promote other causes (Dubber 2002:1–7; Henderson 1998, 1985:942–53; White 1999). Nowhere is the debate surrounding the victims' rights movement more intense than in the context of murder and capital punishment.

Murder Victims, Co-Victims, and Capital Punishment: Legal Doctrine and Lingering Questions

The Supreme Court voided death penalty laws throughout the nation in *Furman v. Georgia* (1972), when the victims' rights movement was still in its nascent stages. The decision bitterly divided the Court as well as the country (Meltsner 1973:290–309; Zimring and Hawkins 1986:38–45). Justice Blackmun's opinion embodied this conflict, albeit on a deeply personal level. Although declaring his individual opposition to the death penalty, Blackmun joined three other dissenting justices in *Furman* in finding no constitutional basis for invalidating capital punishment. His dissent admonished the controlling opinions in the case because:

> [N]one … makes reference to the misery the [offenders'] crimes occasioned to the victims, to the families of the victims, and the communities where the offenses took place…. These cases are here because offenses to innocent victims were perpetrated. This fact, and the terror that occasioned it, and the fear that stalks the streets of many of our cities today perhaps deserve not to be entirely overlooked (*Furman v. Georgia* 1972:413–14, Blackmun, J., dissenting).

Just four years later, the justices approved capital punishment statutes that had been revised in response to the *Furman* Court's concerns that the death penalty was being administered arbitrarily (*Gregg v. Georgia* 1976; Steiker and Steiker 2003). Then, some fifteen years following Justice Blackmun's lament in *Furman,* and after capital punishment had become securely re-established in a majority of states' laws, the Supreme Court's death penalty jurisprudence squarely confronted issues involving murder victims and their survivors. *Booth v. Maryland* (1987) presented the question of "whether the Constitution prohibits a jury from considering a 'victim impact statement' during the sentencing phase of a capital murder trial" (p. 497). A bare majority of the justices (including Justice Blackmun, who over the years had grown doubtful that the death penalty was administered fairly) ruled that the admission of victim impact evidence in death penalty trials was constitutionally impermissible.

Justice Powell's majority opinion in *Booth* reasoned that testimony about a murder victim's personal characteristics and the emotional impact of the murder on surviving family members arbitrarily interjected sentencing considerations that were irrelevant to the offender's moral blameworthiness. The opinion added that "in some cases the victim will not leave behind a family," and expressed concern that in other cases death sentences might "turn on the perception that the victim was a sterling member of the community rather than someone of questionable character" (pp. 505–6). The majority opinion also noted "that it would be difficult—if not impossible—to provide a fair opportunity to rebut [victim impact] evidence without shifting the focus of the sentencing hearing away from the defendant" (p. 506; see also Logan, this volume).

The four dissenting justices in *Booth* vigorously disputed the majority's conclusions. Justice Scalia specifically reprised themes embraced by the victims' rights movement:

> Recent years have seen an outpouring of popular concern for what has come to be known as "victims' rights"—a phrase that describes what its proponents feel is the failure of courts of justice to take into account ... the amount of harm [the offender] has caused to innocent members of society. Many citizens have found one-sided and hence unjust the criminal trial in which a parade of witnesses comes forth to testify to the pressures ... that drove the defendant to commit his crime, with no one to lay before the sentencing authority the full reality of human suffering the defendant has produced—which (and *not* moral guilt alone) is one of the reasons society deems his act worthy of the prescribed penalty (*Booth v. Maryland* 1987:520, Scalia, J., dissenting).

These sentiments prevailed just four years later in *Payne v. Tennessee* (1991), when the Court abruptly overruled *Booth* and approved the use of victim impact evidence in capital trials "relating to the personal characteristics of the victim and the emotional impact of the crimes on the victim's family" (p. 817). During the oral arguments conducted in *Payne*, one of the justices sympathetic to the use of victim impact testimony even hearkened back to the early evolution of victims' rights, musing that "one of the purposes of retribution was to prevent people from taking law into their own hands. You go all the way back and the State's punishment simply substitutes for what used to be called 'wergild,' where the person doing the injury would pay money to the family of the person harmed, and things of that sort. What the family of the person harmed thinks about the matter on that theory would be very important" (*Payne v. Tennessee*, Transcript of Oral Argument 1991:9–10).

If the ruling in *Payne* was designed, at least in part, to make capital punishment law more responsive to the interests of murder victims' survivors (Fahey 1992), various legislative initiatives have been similarly motivated. For example, several states soon enacted statutes entitling murder victims' family members to witness the execution of their loved one's killer (Janick 2000). The United States Attorney General similarly arranged to have Timothy McVeigh's federal execution broadcast on closed circuit television for the benefit of hundreds of co-victims of the Oklahoma City bombing for which McVeigh was responsible (Skaret 2002). A justification offered in support of such initiatives, and of capital punishment more generally, was to help bring "closure" to murder victims' survivors (Gross and Matheson 2003:490–94). The results of a 2001 public opinion poll suggest that 60 percent of Americans endorse using the death penalty to promote that objective (Zimring 2003:61).

We must nevertheless be cautious before concluding that capital punishment laws deliver benefits to co-victims of murder, either generally or in specific cases. In the first place, and perhaps most fundamentally, the death penalty is reserved for a special category of narrowly defined aggravated murders, and is pursued by prosecutors in only a fraction of the eligible cases. It thus has no application in the overwhelming majority of criminal homicides. One scholar (Bedau 1997) has estimated that one execution was carried out in this country for every thousand criminal homicides committed during the decade 1984–1993 (pp. 31–32). More recent data suggest that death sentences and executions remain rare in response to criminal homicide. For example, nearly 16,000 murders and non-negligent manslaughters were committed in the United States in 2001, yet 163 offenders were admitted onto the nation's death rows that same year and significantly fewer executions (66) were carried out (Bonczar and Snell 2003:8–11; Maguire and Pastore 2004:534).

These figures suggest that it is not only implausible, but also perhaps insensitive to argue that the death penalty is justified because of its importance to individual co-victims of murder. The argument obviously is misdirected if the survivors in upwards of ninety-nine criminal homicides out of a hundred receive none of the presumed benefits of capital punishment. It borders on offensive because of the implication that cases not resulting in death sentences involve victims and co-victims who are less deserving of the full weight of the law. This interpretation is especially likely when a capital sentence is not sought (or if sought, is not imposed) within the relatively narrow category of death penalty-eligible homicides. For example, when the San Francisco district attorney announced that she would not seek the death penalty in a case involving a slain police officer, the chief of the city's police department charged that the decision "dishonors the memory of all fallen officers and diminishes the lives of those, who, on a daily basis, risk their lives for the sake of the public's safety" (Van Derbeken 2004: A1). A letter to the editor published in the *San Francisco Chronicle* maintained that the prosecutor's decision was "a slap in the face to the family" of the fallen officer (Gressler 2004: B8; see also Zimring 2003:56).

When the death penalty is sought, it is debatable whether the protracted and unpredictable trial and appeals process, combined with the uncertain consequences of an execution, harbinger net burdens or benefits for individual murder co-victims. The right won by prosecutors in *Payne v. Tennessee* (1991) to have survivors present victim impact evidence in capital trials entails potentially significant costs. First, there is no guarantee that an offender will be sentenced to death even when co-victims offer such testimony (Eisenberg, Garvey and Wells 2003; Karp and Warshaw, this volume), which risks the unfortunate perception that some victims and their families are "unworthy" of the law's ultimate punishment (Sundby 2003). Moreover, murder victims' survivors are not of a single mind regarding the death penalty. Although many co-victims may seek a killer's execution and value the chance to offer victim impact evidence, others may strongly oppose the death penalty (King 2003; Pelke 2003) and feel conflicted, devalued, or even violated by a capital prosecution (Cushing and Sheffer 2002). Charging, sentencing, and executive clemency decisions in potentially capital cases can further strain already raw emotions when views about the death penalty diverge within families (Hoffmann 2003:542; Johnson 2003).

Capital cases also are likely to occasion more sustained and intense press coverage than other criminal homicides, thus involuntarily thrusting survivors into the glare of publicity when they may desperately seek privacy. Moreover, finality is elusive in death penalty cases. Executions usually do not take place for a decade or considerably longer following a capital trial (Bonczar and Snell 2003:11, 15), if they are carried out at all. Roughly two out of three capital convictions or death sentences returned between 1973 and 1995 were later vacated by court action, with the defendant eventually being resentenced to prison (or occasionally exonerated) in the vast majority (82 percent) of the reversals (Liebman, Fagan and West 2000). Between 1973 and 2002, marking the first three decades of the death penalty's reinstatement following *Furman v. Georgia* (1972), just over 11 percent (820 out of 7,254) of the defendants sentenced to death were executed. In contrast, death sentences were removed by court action, executive clemency, or for other reasons in 36 percent (2,609) of the cases; defendants died while awaiting execution in 3.7 percent (268) of the cases; and offenders remained on death row in 49 percent (3,557) of the cases (Bonczar and Snell 2003:14). The promise of delays, reversals, and the lingering uncertainty about whether executions will be carried out may only enhance the psychological trauma experienced by murder co-victims (Bandes 2000:1604; Kanwar 2001–02:241).

Another unknown element of capital murder trials involves how co-victims will respond to executions. The only certainty is that they will react differently, with emotions varying with the passage of time. Some co-victims may have a need to witness the execution of their loved one's murderer and may gain a measure of satisfaction from learning that a death sentence has been carried out. For example, after his parents were murdered, Brooks Douglass was elected to the Oklahoma Legislature and championed a bill entitling co-victims to witness the execution of their family members' killer (Barnes 1996; Goodwin 1997–98:588). However, for many co-victims, the offender's execution will bring little relief; it may even be disturbing, perhaps because they oppose capital punishment (Coyne 2003:103–10; Cushing 2002:285) or because they will be required to confront the pain and grief brought on by their loved one's murder directly, no longer insulated by the anticipation of the impending execution (Kanwar 2001–02:242–45; Lifton and Mitchell 2000:198–204; Prejean 1993:226). In addition, as media attention focuses on the plight of the condemned prisoner, sometimes inspiring public sympathy (Gross and Matheson 2003:494–95), and with vulgar, party-like celebrations occasionally marring death-house grounds, there is an enhanced risk that an execution will not appropriately solemnize a murder victim's death (Bessler 1997:75–80; Cushing 2002:286; Fitzpatrick 1999:125–28).

In contrast to the earliest Anglo-Saxon traditions, contemporary law has robbed individual victims of the ability either to dictate or reap direct benefits from the accused killer's trial and punishment. This approach may be both inevitable and desirable in a system of criminal justice that respects due process of law and equal protection principles. Not all cultures have chosen to prioritize such fundamental values over the interests of murder co-victims. For example, Islamic law grants murder victims' families the right of retaliation, authorizing them to permit a death sentence to be carried out or, alternatively, to spare an offender from execution by accepting *diyya* ("blood money") or other compensation (Drapkin 1989:281–84; Gottesman 1992:441–42; Postawko 2002:300–305). Historically, "[v]irtually all Near Eastern civilizations permitted a murderer or his family to pay compensation to the family of the deceased victim" (Johnson and Wolfe 2003:24) in lieu of capital punishment, although both the ancient Greeks and the Old Testament repudiated that blood money could substitute for the death of the murderer (Blecker 2003:181).

Despite American law's deliberate distancing of co-victims from the capital punishment process, the death penalty frequently is demanded in the name of murder victims and their survivors. Such calls typically sound the themes of "promoting closure" or "doing justice." This divergence between the law's policy of exclusion, or denying co-victims a direct link to the offender's punishment, and the popular rhetoric of inclusion requires explanation. The answer to this apparent paradox almost certainly lies in the cultural symbolism of murder victims and their family members, as well as capital punishment. The image of an innocent citizen savagely slain at the hands of a merciless killer evokes a powerful mix of emotions, including empathy, fear, and outrage. What better way for the law to denounce criminality and reinforce basic norms of human decency and social cohesion than to severely punish lawbreakers? "A primary function of punishment … is to express solidarity with the victim. It is a way of saying to the victim and his or her family: 'You are not alone. We stand with you, against the criminal'" (Fletcher 1995:203). Murder, the ultimate crime, must be punished commensurately.

> [T]he punishments imposed by the legal order remind us of the reign of the moral order; not only do they remind us of it, but by enforcing its prescriptions, they enhance the dignity of the legal order in the eyes of moral men, in they eyes of those decent citizens who cry out "for gods who will avenge injustice." … Capital punishment … serves to remind us of the majesty of the moral order that is embodied in our law and of the terrible consequences of its breach. (Berns 1979:169, 172–73)

Yet if capital punishment is so rarely sought in response to criminal homicide, and holds such tenuous benefits for murder co-victims when it is imposed—perhaps even being inimical to their interests—the symbolism surrounding crime victims and the death penalty requires more searching analysis. We must ask whether efforts to sustain this symbolism come at the expense of serving the real needs of the individual co-victims of criminal homicide. The danger is that individual murder victims and their survivors are shunted aside, ignored, or exploited, even if inadvertently, to advance and help legitimate an agenda having little to do with their interests. Skeptics have voiced concerns that the victims' rights movement has been co-opted by the politics of crime control and public vengeance (Berger 1992:55–60; Burr 2003:517; Dubber 2002:192; Henderson 1999, 1985); that there has been a "symbolic transformation of execution into a victim service program" (Zimring 2003:62) to promote objectives having little to do with crime victims themselves.

> Bringing the families of murder victims into the capital punishment system both amplifies and co-opts their voices. Ceding a place to victims exemplifies a legitimacy crisis felt in neoliberal regimes as public confidence in political and legal institutions wanes. It is also a deft way of giving those aggrieved by crime voice without giving them

control. In this way state killing walks a dangerous and uncertain line, fueling—while also trying to manage—anger, resentment, and the desire for revenge. (Sarat 2001:25)

Zimring (2003) echoes a similar theme:

Creating the felt need to commemorate a victim's loss with a death sentence is bad for most homicide survivors but good for the death penalty....

The current circumstances of victim influence in the jurisprudence of American capital punishment are a combination of minimum power and maximum symbolism.... While the symbols used in this process sound close to the basic themes of contemporary appeals to victim's rights, the role of the relations of homicide victims is wholly dependent on prosecutorial powers beyond their reach (p. 57).

Many people, of course, willingly support the political undercurrents of the death penalty, including its uncompromising emphasis on retribution and its strict crime control signification. If such objectives are embraced, however, they should be pursued in their own right and not conflated with the message that capital punishment is needed on behalf of murder victims and their families. A preoccupation with capital punishment risks obscuring the most urgent concerns of murder co-victims in the aftermath of criminal homicide and distracting attention from services and assistance that in most cases are likely to be far more beneficial to them.

Toward Victim-Centered Alternatives

With the law's evolution, individual victims of crime, including murder victims' survivors, have lost their unique prominence in administering justice. Few today would deny the state's legitimate interest in regulating crime, encourage private vengeance as personified in the blood feud, or lament the demise of the payment of compensation (*wergild*) in lieu of a killer's punishment. However, in retrospect it is clear that the law's displacement of individual victims from the criminal justice process was regrettably and unnecessarily absolute. A resurgence of interest in victims' rights has helped focus attention on the plight of crime victims, thereby fueling important legislative reforms. This movement has helped solidify victims' roles in some aspects of the criminal justice process, but it also has been clouded by unfulfilled and occasionally misleading promises. If the death penalty represents the triumph of symbolism over substance in the quest to improve the lives of victims of crime, other reforms are likely to be more responsive to the real needs of murder co-victims.

An important objective in murder's wake is to minimize the risk that the criminal justice process will inflict additional harm on survivors. The "secondary victimization" occasioned by co-victims' interaction with police, prosecutors, defense attorneys, and others throughout the investigation, trial, appeals, and other phases of a murder case can be devastating (Beck et al. 2003:385–86). Deborah Spungen (1998), a co-victim of criminal homicide and a victim advocate, has observed that:

> [I]n some ways, the second injury is even worse than the murder itself. The second wound is inflicted on the co-victims by those from whom the co-victims had expected help in dealing with the loss and in remedying the injustice caused by the murder. Co-victims are especially vulnerable to this second injury because of the circumstance surrounding the murder of a loved one and the multiple contacts that they have with the so-called helping systems (10–11).

For reasons we have noted, the risk of secondary victimization is heightened in capital cases: surviving family members may not uniformly support the death penalty; trials and appeals are bitterly contested, protracted, intensely public, and fraught with uncertainties; and prospects that an execution will afford relief to co-victims may prove to be illusory.

Co-victim interaction with the judicial system is inevitable during murder prosecutions. A common complaint is that co-victims are not afforded such basic courtesies as being notified about important developments during the crime's investigation and the scheduling of case proceedings. They may be left in the dark about how the system operates, feel ignored, and be confused about and unprepared for what criminal justice officials expect of them (Gross and Matheson 2003:486; Illinois Criminal Justice Information Authority 2002:3–6; Spungen 1998:181–91). Although victims' rights legislation and state constitutional provisions enacted during the past quarter century have entitled crime victims to be informed about and participate in many case proceedings, enforcement of these rights often lags (Beloof 2003; Spungen 1998:205). Criminal justice officials must be sensitive to the human needs of murder co-victims and vigilant about effectuating their legal rights.

A premium should be placed on identifying the short- and long-term needs of homicide co-victims while tailoring assistance and investing resources accordingly. Individuals vary tremendously in what they experience and how they attempt to cope with the murder of a loved one. An urgent need exists for reliable research studies to help inform victim assistance programs about how best to serve homicide co-victims' needs (Henderson 1999:384–85, 402). Several services merit increased attention, including emergency support and crisis counseling; assistance with claims for compensation and restitution; training for police, prosecutors, defense attorneys, and judges who interact with victims; and follow-up care over extended periods of time (Henderson 1998:604–05; Illinois Criminal Justice Information Authority 2001:3–8). Although victim assistance programs frequently are connected to prosecutors' offices, severing those ties might allow victims' services to be provided more effectively. When such programs are not independent there is a risk that they may be, or may be perceived to be, compromised by prosecution strategies — including decisions made about pursuing the death penalty (Cushing and Sheffer 2002:19–21; Johnson 2003:566–68).

Less traditional suggestions have been made about constructing a legal apparatus that is more directly centered on serving the needs of homicide co-victims. No single approach can be responsive to the diverse needs of murder victims' survivors. Still, crime victims and co-victims understandably yearn to see justice served (Beloof 2003:298; Cushing 2002:285; Gross and Matheson 2003:489; Jacoby 1983:50; Sarat 2001:34; Spungen 1998:179). Although paths to that end will differ, co-victims, commentators, and researchers have increasingly advocated legal alternatives based on restorative justice principles. In contrast to retributively based models of punishment, including the death penalty, restorative justice "focuses on the harmful effects of offenders' actions and actively involves victims and offenders in the process of reparation and rehabilitation" (Van Ness and Strong 2002:27).

> [T]he response to crime would be, not to add to the harm caused, by imposing further harm on the offender, but to do as much as possible to restore the situation. The community offers aid to the victim; the offender is held accountable and required to make reparation. Attention would be given not only to the *outcome,* but also to evolving a *process* that respected the feelings and humanity of both the victim and the offender (Wright 1991:112).

Perhaps counterintuitively, restorative justice approaches, including victim-offender mediation and related initiatives, have been applied successfully in crimes of violence and embraced by some co-victims of criminal homicide (Grunewald and Nath 2003; Spungen 1998:241; Umbreit et al. 2003, this volume). Relying on restorative justice principles, co-victims have sometimes reported feeling liberated from a preoccupation with the murderer's punishment and consequently being able to attend more successfully to their own healing process (King 2003:221–73; Pelke 2003). These approaches clearly should not be foisted on unwilling participants and are not appropriate in all cases. Moreover, legal interventions should not set their aims unrealistically high; a loved one's death is irreversible and the pain is too profound to expect a murder co-victim's healing to be complete. Nevertheless, legal policies should creatively and aggressively explore innovations designed to support and assist murder victims' survivors in coping with the awful harms they have suffered.

Capital punishment, like other traditional criminal justice measures, cannot adequately salve the wounds opened by criminal homicide. Yet the death penalty also risks violating the fundamental principle of not inflicting additional harm on criminal homicide co-victims. It threatens to disrupt and prolong their healing process even as it is justified in their names. More reasoned and effective legal responses are needed. Legal initiatives should be less preoccupied with accomplishing the offender's death, and involve greater effort and invest more resources in constructive reforms focused on helping murder co-victims reclaim their lives.

References

Anderson, John R. and Paul L. Woodard. 1985. "Victim and Witness Assistance: New State Laws and the System's Response." *Judicature* 68:221–44.

Bandes, Susan. 2000. "When Victims Seek Closure: Forgiveness, Vengeance and the Role of Government." *Fordham Urban Law Journal* 27:1599–606.

Barnes, Patricia G. 1996. "Final Reckoning: States Allow Victims' Families to Watch Executions." *ABA Journal* March 1996:36–37.

Bedau, Hugo Adam. 1997. "The Laws, the Crimes, and the Executions." Pp. 26–41 in *The Death Penalty in America: Current Controversies,* edited by Hugo Adam Bedau. New York: Oxford University Press.

Beck, Elizabeth, et al. (2003). "Seeking Sanctuary: Interviews with Family Members of Capital Defendants." *Cornell Law Review* 88:382–418.

Beloof, Douglas E. 2003. "Constitutional Implications of Crime Victims as Witnesses." *Cornell Law Review* 88:282–305.

Berger, Vivian. 1992. "*Payne* and Suffering—A Personal Reflection and a Victim-Centered Critique." *Florida State Law Review* 20:21–65.

Berns, Walter. 1979. *For Capital Punishment: Crime and the Morality of the Death Penalty.* New York: Basic Books.

Bessler, John D. 1997. *Death in the Dark: Midnight Executions in America.* Boston: Northeastern University Press.

Bessler, John D. 1994. "The Public Interest and the Unconstitutionality of Private Prosecutors." *Arkansas Law Review* 47:511–602.

Blecker, Robert. 2003. "Roots." Pp. 169–231 in *America's Experiment With Capital Punishment: Reflections on the Past, Present, and Future of the Ultimate Penal Sanction,* 2d ed., edited by James R. Acker, Robert M. Bohm, and Charles S. Lanier. Durham, NC: Carolina Academic Press.

Bonczar, Thomas P. and Tracy L. Snell. 2003. *Bureau of Justice Statistics Bulletin: Capital Punishment, 2002*. Washington, D.C.: U.S. Department of Justice.

Booth v. Maryland. 1987. 482 U.S. 496.

Burr, Richard. 2003. "Litigating with Victim Impact Testimony: The Serendipity That Has Come from *Payne v. Tennessee*." *Cornell Law Review* 88:517–29.

Byrne, Christina A. et al. 1999. "Female Victims of Partner Versus Nonpartner Violence: Experience With the Criminal Justice System." *Criminal Justice and Behavior* 26:275–92.

Coyne, Randall T. 2003. "Shooting the Wounded: First Degree Murder and Second Class Victims." *Oklahoma City University Law Review* 28:93–117.

Cushing, Renny. 2002. "Amazing Grace: Reflections on Justice, Survival, and Healing." Pp. 283–87 in *Machinery of Death: The Reality of America's Death Penalty Regime*, edited by David R. Dow and Mark Dow. New York: Routledge.

Cushing, Robert Renny and Susannah Sheffer. 2002. *Dignity Denied: The Experience of Murder Victims' Family Members Who Oppose the Death Penalty*. Cambridge, MA: Murder Victims' Families for Reconciliation.

Donahoe, Joel F. 1999. "The Changing Role of Victim Impact Evidence in Capital Cases." *Western Criminology Review* 2(1). Available online at http://wcr.sonoma.edu/v2n1/donahoe.html.

Drapkin, Israel. 1989. *Crime and Punishment in the Ancient World*. Lexington, MA: Lexington Books.

Dressler, Joshua. 1995. *Understanding Criminal Law*. New York: Matthew Bender & Co.

Dubber, Markus Dirk. 2002. *Victims in the War on Crime: The Use and Abuse of Victims' Rights*. New York: New York University Press.

Eisenberg, Theodore, Stephen P. Garvey and Martin T. Wells. 2003. "Victim Characteristics and Victim Impact Evidence in South Carolina Capital Cases." *Cornell Law Review* 88:306–42.

Fahey, Patrick M. 1992. "*Payne v. Tennessee*: An Eye for an Eye and Then Some." *Connecticut Law Review* 25:205–64.

Fitzpatrick, Peter. 1999. "'Always More to Do': Capital Punishment and the (De)Composition of Law." Pp. 117–36 in *The Killing State: Capital Punishment in Law, Politics, and Culture*, edited by Austin Sarat. New York: Oxford University Press.

Fletcher, George P. 1995. *With Justice for Some: Victims' Rights in Criminal Trials*. New York: Addison-Wesley Publishing Company.

Frankel, Tamar. 1996. "Lessons from the Past: Revenge Yesterday and Today." *Boston University Law Review* 76:89–101.

Friedman, Lawrence M. 1993. *Crime and Punishment in American History*. New York: Basic Books.

Furman v. Georgia. 1972. 408 U.S. 238.

Gardner, Martin R. 1993. "The *Mens Rea* Enigma: Observations on the Role of Motive in the Criminal Law Past and Present." *Utah Law Review* 1993:635–750.

Goodwin, Michael Lawrence. 1997–98. "An Eyeful for an Eye—An Argument Against Allowing the Families of Murder Victims to Witness Executions." *Brandeis Journal of Family Law* 36:585–608.

Gottesman, Evan. 1992. "The Reemergence of *Qisas* and *Diyat* in Pakistan." *Columbia Human Rights Law Review* 23:433–61.

Gregg v. Georgia. 1976. 428 U.S. 153.

Gressler, Jacob. 2004. "Letter to the Editor." *San Francisco Chronicle*, 24 April 2004, B8.

Gross, Samuel R. and Daniel J. Matheson. 2003. "What They Say at the End: Capital Victims' Families and the Press." *Cornell Law Review* 88:486–516.

Grunewald, Kristen F. and Priya Nath. 2003. "Defense-Based Victim Outreach: Restorative Justice in Capital Cases." *Capital Defense Journal* 15:315–52.

Hagan, John. 1983. *Victims Before the Law: The Organizational Domination of Criminal Law*. Toronto: Butterworth & Co.

Henderson, Lynne N. 1999. "Revisiting Victim's Rights." *Utah Law Review* 1999:383–442.

———.1998. "Co-opting Compassion: The Federal Victim's Rights Amendment." *Saint Thomas Law Review* 10:579–606.

———. 1985. "The Wrongs of Victim's Rights." *Stanford Law Review* 37:937–1021.

Hoffmann, Joseph L. 2003. "Revenge or Mercy? Some Thoughts About Survivor Opinion Evidence in Death Penalty Cases." *Cornell Law Review* 88:530–42.

Holdsworth, Sir William. 1936/1963. *A History of English Law* (Vol. II). London: Methuen & Co. Ltd.

Illinois Criminal Justice Information Authority. 2002. *Victim and Survivor Issues in Homicide Cases: Focus Group Report—A Report to the Governor's Commission on Capital Punishment*. Chicago: State of Illinois.

———. 2001. *Report on Victim and Survivor Issues in Homicide Cases: A Report to the Governor's Commission on Capital Punishment*. Chicago: State of Illinois.

Jacoby, Joan E. 1980. *The American Prosecutor: A Search for Identity*. Lexington, MA: Lexington Books.

Jacoby, Susan. 1983. *Wild Justice: The Evolution of Revenge*. New York: Harper & Row.

Janick, Doug. 2000. "Allowing Victims' Families to View Executions: The Eighth Amendment and Society's Justifications for Punishment." *Ohio State Law Journal* 61:935–77.

Johnson, Herbert A. and Nancy Travis Wolfe. 2003. *History of Criminal Justice*. Cincinnati, OH: Anderson Publishing Co.

Johnson, Sheri Lynn. 2003. "Speeding in Reverse: An Anecdotal View of Why Victim Impact Testimony Should Not Be Driving Capital Prosecutions." *Cornell Law Review* 88:555–68.

Kanwar, Vik. 2001–2002. "Capital Punishment as 'Closure': The Limits of a Victim-Centered Jurisprudence." *New York University Review of Law and Social Change* 27:215–55.

Karp, David R. and Jarrett Warshaw. (This volume.)

King, Rachel. 2003. *Don't Kill in Our Names: Families of Murder Victims Speak Out Against the Death Penalty*. New Brunswick, NJ: Rutgers University Press.

Liebman, James S., Jeffrey Fagan and Valerie West. 2000. *A Broken System: Error Rates in Capital Cases. 1973–1995*. Available at http://www2.law.columbia.edu/instructionalservices/liebman/liebman1.pdf.

Lifton, Robert Jay and Greg Mitchell. 2000. *Who Owns Death? Capital Punishment, the American Conscience, and the End of Executions*. New York: William Morrow.

Linda R.S. v. Richard D. 1973. 410 U.S. 614.

Logan, Wayne A. (This volume.)

———.1999. "Through the Past Darkly: A Survey of the Uses and Abuses of Victim Impact Evidence in Capital Trials." *Arizona Law Review* 41:143–92.

Lovell, Colin Rhys. 1962. *English Constitutional and Legal History: A Survey*. New York: Oxford University Press.

Maguire, Kathleen and Ann L. Pastore, eds. 2004. *Sourcebook of Criminal Justice Statistics 2002 [Online]*. Washington, D.C.: U.S. Department of Justice. Available at http://www.albany.edu/sourcebook/.

McCormack, Robert J. 2000. "United States Crime Victim Assistance: History, Organization and Evaluation." Pp. 247–60 in *Understanding Victimology: Selected Readings*, edited by Peggy M. Tobolowsky. Cincinnati: Anderson Publishing Co.

McDonald, William F. 1979. "The Prosecutor's Domain." Pp. 15–51 in *The Prosecutor*, edited by William F. McDonald. Beverly Hills, CA: Sage Publications.

Meltsner, Michael. 1973. *Cruel and Unusual: The Supreme Court and Capital Punishment*. New York: Random House.

Mosteller, Robert P. 2003. "Victim Impact Evidence: Hard to Find the Real Rules." *Cornell Law Review* 88:543–54.

Payne v. Tennessee. 1991. 501 U.S. 808.

Payne v. Tennessee, Transcript of Oral Argument. 1991. Available at 1991 WL 636525 (United States Supreme Court).

Peerenboom, R. P. (1993). "The Victim in Chinese Criminal Theory and Practice: A Historical Survey." *Journal of Chinese Law* 7:63–109.

Pelke, Bill. 2003. *Journey of Hope ... From Violence to Healing*. Xlibris Corporation.

Plucknett, Theodore F. T. 1956. *A Concise History of the Common Law*. Boston: Little, Brown and Company.

Pollock, Sir Frederick and Frederic William Maitland. 1895/1968. *The History of English Law* (Vol. II). London: Cambridge University Press.

Postawko, Robert. 2002. "Towards an Islamic Critique of Capital Punishment." *UCLA Journal of Islamic and Near Eastern Law* 1:269–320.

Prejean, Helen. 1993. *Dead Man Walking*. New York: Vintage Books.

President's Task Force on Victims of Crime: Final Report. 1982. Washington, D.C.: United States Government Printing Office.

Roland, David L. 1989. "Progress in the Victim Reform Movement: No Longer the 'Forgotten Victim.'" *Pepperdine Law Review* 17:35–58.

Sarat, Austin. 2001. *When the State Kills: Capital Punishment and the American Condition*. Princeton, NJ: Princeton University Press.

Seipp, David J. 1996. "The Distinction Between Crime and Tort in the Early Common Law." *Boston University Law Review* 76:59–87.

Skaret, Brian D. 2002. "A Victim's Right to View: A Distortion of the Retributivist Theory of Punishment." *Journal of Legislation* 28:349–57.

Spungen, Deborah. 1998. *Homicide: The Hidden Victims—A Guide for Professionals*. Thousand Oaks, CA: Sage Publications.

Steiker, Carol S. and Jordan M. Steiker. 2003. "Judicial Developments in Capital Punishment Law." Pp. 55–83 in *America's Experiment With Capital Punishment: Reflections on the Past, Present, and Future of the Ultimate Penal Sanction*, 2d ed., edited by James R. Acker, Robert M. Bohm and Charles S. Lanier. Durham, NC: Carolina Academic Press.

Stephen, Sir James Fitzjames. 1883/1996. *A History of the Criminal Law of England* (Vol. I). London: Routledge/Thoemmes Press.

Sundby, Scott E. 2003. "The Capital Jury and Empathy: The Problem of Worthy and Unworthy Victims." *Cornell Law Review* 88:343–81.

Tobolowsky, Peggy M. 1999. "Victim Participation in the Criminal Justice Process: Fifteen Years After the President's Task Force on Victims of Crime." *New England Journal on Criminal and Civil Confinement* 25:21–105.

Umbreit, Mark S., Betty Vos, Robert B. Coates, and Katherine A. Brown. 2003. *Facing Violence: The Path of Restorative Justice and Dialogue.* Monsey, NY: Criminal Justice Press.

Van Derbeken, Jaxon. 2004. "S.F. Police Push Hard for Death Penalty: D.A.'s Decision in Slaying of Officer Infuriates Top Brass." *San Francisco Chronicle*, 21 April 2004, A1.

Van Ness, Daniel K. and Karen Heetderks Strong. 2002. *Restoring Justice.* Cincinnati: Anderson Publishing Co.

White, Ahmed A. 1999. "Victims' Rights, Rule of Law, and the Threat to Liberal Jurisprudence." *Kentucky Law Journal* 87:357–415.

Wright, Martin. 1991. *Justice for Victims and Offenders: A Restorative Response to Crime.* Philadelphia: Open University Press.

Zimring, Franklin E. 2003. *The Contradictions of American Capital Punishment.* New York: Oxford University Press.

Zimring, Franklin E. and Gordon Hawkins. 1986. *Capital Punishment and the American Agenda.* New York: Cambridge University Press.

CHAPTER 10

VICTIMS, SURVIVORS, AND THE DECISIONS TO SEEK AND IMPOSE DEATH

Wayne A. Logan[*]

According to the U.S. Supreme Court, the death penalty should only be imposed as a "reasoned moral response" to a killing, based on the heinousness of the act and culpability of the offender (*California v. Brown* 1987:545). In keeping with this mandate, death penalty jurisdictions have instituted an expansive, highly sophisticated regime of legal procedures intended to guide prosecutors in their capital charging decisions, and to assist judges and juries in deciding whether to impose death. Enormous effort, in short, has been dedicated to what former Supreme Court Justice Harry Blackmun aptly referred to as "tinker[ing] with the machinery of death" (*Callins v. Collins* 1994:1130).

Despite such efforts, decisions to seek and impose death unavoidably remain intensely human and emotional undertakings. This is especially so since the Supreme Court's landmark 1991 decision in *Payne v. Tennessee*, which rescinded prior limits on the admission of "victim impact evidence," described by the Court as "evidence about the victim and ... the impact of the murder on the victim's family" (*Payne v. Tennessee* 1991:827). This chapter examines the variety of victim impact evidence introduced in capital trials today and the rules governing its admission and use. The chapter also addresses two closely related matters: the role in capital charging decisions of the pro/anti-death penalty opinions of murder victims' survivors (and in some instances

---

[*] The author thanks Carl Nowlin for helpful research assistance and Meg Daniel for editorial support.

of victims themselves) and the propriety of victim characteristics being considered in decisions to seek and ultimately impose death.

Victim Impact Evidence

On two occasions during the 1980s the U.S. Supreme Court held that the Eighth Amendment to the U.S. Constitution prohibits admission in capital trials of victim impact evidence (VIE). In *Booth v. Maryland* (1987), the Court flatly rejected the contention that such evidence was needed to allow jurors to assess the "gravity" of the offense. According to the Court, VIE improperly refocuses the death decision from the defendant and his crime to the "character and reputation of the victim and the effect on his family." This shift, the Court reasoned, violates the Eighth Amendment because it risks imposition of the death penalty "in an arbitrary and capricious manner" (*Booth v. Maryland* 1987:502–3). A defendant could be put to death based on information—the personal qualities and worth of the victim—about which he was wholly unaware at the time of the killing.

Only two years later, in *South Carolina v. Gathers* (1989), the Court again condemned the use of VIE on Eighth Amendment grounds. In *Gathers*, the VIE involved the statements of a local prosecutor who, in an emotional closing argument praised, among other things, the religiosity and civic-mindedness of the victim, a self-styled "reverend minister." Although not testimony from survivors, as in *Booth*, the Court considered the statements "indistinguishable" in their effect, and hence invalid under the Eighth Amendment. Again, permitting the jury to take account of the victim's traits "could result in imposing the death sentence because of factors about which the defendant was unaware, and that were irrelevant to the decision to kill" (*South Carolina v. Gathers* 1989:811).

In 1991, after several crucial changes in its membership, the Court did an about-face on the admissibility of VIE. In *Payne v. Tennessee* (1991), the Court renounced the premise of *Booth* and *Gathers* that "evidence relating to a particular victim or to the harm that a capital defendant causes to a victim's family" creates a risk that death will be arbitrarily and capriciously imposed. Rather, according to the *Payne* Court, VIE "is simply another form or method of informing the sentencing authority about the specific harm caused.... [A] State may properly conclude that for the jury to assess meaningfully the defendant's moral culpability and blameworthiness, it should have ... evidence of the specific harm caused by the defendant" (*Payne v. Tennessee* 1991:825). In addition, VIE is constitutionally permissible because it helps level the playing field in capital trials. Given that capital defendants are entitled to adduce mitigating evidence to show their "uniqueness" and lessened personal culpability, fairness dictated that evidence of the "uniqueness" of the lives taken by defendants be considered as well. To the *Payne* majority, the decisions in *Booth* and *Gathers* to bar VIE had "deprive[d] the State of the full moral force of its evidence and may prevent the jury from having before it all the information necessary" to reach its death decision. In order to "keep the balance true" in capital trials, the state must be permitted to "offer a 'quick glimpse of the life' which a defendant 'chose to extinguish'" (*Payne v. Tennessee* 1991:822).

While *Payne* only purported to lift the constitutional prohibition of VIE, and in no way required that it be admitted, VIE has since become a staple in capital trials. Today, thirty-three of the thirty-eight states authorizing the death penalty, as well as the U.S. government and military, allow VIE (Blume 2003:267).[1] That VIE has proven so popular should not come as a surprise, given the appeal of affording survivors an opportunity to testify publicly about their personal losses, and the strategic value to prosecutors of such emotionally potent evidence. What is surprising, however, is that strikingly few limits have been imposed on the admission and use of VIE, which is introduced at the most delicate time in the capital process—when jurors must decide whether defendants are to live or die, after having found them guilty of society's most serious crime.[2]

Among the handful of states to impose procedural limits is Oklahoma, where the state must notify the defendant of its intent to introduce VIE, "detailing" the evidence sought to be introduced, and an *in-camera* hearing must be held on admissibility. In addition, in Oklahoma the "trial court may wish to consider whether a question-and-answer format may be a preferable

---

1. Of note, differences have arisen over whether VIE can be admitted in the absence of express legislative authorization. Compare *Commonwealth v. Fisher* (1996) (requiring express statutory authorization) with *State v. Hill* (1998) (rejecting need for legislative authorization).

2. As noted by the Supreme Court in *Caldwell v. Mississippi* (1985:333):

> A capital sentencing jury is made up of individuals placed in a very unfamiliar situation and called upon to make a very difficult and uncomfortable choice. They are confronted with evidence and argument on the issue of whether another should die, and they are asked to decide that issue on behalf of the community. Moreover, they are given only partial guidance as to how their judgment should be exercised, leaving them with substantial discretion.

See also *Gregg v. Georgia* (1976:192) (noting that "[s]ince the members of a jury will have had little, if any, previous experience in sentencing, they are unlikely to be skilled with the information they are given.")

method of controlling the way relevant victim impact evidence is presented to a jury" (Logan 1999b:151–52). Similarly, New Jersey requires prior notice of the state's intent to admit VIE and permits input from only one witness (a family member), relayed by means of a written statement that is reviewed in advance by the court for prejudicial content. Furthermore, New Jersey courts are required to admonish witnesses that they will not be permitted to testify if they cannot control their emotions, and minors typically are not permitted to testify (Logan 1999b:152).

Such limits, however, are unusual. In the vast majority of jurisdictions the state enjoys virtual free reign in the introduction of VIE, subject only to *Payne*'s modest admonition that VIE not be so "unduly prejudicial that it renders the trial fundamentally unfair" (*Payne v. Tennessee* 1991:825). Prosecutors have broad discretion over how VIE is conveyed (e.g., videos, photos, poems, diary entries); who is permitted to testify (e.g., family, friends, co-workers, neighbors, rescue personnel, "community" representatives); and the number of witnesses (e.g., fifty-five in the trial of Oklahoma City bombing conspirator Terry Nichols and thirty-eight in the trial of Timothy McVeigh) (Logan 1999b:151–56; Logan 2000b:21–22). Illustrative of this broad latitude is a recent Missouri case, which upheld the admission of a "family tree," containing forty-six named family members, even though the chart listed individuals not yet born at the time of the murder and spouses who were no longer formally part of the family (*State v. Deck* 2004).

Moreover, although *Payne* only condoned use of impact evidence concerning the victim's family, lower state and federal courts have been far more generous in their understanding of the permissible scope of impact evidence. For instance, in the capital murder trial of Timothy McVeigh the trial court admitted a wide range of VIE, including evidence relating to efforts by rescue workers "to discover the fate of victims" and concerning the "pure love and innocence of children" (Logan 2000b:22). The latter category contained such heartrending stories as that of a little girl who had been outside the federal building when the bomb exploded, and later approached a police officer and his dog, hugged his dog, and asked, "Mr. Police Dog, will you find my friends?" (Logan 2000b:22–23). Stretching "impact" further still from *Payne*, which addressed the impact of murder only on a victim's immediate family, one federal court recently approved of testimony from three prison guards relating to the effects the killing of a prison guard had on inmate behavior and daily prison life (Logan 2000b:23). Other courts, betraying the tenet that VIE highlight the "uniqueness" of the victim, have permitted evidence of emotional harm stemming from unrelated killings allegedly committed by the defendant (Logan 2000b:23). "Community"-related impact is also fair game, permitting jurors to hear of the impact on the "law enforcement community" and even listeners of a radio talk show (Logan 1999b:161–62).

While the much of the foregoing can perhaps be said to constitute foreseeable consequences of killings, VIE often assumes a much broader form, posing the risk identified by the Court in *Booth* that jurors will "impos[e] the death sentence because of factors about which the defendant was unaware, and that were irrelevant to the decision to kill" (*Booth v. Maryland* 1987:505). The Texas Court of Criminal Appeals, for instance, deemed "tenuous" but nonetheless admissible the fact that the victim's sister later experienced a divorce (*McDuff v. State* 1997), while the Missouri Supreme Court permitted consideration of evidence that the victim's family had previously endured the loss of another child as a result of cerebral palsy (*State v. Clay* 1998).[3]

Victim characteristic evidence, a form of VIE *Payne* stated is "designed to show ... each victim's uniqueness as an individual human being" (p. 823), also assumes a wide range of forms. This is so despite the verity of Justice Stevens's dissenting observation in *Payne* that "[t]he fact that each of us is unique is a proposition so obvious that it surely requires no evidentiary support" (p. 866). Examples include testimony that the victim was a "martyr" (while the defendant was "evil"); a nationally recognized piano player; a "smart person" with a "higher IQ" than others in her family; a "minister who read and carried a Bible every day"; and a person "without a hateful bone in her body" (Logan 2000b:25). At the same time, defense efforts to rebut such evidence with "bad" victim evidence have been uniformly rebuffed by trial courts and even if permitted, would be of dubious tactical wisdom. So too would be the cross-examination of witnesses on the validity of the adverse consequences of killings, even though such a right of cross-examination technically exists in several jurisdictions (Logan 2000b:28). As a result, as noted by Randall Coyne, a defendant's capacity to cross-examine VIE witnesses is "more apparent than real" (Coyne 1992:599).

Finally, in stark contrast to the increasingly specific and regimented quality of capital punishment law more generally (Simon and Spaulding 1999), uncertainty persists over the fundamental purpose and role of VIE in capital trials. Oklahoma jurors, for instance, are vaguely advised that VIE "is simply another method of informing you about the specific harm caused by the crime

---

3. Some effort has been made to attach probative weight to the fact that the defendant had prior knowledge of the victim's immediate family (see, e.g., *State v. Nesbit* 1998). In the words of the Tennessee Supreme Court, "probative value is particularly great, where the proof shows ... that a defendant had specific knowledge about the victim's family when the crime was committed" (p. 893).

in question. You may consider this evidence in determining an appropriate punishment" (*Cargle v. State* 1995:828–29). According to the Missouri Supreme Court, it "is sufficient that [VIE] is relevant to inform the jury as to the effect of the crime ... even if no instruction is given regarding the evidence" (*State v. Basile* 1997:359). In Florida, VIE qualifies as "other evidence, which is not required to be weighed against, or offset by, statutory factors" (*State v. Maxwell* 1994:872). Despite this uncertainty, the Supreme Court has rejected arguments that consideration of VIE amounts to "double-counting" of closely related aggravators, and that the amorphous nature of VIE itself violates constitutional due process due to vagueness or overbreadth (*United States v. Jones* 1999:398–402).

In sum, fifteen years after *Payne* was decided, it is clear that VIE is being used to provide far more than a mere "quick glimpse" of victims and the loss resulting from a murder. Jurors now regularly receive highly emotional, gripping evidence, with precious little in the way of substantive limits and procedural controls, or guidance on how the potent evidence should influence their death decisions.

Survivor and Victim
"Opinion" Sentiments on Death

VIE is intended to provide jurors insight into the "specific harm" caused by a murder and to provide a sense of the life the "defendant chose to extinguish" (*Payne v. Tennessee* 1991:822, 825). With the advent of VIE, capital trials have thus become more personalized, in both tone and content. This section examines a by-product of this personalization: the role played by the personal opinions of murder victims' survivors (and perhaps victims, when their views on capital punishment are known) in the decisions whether to impose death upon conviction, as well as whether to file a capital charge in the first instance.

Opinions on Whether to Impose Death

One would presume that the sentiments of victims and survivors, the individuals most directly affected by criminal acts, would play a paramount role in sentencing outcomes. Common practice, in fact, largely supports this presumption, as jurisdictions, in response to the powerful influence of the victims' rights movement, have taken significant steps to increase the role of victims and survivors in the sentencing process (Tobolowsky 2001:81–104).

In capital trials, however, courts have been reluctant to permit the sentencing authority to consider the opinions of victims (or, more commonly, their survivors) on whether death should be imposed. In *Booth v. Maryland*, discussed above, the U.S. Supreme Court emphasized that the distinction was justified because "death is a 'punishment different from all other sanctions,' and that therefore the considerations that inform the sentencing decision may be different from those that might be relevant to other liability or punishment determinations" (1987:509 n.12). Although sympathetic to the desire of survivors to espouse their views, and mindful that "there is no doubt that jurors are generally aware" of the pro-death sentiments of survivors, the Court concluded that

> the formal presentation of [opinion testimony] by the State can serve no other purpose than to inflame the jury and divert it from deciding the case on the relevant evidence concerning the crime and the defendant.... The admission of these emotionally charged opinions as to what conclusions the jury should draw from the evidence clearly is inconsistent with the reasoned decisionmaking we require in capital cases" (pp. 508–9).

In *Payne*, although overruling *Booth's* prohibition of VIE, the Court expressly avoided reexamination of its earlier bar on opinion evidence because, according to the Court, no evidence of the sort was presented in Payne's sentencing (*Payne v. Tennessee* 1991: 830 n. 2).

Despite the *Payne* Court's refusal to reconsider the bar it imposed in *Booth* on opinion testimony, uncertainty exists over the place of opinion testimony in capital trials, with several state courts expressing ambivalence over the extent, and indeed continued existence, of the *Booth* prohibition (Logan 2000a:528). This sentiment is most pronounced in Oklahoma, where the Court of Criminal Appeals has concluded that *Payne* "implicitly" overruled *Booth* altogether, and Oklahoma statutory law expressly permits sentence opinion testimony in capital trials (Logan 2000a:528–29).[4]

More commonly, jurisdictions sidestep the question by adopting decidedly narrow definitions of "opinions." In one Nevada capital case, for instance, the wife of the decedent asked the jury to "show no mercy." The Nevada Supreme Court unanimously concluded that the comment did not amount to an opinion as such, but rather amounted to a request that the jury return the most

---

4. In 2003 the Arizona Legislature signaled its support for victim sentence recommendations in capital trials by adopting legislation that expressly authorizes their admission in the event they are deemed constitutional (Bernheim 2004:566).

severe sentence it felt appropriate (*Witter v. State* 1996:895–96). Similarly, the Illinois Supreme Court upheld the admissibility of the following sentiment offered by the wife of a murdered police officer:

> My family and I are very confident that all of you will return a quick verdict which will send a message to my children, society, and the law enforcement community that we simply will not tolerate or accept our last means of protection being annihilated on our streets. Renew our faith in the criminal justice system and bring a phase of closure to this ongoing nightmare that fills our lives (*People v. Williams* 1998:1124).

According to the court, the testimony was permissible because the requests for "closure" and a "quick verdict" did not relate to the death penalty, ultimately imposed by the jury, but rather to the witness's "desire that the jury deliberate in an expedient manner so that she and her family could move on with their lives" (p. 1124). The Supreme Court of Missouri displayed only slightly less indulgence when it concluded that the following did not constitute a sentence recommendation: "I believe this man has caused enough chaos and I ask he be fairly punished for what he has done" (*State v. Worthington* 1999:89 n.2).

This weakening of the opinion testimony prohibition is also evident in the strikingly reductionistic analysis commonly employed by courts in their evaluation of whether particular testimony comes within the scope of the prohibition. The Alabama Court of Criminal Appeals reflected this approach in a recent decision when it rejected a challenge arising from a father and brother of the victim (a police officer) who "begged" the jury to impose death in the name of the victim's family and "every police officer." According to the Alabama court, "[t]he jury surely recognized the testimony of the victim impact witnesses as a normal, human reaction to the death of a loved one. That these witnesses wanted [the defendant] to receive the death penalty would come as no surprise to the members of the jury" (*State v. Whitehead* 1999:849). Similarly, in Oklahoma sentence opinion testimony is permitted because "a jury expects such a statement from the victim's family" (*Wood v. State* 1998:12).

In short, there is increasing evidence that the prohibition of opinion testimony is weakening, despite the compelling reasons supporting its continued existence. Perhaps the most prominent reason supporting retention is the irrelevance of a witness's opinion—even when the witness is a loved one of the murder victim—to the question of whether the death penalty is warranted. An opinion does not relate to the nature of the offense or the offender, the cornerstone criteria of death decisions. Nor, for that matter, does a witness's view that a punishment less than death is warranted come within the traditional ambit of mitigation, as defined by the Supreme Court.

A related but distinct reason for retention of the prohibition is the inherently arbitrary quality of opinion testimony. Since *Furman v. Georgia* (1972), the Supreme Court has guarded against the introduction of factors that might contribute to arbitrary and capricious decision making in capital cases. Opinion testimony raises just such a risk: it allows jurors to impose (or abstain from) death not because the evidence warrants such an outcome, but because of the unpredictable, idiosyncratic desires of witnesses who happen to testify.

In addition, the highly subjective quality of opinion testimony heightens the risk that sentencing decisions will be influenced by the fortuity of the persuasiveness, attractiveness, or eloquence of witnesses. While of course such fortuities are intrinsic to the adversarial system, and indeed the opinions of witnesses (whether for the prosecution or the defense) can likely be readily surmised, concern should arise over the purposeful injection of arbitrariness into the delicate, already highly emotional capital decision-making process. Indeed, given that such opinions can be forecasted, to permit their statement under such circumstances smacks of excessiveness and arbitrariness, which have no place in capital trials.

A third and final argument favoring the continued bar stems from the reality that opinion testimony not merely distracts the sentencing authority from its constitutional duty to weigh only relevant aggravating and mitigating factors (opinion testimony is neither), but actually undercuts this mission in its entirety. As the Supreme Court observed in *McCleskey v. Kemp* (1987), "it is the jury's function to make the difficult and uniquely human judgments that defy codification and buil[d] discretion, equity, and flexibility into [the] legal system" (p. 311). Opinion testimony disavows this critical responsibility insofar as it urges the sentencer to defer to the personal views of the individual witnesses, at the expense of the constitutionally mandated consideration of aggravating and mitigating evidence.

Despite the persuasiveness of the foregoing arguments, it is likely that the bar on opinion testimony will continue to weaken, and likely fall, in the years to come. This is because the exception runs against the grain of the Court's bias in favor of increasing the amount of information put before decision makers in capital trials (Logan 2000b:7–9). Moreover, as the discussion above indicates, in the wake of *Payne*, it has become increasingly difficult to draw distinctions between impermissible opinion testimony and the permitted, highly personalized accounts characteristic of VIE.[5] The absence of any mean-

---

5. In addition to the line-drawing difficulties highlighted in the text, opinion testimony closely resembles several other commonly accepted strategies in capital trials, e.g., "pleas for mercy" by defense witnesses; allocution, when the capital defendant himself addresses

ingful basis to distinguish the two naturally militates in favor of abandoning the prohibition altogether.

Attention also likely will be increasingly drawn to a glaring jurisprudential asymmetry created by the prohibition, whereby opinion testimony is permitted in noncapital yet not capital trials. With the Supreme Court in the lead, the "death is different" rationale is showing signs of wear. Indeed, *Payne* itself provides a compelling example of this evolution, renouncing *Booth's* prohibition of VIE in capital trials alone.

Finally, and perhaps most important, the admission of sentence opinion testimony lies with the grain of larger systemic changes now occurring nationwide as a result of the powerful victims' rights movement. Numerous states, either in their constitutions or statutory law, now contain victims' rights provisions, and a federal Victims' Rights Amendment has been debated by Congress on several occasions (Logan 2000a:535–37). The prospect of affording survivors a constitutional right to express their views on the appropriate sentence to be imposed on the killers of their loved ones would likely enjoy considerable appeal among victims' advocates and politicians alike.

Opinions on Prosecutors' Decisions to Seek Death

In contrast to the significant critical scrutiny given opinion sentiments in the sentencing phase of capital trials, relatively little attention has been paid to the weight given by prosecutors to the opinions of victims and survivors on whether death should be sought in the first instance.[6] This lack of attention should perhaps come as no surprise given the broad charging discretion enjoyed by prosecutors more generally, whose work is largely guided only by the open-ended mandate that they "seek justice" (Logan 1999a:43).[7]

Within the high-stakes context of capital litigation, however, this neutral requirement is subject to unique pressures. An increasing body of literature supports the view that prosecutors, the vast majority of whom are popularly elected, are highly sensitized to the political ramifications of death penalty-

---

the sentencing authority; and opinions by prosecutors on whether death is warranted (Logan 2000a:545–46).

6. The discussion here is mainly limited to state and local prosecutors, in contrast to their federal counterparts who typically are subject to far more procedural requirements and constraints. For a discussion of the federal regime see Little (1999).

7. In constitutional terms, the only functional limits on prosecutorial decisions are that they not be selective, vindictive or otherwise motivated by bad faith. See Gershman (1998:4.3–4.5).

charging decisions. (Dieter 1996; Liebman 2000:2079–81) In an era when being "tough on crime" is seen as a prerequisite for political success, a decision to refrain from filing a capital charge has obvious risks. Such risks, in turn, are significantly heightened when the survivor(s) of a murder victim publicly advocate that death be pursued. No prosecutor facing reelection would relish the prospect of being criticized for repudiating the wishes of a grieving loved one who has asked the state to exact death.

As a result of these political realities, it is not uncommon today to have prosecutors publicly consult with survivors on the critically important threshold decision of whether to seek death. As noted by one commentator, the victims' rights movement has "changed dramatically the manner in which capital cases are investigated and prosecuted. Prosecutors may work directly with victims' families in deciding whether to seek the death penalty" (Karamanian 1998:1028). When survivors advocate death, and especially when they make their views publicly known, the dynamic of death decision making is unavoidably tilted in favor of a pro-death outcome (Logan 1999a:44).

Needless to say, however, public acceptance of the death penalty is not uniform, and the decisional dynamic for prosecutors becomes more complicated when those most directly affected by a murder do not want death charges to be filed. In such situations, a death-predisposed prosecutor is put in the difficult position of advocating state-sanctioned killing in the name of a victim, when her survivors (and perhaps the victim herself, should she have let her preference be known), do not wish to have the ultimate penalty imposed. Significantly, prosecutors have often resisted such anti-capital views in their charging decisions (Barnes 2002:255; Logan 1999a:44; Cushing and Sheffer 2002).[8]

The question of whether such opinions should influence prosecutorial decisions to seek death presents an array of challenges to American justice. Indeed, the public acknowledgment by prosecutors that such opinions should guide charging decisions itself underscores an important shift in the nation's public prosecution norm. Heretofore, while prosecutors have typically allowed private parties to provide input on charging decisions, they have steadfastly

---

8. They can do so confident in the knowledge that their public persona for toughness will go undiminished. In addition, to the extent that negatives attach, prosecutors can justify their repudiation by invoking their institutional mandate to "seek justice" in the name of the state, irrespective of the wishes of individuals most affected by a given crime. A murder, after all, implicates the interests of organized society, affording the state the prerogative to punish as it sees fit (Logan 1999a:45).

resisted having such private views play a dispositive role, at least publicly (Lynch 2002:1246).

As a result of this shift, prosecutors increasingly face difficult questions. For instance, how is a prosecutor to decide whose opinion is worthy of deference, when survivors cannot reach unanimity on whether death is warranted; or when the views of survivors do not jibe with that of the victim?[9] Why indeed should the views of some survivors be valued over those of others? In such circumstances the system renders itself vulnerable to charges of arbitrariness and the cynical inference that it is manipulating victimhood, with its powerful emotional and political cache, and ignoring the desires of those most directly affected by murder only when it suits its own purposes (Logan1999a: 45). Even in the absence of such confusion, however, a basic concern is presented: that the public prosecution apparatus has been hijacked by a private party, inducing a result not necessarily consistent with the prosecutorial mandate of "doing justice."

The Role of Victim Traits

Today, it is taken as a given that murder victims should be considered equal in the eyes of the law; capital punishment is made neither more nor less warranted based on the background and characteristics of individual victims.[10] Even a cursory review of death penalty statutes, however, reveals that this is not the case. Laws containing substantive definitions of capital murder typically single out the murder of particular persons, such as judges, prosecutors, witnesses, elected officials, police officers, and children for special attention— transforming otherwise noncapital killings into capital ones for charging purposes (Acker and Lanier 1993:402–6). Furthermore, in the sentencing phase,

---

9. Elsewhere, in an article addressing "declarations of life," I have discussed how such a conflict might be redressed. Declarations are notarized documents completed by death penalty opponents requesting that should they be murdered their convicted murderer "not be subject to or put in jeopardy of the death penalty under any circumstances, no matter how heinous their crime or how much I have suffered." I argue that declarations should have dispositive force in death-charging decisions, analogizing them to "advance medical directives," which provide medical personnel guidance on whether an individual beset by a fatal medical circumstance wishes to forego aggressive life-sustaining treatment (Logan 1999a).

10. Of course, such distinctions are the norm in civil (tort) actions seeking recovery for wrongful death. There, compensatory awards are typically based on anticipated future earnings, loss of society and companionship, and the like, which as a matter of course permit distinctions to be drawn among decedents.

jurisdictions have seen fit to single out the killings of many such victims as aggravating circumstances in the decision whether a convicted murder should be put to death (Acker and Lanier 1994:140–51).

On its face, the mere existence of such provisions raises concern that the State is engaging in a form of discrimination; victim status should not, for moral, ethical, and legal purposes, enter into the death decision-making process. This selectivity, however, has been undertaken with the blessing of the Supreme Court, which since *Furman v. Georgia* (1972) has urged that capital jurisdictions specify criteria to ensure that only the most death-worthy killers are executed. Supreme Court doctrine has sought to "force communities, speaking through state legislatures, to designate in advance those offenders most deserving of death" (Steiker and Steiker 1995:372). And so capital jurisdictions have complied, singling out particular murder victims for special attention—be they especially vulnerable (e.g., children) or integral to the operation of the criminal justice system apparatus (e.g., prosecutors) or to the polity itself (elected officials).

Moreover, it is also important to recognize that victim traits can, and do, play a less formal (i.e., nonstatutory) yet still significant role in the capital process. Research makes clear that the personal traits of certain victims—those for whom we perhaps are inclined to have sympathy or admire for their social standing or accomplishments—can play a significant role in death decisions (*Ring v. Arizona* 2002:617; Baldus et al. 1998:1681; Turow 2003:72–73). Race, as well, has been shown to have significant influence. An extensive body of empirical evidence makes clear that black killers of white victims are far more likely to be charged with or receive the death penalty (Baldus and Woodworth 2004:1424–26). In *Payne,* the U.S. Supreme Court itself made clear that death decision-makers can consider the personal background of a victim (e.g., his or her "uniqueness as an individual human being") when assessing "harm." Only now is work becoming available on the influence of VIE relating to victims' personal traits. While much research shows a significant role (Baldus et al. 1998:1671; Beck and Shumsky 1997:536; Luginbuhl and Burkhead 1995:7–9; Sundby 2003:346–52), some work has reached more ambiguous results (Eisenberg et al. 2003).

Whatever the influence of victim traits on death decisions, their newfound place in capital trials raises the appearance of unequal application of the law. Despite *Payne*'s caution that victim trait information should not serve "to encourage comparative judgments," such comparisons inevitably occur, and are ultimately condoned by courts[11] (Logan 2000b:157–59). As a result, death de-

---

11. This tendency is enhanced by the willingness of courts to admit testimony of survivors that characterizes murders and defendants. Although *Payne* refused to allow such evidence, the prohibition, much like that regarding opinion testimony, increasingly is being

cisions can now turn on the finding that "the victim was a sterling member of the community rather than someone of questionable character" (*Booth v. Maryland* 1987:506), or that the defendant deserves death because he is "less worthy" than his victim (*Humphries v. Ozmint* 2005:246).

In the end, regardless of whether one agrees with the observation of eighteenth-century legal commentator William Blackstone that "the execution of a needy decrepit assassin is a poor satisfaction for the murder of a nobleman in the full bloom of his youth and full enjoyment of his friends, his honours, and his fortune" (Blackstone 1783:13), current capital punishment law affords death decision makers much more latitude to engage in, and act upon, this comparative calculus.

Conclusion

Today, to an unprecedented extent, the legal barrier between violent criminal offenders and their victims is showing signs of wear in American criminal justice. Although not marked by the "blood feuds" and vigilantism of bygone times, there is no mistaking that America's justice system, including its capital trials, has become increasingly personalized. As Markus Dubber has aptly noted, "[I]n the past, capital sentencing pitted the defendant against the State.... In the new paradigmatic sentencing hearing, the capital defendant now encounters an even more formidable opponent: the person whose death made her eligible for the death penalty, the capital victim" (Dubber 1993:86).

A major catalyst in this legal evolution has been the Supreme Court's landmark 1991 decision in *Payne v. Tennessee*, which for the first time permitted the admission of victim impact evidence in the sentencing phase of capital trials. With the Eighth Amendment bar lifted, capital decision-makers are now exposed to far more than a "quick glimpse" of the murder victim, and the personal losses resulting from killings. Furthermore, such emotionally charged information is being admitted largely free of procedural limits, or substantive guidance, in jurors' decisions on whether to impose the State's ultimate sanction. Despite such concerns, victim impact evidence is very likely here to stay, given the popular appeal of affording victims and their survivors a voice in

---

honored in the breach. Courts regularly allow such testimony, either outright or on the basis of harmless error analysis. The Oklahoma Court of Criminal Appeals, for instance, upheld admission of a husband's testimony that a "cur" or "stray dog" did not deserve the death suffered by his wife, and a grieving daughter's reference to the defendant as a "piece of trash" (Logan 1999b:166).

capital sentencing decisions. Critics of *Payne*, at most, can hope only that courts and legislatures will see fit to institute rules limiting its form and use in capital trials.

Even with such changes, it is likely that capital trials will continue their evolution toward personalization, with the characteristics of victims, and victim and survivor opinions on whether death is warranted, coming to play an even more central, publicly acknowledged role. What this ultimately means for the American system of public prosecution, a system heretofore predicated on at least the appearance of dispensing dispassionate and impartial justice, remains to be seen.

References

Acker, James R. and Charles S. Lanier. 1993. "The Dimensions of Capital Murder." *Criminal Law Bulletin* 29:379–417.

_____. 1994. "Parsing This Lexicon of Death: Aggravating Factors in Capital Sentencing Statute." *Criminal Law Bulletin* 30:107–52.

American Bar Association. 1993. *Standards for Criminal Justice, Prosecution Function and Defense Function*. 3d edition. Washington, D.C., American Bar Association.

Baldus, David C. and George Woodworth. 2004. "Race Discrimination and the Legitimacy of Capital Punishment: Reflections on the Interaction of Fact and Perception." *DePaul Law Review* 53:1411–95.

Baldus, David C., George Woodworth, David Zuckerman, Neil Alan Weiner, and Barbara Broffitt. 1998. "Racial Discrimination and the Death Penalty in the Post-Furman Era: An Empirical and Legal Overview, with Recent Findings from Philadelphia." *Cornell Law Review* 83:1638–770.

Barnes, Adrienne N. 2002. "Reverse Impact Testimony: A New and Improved Victim Impact Statement." *Capital Defense Journal* 14:245–64.

Beck, James C. and Robert Shumsky. 1997. "A Comparison of Retained and Appointed Counsel in Cases of Capital Murder." *Law and Human Behavior* 21:525–38.

Bernheim, Robert. 2004. "Lynn v. Reinstein: Limiting Victims' Rights to Recommend Sentences in Capital Cases," *Arizona Law Review* 46: 581.

Blackstone, William. *Commentaries on the Laws of England, Volume 4, 1783*. Chicago, IL.

Blume, John H. 2003. "Ten Years of *Payne*: Victim Evidence in Capital Cases." *Cornell Law Review* 88:257–81.

Booth v. Maryland. 1987. 482 U.S. 496.

Caldwell v. Mississippi. 1985. 472 U.S. 320.

California v. Brown. 1987. 479 U.S. 538.

Callins v. Collins. 1994. 510 U.S. 1141.

Cargle v. State. 1995. 909 P.2d 806 (Okla. Court of Criminal Appeals).

Commonwealth v. Fisher. 1996. 681 A.2d 130 (Pa.).

Coyne, Randall. 1992. "Inflicting *Payne* on Oklahoma: The Use of Victim Impact Evidence During the Sentencing Phase of Capital Cases." *Oklahoma Law Review* 45:589–628.

Cushing, Robert Renny and Susannah Sheffer. 2002. *Dignity Denied: The Experience of Murder Victims' Family Members Who Oppose the Death Penalty*. Cambridge, MA: Murder Victims' Families for Reconciliation.

Dieter, Richard C. 1996. *Killing for Votes: The Dangers of Politicizing the Death Penalty*. Washington, D.C.: Death Penalty Information Center.

Dubber, Markus D. 1993. "Regulating the Tender Heart When the Axe is Ready to Strike." *Buffalo Law Review* 41:85–156.

Eisenberg, Theodore, Stephen P. Garvey and Martin T. Wells. 2003. "Victim Characteristics and Victim Impact Evidence in South Carolina Capital Cases." *Cornell Law Review* 88:306–42.

Furman v. Georgia. 1972. 408 U.S. 238.

Gershman, Bennett L. 1998. *Prosecutorial Misconduct*. New York: Clark Boardman.

Greene, Edith. 1999. "The Many Guises of Victim Impact Evidence and Effects on Jurors' Judgments." *Psychology, Crime and the Law* 5:331–48.

Gregg v. Georgia. 1976. 428 U.S. 153.

Humphries v. Ozmint. 2005. 397 F.3d 206 (Fourth Circuit, en banc).

Karamanian, Susan L. 1998. "Victims' Rights and the Death-Sentenced Inmate: Some Observations and Thoughts." *St. Mary's Law Journal* 29:1025–35.

Liebman, James S. 2000. "The Overproduction of Death." *Columbia Law Review* 100:2030–156.

Little, Rory K. 1999. "The Federal Death Penalty: History and Some Thoughts About the Department of Justice's Role." *Fordham Urban Law Journal* 26:347–508.

Logan, Wayne A. 1999a. "Declaring Life at the Crossroads of Death: Victims' Anti-Death Penalty Views and Prosecutors' Charging Decisions." *Criminal Justice Ethics* 18:41–57.

_____. 1999b. "Through the Past Darkly: A Survey of the Uses and Abuses of Victim Impact Evidence in Capital Trials." *Arizona Law Review* 41:143–92.

_____. 2000a. "Opining on Death: Witness Sentence Recommendations in Capital Trials." *Boston College Law Review* 41:517–47.

_____. 2000b. "When Balance and Fairness Collide: An Argument for Execution Impact Evidence in Capital Trials." *University of Michigan Journal of Law Reform* 33:1–56.

Luginbuhl, James and Michael Burkhead. 1995. "Victim Impact Evidence in a Capital Trial: Encouraging Votes for Death." *American Journal of Criminal Justice* 20:1–16.

Lynch, Gerard E. 2002. "Prosecution: Prosecutorial Discretion." Pp. 1246–53 in *Encyclopedia of Crime and Justice, Second Edition*, vol. 3 edited by Joshua Dressler. New York, New York: Macmillan Reference USA.

McCleskey v. Kemp. 1987. 481 U.S. 279.

McDuff v. State. 1997. 939 S.W.2d 607 (Tex. Court of Criminal Appeals).

Payne v. Tennessee. 1991. 501 U.S. 808.

People v. Williams. 1998. 692 N.E.2d 1109 (Ill.).

Ring v. Arizona. 2002. 536 U.S. 584.

Simon, Jonathan and Christina Spaulding. 1999. "Tokens of Our Esteem: Aggravating Factors in the Era of Deregulated Death Penalties." Pp. 81–113 in *The Killing State: Capital Punishment in Law, Politics and Culture*, edited by Austin Sarat. New York, New York: Oxford University Press.

South Carolina v. Gathers. 1989. 490 U.S. 805.

State v. Basile. 1997. 942 S.W.2d 342 (Mo.).

State v. Clay. 1998. 975 S.W.2d 121 (Mo.).

State v. Deck. 2004. 136 S.W.3d 481 (Mo.).

State v. Hill. 1998. 501 S.E.2d 122 (S.C.).

State v. Maxwell. 1994. 647 So. 2d 871 (Fla. District Court of Appeals).

State v. Nesbit. 1998. 978 S.W.2d 872 (Tenn.).

State v. Whitehead. 1999. 777 So.2d 781 (Ala. Court of Criminal Appeals).

State v. Worthington. 1999. 8 S.W.3d 83 (Mo.).

Steiker, Carol S. and Jordan M. Steiker. 1995. "Sober Second Thoughts: Reflections on Two Decades of Constitutional Regulation of Capital Punishment." *Harvard Law Review* 109:355–438.

Sundby, Scott E. 2003. "The Capital Jury and Empathy: The Problem of Worthy and Unworthy Victims." *Cornell Law Review* 88:343–81.

Tobolowsky, Peggy M. 2001. *Crime Victim Rights and Remedies.* North Carolina: Carolina Academic Press.

Turow, Scott. 2003. *Ultimate Punishment.* New York: Farrar, Straus, and Giroux.

United States v. Jones. 1999. 527 U.S. 373.

Witter v. State. 1996. 921 P.2d 886 (Nev.).

Wood v. State. 1998. 959 P.2d 1 (Okla. Court of Criminal Appeals).

CHAPTER 11

Extinguishing the Victims' Payne or Acquiescing to the "Demon of Error": Confronting the Role of Victims in Capital Clemency Proceedings

Charles S. Lanier* *and*
Beau Breslin

"Clemency is deeply rooted in our Anglo-American tradition of law, and is the historic remedy for preventing miscarriages of justice where judicial process has been exhausted."—*Herrera v. Collins* (1993:411–12)

"George Ryan has severed the bond of trust between those who hold great power on behalf of the people and the people themselves.... [H]e may have irreparably injured the law itself.... He has certainly committed a great wrong against the victims, and he has profoundly insulted his subordinates in the system—the state's attorneys, the police officers, the jurors and judges—with his pen and his reckless language."—Whitworth (2003, as cited in Boger (2004:1281))

---

* The authors would like to thank the editors of this volume for their helpful comments on an earlier draft; thanks also to Todd R. Engwer, who assisted with the research on Governor Ryan and the fallout from his clemency decision.

Introduction

In the wake of Governor George Ryan's 2003 blanket commutation of all 167 prisoners on death row in Illinois—because, as he put it, "[o]ur capital system is haunted by the demon of error" (Ryan 2003)—public scrutiny, as well as outrage, centered on the power of executive clemency. At the center of this firestorm were the families of the victims. For many family members involved in this ordeal, Ryan's announcement was most unwelcome. Indeed, it was accompanied by a sense of betrayal that their pleas to look at each case individually, and to respect the wishes of those who seek closure through execution, mostly were unheard (see, e.g., Wagner, this volume). This chapter takes its point of departure from the numerous reports suggesting that surviving family members in Illinois felt "twice betrayed" and "cheated" by Governor Ryan's actions.

Providing a voice for victims at clemency hearings is analogous to the voice given them by the Supreme Court, in *Payne v. Tennessee* (1991), at a capital sentencing hearing. That is, it appears to be another type of "victim impact statement" (VIS), a declaration by a victim that details how a violent crime has affected his or her life. The appropriateness of such statements and testimony at the penalty phase has received wide attention in the scholarly literature. Accordingly, we review relevant scholarship, including the Court's discordant decisions on VIS at a capital sentencing (*Booth v. Maryland* 1987; *South Carolina v. Gathers* 1989; *Payne* 1991), as a backdrop for our chapter.

At the outset we should acknowledge that our aim is not to draw normative conclusions about the similarities between victim impact evidence (VIE)[1] during the sentencing phase of a capital trial, and the testimony of victims' families during the clemency process. These two parts of capital cases have different purposes. The goals that drive capital sentencing, for example, typically involve retribution, incapacitation, and deterrence. The objectives of the clemency process, on the other hand, are somewhat different—insuring reliability, equity, mercy, and/or redemption. Our goal, then, is to address only whether the emotional, gut-wrenching aspect of victim involvement taints the clemency process in such a way that a "just outcome" eludes the system.

Drawing initially on the literature considering the role of VIE in capital sentencing, we ask whether a "just outcome" can only be reached by looking

---

1. The terms "victim impact statement" (VIS) and "victim impact evidence" (VIE) are used interchangeably in this chapter.

through the eyes of a murdered person's surviving family members. Put differently, do some elected officials face a Hobson's choice between cleansing the death penalty of error, and/or allowing the pain and anguish of surviving family members to govern grants of clemency? In exploring the appropriateness of providing surviving family members a decisive voice in the clemency process, we consider whether the pain of a victim's surviving family members should dictate the outcome of the search for justice, or whether their participation should be dampened or even extinguished at this terminal stage of a capital proceeding.

The Role of Co-Victims in the Sentencing Phase

In late 1987 Mary Zvolanek took the stand in the capital trial of Pervis Tyrone Payne, a Tennessee man found guilty of murdering Ms. Zvolanek's twenty-eight-year-old daughter Charisse, and her two-year-old granddaughter Lacie. Her role in the case was both simple and horrifying—she was asked to speak about the impact of the loss on her surviving grandson, three-year-old Nicholas. Ms. Zvolanek spoke movingly of Nicholas crying for his mom, of the young boy who still "worr[ied] about [his] Lacie" (*Payne v. Tennessee* 1991:816), and of the devastation felt by Nicholas whenever he recalled his mother and sister. It was powerful testimony, and, in the end, this emotional narrative likely contributed significantly to the jury returning a sentence of death.

Yet Payne's death sentence was not the only one affected by Ms. Zvolanek's moving testimony: her words—or perhaps more accurately, her involvement in the case—would eventually became the centerpiece of a renewed constitutional challenge to victim impact evidence in capital trials. Just four years earlier, in *Booth v. Maryland* (1987), a narrow majority of the U.S. Supreme Court concluded that "victim impact evidence"—i.e., information "describ[ing] the personal characteristics of the victims and the emotional impact of the crimes on the family" (p. 502)—was "irrelevant to a capital sentencing decision, and that its admission creates a constitutionally unacceptable risk that the jury may impose the death penalty in an arbitrary and capricious manner" (p. 503), in violation of the Eighth Amendment.

Two years later, in *South Carolina v. Gathers* (1989) the Court extended the ruling in *Booth* to statements made by a prosecutor to a capital sentencing jury. In *Gathers*, the prosecutor "read to the jury at length from the religious tract the victim was carrying and commented on the personal qualities" (p. 811) of the victim that he inferred from the papers. The Court ruled that because "the content of the various papers the victim happened to be carrying when he was attacked was purely fortuitous and cannot provide any information relevant to the defendant's moral culpability" (p. 812), their introduction at sentencing was unconstitutional.

By 1991, though, when *Payne v. Tennessee* reached the High Court, a new majority of justices emerged. Victim impact evidence of the kind presented by Mary Zvolanek would now be constitutionally admissible. Writing for a six-member majority, Chief Justice Rehnquist quoted Justice White's dissent in *Booth* to show that "the State has a legitimate interest in counteracting the mitigating evidence which the defendant is entitled to put in, by reminding the sentencer that just as the murderer should be considered as an individual, so too the victim is an individual whose death represents a unique loss to society and in particular to his family" (p. 825). Thus, as the Court overruled *Booth* and *Gathers*, Rehnquist could rationalize that "there is nothing unfair about allowing the jury to bear in mind that harm [to the victim's family] at the same time it considers the mitigating evidence introduced by the defendant" (p. 826). The Eighth Amendment, in other words, does not bar the state from introducing evidence directly from the victim's family that might successfully balance the impact of the defendant's mitigating testimony.

Rehnquist's stance centered on a particular view of what evidence ought to contribute to a jury's deliberation about death. In *Booth* and *Gathers*, the Court seemingly favored a narrow interpretation where "the only evidence that is relevant for a jury to consider during the sentencing phase of a capital trial is the evidence that directly relates to the blameworthiness of the defendant" (Teuber 2000:5). *Payne*, on the other hand, expanded the range of the jury's prerogative, insisting that "the assessment of harm caused by the defendant as a result of the crime charged has understandably been an important concern of the criminal law, both in determining the elements of the offense and in determining the appropriate punishment" (p. 819). Introducing victim impact evidence might carry some risk, Rehnquist admitted, but the specific safeguards of the Fourteenth Amendment's Due Process Clause would balance those concerns. Thus, in expanding the jury's deliberative range, the majority of the Supreme Court announced a dramatic shift in the importance of victim impact evidence in capital trials. The principle that the physical and emotional effect on victims of violent crime ought to be included in a jury's deliberation clearly outweighed the potential for bias that such information carries.

The Court's decision to allow victim impact evidence represented a sharp blow to the abolitionist forces. Many who opposed capital punishment viewed both *Booth* and *Gathers* as critical cases in the quest to reduce the number of

death sentences in America. In contrast, members of the victims' rights movement hailed the decision in *Payne* as a great victory since the justice system
would now include victims' families in the process. The movement, born
largely in the 1960s and 1970s in response to the perception that the criminal
justice system was marginalizing victims,[2] reacted favorably to the Court's majority opinion by insisting that states willing to impose the death penalty
(re)introduce the practice of admitting victim impact evidence. Advocates of
victims' rights called on governors and state legislatures to pass measures
aimed at providing victims with a voice, and at the same time urged prosecutors to rely heavily on family members of murder victims when seeking the
harshest possible punishment. Their strategy worked. Today, the federal government and thirty-three of the thirty-six states that authorize capital punishment allow some form of victim impact evidence in capital trials (Blume
2003; Logan 1999; Logan, this volume).[3]

Despite the widespread use of victim impact evidence, disparities exist in
specific measures (Dugger 1996). Some statutes permit victim impact testimony
only at pre-sentencing, while others allow the evidence as part of the actual
penalty trial of capital cases. Still others only permit statements in written form.
In *Payne*, the Court refused to provide detailed guidelines to the states, prefer-
ring instead to define what constitutes a victim impact statement in the most
general, sweeping terms. The justices articulated a simple rule—that victim impact evidence not be so "unduly prejudicial that it renders the trial fundamentally unfair" (p. 825). The Court refused to speculate on which aspects of the
testimony might be considered unduly prejudicial. Not surprisingly, the majority similarly avoided speculation on the most appropriate procedural model
for admitting victim impact evidence. Accordingly, the responsibility for craft-
ing the procedural details of victim impact evidence fell directly to the states.

After states began to craft rules for victim impact evidence in the wake of
Payne, critics of the practice raised serious concerns (see, e.g., Blume 2003;

---

2. Although victims of crime had long insisted on a greater voice in the criminal justice system, it was not until the U.S. Congress passed a series of laws—the Victim and Witness Protection Act of 1982, the Comprehensive Crime Control Act of 1984, and the Crime
Control Act of 1990—that the movement gained significant momentum. These statutes
provided services to victims, ranging from federal funding for direct compensation to victims to greater opportunities for victims to participate more meaningfully in the judicial
process. Presently, it should be noted that a constitutional amendment protecting the rights
of victims sits in Congress.

3. Thirty-one states and the federal government place no restrictions on the admissibility of victim impact evidence, while two states—Indiana and Mississippi—allow victim impact evidence only in limited circumstances.

Long 1995; Myers and Greene 2004; Sullivan 1998). Logan (1999; see also this volume) summarized many of the concerns about using VIS in the capital sentencing context. First, few states accepted the Court's implicit invitation to introduce "procedural controls" on the presentation of victim impact evidence. A handful of states—among them, Oklahoma, Georgia, and Tennessee—insist that the prosecution notify the defendant of its plan to present victim impact statements at trial. New Jersey permits testimony from only one family member, and only after the details, written in advance, have been vetted by the court. Logan additionally notes that the definition of who qualifies as a victim is ambiguous. In most states, "as a result of [a] broad conceptualization [of the term victim], family, friends, neighbors, and even co-workers all regularly provide impact evidence" (1999:155). Finally, there are "enduring questions" about "the purpose and function of victim impact evidence" (p. 171), and "the timing of the admission of victim impact evidence" (p. 172). The result is a situation, brought on by the decision in *Payne*, in which no court can be sure that prejudicial statements against the defendant will be eradicated.[4]

Logan (2000) offers three reasons why VIS should be barred at capital sentencing hearings: 1) "The first, and most fundamental, reason in support of the prohibition of sentence opinion testimony is its distinct irrelevance to capital decision making" (p. 539); 2) "A related but distinct reason to bar sentence opinion testimony is its arbitrary quality" (p. 540); 3) "A final concern [is] that opinion testimony not merely distracts the sentencing authority from its constitutional duty to weigh only relevant factors, but actually usurps its fundamental mission" (p. 544). As the author warns: "Indeed, the emotionalism sanctioned by *Payne* in particular makes it all the more crucial that the law be vigilant in its effort to preserve what remains of the 'reasoned moral response' once thought intrinsic to death decision making" (pp. 546–47).

Leaping forward to consider the role of victims in clemency proceedings, it seems clear that the same concerns, regarding the prejudicial nature of highly emotional testimony, would surface again. In other words, the same emotional forces and community pressures involved in using VIS at capital sentencing proceedings may exist in the context of clemency decision making. That is, inflammatory, emotion-laden sentiments expressed by family mem-

---

4. One author suggests that, "victim impact statements appeal to hatred, the desire for undifferentiated vengeance, and even bigotry" (Bandes 1996:365), while another warns that "[t]he admission of victim impact evidence in capital sentencing hearings, while a politically popular idea, risks the imposition of the death penalty according to the perceived 'social worth' of the victim" (Phillips 1997:118).

bers to an Executive, or other clemency-granting entity, likewise possess the potential to unfairly prejudice the outcome. Such undue influence might be even more likely in the clemency context, because politicians are frequently susceptible to pressures that judges are not (see, e.g., Korengold, Noteboom, and Gurwitch 1996; Love 2000; Palacios 1996). Thus, affording surviving family members a central role at the clemency stage is analogous to using similarly powerful and emotional testimony at the capital sentencing trial, despite real differences in the goals of each process.

The Role of Co-Victims in the Clemency Phase

Clemency Defined

Clemency broadly refers to "an act of mercy exercised at the discretion of the Executive—a state governor or pardons board or, in the federal system, the president" (Lanier and Acker 2004; see also Kobil 1991; Moore 1989). In the capital context, clemency can take several forms, including reprieve,[5] commutation,[6] and pardon.[7] Governor Ryan granted both commutations and pardons in his sweeping 2003 decision that effectively emptied death row in Illinois.

Some form of clemency is authorized in all death-penalty jurisdictions in the United States.[8] However, the actual granting authority differs by venue (see, e.g., Acker and Lanier 2000:216–20). For instance, the Constitution grants the President clemency power in cases within federal jurisdiction. While

---

5. "Reprieve is the most limited type of clemency and thus is most apt to be invoked in capital cases. It refers to the temporary postponement of punishment. A reprieve simply stays execution of the death sentence for a specified period of time. Typically, a reprieve is used to give the prisoner an opportunity to complete pending appeals or to allow the Governor to examine last-minute allegations that raise doubt about guilt" (Kobil 1991:674).

6. "Commutation is a broader form of clemency that consists of the substitution of a milder punishment for the one imposed by the court. Commutations are occasionally granted in capital cases to mitigate the death sentence and impose instead a sentence of life imprisonment, usually without possibility of parole" (ibid.).

7. "[A] pardon is the most expansive form of clemency. A pardon effectively erases both the crime and the punishment originally imposed on the prisoner; if granted, it would allow a capitally sentenced prisoner to walk freely off of death row and back into society" (ibid.).

8. "Although the structure of clemency decision-making authority varies by state, every state that presently uses the death penalty has either constitutional or statutory provisions for clemency" (Heise 2003:255).

such power "largely mimics its federal counterpart" by being invested in governors at the state level (Heise 2003:255), two variants exist: some states "assign clemency decision-making power to administrative boards," and still others "seek to capture the benefits flowing from both the executive and administrative models through a third variation: a hybrid blend of the two" (ibid.). Not surprisingly, the procedures through which clemency decisions are made also differ greatly by jurisdiction (Acker and Lanier 2000:220–29).

The Supreme Court has frequently acknowledged the importance of an Executive's power to grant clemency in cases where a person has been sentenced to death. For example, Justice Stewart's plurality opinion in *Gregg v. Georgia* (1976) declared that a system of capital justice in which "acts of executive clemency would have to be prohibited … of course, would be totally alien to our notions of criminal justice" (p. 199, n. 50). Further, as Kobil (2003:681) notes, Justice White's dissenting opinion in *Roberts v. Louisiana* (1976) "considered it 'reasonable to expect the [clemency] power to be exercised by the Executive Branch whenever' a person is unjustly convicted and sentenced to death."

Almost two decades later in *Herrera v. Collins* (1993), a case from Texas involving a claim of innocence, the Court once again observed the important role played by clemency in the American death-penalty system. In its decision the Court relied partly on the availability of a "clemency mechanism" to underpin its rationale for denying Herrera's request for judicial relief. As Chief Justice Rehnquist wrote for the majority, "Today, all 36 States that authorize capital punishment have constitutional or statutory provisions for clemency" (p. 414) (footnote omitted). As such, the Court reassuringly continued, "[e]xecutive clemency has provided the 'fail safe' in our criminal justice system" (p. 415). The *Herrera* majority presumed that meritorious claims of innocence, if not addressed by the courts, would be cured by grants of mercy dispensed by the jurisdiction's clemency-granting authority.[9]

Several years later, a death-row prisoner in Ohio by the name of Eugene Woodard challenged that state's clemency procedure as being unconstitutional (*Ohio Adult Parole Authority v. Woodard* 1998). He claimed, in part, that the Ohio executive clemency scheme forced him to admit involvement in the

---

9. Nevertheless, Justice Blackmun, uncomfortable with the Court's reliance on the "fail safe" of clemency to identify and prevent those men and women who actually were innocent from being executed, wrote in dissent: "The possibility of executive clemency is *not* sufficient to satisfy the requirements of the Eighth and Fourteenth Amendments" (p. 439). He declared further that "[t]he execution of a person who can show that he is innocent comes perilously close to simple murder" (p. 446).

crime, thereby compelling him to "incriminate himself"[10] (1998:285). However, the Court concluded that, "Ohio's clemency procedures do not violate due process" (p. 282). Chief Justice Rehnquist observed more particularly that the "pressure to speak in the hope of improving the chance of being granted clemency does not make the interview compelled. We therefore hold that the Ohio clemency interview ... does not violate the Fifth Amendment privilege against compelled self-incrimination" (p. 288). In language that appears somewhat offensive to the "fail safe" role articulated in *Herrera*, though, the Court also observed that: "[a] death-row inmate's petition for clemency is ... a 'unilateral hope'" (p. 282).

Nevertheless, it appears well established through these and other decisions of the High Court[11] that executive clemency in death-penalty cases is a legitimate, and perhaps integral, part of the administration of capital punishment in America. Yet, some have criticized the clemency process as producing "outcomes that correlate with race, ethnicity, gender, and other constitutionally impermissible or suspect factors"[12] (Lanier and Acker 2004:587). Moreover, with the notable exception of Governor Ryan's action in Illinois, grants of clemency remain fairly infrequent in the post-*Furman* era (Burnett 2002; Klasmeier 1995; Korengold et al. 1996; Ledewitz and Staples 1993; Radelet and Zsembik 1993). As some have observed: "The relative dearth of commutations in capital cases in recent times, doubtlessly attributable in substantial part to the perceived political risks associated with taking such action amidst a climate of popular support for the death penalty, does not bode well for those who continue to look to executive clemency as a corrective mechanism for the rough edges and potential injustices associated with contemporary death-penalty systems" (Acker and Lanier 2000:215–16) (footnotes omitted).

For instance, at the time of the Court's decision in *Herrera*, January 25, 1993, only twenty-nine death-sentenced prisoners in the United States had re-

---

10. Chief Justice Rehnquist explained in the Court's decision: "Because there is only one guaranteed clemency review, respondent asserts, his decision to participate is not truly voluntary. And in the interview he may be forced to answer questions; or, if he remains silent, his silence may be used against him. Respondent further asserts there is a substantial risk of incrimination since postconviction proceedings are in progress and since he could potentially incriminate himself on other crimes. Respondent therefore concludes that the interview unconstitutionally conditions his assertion of the right to pursue clemency on his waiver of the right to remain silent" (pp. 285–86).

11. See, e.g., *Ford v. Wainwright* (1986:432), citing *Solesbee v. Balkcom* (1950); *Thompson v. Oklahoma* (1986).

12. See, e.g., Marquart et al. 1994:116–19; Pridemore 2000; Vandiver 1993; Wolfgang et al. 1962.

ceived clemency since *Gregg* authorized the reimposition of capital punishment in 1976.[13] Excluding Ryan's 167 commutations, there have been sixty-one grants of clemency in capital cases through early 2005. Although perhaps of little comfort to those surviving family members in Illinois who felt "re-victimized" by Governor Ryan's clemency decision, as observed above, it remains the case that "clemency in a capital case is extremely rare" (Radelet and Zsembik 1993:304).

Notwithstanding the infrequent use of capital clemency in the United States, and the certainty that almost all commuted death-sentenced prisoners will never go free, the potential for a condemned killer to escape execution at the hands of an Executive unsettles many surviving family members. This was true in Illinois, where many surviving family members met on several occasions with Governor Ryan, and felt assured that all cases would receive individual scrutiny—regardless of the overall infirmities affecting the state's system of capital punishment (Keilman 2003; Mills 2002b; Parsons and Mills 2002a, 2002b). As the clemency process in Illinois unfolded, the active participation of surviving family members may have raised their expectations and thus magnified their eventual disappointment.

Capital Clemency in Illinois

The recognition that more people "wrongfully convicted" were released from Illinois death row (thirteen) than had been executed (twelve) spurred Governor Ryan to issue a moratorium on executions effective January 31, 2000. An investigative series in the *Chicago Tribune* by two staff writers was key to stirring interest in the failures of the Illinois system of capital justice (Armstrong and Mills 1999). Several high-profile exonerations, including that of the men convicted of the kidnapping, rape, and murder of ten-year-old Jeanine Nicarico (Frisbie and Garrett 1998; Turow 2003), also underpinned the discomfort of the Governor and citizens alike. Governor Ryan thus declared a halt to executions, and ordered a study of "questions related to the imposition of capital punishment in Illinois" (Commission on Capital Punishment 2002:1).

He appointed a Commission, whose membership included prominent individuals from the state's legal and political communities, to examine the condition of capital punishment in Illinois. The Commission began its work

---

13. After it had ruled the death penalty unconstitutional in 1972 in *Furman v. Georgia*, the Supreme Court subsequently opined that capital punishment was constitutional in a series of 1976 decisions known as *Gregg* and its companion cases (*Gregg v. Georgia, Jurek v. Texas, Proffitt v. Florida, Roberts v. Louisiana,* and *Woodson v. North Carolina*).

shortly after the inception of the moratorium, and it reported back to the Governor in April 2002. The report made eighty-five recommendations concerning the investigation and prosecution of cases in Illinois. The Commission suggested only the following change when it came to clemency: "Illinois law should provide that after all appeals have been exhausted and the Attorney General applies for a final execution date for the defendant, a clemency petition may not be filed later than 30 days after the date that the Illinois Supreme Court enters an order setting an execution date" (Commission on Capital Punishment 2002:173).

Critically, though, the Commission concluded its report with the following declaration:

> Although the Commission has not made a specific recommendation with respect to the application of its recommendations to pending cases, Commission members believe the Governor should give consideration to the proposed reforms when considering clemency applications in capital cases. If changes in the present system are required to ensure its fairness and accuracy, it is entirely appropriate to consider how those changes might have made a difference to defendants when reaching determinations about whether or not a death sentence should be upheld on the merits or whether mercy should be extended in light of all the circumstances (Commission on Capital Punishment 2002:207).

Perhaps spurred by this conclusion, the Illinois Prisoner Review Board initiated a series of public hearings on clemency for the state's death-row prisoners, beginning in October 2002—six months after the Commission handed in its report to the Governor. The "unprecedented series of clemency hearings" brought "prosecutors, victims' families, and defense lawyers for Death Row inmates" (Parsons and Mills 2002a) together in a forum that was destined, in the eyes of many, to open old wounds, and perhaps further traumatize surviving family members. In fact, Richard Devine, the State's Attorney for Cook County, openly exhorted the Governor "to spare the victims' families and cancel the proceedings if he has already decided to grant a blanket commutation" (Mills 2002a). Not only did the hearings go forward, but Governor Ryan met with surviving family members on several separate occasions as he wrestled with his momentous decision.

Just before Christmas, the Governor pardoned three men who previously had been released from death row after they had been exonerated: Rolando Cruz, Gary Gauger, and Steven Linscott (Frisbie and Garrett 1998; Mills and Long 2002). On January 10, 2003, the Governor issued four additional pardons for men who he stated had been tortured into confessing to murder and subsequently sentenced to die in Illinois: Madison Hobley, Stanley Howard,

Aaron Patterson, and Leroy Orange (Mills and Parsons 2003). The following day, with just three days left in his term, Ryan used a speech at the Northwestern University College of Law to announce his blanket commutation of all remaining men on death row. In memorable language, he told the world: "I must act. Our capital system is haunted by the demon of error, error in determining guilt, and error in determining who among the guilty deserves to die. Because of all of these reasons today I am commuting the sentences of all death row inmates" (Ryan 2003). At day's end, through action that represented a betrayal to many surviving family members, no person was living under a sentence of death in Illinois.

Article 5, section 12 of the Illinois Constitution authorizes the Governor to commute the sentences of prisoners, including those on death row: "The Governor may grant reprieves, commutations and pardons, after conviction, for all offenses on such terms as he thinks proper." Rejecting a challenge to Ryan's grant of "blanket clemency," the Supreme Court of Illinois affirmed that the Governor was authorized to grant reprieves and commutations (*People ex rel. Madigan v. Snyder* 2004). At the same time, the court appeared to caution against the indiscriminate use of the clemency powers.[14]

Governor Ryan's decision to empty the Illinois death row may have been a response to the State Assembly's failure to act on his package of death penalty reforms. One observer noted: "Since the legislature showed no signs of cooperating with the Governor in making changes to Illinois' administration of the death penalty, the Governor announced he was considering a blanket commutation for every person on death row. His announcement appeared to be in hopes of encouraging the General Assembly to pass the reforms the Commission recommended" (Rupcich 2003:143, footnote omitted).

Firestorm over Ryan's Decision

Governor Ryan's decision to empty the Illinois death row of its entire population meant different things to different people. Some in Illinois and

---

14. "As a final matter, we note that clemency is the historic remedy employed to prevent a miscarriage of justice where the judicial process has been exhausted.... We believe that this is the purpose for which the framers gave the Governor this power in the Illinois Constitution. The grant of this essentially unreviewable power carries with it the responsibility to exercise it in the manner intended. Our hope is that Governors will use the clemency power in its intended manner—to prevent miscarriages of justice in individual cases" (p. 480; citation omitted). Others suggested that a variety of concrete actions and changes in the Illinois "clemency scheme" were in order to "... reduce the possibility of abuse in the future" (Rupcich 2003:131).

around the country hailed the decision as representing the single greatest blow to the future of capital punishment since the landmark decision of *Furman v. Georgia* (1972). Others, particularly in his home state, viewed the blanket commutations as irresponsible, bordering on immoral. Ryan became a hero to many around the world for his opposition to capital punishment, but he also was vilified for what many saw as an unprincipled, insensitive decision.

Caught in the middle of the firestorm over Ryan's commutation were the heartbroken relatives whose intimate connection to the victims of these offenders made the Governor's decision particularly painful. Consider the words of Vern Fueling, whose child was killed in 1985 by one of the death-row inmates: "[M]y son is in the ground for 17 years and justice is not done ... [The decision] is a mockery" (Davey and Mills 2003). Or Crystal Finch, whose sister was killed in 1994 by Anthony Brown, another death-row inmate who benefited from Ryan's executive decision: "Ryan lied, he's a liar and a coward. Now Anthony Brown is going to live off of my tax money" (Sadovi 2003). Or, finally, Sam Evans and Katy Salhani, father and sister of Debra Evans, who, while nine months pregnant, was murdered by a couple who pulled the unborn baby from Debra's womb so they could call the child their own: "I have nothing to say to Governor Ryan. I have nothing but contempt and disgust for a man who abused the powers that the State of Illinois granted him. He spit in our faces" (United Press International 2003).

These sentiments are representative of the negative emotions that accompanied Ryan's unprecedented decision. The media's portrayal of the pain suffered by victims' families centered on their anguish over having to revisit the events that led to capital convictions in the first place, and anger over the betrayal by a chief executive who provided distinctly mixed messages to a constituency that overwhelmingly wanted to hear just one.

According to published reports, most relatives who felt compelled to tell their story were racked by grief at the prospect of reliving the loss of their beloved family member. One member of a victim's family said that the discussion about clemency "is making it worse. It's reopening the wounds I didn't want reopened" (Kelly 2002). Ryan's initial decision to consider the possibility of granting clemency to certain individuals on death row, and then inviting family members of the victims to testify, resulted in secondary victimization, the feeling on the part of victims that they are both powerless to change the past and constantly reminded of it by the institutions with the responsibility for protecting them. In his capacity as Governor, Ryan represented numerous official institutions to relatives of the victims. But most significantly, he failed to provide the safety typically associated with his power as Chief Executive.

Relatives of the victims were quick to point out that Ryan made implicit, and in some cases even explicit, promises to them. Specifically, a number of family members recall that the Governor insisted, in a series of meetings held across the state, that he would evaluate each case independently and make separate determinations about individual grants of clemency. The message to these family members, of course, was that Ryan would never completely empty the state's death row; some murderers, like the killers of Debra Evans, would continue to face execution. That obviously did not happen, and thus what emerged was a general consensus among family members that they had been deceived. Governor Ryan even implicitly acknowledged the betrayal, admitting that he " 'probably misled' victims' families by vacillating on the question of whether to commute all or just some of the death sentences to life in prison without the possibility of parole" (Daly 2003).

That sense of betrayal even extended to many who had no familial relationship to the victims. A number of key state political leaders weighed in on the appropriateness of the blanket grant of clemency. Incoming Governor Rod Blagojevich, for example, called Ryan's decision a "gross injustice" and a "terrible" mistake. Cook County State Attorney Richard Devine, who, as head of one of the country's largest prosecutor's offices had a professional stake in Governor Ryan's decision, called the blanket clemency "outrageous" and "unconscionable." He elaborated: "I am sure that the governor expects that the acts of pardon and clemency ... will be long remembered—and they will be," he said. "They will be remembered among the most irresponsible decisions ever taken by a state's chief executive. They will be remembered as decisions that fly in the face of statements the governor made to the families of the victims that he would review these cases on an individual basis and decide them on the merits of each case" (Guerrero 2003).

Discussion

The present system of capital clemency appears to favor a more "popular" rather than a more "just" outcome. For some victims "justice" requires that a killer be put to death as prescribed by the State. Only the demise of the condemned would satisfy their heartfelt anguish. In their eyes, an unjust outcome would occur if they were forced to "suffer further" because the condemned killer was spared execution—regardless of whether the system itself was unjust. If their pain—articulated in the form of an ardent and moving plea to an Executive—supersedes a "just" outcome, then that is how justice must be delivered to surviving family members.

Understandably, such powerfully emotional evidence and testimony may have more of a persuasive effect on an elected official than on a capital juror (see, e.g., Bright 2003; Love 2000). In short, impassioned pleas and political considerations threaten to eclipse other issues in determining the fate of a person facing imminent execution. Thus, it may be okay if some condemned men and women go to their deaths, in spite of an inequitable capital punishment system, in large part because the agonizing, highly personal testimony of surviving family members may taint the clemency process.

Importantly, Governor Ryan was acutely aware of the challenges posed by the Illinois system of capital punishment. He had been dealing with it for years as Governor, and he even presided over an execution. On March 17, 1999, only about a month after assuming office, Governor Ryan confronted an upcoming scheduled execution. After a short investigation, he signed a death warrant, and thirty-five-year-old Andrew Kokoraleis was lethally injected.[15] In addition to his direct experiences, the Governor had the advice and recommendations of the Illinois Commission on Capital Punishment before making his 2003 clemency decision. As such, he must have understood the considerable slippage between the constitutional principles governing capital punishment and their application in practice.

One observer commented on Ryan's commutation decision:

> Some might view the commutation as an act of grace wholly outside the field of justice. But Governor Ryan surely had some notion of justice in mind—in effect, he thought the death sentences he was commuting had been unjust, if not technically illegal. Critics of his action might therefore view his act of mercy as violating justice by invoking the wrong legal principles or exercising unwarranted legal authority.... But the commutation might also be viewed as a very distinct type of mercy, though one with a certain pedigree in American death penalty law. That is, it can be seen as an apology for systemic injustice (Weisberg 2004:1439–440).

It appears from Governor Ryan's statement announcing his clemency decision that he was guided by the latter principle—that in his opinion the "demon of error" had so thoroughly defiled the Illinois system of capital punishment that justice required his decisive action.

---

15. "Well, in the end, I ultimately sat in judgment of Anthony Kokoraleis, and signed his death warrant, and he was executed. And that's what really started to bother me. It's a gnawing that I've still got with me, [it] still bothers me that I executed this man. And so that's when I decided that I should take a little harder look" (Ryan 2004:1724).

Such knowledge may have buttressed Governor Ryan against the pressures of hearing testimony from surviving family members during the clemency hearings. As noted above, the emotionalism and inflamed passions that can erupt during such proceedings have the potential to prejudice the outcome— whether it occurs before twelve jurors or a single Chief Executive. Some have even argued that VIS at a capital trial is so potentially prejudicial that a constitutional amendment is necessary in order to protect the integrity of the proceedings (Sullivan 1998:636). Whatever remediation may be in order, it must be recognized that the pain of surviving family members has the potential to emasculate the dictates of the Court when it demanded, in *California v. Brown* (1987), a "reasoned *moral* response" (p. 545) in cases of capital punishment.[16]

A personal reflection of Judge Alex Kozinski speaks to this danger: "Whatever qualms I had about the efficacy or the morality of the death penalty were drowned out by the pitiful cries of the victims screaming from between the lines of dry legal prose" (Bedau and Cassell 2004:2). In the context of clemency decisions, hearing the horror of a capital crime announced painfully by some surviving family members may abrogate any humanitarian or legal considerations in the dispensation of justice by an Executive. Matters like coerced confessions, incompetent counsel, prosecutorial misconduct, racial discrimination, and other defects in the administration of the capital sanction all may recede in importance to an emotionally powerful presentation by articulate, grieving, and passionate surviving family members. As such, "the tortured voices of the victims crying out ... for vindication" (Bedau and Cassell 2004:14) may trump both rational decision making by the Executive, as well as the right of due process guaranteed to all under the U.S. Constitution.

Conclusion

Some have argued that there should be few restrictions on the absolute power of a jurisdiction's Executive to grant clemency in capital cases (Breslin and Howley 2002). Others have argued that life-and-death decisions at the terminal stage of a capital proceeding should be guided by the dictates of due process (Acker and Lanier 2000; Kobil 2003; Lim 1994). Still others advocate allowing the testimony of offenders' family members regarding the im-

---

16. "Indeed, the emotionalism sanctioned by *Payne* in particular makes it all the more crucial that the law be vigilant in its effort to preserve what remains of the 'reasoned moral response' once thought intrinsic to death decision making" (Logan 2000:546–47).

pact on them of a loved one's execution (King and Norgard 1999; Logan 1999/2000; Thomas 2000). However the personnel and procedures evolve in the future, it seems clear that executive clemency in capital cases will remain a part of the constitutional landscape. What, then, might alleviate some of the anguish that inevitably will accompany such decisions in the future? Is there a remedial approach that might help temper the pain felt by surviving family members?

Some have attributed the active participation of surviving family members in capital cases to the rise of the victims' rights movement in America (King and Norgard 1999; Logan 1999; Sullivan 1998). For example, "Starting in the early 1970s, victims' advocates successfully made their case for an increased role for crime victims in the criminal justice process, and achieved rapid and widespread changes in state and federal law.... Perhaps most prominent and controversial among these measures was the advent of 'victim impact evidence' in criminal trials" (Logan 1999:144) (footnotes omitted). It seems likely that victims' proponents will continue to press for the active participation of surviving family members in capital proceedings at all levels.

However, serious consideration should be given to the emotional and psychological well-being of surviving family members of homicide victims. In the long run, their quality of life is more likely to benefit through services and direct assistance for coping with their grief. There are more constructive ways of confronting grief than holding out hope that a loved one's killer will be put to death by the State. In that vein, emphasis should be placed on policies and programs that constructively assist surviving family members in coping with the murder of a loved one. For example, counselors, and other professionals should embrace victims, both in the short and long term. It is not enough to offer assistance solely in the immediate aftermath of a tragedy. Moreover, survivors should not be compelled to live in an insular world—the community must be engaged in the healing process as well. A wide body of literature and clinical practice suggests lessons for confronting and overcoming grief (see, e.g., Attig 1996; Doka 1996; Sanders 1992), and the criminal justice system should make greater use of these strategies in the wake of a homicide.

One practitioner, writing from personal experience about the death of her own family members, observes, "We have choices over how we will survive our significant losses. We can choose to maintain a bitterly cynical viewpoint, remaining in the conservation/withdrawal phase of grief, or we can confront the lessons of grief, painful as they are, and treat them instead as opportunities for our growth" (Sanders 1992:193). The author suggests that by following the latter course "[w]e are capable of deeper, richer relationships, immeasurable compassion, and an extraordinary ability to open our arms to life and adventure" (p. 193). In short, learning to live again by transcending grief and triumphing over sorrow may be a more important objective for surviving family members than collaborating with the State to end another life. Nurturing grievously wounded family members back to life, rather than capitalizing on their pain to secure an execution, thus should be the priority of the justice system.

If the emotionally searing and perhaps ultimately prejudicial testimony of surviving family members is permitted at the clemency stage of a capital proceeding, then at a minimum its temperature should be lowered. For instance, testimony might be authorized in the form of a short statement, rather than an anguished presentation before the decision maker. The substance of the statement also might be restricted, as suggested by Sullivan (1998) in a discussion about the use of VIS at sentencing: "Under proper guidelines ... [it] should contain no more than a general description of the victim. Any statements dealing with social status, religion, and political beliefs should be prohibited because they serve no more than to capitalize upon the jury's emotions and preconceived ideals. Moreover, commentary about the victim's funeral, and gory, distasteful details or characterizations of the crime itself should be exempt on the grounds that such statements open the door to passion and prejudice" (p. 633).

The preceding review raises a question about the "appropriateness" or "inappropriateness" of providing surviving family members a decisive voice in the clemency process in the first place. Simply put, should the pain of a victim's surviving family members dictate the outcome of the search for justice, or should their participation be dampened or even extinguished at this terminal stage? As the process stands now, it appears that at times the search for justice is analogous to meeting the demands of the surviving family members. Consequently, any corruption or unequal application of the death penalty in practice—whether on an individual or systemic level—is depreciated in importance to the desires of the victims.

However, some suggest that the interests of a death-sentenced person may in fact coincide with those of the general public. Weisberg (2004) alluded to this above, with his comment that Ryan's mass clemency could be viewed as "an apology for systemic injustice" (p. 1440). In discussing his book on capital punishment, author William McFeely writes that " ... this is an account of a historian who suddenly found himself pulled out of history and into the reality of the law taking a person's life. Right in front of me, as a result of twenty minutes on the stand as a witness in a death penalty case, appeared what seemed to me a strand of the hatred that has done, and continues to do, great damage in the land" (2000:23). It thus seems prudent to acknowledge that sparing the life of a condemned killer actually may be in the best interest of society as a whole; that it might be an attempt to counter some of the damage rendered by an unhealthy capital punishment system.

It may be that "justice" can only be done for one group or the other: either some family members victimized by the murder of a loved one will have their execution, regardless of whether capital punishment is administered fairly and according to the dictates of due process, or some condemned killers will be spared execution to spend the rest of their lives in prison, because of the unsettling recognition that "justice" in the capital context cannot be achieved. If this is the case, then an Executive faced with such a decision must decide who best deserves Weisberg's "apology": Should killers obtain an apology for a system plagued by the "demon of error," or should family members receive redress for the grievous injury and trauma inflicted on them? Forced choices like these—where there is no fair and equitable outcome—ultimately may doom the capital sanction in America. In the interim, it may be that justice in the capital context must be dispensed either narrowly, to aggrieved family members, or more generously, to the body politic as a whole.

References

Acker, James R. and Charles S. Lanier. 2000. "May God—Or the Governor—Have Mercy: Executive Clemency and Executions in Modern Death-Penalty Systems." *Criminal Law Bulletin* 36:200–37.

Armstrong, Ken and Steve Mills. 1999. "Death Row Justice Derailed: Bias, Errors and Incompetence in Capital Cases Have Turned Illinois' Harshest Punishment into its Least Credible." Chicago Tribune, 14 November 1999, 1.

Attig, Thomas. 1996. *How We Grieve: Relearning the World.* New York/Oxford: Oxford University Press.

Bandes, Susan. 1996. "Empathy, Narrative, and Victim Impact Statements." *University of Chicago Law Review* 63:361–412.

Bedau, Hugo A. and Paul G. Cassell. 2004. *Debating the Death Penalty: Should America Have Capital Punishment? The Experts on Both Sides Make Their Best Case.* Oxford University Press.

Blume, John H. 2003. "Ten Years of Payne: Victim Impact Evidence in Capital Cases." *Cornell Law Review* 88:257–81.

Boger, John Charles. 2004. "Foreword: Acts of Capital Clemency: The Words and Deeds of Governor George Ryan." *North Carolina Law Review* 82:1279–95.

Booth v. Maryland. 1987. 482 U.S. 496.

Breslin, Beau and John J. P. Howley. 2002. "Defending the Politics of Clemency." *Oregon Law Review* 81:231–54.

Bright, Stephen B. 2003. "The Politics of Capital Punishment: The Sacrifice of Fairness for Executions." Pp. 127–46 in *America's Experiment With Capital Punish-*

ment: Reflections on the Past, Present, and Future of the Ultimate Penal Sanction (2d ed.), edited by James R. Acker, Robert M. Bohm, and Charles S. Lanier. Durham, NC: Carolina Academic Press.

Burnett, Cathleen. 2002. *Justice Denied: Clemency Appeals in Death Penalty Cases.* Boston, MA: Northeastern University Press.

California v. Brown. 1987. 479 U.S. 538.

Commission on Capital Punishment. 2002. "Report of the Commission on Capital Punishment April 2002." Illinois Commission on Capital Punishment. http://www.idoc.state.il.us/ccp/ccp/reports/commission_report/chapter_01.pdf (15 June 15 2005).

Comprehensive Crime Control Act of 1984 (Pub.L. 98-473, Title II, 12 October 1984, 98 Stat. 1976).

Constitution of the State of Illinois, Article 5, section 12.

Crime Control Act of 1990 (Pub.L. 101-647, 29 November 1990, 104 Stat. 4789).

Daly, Louise. 2003. "Celebrated by Many, Illinois Governor is Still Vilified at Home." *Agence France Presse,* 13 January 2003.

Davey, Monica and Steven Mills. 2003. "Illinois Governor Commutes State's Entire Death Row; Blanket Reprieve Follows Three-Year Study of Penalty." *Bergen Record,* 12 January 2003.

Doka, Kenneth J. (ed.). 1996. *Living with Grief after Sudden Loss: Suicide, Homicide, Accident, Heart Attack, Stroke.* Washington, DC: Hospice Foundation of America.

Dugger, Ashley Page. 1996. "Victim Impact Evidence in Capital Sentencing: A History of Incompatibility." *American Journal of Criminal Law* 23:375–404.

Ford v. Wainwright, 1986. 477 U.S. 399.

Frisbie, Thomas and Randy Garrett. 1998. *Victims of Justice: The True Story of Two Innocent Men Condemned to Die and a Prosecution out of Control.* New York: Avon Books.

Furman v. Georgia. 1972. 408 U.S. 238.

Gregg v. Georgia. 1976. 428 U.S. 153.

Guerrero, Lucio. 2003. "Prosecutors, Survivors Rip Ryan." *Chicago Sun Times,* 13 January, 2003.

Heise, Michael. 2003. "Mercy by the Numbers: An Empirical Analysis of Clemency and its Structure." *Virginia Law Review* 89:239–310.

Herrera v. Collins. 1993. 506 U.S. 390.

Jurek v. Texas. 1976. 428 U.S. 262.

Keilman, John. 2003. "Murder Victims' Families Feel Twice Betrayed by Ryan." *Chicago Tribune,* 12 January 2003, 17.

Kelly, Maura. 2002. "More Murder Victims' Families Meet with Governor on Clemency." *The Associated Press Wire,* 11 December 2002.

King, Rachel and Katherine Norgard. 1999. "What About our Families? Using the Impact on Death Row Defendants' Family Members as a Mitigating Factor in Death Penalty Sentencing Hearings." *Florida State University Law Review* 26:1119–73.

Klasmeier, Coleen E. 1995. "Towards a New Understanding of Capital Clemency and Procedural Due Process." *Boston University Law Review* 75:1507–39.

Kobil, D.T. 2003. "The Evolving Role of Clemency In Capital Cases." Pp. 673–92 in *America's Experiment With Capital Punishment: Reflections on the Past, Present, and Future of the Ultimate Penal Sanction* (2d ed.), edited by James R. Acker, Robert M. Bohm, and Charles S. Lanier. Durham, NC: Carolina Academic Press.

_____. 1991. "The Quality of Mercy Strained: Wresting the Pardoning Power from the King. *Texas Law Review* 69:569–641.

Korengold, Michael A. G., Todd A. Noteboom, and Sara Gurwitch. 1996. "And Justice for Few: The Collapse of the Capital Clemency System in the United States." *Hamline Law Review* 20:349–69.

Lanier, Charles S. and James R. Acker. 2004. "Capital Punishment, the Moratorium Movement, and Empirical Questions: Looking Beyond Innocence, Race, and Bad Lawyering in Death Penalty Cases." *Journal of Public Policy, Psychology, and the Law* 10, 4:577–614.

Ledewitz, Bruce and Scott Staples 1993. "The Role of Executive Clemency in Modern Death Penalty Cases." *University of Richmond Law Review* 27:227–39.

Lim, Daniel. 1994. "State Due Process Guarantees for Meaningful Death Penalty Clemency Proceedings." *Columbia Journal of Law and Social Problems* 28:47–82.

Logan, Wayne A. (This volume.)

_____. 2000. "Opining on Death: Witness Sentence Recommendations in Capital Trials." *Boston College Law Review* 41:517–47.

_____. 1999/2000. "When Balance and Fairness Collide: An Argument for Execution Impact Evidence in Capital Trials." *University of Michigan Journal of Law Reform* 33:1–55.

_____. 1999. "Through the Past Darkly: A Survey of the Uses and Abuses of Victim Impact Evidence in Capital Trials." *Arizona Law Review* 41:143–92.

Long, Katie. 1995. "Community Input at Sentencing: Victim's Right or Victim's Revenge?" *Boston University Law Review* 75:187–229.

Love, M. C. 2000. "Of Pardons, Politics and Collar Buttons: Reflections on the President's Duty to be Merciful." *Fordham Urban Law Journal* 27:1483–513.

Marquart, J. W., Sheldon Ekland-Olson, and Jonathan R. Sorensen. 1994. *The Rope, The Chair, and The Needle: Capital Punishment in Texas, 1923–1990.* Austin, TX: University of Texas Press.

McFeely, William S. 2000. *Proximity to Death.* New York: W. W. Norton & Company.

Mills, Steve. 2002a. "Life-or-death Debate Rages at Hearings: Attorneys Argue over Clemency as Victims' Families Relive Grief, Pain." *Chicago Tribune*, 16 October 2002, 1.

_____. 2002b. "A Late Plea on Clemency Hearings of all are Getting Pardons, Cancel Them, Ryan Urged." *Chicago Tribune*, 15 October 2002, 1.

Mills, Steve and Ray Long. 2002. "Cruz, 2 Others Pardoned: Ryan Says 3 Men Were Victims of 'Justice System Run Amok.'" *Chicago Tribune*, 20 December 2002, 1.

Mills, Steve and Christi Parsons. 2003. "'The System has Failed' Ryan Condemns Injustice, Pardons 6; Paves the Way for Sweeping Clemency." *Chicago Tribune*, 11 January 2003, 1.

Moore, K. D. 1989. *Pardons: Justice, Mercy, and the Public Interest.* New York: Oxford University Press.

Myers, Bryan and Edith Greene. 2004. "The Prejudicial Nature of Victim Impact Statements: Implications for Capital Sentencing Policy." *Journal of Public Policy, Psychology, and the Law* 10, 4:492–515.

Ohio Adult Parole Authority v. Woodard. 1998. 523 U.S. 272.

Palacios, Victoria J. 1996. "Faith in Fantasy: The Supreme Court's Reliance on Commutation to Ensure Justice in Death Penalty Cases." *Vanderbilt Law Review* 49:311–72.

Parsons, Christi and Steve Mills. 2002a. "Ryan Backs off Blanket Clemency: Governor to Review Cases Separately, Says Hearings Raise Troubling Issues." *Chicago Tribune*, 23 October 2002, 1.

_____. 2002b. "Clemency Hearings Forum for Unknown: Death Row Review to Begin Tuesday." *Chicago Tribune*, 14 October 2002, 1.

Payne v. Tennessee. 1991. 501 U.S. 808.

People ex rel. Madigan v. Snyder. 2004. 208 Ill.2d 457.

Phillips, Amy K. 1997. "Thou Shalt Not Kill Any Nice People: The Problem of Victim Impact Statements in Capital Sentencing." *American Criminal Law Review* 35:93–118.

Pridemore, William A. 2000. "An Empirical Examination of Commutations and Executions in Post-*Furman* Capital Cases." *Justice Quarterly* 17:159–83.

Proffitt v. Florida. 1976. 428 U.S. 242.

Radelet, Michael L. and Barbara A. Zsembik. 1993. "Executive Clemency in Post-*Furman* Capital Cases." *University of Richmond Law Review* 27:289–314.

Roberts v. Louisiana. 1976. 428 U.S. 325.

Rupcich, Joseph N. 2003. "Abusing a Limitless Power: Executive Clemency in Illinois." *Southern Illinois University Law Journal* 28:131–57.

Ryan, George. 2004. "Symposium: Race to Execution—Closing Remarks by Former Illinois Governor George Ryan." *DePaul Law Review* 53:1719–37.

_____. 2003. *Prepared text of Gov. George Ryan's speech at Northwestern University College of Law*. Death Penalty Information Center. http://www.deathpenalty-info.org/article.php?scid=13&did=551 (15 June 2005).

Sadovi, Carlos. 2003. "For Inmates, a Second Chance; For Victims' Families, More Grief." *Chicago Sun Times*, 12 January 2003.

Sanders, Catherine M. 1992. *Surviving Grief... and Learning to Live Again*. New York: John Wiley & Sons, Inc.

Solesbee v. Balkcom. 1950. 339 U.S. 9.

South Carolina v. Gathers. 1989. 490 U.S. 805.

Sullivan, Beth E. 1998. "Harnessing *Payne*: Controlling the Admission of Victim Impact Statements to Safeguard Capital Sentencing Hearings from Passion and Prejudice." *Fordham Urban Law Journal* 25:601–39.

Teuber, Andreas. 2000. "Victim's Rights: Justice or Revenge?" *Imprint* 20, 20:1–13.

Thomas, Tad. 2000. "Execution Impact Evidence in Kentucky: It is Time to Return the Scales to Balance." *Northern Kentucky Law Review* 27:411–29.

Thompson v. Oklahoma. 1986. 487 U.S. 815.

Turow, Scott. 2003. *Ultimate Punishment: A Lawyer's Reflections on Dealing with the Death Penalty*. New York: Farrar, Straus and Giroux.

United Press International. 2003. "Ryan Ripped for Death Row Clemency." *United Press International*, 13 January 2003.

Vandiver, Margaret. 1993. "The Quality of Mercy: Race and Clemency in Florida Death Penalty Cases, 1924–1966." *University of Richmond Law Review* 2:315–43.

Victim and Witness Protection Act of 1982 (VWPA) (Pub.L. 97-291, 14 October 1982, 96 Stat. 1248).

Wagner, Shane. This volume.

Weisberg, Robert. 2004. "Apology, Legislation, and Mercy." *North Carolina Law Review* 82:1415–40.

Whitworth, Steve. 2003. "Haine Enraged by Governor's Move." *The Telegraph.* http://www.stopcapitalpunishment.org/coverage/44.html (15 June 2005).

Wolfgang, M. E., A. Kelly, and H. C. Nolde. 1962. "Comparison of the Executed and the Commuted Among Admissions to Death Row." *Journal of Criminal Law, Criminology and Police Science* 53:301–11.

Woodson v. North Carolina. 1976. 428 U.S. 280.

CHAPTER 12

Putting a Square Peg in a Round Hole: Victims, Retribution, and George Ryan's Clemency[*]

Austin Sarat

"Though the victim occupies the unhappy special position of the victim and is owed compensation, he is not owed punishment."—
Robert Nozick (1974:138)

Introduction

On January 11, 2003, Governor George Ryan of Illinois emptied that state's death row by exercising his clemency powers under the state constitution, first pardoning four and then commuting 167 condemned inmates' sentences in the broadest attack on the death penalty in decades.[1] Ryan's act was the single sharpest blow to capital punishment since the U.S. Supreme Court declared it unconstitutional in 1972 with the result that approximately 600 death sentences across the nation were reduced to life in prison. It was also a dramatic reminder of the powers of chief executives at the state and federal level to grant

---

[*] A version of this chapter was published in the *North Carolina Law Review* (2004) 82:1345–76. Reprinted by permission of the author.

1. Ryan commuted 164 death sentences to life without parole. The previous day he pardoned four death-row inmates. Another three inmates had their sentences shortened to forty-year terms.

clemency,[2] and of the role of two inconsistent, but powerful forces—the claims of victims and the demands of retributive justice—in contemporary American law and politics.

The victims' rights movement contests the hegemony of the very normative constraints that retributive justice insists must govern criminal justice[3] as well as what Allen (1999:204) calls "the near-total erasure of the victim from the process of punishment." It demands that the legal system respond to crime victims' grief and rage.[4] By turning punishment into a site for the rituals of grieving,[5] that movement would make private experiences part of public discourse. Yet in so doing not only is a private colonization of public processes encouraged, but also public scrutiny invades some of the most personal aspects of our lives—the ways we suffer and grieve. The victims' rights movement points to the difficulty of "reconciling grief and rage and vengefulness with practicable moral enforcements of civil association [and] of reconciling a cultural preoccupation with vengeance and ... forms of legal punishment which deny it" (Aladjem 1992:3). Retributive norms, so this argument goes, no longer, if they ever did, adequately express common moral commitments.

Modern legality is founded on an effort to make reason triumph over emotion and to make punishments proportional in their severity to the crimes that occasion them (Bandes 1999:7). Just deserts, not deterrence or rehabilitation, becomes the primary, if not the sole, norm governing punishment.[6] "Only the Law of retribution," Kant (1965) noted:

---

2. "Clemency is a general term for the power of an executive to intervene in the sentencing of a criminal defendant to prevent injustice from occurring. It is a relief imparted after the justice system has run its course. Clemency provisions exist in every judicial system in the world except China. The U.S. Constitution gives the President the power to grant clemency. In thirty-five states, the governor can make clemency decisions directly, or exercise this power in conjunction with an advisory board. In five states, boards make clemency decisions, and in sixteen states, the power to grant clemency is shared between the governor and an advisory board" (*Clemency for Battered Women in Michigan: A Manual for Attorneys, Law Students and Social Workers* 2003).

3. On the requirements of retributive justice see Kant 1965; see also Henberg 1990, Murphy 1979.

4. "To a victim, the notion that crimes are committed against society, making the community the injured party, can seem both bizarre and insulting: it can make them feel invisible, unavenged, and unprotected" (Kaminer 1995:75; see also Harris 1991).

5. For a discussion of rituals of grieving, see Taylor 1983.

6. "Insofar as humanly possible ... law attempts to remove personal animus from the process of apportioning blame and exacting retribution. It is the removal of personal animus ... that distinguishes the rule of law from the rule of passion" (Jacoby 1983:115). On just deserts, see Singer 1979 and von Hirsch 1985.

can determine exactly the kind and degree of punishment; it must be well understood, however, that this determination must be made in the chambers of a court of justice and not in your private judgement. All other standards fluctuate back and forth and, because extraneous considerations are mixed with them, they cannot be compatible with the principle of pure and legal justice (p. 101).

Aladjem (1990) observes that:

This inclination to make revenge over into a rational principle of justice has roots in democratic theory and in certain suppositions of natural law. It arose in claims about the founding of the state, where it was said that a process of consent converts the laws of nature into those of civil society and that the state acquires its right to punish from consenting individuals who thereby relinquish a natural right to avenge themselves. From the beginning, however, that reasoning presents a paradox: the state is supposed to arise from the inclinations of individuals as they might be found in nature, but it must rescue them from the very same inclinations.... [A] vengeful "natural man" turns to the state as a place of appeal from the injustices of nature *and* from the excesses of his own revenge (p. 9).

Victims and their pain must be kept at bay, so the argument goes, because they threaten to overwhelm us with anger and passion that knows no limits.[7] As Augustine (1947) put it:

We do not wish to have the sufferings of the servants of God avenged by the infliction of precisely similar injuries in the way of retaliation ... [O]ur desire is that justice be satisfied ... [W]ho does not see that a restraint is put upon the boldness of savage violence, and the remedies fitted to produce repentance are not withdrawn, the discipline should be called a benefit rather than a vindictive punishment (pp. 168–69).

Justice becomes public, and the voice of the victim is merged with the distanced state bureaucracy which speaks for "The People" against whom all criminal offenses are said to be directed (Becker 1974). "It is sometimes the custom," Beccaria states:

to release a man from the punishment of a slight crime when the injured pardons him: an act, indeed, which is in accordance with mercy

---

7. For a discussion of the role of emotion in justice, see Pillsbury 1989.

and humanity but contrary to public policy; as if a private citizen could by his remission do away with the necessity of the example in the same way that he can excuse the reparation due for an offense. The right of punishing does not rest with an individual, but with the community as a whole, or the sovereign (quoted in Ferrer 1880:190).

Governor Ryan acted against this complex backdrop in trying to heed the voice of victims and, at the same time, satisfy the requirements of retributive justice. He also acted at a time when clemency in capital cases has come to be both one of the most dramatic, and least often used, sovereign prerogatives. During the twentieth century, a few governors took a broad view of this power, and some used it to overturn large numbers of death sentences while rendering various judgments on state killing. Unlike Ryan, they neither catered to victims nor, in the exercise of their clemency power, saw themselves as limited to retributive considerations.

Terry Sanford, former governor of North Carolina, provides an example of this broad view. "The courts of our state and nation exercise in the name of the people the powers of administration of justice" (Sanford 1966:552). Sanford said:

The Executive is charged with the exercise in the name of the people of an ... important attitude of a healthy society—that of mercy beyond the strict framework of the law. The use of executive clemency is not a criticism of the courts, either express or implied. I have no criticism of any court or any judge. Executive clemency does not involve the changing of any judicial determination. It does not eliminate punishment; it does consider rehabilitation. To decide when and where such mercy should be extended is a decision which must be made by the Executive. It cannot be delegated even in part to anyone else, and thus the decision is a lonely one. It falls to the Governor to blend mercy with justice, as best he can, involving human as well as legal considerations, in the light of all circumstances after the passage of time, but before justice is allowed to overrun mercy in the name of the power of the state. I fully realize that reasonable men hold strong feelings on both sides of every case where executive clemency is indicated. I accepted the responsibility of being Governor, however, and I will not shy away from the responsibility of exercising the power of executive clemency. (ibid.)

Lee Cruce, Oklahoma governor from 1911 to 1915, commuted twenty-two death sentences to life in prison, boldly telling the state legislature, "The ground I take is that the infliction of the death penalty by the state is wrong in morals and is destructive of the highest and noblest ideals in government" (Hines 2003). Speaking in the lofty terms of a confident sovereignty, Cruce asserted his right to spare lives because he disagreed with the state's policy.

During Pat Brown's tenure as governor of California from 1959 to 1966, he anguished over the death penalty and clemency, commuting the sentences of twenty-three death-row inmates and allowing thirty-six others to be executed in the gas chamber at San Quentin (Sward 2003). Brown later said that his power of life and death "was an awesome, ultimate power over the lives of others that no person or government should have, or crave. And looking back over their names and files now, despite the horrible crimes and the catalog of human weaknesses they comprise, I realize that each decision took something out of me that nothing—not family or work or hope for the future—has ever been able to replace" (Meehan 1989).

As he cleared Arkansas's death row with commutations at the end of his term in 1970, Gov. Winthrop Rockefeller, like Governors Sanford, Cruce, and Brown, used the rhetoric of high moralism to explain his grant of clemency: "I yearn to see other chief executives throughout the nation follow suit, so that as a people we may hasten the elimination of barbarism as a tool of American justice" (Hines 2003). In 1986 Governor Toney Anaya of New Mexico, with just weeks left in office, commuted the death sentences of all five condemned men in his state. He called capital punishment "a false god that too many worship" (*New York Times* 1986:A18). Anaya said that he exercised his clemency power because he "opposed capital punishment as being inhumane, immoral, anti-God and incompatible with enlightened society" (1993:177). At the time of his commutation decision he had a hopeful vision: "I am dropping a pebble into a pond that will cause a ripple, which I pray will be joined in other ponds across this great country, ripples that, coming together, will cause a rising tide" (Hines 2003).[8]

Despite Anaya's prayer, the tide moved in precisely the opposite direction, with governors increasingly reluctant to grant clemency in capital cases. Across the nation, the long-held constitutional right of chief executives to bestow mercy has "died its own death, the victim of a political lethal injection and a public that overwhelmingly supports the death penalty" (Salladay 1998). Thus, at the outset of his administration, then-Texas Governor George W. Bush embraced a standard for clemency that all but ensured that few if any death sentences would be seriously examined. Writing about Bush's views Alan Berlow (2003) noted:

---

8. Ohio Governor Richard Celeste commuted the death sentences of eight inmates days before he left office in January 1991.

"In every case," he wrote in *A Charge to Keep*, "I would ask: Is there any doubt about this individual's guilt or innocence? And, have the courts had ample opportunity to review all the legal issues in this case?" This is an extraordinarily narrow notion of clemency review: it seems to leave little, if any, room to consider mental illness or incompetence, childhood physical or sexual abuse, remorse, rehabilitation, racial discrimination in jury selection, the competence of the legal defense, or disparities in sentences between co-defendants or among defendants convicted of similar crimes. Neither compassion nor "mercy," which the Supreme Court as far back as 1855 saw as central to the very idea of clemency, is acknowledged as being of any account.... During Bush's six years as governor 150 men and two women were executed in Texas—a record unmatched by any other governor in modern American history.... Bush allowed the execution to proceed in all cases but one.

Similarly, then-Arkansas Governor Bill Clinton explained his reluctance to grant clemency by saying, "The appeals process, although lengthy, provides many opportunities for the courts to review sentences, and that's where these decisions should be made" (cited in *Corrections Digest* 1987:2).

The Bush and Clinton views were, and are, still very much the norm. The result is that:

at the same time the number of death sentences and executions has increased the number of clemency grants has decreased. For example, after 1984, the ratio of successful clemency petitions to executions dropped dramatically. Before 1984, the number of successful clemency petitions was slightly more than three times greater than the number of executions (105 to 32). After 1984, however, the ratio reversed: The number of executions (556) was seven times larger than the number of removals through clemency (Heise 2003:309).[9]

During the 1990s, from one to three death-row inmates were granted clemency every year in the entire nation—out of approximately sixty to eighty executions each year.[10] This is a dramatic shift from several decades ago, when governors granted clemency in 20–25 percent of the death penalty cases they

---

9. As Radelet and Zsembik (1993:304) put it, "Clemency in a capital case is extremely rare...."

10. Of the sixty-eight people executed in 1998, only one was granted clemency: a Texas man who "confessed" to 600 murders but was found to be in Florida during the one killing for which he received a death sentence.

reviewed. In Florida, one of the pillars of the "death belt," governors commuted 23 percent of death sentences between 1924 and 1966, yet no Florida death penalty sentences were commuted in the 1990s (Salladay 1998; see Ledewitz and Staples 1993:227).

Unlike Governors Sanford, Cruce, Brown, Rockefeller, and Anaya, governors today are reluctant to substitute their judgment for those of state legislators and courts, and to use clemency as a tool of sovereign prerogative (Breslin and Howley 2002:239. See also Dinsmore 2002:1842; Kobil 2000:572).[11] Rejecting appeals from the Pope, Mother Teresa, televangelist Pat Robertson, former prosecutors, and even judges and jurors in death cases, they reserve their clemency power for "unusual" cases in which someone clearly has been unfairly convicted. To some extent this is because of the political climate surrounding the death penalty. While during the 1950s and 1960s about 50 percent of the public supported the death penalty, today polls show the public overwhelmingly approves of it (Gross and Ellsworth 2003:13). As a result, many politicians have used the death penalty in their campaigns, promising more and quicker executions (Simon 2003). This is "the answer to the public's fear of crime," Richard Dieter, executive director of the Death Penalty Information Center, observes, "so [clemency] just goes against the grain" (quoted in Salladay 1998).[12]

Reactions to Ryan's Pardons and Commutations

Not surprisingly, then, Ryan's action sparked immediate and intense controversy. Law professors from around the country encouraged Ryan to issue a blanket commutation. "We feel compelled to share with you our considered judgment that, in our country, the power of executive clemency is not so lim-

---

11. Love (2000–1) notes a similar reluctance at the federal level. Beginning with the Reagan Administration, she says, "the number of pardons each year began to drop off" (p. 126). Rita Radostitz, co-director of the Capital Punishment Clinic at the University of Texas and an attorney for Henry Lee Lucas, who was granted clemency in Texas, says about clemency: "I think that clearly a miscarriage of justice should be raised, but in other cases, mercy could also come into play.... That's what clemency has historically been about— mercy" (quoted in Salladay 1998).

12. As Joseph Story (1848) long ago remarked: "The danger is not that in republics the victims of the law will too often escape punishment by a pardon; but that the power will not be sufficiently exerted in cases where public feeling accompanies the prosecution and assigns the ultimate doom to persons...."

ited," their letter said. "To the contrary, where circumstances warrant, executive clemency should be and has in fact been used as a means to correct systemic injustice" ("An Open Letter to Governor Ryan" 2002).[13] Death penalty opponents generally praised Ryan's decision. "Governor Ryan has moved this nation in the direction of the other world democracies. The U.S. has been alone in the world in its use of the death penalty," said former Illinois Senator Paul Simon. "What the families of the victims want is revenge, and that's understandable. But the role of government can't be about revenge. The role of government is to protect society—and there is no evidence at all that the death penalty protects society" (O'Brien 2003). Finally, a spokesperson for Amnesty International said Ryan's decision marked a "significant step in the struggle against the death penalty" and urged governors in U.S. states still implementing the death penalty to follow suit (Evans 2003).

However, not everyone shared these enthusiasms. Some relatives of Illinois murder victims responded vehemently. Cathy Drobney, whose daughter Bridget was murdered in 1985 by one of the people granted clemency, accused Governor Ryan of gross insensitivity to murder victims and their families. "He has killed them [those whose killers had their sentences commuted] all over again" ("Illinois Governor's Blanket Pardon Spares Lives of 167 Condemned Inmates" 2003). John Woodhouse's wife Kathy Ann was raped and murdered in 1992; when he learned of Ryan's decision Woodhouse complained that the death penalty debate in Illinois had become very one-sided because it focused on offenders rather than the victims and the harm done to their families. "The problem is the system, not the sentences," said Woodhouse. "If it's true—and it seems to be true—that the system is jailing and executing innocent people, well, fix the system. They had years and years to fix the flaws in the system. But don't destroy the sentences. Don't let murderers off the hook. This makes a mockery of my wife's life" (O'Brien 2003).

Randy Odle, who lost five family members to a murder in 1985 committed by his cousin, criticized Ryan for acting unjustly. "There was never any question about Thomas Odle's guilt. He bragged about killing our family. He admitted it when the police arrived and he bragged about it in jail. This deci-

---

13. Some lawyers in Illinois agreed with this position. "We who have signed this letter are convinced that you would best serve the Illinois criminal justice system and the citizens of this State by commuting the sentences of all of the petitioners. A system of capital punishment so fundamentally flawed as ours—one that has sentenced *at least* 13 innocent persons to death—cannot be permitted to inflict the ultimate punishment" ("Open Letter Signed by More than 650 Illinois Attorneys" 2002).

sion mocks our judicial system, and tells the jurors they did not do their jobs" (O'Brien 2003).

Such criticism was not confined to the victim community. Rod Blagojevich, Ryan's successor, said, "I support the governor's decision on the moratorium. I think he is right to review all of the cases on a case-by-case basis. I think that is a moral obligation. He's been right to do that. But I disagree with his decision to provide blanket clemency. I think a blanket anything is usually wrong. There is no one-size fits all approach to this. We're talking about convicted murderers. And I just think that that is a mistake" (Babwin 2003).

Cook County State's Attorney Richard Devine joined the attack on Ryan, combining the argument about victims with Blagojevich's complaint about the injustice of the mass clemency. "All of these cases," he said, "would have been best left for consideration by the courts which have the experience, the training and the wisdom to decide innocence or guilt. Instead, they were ripped away from the justice system by a man who is a pharmacist by training and a politician by trade.... By his actions today the governor has breached faith with the memory of the dead victims, their families and the people he was elected to serve" (Phillips 2003).

State Senator William Haine, who had helped convict two of those Ryan freed from death row during his tenure as a state's attorney, provided one of the most extensive critiques. He called Ryan's clemency decision "a great wrong [and] ... an extraordinary and ... breathtaking act of arrogance." Pointing in two somewhat different directions, Haine argued that clemency was meant to be used "sparingly to prevent clear miscarriages of justice" and "for an occasional act of mercy" (Whitworth 2003). "George Ryan," he continued, "has severed the bond of trust between those who hold great power on behalf of the people and the people themselves ..." (ibid.).

Like Haine, other commentators also called Ryan's act anti-democratic. "Illinois Gov. George Ryan's commutation of the death sentences of all 167 inmates in Illinois prisons," the columnist George Will (2003:33) wrote, "is another golden moment for liberals that underscores how many of their successes are tarnished by being explicitly, even exuberantly, anti-democratic." Will compared Ryan's act to the Supreme Court's abortion decision, "a judicial fiat that overturned the evolving consensus on abortion policy set by 50 state legislatures" (ibid.). Ryan's clemency decision will be remembered, Will continued, for its "disregard of democratic values" and "cavalier laceration of the unhealable wounds of those who mourn the victims of the killers the state of Illinois condemned" (ibid.).

Senator Haine observed that Ryan "profoundly insulted his subordinates in the system—the state's attorneys, the police officers, the jurors and judges—with his pen and his reckless language.... [H]e may have irreparably injured the law itself.... It's not in the tradition of Abraham Lincoln, who believed in a government of law, not of men" (Whitworth 2003). Haine was angered that Ryan used his gubernatorial power to circumvent the state's legal system. "Even those who are opposed to the death penalty as an option must stand shocked at the use of raw power to cut down the law itself, the Constitution, to get at the end they desire—a state without a death penalty.... If they cheer him at Northwestern Law School [where Ryan announced his clemency decision], they are cheering the raw exercise of power against the law itself" (ibid.).

While the governor has "unfettered discretion," Haine continued:

> The bond between the governor and the citizens is that these great powers are to be used with constraint consistent with the law. George Ryan has, by his conduct, breached that ethic, which is as old as the Republic itself.... Every citizen should see this as an abuse of power. This was not intended by the framers of our Constitution.... I can't think of any analogy to compare it to other than the Civil War, when senators and military officers abandoned their oaths and took up arms against the United States. In the history of the Republic, I can't compare it to anything else, an act of this nature, where you simply take the position that the law doesn't mean anything. (Whitworth 2003).

In what follows I examine Ryan's clemency announcement, titled "I Must Act" (Ryan 2003), for what it says about the concerns raised by his critics—in particular their interest in victims' rights, retributive justice, and legality. As to the first, I will argue that Ryan's statement vividly illustrates the importance of the rights and interests of victims in the contemporary United States. Second, I will suggest that his rhetoric is impelled by democracy's fragile sovereignty and a limited view of clemency, one not at all hostile to legality. Ryan's act, I will argue, was neither bold nor lawless. Quite to the contrary, it lent itself easily to positions taken by conservative politicians and judges who see retributive principles providing the only legitimate basis for executive clemency in America's capital punishment system. It was caught in the crossfire of two of our society's most powerful but opposing forces, the claims of victims and the demands of retributive justice.

"I Must Act"

Because clemency declarations have no standard genre, George Ryan had to stitch together a rhetorical performance. He did so by borrowing from the rhetoric of judicial opinions (see Ferguson 1990). His statement most closely resembles the justificatory act of a judge speaking through his opinion to the counter-majoritarian difficulty that in a democracy places judicial review, like executive clemency, in a structurally anomalous position.[14] Like a judge, Ryan presented his decision as "compelled," an act of duty, not a personal choice. It was, as Ferguson (1990:205, 207) says of judicial rhetoric, "self-dramatizing. It has, in effect, no other choice. Judges often solve this difficulty by stressing the importance of a decision only they can make."

Like a judicial opinion, Ryan's statement worked "to appropriate all other voices into its own monologue," subsuming "difference into an act of explanation and moment of decision.... The monologic voice of the opinion can never presume to act on its own. It must appear as if forced to its inevitable conclusion by the logic of the situation and the duties of office, which together eliminate all thought of an unfettered hand" (Ferguson 1990:205). Like a judge unelected and accountable only through the adequacy of his justifications, Ryan granted clemency as he was about to leave office, no longer subject to electoral accountability, with the imagined judgment of history as his target audience.

Ryan's "I Must Act" explains his decision through two somewhat contradictory stories. One is a story of victims and their suffering, the other of institutions and their failures; one expresses a commitment to the interests of the victimized, the other a retributive theory of clemency.[15] In both of these elements, Ryan puts himself at the center. In one he sought to authenticate his act by identifying himself as a suffering subject, able in his suffering to know the pain that families of murder victims suffer at the hands of criminals and that the families would suffer at his hands. In the other he painted himself as a reluctant actor seeking to insure justice in a failing justice system and a political system in paralysis.[16]

---

14. Ferguson (1990:207) describes the rhetoric of judicial opinions as a response to "the judiciary's non-majoritarian status in a democratic republic."

15. For a description of the retributive theory of clemency, see Moore 1989. Pardons, like punishment, Moore argues, "need to be "justified by reasons having to do with what is just" (p. 91). She lists four principles that justify pardons. Pardons are allowed in order to correct the punishment of the innocent (those who stand convicted of a crime they "may not have committed") and of those who are "guilty under the law but are not morally blameworthy." They may be used when the punishment of a guilty and deserving offending is unduly severe or to prevent cruelty or relieve those whose suffering exceeds what they merit. In our legal system pardon is "a backup system that works outside the rules to correct mistakes, making sure that only those who deserve punishment are punished" (pp. 286, 287, 284). See also Moore 1993; Kobil 1991.

16. He neither linked clemency to mercy nor did he elevate it to the moral stature of governors Stanford, Cruce, Brown, or Anaya. His critique of capital punishment is sys-

In the story of victims and their suffering he displays the frail sovereignty of a democracy, desperately seeking grounding in a shared conception of citizenship, in which what binds us together is our common suffering and victimization (Culbert 1995:8). In the story of institutional failure, he portrays himself as a committed retributivist[17] and embraces a "fail safe" attitude toward clemency advocated by former governors Clinton and Bush and Chief Justice Rehnquist.[18] If responsiveness to victims provided the point of departure for his clemency, retributive principles provided its disciplining core.

Listening to Victims

Legal systems in the United States and Europe recently have been confronted by stern challenges in the name of victims' rights (see Fletcher 1995; Forer 1980; Roland 1989; Scheingold et al 1994). Here and elsewhere a tide of resentment is rising against a system of justice that traditionally has tried to substitute public processes for private action and, in so doing, to justify the criminal sanction as a response to injuries to public order rather than harms done to particular individuals. The tendency of criminal justice systems in western democracies has been to displace the victim, to shut the door on those with the greatest interest in seeing justice done. In response, victims have demanded that their voices be heard throughout the criminal process. And in place after place their demands have been met.[19]

But the victims' rights movement wants more. It seeks participation and power by making the victim the symbolic heart of modern legality. It contests

---

temic, not moral; his justification oddly evocative of a seventeenth-century view of sovereign prerogative.

17. Ryan relied, Kobil only somewhat inaccurately claims, "entirely on retributive arguments" (Kobil 2003:227).

18. "Clemency," Rehnquist said, "is deeply rooted in our Anglo-American tradition of law, and is the historic remedy for preventing miscarriages of justice where judicial process has been exhausted" (*Herrera v. Collins* 1993:412).

19. In 1981 President Reagan proclaimed the week of April 19 the first "National Victims' Rights Week" (see Reagan 1981). Each president has proclaimed a Crime Victims' Week annually since then. Legislation now exists that grants victims a role in the plea-bargaining process and in sentencing decisions as well as a right to be notified about the release of the offenders who victimized them (see Lamborn 1987). Moreover, "Today, the constitutions of at least 20 states now contain 'victim's rights amendments,' and similar legislation has been introduced at the federal level" (Logan 1999:144 n. 4; see also McLeod 1986, Carrington and Nicholson 1984, Henderson 1985.)

the attempted appropriation of the role of the victim by offenders and what it sees as the promiscuous use of the language of victimization throughout our culture. The movement draws on standard stories and mobilizes around incidents that are "horrifying and aberrational" (Scheingold, Olson, and Pershing 1994:734), generating sentimental narratives of lives lost, families ruined, evil done.

"'I draw most of my strength from victims,'" former Attorney General Reno once said, "'for they represent America to me: people who will not be put down, people who will not be defeated, people who will rise again and stand again for what is right.... You are my heroes and heroines. You are but little lower than the angels'" (Simon 2003:3–27). So important is the image of the victim in our political life that one scholar argues that crime victims have come to be "the most idealized form of political subjectivity.... It is as crime victims that Americans are most readily imagined as united by threat that simultaneously downplays their differences and authorizes them to take dramatic political steps.... The innocent victim of violent crime becomes the paradigm example of the citizen who needs government" (ibid.:3-5 to 3-7).[20]

That Ryan's mass commutation is situated in the saga of an increasingly victim-centered political and legal environment is suggested by the great prominence that the language of victimization had in his speech.[21] "I have read, listened to and discussed the issue with the families of the victims as well as the families of the condemned," Ryan said, before sharing a story in which he identified himself as a crime victim twice removed.[22] "I grew up in Kankakee which even today is still a small Midwestern town, a place where people tend to know each other," Ryan explained.

---

20. We become what Berlant (1997:25) calls "infantile citizens." In this version of citizenship, "a citizen is defined as a person traumatized by some aspect of life in the United States. Portraits and stories of citizen-victims ... now permeate the political public sphere" (p. 1).

21. His decision followed closely on the heels of an extraordinary series of hearings by the Illinois Prison Review Board, hearings that were dominated by victims and their family members. During these hearings, as one newspaper described them, "hour after hour, victims and family members of dead victims have been forced to come before a panel and revisit the most horrific event in their lives. These people had to retell their stories and beg, sobbing, for the panel to let the current sentence of death stand" Walsh (2002). As Jennifer Culbert (2001:104) puts it, in our era, "The pain and suffering expressed by the murder victim's survivors can serve as an absolute in a society in which every other kind of claim is subject to contestation, doubt, and criticism."

22. This and the following quotations are from Governor George Ryan's (2003) speech at the Northwestern University College of Law on January 11, 2003: "I Must Act."

Steve Small was a neighbor. I watched him grow up. He would babysit my young children, which was not for the faint of heart since Lura Lynn and I had six children, five of them under the age of 3. He was a bright young man who helped run the family business. He got married and he and his wife had three children of their own. Lura Lynn was especially close to him and his family. We took comfort in knowing he was there for us and we for him. One September midnight he received a call at his home. There had been a break-in at the nearby house he was renovating. But as he left his house, he was seized at gunpoint by kidnappers. His captors buried him alive in a shallow hole. He suffocated to death before police could find him. His killer led investigators to where Steve's body was buried. The killer, Danny Edward[sic], was also from my hometown. He now sits on death row. I also know his family. I share this story with you so that you know I do not come to this as a neophyte without having experienced a small bit of the bitter pill the survivors of murder must swallow....

This is a ghostly as well as ghastly account, bringing before its listeners the specter of a dead man, mercilessly slaughtered. That Ryan ties himself to this ghost reminds us of Fitzpatrick's (1999:486–87) account of the finitude that death imposes on law and the unfolding indeterminism of law's beyond. Clemency exercised to stave off death, confronting it, as it were, face-to-face and refusing its demand, helps to mark death as the horizon of law both as "supreme stasis" and "the opening to all possibility that is beyond affirmed order" (ibid.:484). Moreover, metaphors of place, the small town and the knowledge that Small was "there for us," contribute to the ghostliness of Ryan's account precisely by marking the placelessness of death and its irresistible ability to enter any place.[23]

But there is another specter in this story, this one of a life marked for its own untimely extinction.[24] By connecting himself to Danny Edwards, Ryan

---

23. The small-town imagery is reminiscent of what Minow (1993) says about victim impact statements. They "persuade, when they do, because they invoke widely shared images of goodness, Christian piety ... the 'little guy,' and American patriotism, all of which are talismans of the deserving person. Some degree of simplification is inevitable, and no one should be surprised to find that victim impact statements do not reveal the uniqueness of the human being victimized by crime" (p. 1432).

24. "With the death penalty—an act of sovereignty—the State, the Prince or the Dictator claims an extraordinary power of calculation: the right to determine when life expires. The President, Governor or the Judge, who hold the right to grant pardon, the right to forgive and thus to make exceptions, are meant to know and be able to calculate the time of death, the moment which abruptly puts an end to the other's finitude" (Crosara 2000).

rhetorically invokes the kind of dual accountability that governs clemency in capital cases, one side facing the already dead, the other those whose lives are in the balance. If Ryan's rhetoric is rightly thought of as juridical, then, like others who pass judgment in death penalty cases, he turns to "expressions of pain as others may once have turned to God, in trust that this 'sacred name' will make it possible for individuals to answer the question, 'In the name of what or whom do we judge?'" (Culbert 2001:104–5).

Moreover Ryan makes his persona, his private not sovereign body, vividly present. In this story he is caught, almost literally torn, between the victim and the offender, reassuring his listeners that he has tasted murder's "bitter pill." This is hardly the language of a majestic, distant, undemocratic sovereignty, unresponsive to, or uninterested in, the pain of the victims. It is, instead, domesticated by that pain. For it is only by assuming the status of a victim of Danny Edwards's crime that he can be entitled to forgive it or to mitigate its punishment.[25] As Jacques Derrida (1999) says, pointing to the condition that creates Ryan's dilemma, "Who would have the right of forgiving in the name of the vanished victims? They are always absent, in a certain manner. Missing in essence, they are never themselves absolutely present, at the moment pardon is asked for, as the same they were the moment of the crime; and they are sometimes absent in body, which is to say dead."

As victim and as someone in contact with the experience of victimization, Ryan constituted his listeners as particular kinds of political subjects, earning their attention, as it were, through his own earnest attention to the claims of victims, even as he both broadened and blurred the referent of the term.[26] "As I came closer to my decision, I knew that I was going to have to face the question of whether I believed so completely in the choice I wanted to make that I could face the prospect of even commuting the death sentence of Danny Edwards, the man who had killed a close family friend of mine. I discussed it with my wife, Lura Lynn, who has stood by me all these years. She was angry and disappointed at my decision like many of the families of other victims will be."

---

25. "[F]orgiveness in general should only be permitted on the part of the victim. The question of forgiveness as such should only arise in the head-to-head or the face-to-face between the victim and the guilty party, never by a third party for a third.... [Y]et forgiveness perhaps implies, from the outset ... the appearance on the scene of a third party whom it nonetheless must, should, exclude" (Derrida undated:34).

26. As the cultural critic Lauren Berlant (1997:27) notes, the result is to produce a "special form of tyranny that makes citizens like children, infantilized, passive, and overdependent on the 'immense and tutelary power' of the state."

There is a very interesting use of verb tenses here with Ryan again describing himself as caught, this time between the past with its own imagined future—"was going"—and the present with its imagining of the coming anger and disappointment of the community with which he is rhetorically allied. Danny Edwards returns to the story as the touchstone of Ryan's accountability to his dead "close family friend." The test of his commitment to clemency would be found in the answer to the question of whether his beliefs and convictions could pass the Danny Edwards test. Could he find the reasons to commute every death sentence sufficiently persuasive to move him to spare even Edwards's life? This is a stern test indeed, converting clemency into a measure of personal conviction and strength for Ryan himself.

As if not able to say it enough times, Ryan repeatedly tried to assure his listeners that he had indeed heard the voice of victims. "I have conducted private group meetings, one in Springfield and one in Chicago, with the surviving family members of homicide victims. Everyone in the room who wanted to speak had the opportunity to do so. Some wanted to express their grief, others wanted to express their anger. I took it all in…. I redoubled my effort to review each case personally in order to respond to the concerns of prosecutors and victims' families." Unlike the minimal due process that some justices of the U.S. Supreme Court believe must be provided for those seeking clemency,[27] Ryan accords a deep and respectful attentiveness to victims. He takes into himself their grief and anger, again rhetorically refiguring himself as a victim. In Ryan's account there is a rhetorical responsiveness to pain and a grounding not in sovereign grace, but in the need to pay homage to suffering.[28]

---

27. See *Ohio Adult Parole Authority v. Woodard* 1998. As Justice O'Connor put it, "some *minimal* procedural safeguards apply to clemency proceedings" (p. 289). Yet she was not able to name what those procedures might be and could imagine judicial intervention only in cases of the most transparent and unreasoning arbitrariness—for example "a scheme where a state official flipped a coin to determine whether to grant clemency, or in a case where the State arbitrarily denied a prisoner any access to its clemency process" (ibid.). Justice Stevens added to this list of barely imaginable horrors when he stated that "no one would contend that a governor could ignore the commands of the Equal Protection Clause and use race, religion, or political affiliation as a standard for granting or denying clemency" (p. 292).

28. "In the absence of an overarching principle or absolute to which to refer for sense and guidance in a multicultural, morally pluralist society, the survivor is embraced as a unique figure with the power to liberate people from the chains of a well-meaning but paralyzing relativism" (Culbert 2001:134).

Just as Ryan's rhetoric positions him between victim and offender and through him establishes connections between them, in his expansive use of the category of victim he attempts to establish connections between the relatives of those who have died and of those who are sentenced to death. Everyone, it turns out, is in pain; the political community is imagined as constituted by shared suffering.[29]

> I also had a meeting with a group of people who are less often heard from, and who are not as popular with the media. The family members of death-row inmates have a special challenge to face. I spent an afternoon with those family members at a Catholic Church here in Chicago. At that meeting, I heard a different kind of pain expressed. Many of these families live with the twin pain of knowing not only that, in some cases, their family member may have been responsible for inflicting a terrible trauma on another family, but also the pain of knowing that society has called for another killing. These parents, siblings and children are not to blame for the crime committed, yet these innocent stand to have their loved ones killed by the state.... They are also branded and scarred for life because of the awful crime committed by their family member. Others were even more tormented by the fact that their loved one was another victim, that they were truly innocent of the crime for which they were sentenced to die.

Again Ryan deploys his own kind of due process. He is the sovereign holding court to receive the petition of his subjects, in a church not in a castle. He is a sovereign listening, hearing, heeding the voice of another group figuratively silenced by their connection to death, the death of those whose time of death has been made calculable by society's choice. And again it is pain that provides the connective tissue between speakers and listeners.

Yet what can victims provide for those with the power of clemency? While they are present in every clemency decision, whether it is granted or refused and despite Ryan's rhetorical identification with them, the judgment, and responsibility for it, could only be his. Despite his rhetorical identification with victims, he could not, as the reactions of Cathy Drobney and John Woodhouse suggest, dispense forgiveness in their name. Despite the connections he tried to forge in a community with many different kinds of victims, stable grounds for his act could not be established in its shared pain. So, he turned from re-

---

29. Culbert (1995:8) contends that it is "counter-intuitive to think of a subjective experience like pain as establishing a publicly valid authority."

sponsiveness to suffering in a community of victims to a critique of the institutions of the legal and political system for being insufficiently attentive to the claims of retributive justice.

Clemency and the Requirements of Justice

As Ryan changed the subject he used victims and their needs to introduce his broad indictment of Illinois's death penalty system. Victims, it turns out, are also victimized by that system. Speaking of the relative rarity of capital punishment, he says, "There were more than 1,000 murders last year in Illinois. There is no doubt that all murders are horrific and cruel. Yet, less than 2 percent of those murder defendants will receive the death penalty. That means more than 98 percent of victims families do not get, and will not receive, whatever satisfaction can be derived from the execution of the murderer."

"Whatever satisfaction" registers Ryan's doubt about what executions do for victims' families, his doubt that they provide their much advertised virtue of "closure."[30] Imagining the crime victim's family as the paradigmatic needy citizen, Ryan asks, "What kind of victim services are we providing? Are all of our resources geared toward providing this notion of closure by execution instead of tending to the physical and social service needs of victim families?"

But Ryan's rhetorical identification with victims is overridden in his "I Must Act" statement by a commitment to ensuring that offenders get what they deserve. Retribution provides a disciplining presence in his exercise of clemency (Kobil 2003:228), an anchor of lawfulness in the presence of his potentially uncheckable power.[31] As Kobil (ibid.:240) says, describing Ryan's "I Must Act":

---

30. "To a family they talked about closure," Ryan says. "They pleaded with me to allow the state to kill an inmate in its name to provide the families with closure. But is that the purpose of capital punishment? Is it to soothe the families? And is that truly what the families experience?" In Kaminer's (1995:84) view, talk about closure "partakes of a popular confusion of law and therapy and the substitution of feelings for facts. But if feelings are facts in a therapist's office … feelings are prejudices in a court of law…. Justice is not a form of therapy, meaning that what is helpful to a particular victim … is not necessarily just, and what is just may not be therapeutic."

31. See *Ex parte Garland* 1866. Speaking of the President's power to pardon, Justice Field gave legal sanction to its lawlessness. "The power thus conferred," Field said, "is unlimited, with the exception [of cases of impeachment]. It extends to every offence known to the law, and may be exercised at any time after its commission, either before legal proceedings are taken, or during their pendency, or after conviction and judgment. This power of the President is not subject to legislative control. Congress can neither limit the effect of his pardon, nor exclude from its exercise any class of offenders. The benign prerogative

> Governor Ryan relied entirely on retributive arguments.... Although
> there has been substantial public outcry against Ryan's actions and
> even legal challenges to some of his commutations, it appears that for
> now retributive justifications have carried the day.... Ultimately ...
> Ryan was persuaded to grant clemency to every person on Death Row
> not as a grand gesture of forgiveness, but because his faith in the abil-
> ity of the Illinois system to give only deserving defendants a sentence
> of death had been destroyed by a series of blatant errors and mistakes.

Ryan's commitment to a just-deserts theory of punishment moved him from individual cases, on which clemency typically focuses, to the systemic level. "The facts I have seen in reviewing each and every one of these cases," Ryan observed, "raised questions not only about the innocence of people on death row, but about the fairness of the death penalty system as a whole. If the system was making so many errors in determining whether someone was guilty in the first place, how fairly and accurately was it determining which guilty defendants deserved to live and which deserved to die? What effect was race having? What effect was poverty having?"

In this rhetorical movement from the individual to the system and in his reference to the effect of race in the system of state killing, Ryan inverts the logic of the Supreme Court's decision in *McCleskey v. Kemp* (1987). Presented with a wholesale challenge to Georgia's death penalty system, the Court re-fused to inquire into systemic problems that might undermine confidence in decisions at the "heart of the criminal justice system" (ibid.:281). Unlike the Court which refused to move from the particular to the general,[32] this is ex-actly what Ryan's commutation statement insists must be done.

> The death penalty has been abolished in 12 states. In none of these
> states has the homicide rate increased. In Illinois last year we had

---

of mercy reposed in him cannot be fettered by any legislative restrictions" (p. 371). See also *Ex parte Grossman* 1925. "Executive clemency," Chief Justice Taft said, "exists to afford re-lief from undue harshness or evident mistake in the operation of enforcement of the crim-inal law. The administration of justice by the courts is not necessarily always wise or cer-tainly considerate of circumstances which may properly mitigate guilt. To afford a remedy, it has always been thought essential in popular governments, as well as in monarchies, to vest in some other authority than the court's power to ameliorate or avoid particular crim-inal judgments. It is a check entrusted to the executive for special cases. To exercise it to the extent of destroying the deterrent effect of judicial punishment would be to pervert it; but whoever is to make it useful must have full discretion to exercise it" (pp. 120–21).

32. For a useful analysis of the implications of this refusal for our understanding of nar-rative and rhetoric, see Ewick and Silbey 1995:215–16.

about 1,000 murders, only 2 percent of that 1,000 were sentenced to death. Where is the fairness and equality in that? The death penalty in Illinois is not imposed fairly or uniformly because of the absence of standards for the 102 Illinois State Attorneys, who must decide whether to request the death sentence. Should geography be a factor in determining who gets the death sentence? I don't think so, but in Illinois it makes a difference. You are 5 times more likely to get a death sentence for first-degree murder in the rural area of Illinois than you are in Cook County. Where is the justice and fairness in that? Where is the proportionality?

Instead of a system finely geared to assigning punishment on the basis of a careful assessment of the nature of the crime and the blameworthiness of the offender, Ryan, quoting Justice Blackmun (*Callins v. Collins* 1994:1141) concluded that "'the death penalty remains fraught with arbitrariness, discrimination, caprice and mistake.'" Here he assumes the posture of a "new abolitionist" (Sarat 2001:246–60). The new abolitionist does not oppose state killing as an affront to morality or as per se unconstitutional. Instead, arguments against the death penalty occur in the name of constitutional rights other than the Eighth Amendment, in particular due process and equal protection. New abolitionists, like Ryan, argue against the death penalty claiming that it has not been, and cannot be, administered in a manner that is compatible with our legal system's fundamental commitments to fair and equal treatment. Thus, Ryan noted that:

[P]rosecutors in Illinois have the ultimate commutation power, a power that is exercised every day. They decide who will be subject to the death penalty, who will get a plea deal or even who may get a complete pass on prosecution. By what objective standards do they make these decisions? We do not know, they are not public.... [I]f you look at the cases, as I have done both individually and collectively—a killing with the same circumstances might get 40 years in one county and death in another county. I have also seen where co-defendants who are equally or even more culpable get sentenced to a term of years, while another less culpable defendant ends up on death row.... Our capital system is haunted by the demon of error, error in determining guilt, and error in determining who among the guilty deserves to die.

Ryan issues a stunning, though by now familiar, indictment of a system in which decisions about who gets the death penalty and who does not are made without reference to "objective standards." He draws attention to the contrast between his own publicly delivered justification and the daily "commutation" decisions of prosecutors, made without explanation, privately, outside of the public eye. Ryan finds arbitrariness deeply enfolded in the operations of the death penalty system, pointing to the influence of irrelevant factors like geography and the fact that offenders committing the same acts end up with radically different sentences. In a system marked by such arbitrariness perhaps only the arbitrary power of clemency provides a route to justice.

Ryan invoked yet another calculus of desert to justify his commutation, returning Danny Edwards to the center of the story.

> Some inmates on death row don't want a sentence of life without parole. Danny Edwards wrote me and told me not to do him any favors because he didn't want to face a prospect of a life in prison without parole. They will be confined in a cell that is about 5-feet-by-12 feet, usually double-bunked. Our prisons have no air conditioning, except at our supermax facility where inmates are kept in their cell 23 hours a day. In summer months, temperatures in these prisons exceed one hundred degrees. It is a stark and dreary existence. They can think about their crimes. Life without parole has even, at times, been described by prosecutors as a fate worse than death.

Ryan tells his listeners of Edwards's preference not to be spared. He does so in order to assure them that his commutation decision actually satisfies the requirements of justice better than would capital punishment. He describes a future spent in thinking about one's worst deed, a kind of living self-torture, as a "fate worse than death," and in doing so again calls attention to his own future suffering. "I realize it will draw ridicule, scorn and anger from many who oppose this decision. They will say I am usurping the decisions of judges and juries and state legislators.... I may never be comfortable with my final decision, but I will know in my heart that I did my very best to do the right thing."

From responsiveness to the claims of suffering and of death itself, Ryan sought grounding in a retributive calculus (Kobil 2003:227–28, 240). Yet, as Ryan's discussion of Danny Edwards's views on life without parole highlights, retributivism could not ensure stable grounds for judgment any more than could his complicated imaginings of the victims and their needs.[33] Whether

---

33. As Duff and Garland (1995:7) note, "The central problem for any retributivist ... is to explain the heart of desert. Punishment is supposed to be justified as an intrinsically appropriate response to crime; the notion of 'desert' is supposed to indicate the justifica-

life without parole is worse than death for the crime of murder cannot be subject to a calculus that eliminates or grounds decision in a certitude beyond contest, thus alleviating the need to take responsibility for that decision. It is that decision, along with the power to actualize it, that defines the essence of clemency whether in monarchical or democratic governments.

Political Paralysis

The last element of Ryan's rhetorical strategy was, in fact, to emphasize the responsibility and the power that his position accorded him as well as his commitment to retributive principles. "My responsibilities and obligations are to more than my neighbors and my family. I represent all the people of Illinois, like it or not. The people of our state have vested in me the power to act in the interest of justice. Even if the exercise of my power becomes my burden I will bear it.... I know," he said, "that my decision will be just that—my decision."

But why was it necessary for him to make that decision and exercise that power? Here Ryan's critique is not directed at the system through which the death penalty is administered. Instead his critique turns from a retributivist's indictment of the flaws in that system to a criticism of the failures of the political system—failures, in the absence of which, clemency would have been unnecessary.

Turning first to the Illinois State Supreme Court, Ryan portrays it as "divided" on issues which he sees as clear cut, and as failing in courage on the ultimate question of the constitutionality of capital punishment itself. "We have come very close," Ryan reports:

> to having our state Supreme Court rule our death penalty statute—
> the one that I helped enact in 1977—unconstitutional. Former State
> Supreme Court Justice Seymour Simon wrote to me that it was only
> happenstance that our statute was not struck down by the state's high
> court. When he joined the bench in 1980, three other justices had al-
> ready said Illinois's death penalty was unconstitutional. But they got
> cold feet when a case came along to revisit the question. One judge
> wrote that he wanted to wait and see if the Supreme Court of the
> United States would rule on the constitutionality of the new Illinois
> law. Another said precedent required him to follow the old state
> Supreme Court ruling with which he disagreed. Even a pharmacist

---

tory link between past crime and present punishment. But just what is that link? What is 'desert' which supposedly makes punishment the appropriate response to crime?"

knows that doesn't make sense. We wouldn't have a death penalty today, and we all wouldn't be struggling with this issue, if those votes had been different. How arbitrary.

But his strongest criticism was directed toward the state legislature of which he was once a member.

I have also had to watch in frustration as members of the Illinois General Assembly failed to pass even one substantive death penalty reform. Not one. They couldn't even agree on *one.* How much more evidence is needed before the General Assembly will take its responsibility in this area seriously? ... I don't know why legislators could not heed the rising voices of reform. I don't know how many more systemic flaws we needed to uncover before they would be spurred to action. Three times I proposed reforming the system with a package that would restrict the use of jailhouse snitches, create a statewide panel to determine death eligible cases, and reduce the number of crimes eligible for death. These reforms would not have created a perfect system, but they would have dramatically reduced the chance for error in the administration of the ultimate penalty.

Juxtaposed to his earlier emphasis on hearing, listening, and attending as one of the attributes of a responsible public official, his discussion of the legislature's failure to "heed the rising voices of reform" is particularly striking. Doing his duty as chief executive, he proposed reforms to fix the system that he had earlier criticized as "arbitrary" so that it could better meet the commands of a retributive theory. However, almost inexplicably, the legislature, like the U.S. Supreme Court, did not, would not, act responsibly.

The legislature's failure to take responsibility and act responsibly is not its failure alone. It is, on Ryan's account, "a symptom of the larger problem" in the domain of state killing. "Many people express the desire to have capital punishment. Few, however, seem prepared to address the tough questions that arise when the system fails. It is easier and more comfortable for politicians to be tough on crime and support the death penalty. It wins votes. But when it comes to admitting that we have a problem, most run for cover."

Saying that he "never intended to be an activist" on the death penalty, Ryan portrays himself as someone who is propelled against his own inclination to do a painful and costly duty that others refused to do. "We are a rudderless ship because they failed to act." Seizing that rudder is today, as it long has been, one of the imperatives of executive leadership in times of crisis. Saying, "The legislature couldn't reform it. Lawmakers won't repeal it. But I will not stand for it. I must act," Ryan plunged into that lawful lawlessness that today, as it always has, marks the exercise of sovereign prerogative.[34]

Conclusion

George Ryan's commutation was, as I have argued, pulled in two somewhat incompatible directions. That he found himself in this situation is attributable, in part, to the importance of the victims' rights movement in the United States. While he did not do what the victims' community wanted him to do, his justificatory rhetoric paid homage, perhaps undue homage, to victims. While he broadened and complicated the category of victim, he sought to use his clemency decision to identify with and express respect for them. If there was a failure in its justification it is to be found in trying to reconcile the irreconcilable by combining fidelity to victims and their suffering with commitment to retributive justice and by trying to be responsive both to private pain and the strict dictates of public justice. He could not feel the pain of the victims and then seem to ignore it without enraging them and leaving them feeling, as noted above, like they had suffered another undeserved injury.

These tensions are illustrated in Robert Nozick's (1981) discussion of the demands of retributive justice (see also Bedau 1978; Cottingham 1979; Feinberg 1970). Nozick identifies five attributes of retribution and five ways that it distances itself from the claims of private victims. First, retribution, according to Nozick, is only done for a "wrong" while victims may seek punishment "for an injury or harm or slight and need not be for a wrong" (p. 366). What counts in the realm of injury, harm, or slight is the private pain of the victim and not the intent of the person whose action caused that pain.

Second, while retribution "sets an internal limit to the amount of punishment, according to the seriousness of the wrong ... victims often recognize no such limits" (Nozick 1981:367). What Nozick means is that retributive punishment must be proportional to the wrong committed.[35] Third, "The agent of retribution," Nozick tells us, "need have no special or personal tie to the vic-

---

34. Derrida (1999) refers to the clemency power as what he calls "the right of grace." To speak of such a right, he says, is to locate clemency on the terrain of law, that is, to place it within the "order of rights." Yet *this* right works precisely by inscribing in law "a power above the law." Clemency, he says, is "law above the law."

35. See Davis 1995. Kant (1965:101–2) describes the law of retribution as "any undeserved evil that you inflict on someone else among the people is one that you do to yourself."

tim...." (p. 367). It is, of course, just this element of impersonality in retributive justice that causes discomfort and concern in the victims' rights movement. The goal of victims and those who take up their cause is to re-personalize criminal justice so that the sentencer has to declare an alliance—with either the victim or the offender. Criminal sentencing thus becomes a test of loyalty.

Fourth, as Nozick sees it retributive justice involves no "emotional tone" (p. 367). The desire to experience a direct, immediate, passionate connection to the suffering of the criminal fuels the victims' rights movement. Only when victims become agents in the suffering of the people responsible for their own suffering is a kind of social equilibrium reached. "The notion of paying back," Miller argues, "makes no sense unless the victim or his representative is there to hit back. Under this paradigm ... the focus is ... on the obligation to repay the wrong done to him by retaliating against either the wrongdoer or someone closely connected to him" (1998:167). When punishment is guided by retributive principles, the victim's right/need to pay back remains unsatisfied.

Finally, retribution is based on "general principles ... mandating punishment in other similar circumstances" (Nozick 1981:367). This means that if a concern for systemic failure provides the grounds for clemency, it must be given even to Danny Edwards. Victims, in contrast, care most about their injuries and the punishment inflicted for them (p. 368).

If philosophers like Nozick cannot reconcile retributive justice and the desires of victims, it should not be surprising that George Ryan did not succeed in this same endeavor. However, despite his inability to put a square peg in a round hole, Ryan's act was well within the bounds of traditional understandings of clemency. Its forebears are former governors Clinton and Bush, and Chief Justice Rehnquist. Far from disrupting the essential rhythms of American politics, in its emphasis on suffering and victimization, in its embrace of retributive principles, and in its demonstration of "energy in the executive,"[36] it gave new voice to ongoing trends in our political and cultural lives.

State Senator Haine may have been right to characterize it as "a great wrong [and] ... an extraordinary and ... breathtaking act of arrogance," and to say that it broke the bond of trust between the people and the Governor; but he was surely wrong when he alleged that Ryan's clemency rendered the law meaningless (Whitworth 2003). And, if Ryan's pardon was an "injury to law itself," it is an injury that the law authorizes and requires, a form of lawful law-

---

36. "Energy in the executive is a leading character in the definition of good government" (*The Federalist Papers*: 1961:423).

lessness without which the law would indeed be rendered meaningless (Agamben 1998).[37] As Abraham Lincoln himself vividly demonstrated, the survival of constitutional democracy may require just the kind of arrogance that the power to pardon and commute punishments invites and that George Ryan displayed.

While his critics may have misread and misunderstood Ryan's use of clemency, failing to see that its essential incoherence arose from his effort to be sensitive to victims and also responsive to the dictates of justice, they may have been onto something important in highlighting the lawful lawlessness that is endemic to clemency itself. Despite Ryan's gallant efforts to ground and authorize his acts in the suffering of victims, the systemic flaws of the capital punishment system, or the failures of political institutions, he could neither resolve the contradictory forces that mark our contemporary political condition nor satisfy our need for, and yet discomfort with, the sovereign power to spare life.

References

Agamben, Giorgio. 1998. *Homo Sacer: Sovereign Power and Bare Life.* Trans. by Daniel Heller-Roazen. Stanford, CA: Stanford University Press.

Aladjem, Terry. 1992. *Vengeance and Democratic Justice: American Culture and the Limits of Punishment.* Unpublished manuscript, on file with the author.

_____. 1990. *Revenge and Consent.* Unpublished manuscript, on file with the author.

Allen, Danielle S. 1999. "Democratic Dis-ease: Of Anger and the Troubling Nature of Punishment." Pp. 191–214 in *The Passions of Law*, edited by Susan A. Bandes. New York: New York University Press.

Anaya, Toney. 1993. "Statement by Toney Anaya on Capital Punishment." *University of Richmond Law Review* 27:177–83.

Augustine, St. 1947. *The Writings of St. Augustine.* New York: Fathers of the Church.

Babwin, Don. 2003. "Illinois Governor Empties Death Row" (12 January 2003). http://www.stopcapitalpunishment.org/coverage/56.html (last consulted 26 August 2003).

Bandes, Susan A. 1999. "Introduction." Pp. 1–15 in *The Passions of Law*, edited by Susan A. Bandes. New York: New York University Press.

Becker, Lawrence. 1974. "Criminal Attempt and the Theory of the Law of Crimes." *Philosophy & Public Affairs* 3:262–94.

Bedau, Hugo Adam. 1978. "Retribution and the Theory of Punishment." *Journal of Philosophy* 75:601–20.

---

37. Acts of clemency create exceptions, exclusions, but as Agamben notes, the exception does not "subtract itself from the rule; rather the rule, suspending itself, gives rise to the exception and, maintaining itself in relation to the exception, first constitutes itself as a rule ..." (1998:18).

Berlant, Lauren. 1997. *The Queen of America Goes to Washington City: Essays on Sex and Citizenship.* Durham: Duke University Press.

Berlow, Alan. 2003. "The Texas Clemency Memos." *The Atlantic Monthly* July/August 2003 http://www.theatlantic.com/issues/2003/07/berlow.htm (last consulted 26 August 2003).

Breslin, Beau and John J. P. Howley. 2002. "Defending the Politics of Clemency." *Oregon Law Review* 81:231–54.

Callins v. Collins. 1994. 510 U.S. 1129.

Carrington, Frank and George Nicholson. 1984. "The Victims' Movement: An Idea Whose Time Has Come." *Pepperdine Law Review* 11:1–13.

Clemency for Battered Women in Michigan: A Manual for Attorneys, Law Students and Social Workers (2003). http://www.umich.edu/~clemency/clemency_manual/manual_chapter02.html (last consulted 26 August 2003).

Corrections Digest. 1987. "Clemency Becoming Rare as Executions Increase." 8 July 1987:2.

Cottingham, John. 1979. "Varieties of Retribution." *The Philosophical Quarterly* 29:238–46.

Crosara, Stafano. 2000. "I'm Against the Death Penalty." *Trieste Contemporanea* (November 2000). http://www.tscont.ts.it/pag20-e.htm (last consulted 26 August 2003).

Culbert, Jennifer. 2001. "The Sacred Name of Pain: The Role of Victim Impact Evidence in Death Penalty Sentencing Decisions." Pp. 103–36 in *Pain, Death, and the Law*, edited by Austin Sarat. Ann Arbor: University of Michigan Press.

———. 1995. "The Body in *Payne*: The Rhetoric of Victims' Rights and the Predicament of Judgment." Paper presented at the 1995 Annual Meeting of the Law & Society Association, Toronto, Canada.

Davis, Michael. 1995. "Harm and Retribution." Pp. 188–218 in *Punishment*, edited by A. John Simmons et al. Princeton, NJ: Princeton University Press.

Derrida, Jacques. 1999. "The Century and the Pardon." *Le Mondes des Debats* (December 1999). www.excitingland.com/fixion/pardonEng.htm (last consulted 26 August 2003).

———. Undated. *To Forgive: The Unforgivable and the Imprescriptible.* Unpublished manuscript, on file with the author.

Dinsmore, Alyson. 2002. "Clemency in Capital Cases: The Need to Ensure Meaningful Review." *UCLA Law Review* 49:1825–58.

Duff, R. A. and David Garland. 1995. *A Reader on Punishment.* Oxford: Oxford University Press.

Evans, Dominic. 2003. "Amnesty Urges Bush 'Moral Stand' on Death Penalty." *ABCNews. Com.* (January 12, 2003). http://www.stopcapitalpunishment.org/coverage/48.html (last consulted Aug. 26, 2003).

Ewick, Patricia and Susan S. Silbey. 1995. "Subversive Stories, Hegemonic Tales: Toward a Sociology of Narrative." *Law & Society Review* 29:197–226.

Ex parte Garland. 1866. 71 U.S. 333.

Ex parte Grossman. 1925. 267 US 87.

The Federalist Papers. 1961. *No. 70* (Alexander Hamilton), pp. 423–31, edited by Clinton Rossiter. New York: New American Library.

Feinberg, Joel. 1970. *Doing and Deserving.* Princeton, NJ: Princeton University Press.

Ferguson, Robert. 1990. "The Judicial Opinion as a Literary Genre." *Yale Journal of Law and the Humanities* 2:201–20.

Ferrer, James. 1880. *Crimes and Punishments.* London: Chatto & Windus.

Fitzpatrick, Peter. 1999. "Life, Death, and the Law—And Why Capital Punishment Is Legally Insupportable." *Cleveland State Law Review* 47:483–96.

Fletcher, George. 1995. *With Justice for Some: Victims' Rights in Criminal Trials.* Reading, MA: Addison-Wesley.

Forer, Lois. 1980. *Criminals and Victims.* New York: Norton.

Gross, Samuel R. and Phoebe C. Ellsworth. 2003. "Second Thoughts: Americans' Views of the Death Penalty at the Turn of the Century," Pp. 7–57 in *Beyond Repair? America's Death Penalty*, edited by Stephen P. Garvey. Durham, NC: Duke University Press.

Harris, Angela P. 1991. "The Jurisprudence of Victimhood." *Supreme Court Review* 1991:77–102.

Heise, Michael. 2003. "Mercy by the Numbers: An Empirical Analysis of Clemency and Its Structure." *Virginia Law Review* 89:239–310.

Henberg, Marvin. 1990. *Retribution: Evil for Evil in Ethics, Law, and Literature.* Philadelphia: Temple University Press.

Henderson, Lynne. 1985. "The Wrongs of Victim's Rights." *Stanford Law Review* 37:937–1021.

Herrera v. Collins. 1993. 506 U.S. 390.

Hines, Craigg. 2003. "A Heartening Rain as We Await the Flood." *Houston Chronicle.Com* (14 January 2003). http://www.chron.com/cs/CDA/story.hts/editorial/hines/1736223 (last consulted 26 August 2003).

"Illinois Governor's Blanket Pardon Spares Lives of 167 Condemned Inmates." 2003. *FoxNews.Com* (11 January 2003). http://www.foxnews.com/story/0,2933,75170,00 html (last consulted 26 August 2003).

Jacoby, Susan. 1983. *Wild Justice: The Evolution of Revenge.* New York: Harper & Row.

Kaminer, Wendy. 1995. *It's All the Rage: Crime and Culture.* Reading, MA: Addison-Wesley.

Kant, Immanuel. 1965. *Metaphysical Elements of Justice.* Trans. John Ladd. Indianapolis: Bobbs-Merrill.

Kobil, Daniel T. 2003. "How to Grant Clemency in Unforgiving Times." *Capital University Law Review* 31:219–41.

_____. 2000. "Chance and the Constitution in Capital Clemency Cases." *Capital University Law Review* 28:567–77.

_____. 1991. "The Quality of Mercy Strained: Wresting the Pardoning Power from the King." *Texas Law Review* 69:569–641.

Lamborn, Leroy L. 1987. "Victim Participation in the Criminal Justice Process: The Proposal for a Constitutional Amendment." *Wayne Law Review* 34:125–20.

Ledewitz, Bruce and Scott Staples. 1993. "The Role of Executive Clemency in Modern Death Penalty Cases." *University of Richmond Law Review* 27:227–39.

Logan, Wayne A. 1999. "Through the Past Darkly: A Survey of the Uses and Abuses of Victim Impact in Capital Trials." *Arizona Law Review* 41:143–92.

Love, Margaret Colgate. 2000–1. "Fear of Forgiving: Rule and Discretion in the Theory and Practice of Pardoning." *Federal Sentencing Reporter* 13:125–33.

McCleskey v. Kemp. 1987. 481 U.S. 279.

McLeod, Maureen. 1986. "Victim Participation at Sentencing." *Criminal Law Bulletin* 22:501–17.

Meehan, Mary. 1989. "Review of *Public Justice, Private Mercy: A Governor's Education on Death Row*, by Edmund (Pat) Brown with Dick Adler. New York: Weidenfeld & Nicholson, 1989, 171 pp." *Harmony* (November–December 1989). http://members.verizon.net/~meehan4/mercy.html (last consulted 26 August 2003).

Miller, William. 1998. "Clint Eastwood and Equity: Popular Culture's Theory of Revenge." Pp. 161–202 in *Law in the Domains of Culture*, edited by Austin Sarat and Thomas R. Kearns. Ann Arbor: University of Michigan Press.

Minow, Martha. 1993. "Surviving Victim Talk." *U.C.L.A. Law Review* 40:1411–45.

Moore, Kathleen Dean. 1993. "Pardon for Good and Sufficient Reasons." *University of Richmond Law Review* 27:281–88.

_____. 1989. *Pardons: Justice, Mercy, and The Public Interest*. New York: Oxford University Press.

Murphy, Jeffrie G. 1979. *Retribution, Justice, and Therapy: Essays in the Philosophy of Law*. Boston: D. Reidel Publishing Company.

New York Times. 1986. "Five, Lives Spared, Hail Anaya's Move." *New York Times*, 28 November 1986, A18.

Nozick, Robert. 1981. *Philosophical Explanations*. Cambridge: Harvard University Press.

_____. 1974. *Anarchy, State, and Utopia*. New York: Basic Books.

O'Brien, Claire. 2003. "Ryan: Life Over Death: Over Protests of Victims' Families, Governor Commutes All Sentences." *The Southern Illinoisan* (11 January 2003). http://www.stopcapitalpunishment.org/coverage/45.html (last consulted 26 August 2003).

Ohio Adult Parole Authority v. Woodard. 1998. 523 U.S. 272.

"An Open Letter to Governor Ryan." 2002. (30 December 2002.) http://www.law.northwestern.edu/depts/clinic/wrongful/documents/LawProfLet1.pdf (last consulted 26 August 2003).

"Open Letter Signed by More than 650 Illinois Attorneys." 2002. (18 November 2002.) http://www.law.northwestern.edu/depts/clinic/wrongful/documents/LawyerLet1.pdf (last consulted 26 August 2003).

Phillips, Robert Anthony. 2003. "Ryan Commutes All Death Sentences in Illinois." *The Death House.com*. (11 January 2003). http://www.thedeathhouse.com/deathhousenewfi_352.htm (last consulted 26 August 2003).

Pillsbury, Samuel H. 1989. "Emotional Justice: Moralizing the Passions of Criminal Justice." *Cornell Law Review* 74:655–710.

Radelet, Michael L. and Barbara A. Zsembik. 1993. "Executive Clemency in Post-*Furman* Capital Cases." *University of Richmond Law Review* 27:289–314.

Reagan, Ronald. 1981. "Proclamation No. 4831." *C.F.R.* 3: 18.

Roland, David L. 1989. "Progress in the Victim Reform Movement: No Longer the 'Forgotten Victim.'" *Pepperdine Law Review* 17:35–58.

Ryan, George. 2003. "I Must Act" (speech at the Northwestern University College of Law, 11 January 2003). http://www.deathpenaltyinfo.org/article.php?scid=13&did=551 (last consulted 26 August 2003).

Salladay, Robert. 1998. "Clemency: Slim Chance These Days." *San Francisco Examiner*, 29 November 1998. Available at http://www.sfgate.com/cgi-bin/article.cgi%3Ff=/examiner/archive/1998/11/29/NEWS8622.dtl&type=printable (last consulted 26 August 2003).

Sanford, Terry. 1966. "On Executive Clemency." Pp. 552–53 in *Messages, Addresses and Public Papers of Governor Terry Sanford 1961–1965*. Raleigh, NC: Council of State, State of North Carolina.

Sarat, Austin. 2001. *When the State Kills: Capital Punishment and the American Condition*. Princeton, NJ: Princeton University Press.

Scheingold, Stuart A., Toska Olson, and Jana Pershing. 1994. "Sexual Violence, Victim Advocacy, and Republican Criminology: Washington State's Community Protection Act." *Law and Society Review* 28:729–63.

Simon, Jonathan. 2003. *Governing Through Crime: The War on Crime and the Transformation of American Governance 1960–2000*. Unpublished manuscript, on file with the author.

Singer, Richard. 1979. *Just Deserts: Sentencing Based on Equality and Desert*. Cambridge, MA: Ballinger Publishing Company.

Story, Joseph. 1848. *Two Commentaries on the Constitution of the United States*. 3d ed. Boston: Hilliard, Gray, and Company.

Sward, Susan. 2003. "Pat Ryan's Book Helped Ryan Decide: Former Governor Wrote About Struggles Over Death Penalty." *San Francisco Chronicle.Com* (13 January 2003). http://www.sfgate.com/cgi-bin/article.cgi?file=/chronicle/archive/2003/01/13/MN3420.DTL (last consulted 26 August 2003).

Taylor, Lou. 1983. *Mourning Dress: A Costume and Social History*. London: Allen & Unwin.

von Hirsch, Andrew. 1985. *Past or Future Crimes: Deservedness and Dangerousness in the Sentencing of Criminals*. New Brunswick: Rutgers University Press.

Walsh, Katie. 2002. "Clemency Hearings Unjust to Victims' Families." *Columbia Chronicle Online* (21 October 2002). http://www.ccchronicle.com/back/2002-10-21/opinions4.html (last consulted 26 August 2003).

Whitworth, Steve. 2003. "Haine Enraged by Governor's Move." *The Telegraph.com.* (12 January 2003). http://www.stopcapitalpunishment.org/coverage/44.html (last consulted 26 August 2003).

Will, George. "Death Row Clemency Shows a Contempt for Democracy." *Chicago Sun-Times*, 19 January 2003, 33.

PART III

RESEARCH PERSPECTIVES

CHAPTER 13

THE DEATH PENALTY AND THE FAMILIES OF VICTIMS: AN OVERVIEW OF RESEARCH ISSUES

Margaret Vandiver

Introduction

There is surprisingly little research concerning the effects of capital punishment on the families of murder victims. Despite lack of evidence, discussions of the death penalty often revolve around claims about whether executions offer certain benefits to victims' families not provided by any other form of punishment. This chapter provides an overview of the issues facing researchers and emphasizes the need for a systematic program of research.

Nearly every discussion of the death penalty includes the question, "What about the victims' families?" and most discussions of victims' issues ultimately lead to the question of capital punishment. Supporters of the death penalty claim that it offers benefits to victims' families not provided by any other punishment; opponents deny that this is so, sometimes asserting that the death penalty harms the families of victims and the families of offenders as well. Neither the enormous scholarly literature on capital punishment nor the growing research literature on surviving family members of homicide victims has adequately tested these assertions. We know very little about how the death penalty in practice affects victims' families.

This chapter is intended to point the way to remedying this deficit of knowledge. I discuss underlying issues that researchers need to consider, put forward a number of specific questions that future research should attempt to answer, and note some of the basic methodological issues facing researchers in this area. I do not attempt to set out a full research agenda, nor do I try to resolve the very challenging methodological and ethical issues raised by the topic. Rather, the chapter is simply an overview of what we should be trying to find out and how we might begin to do so.

Twenty-five years ago there was almost no scholarly literature on homicide victims' surviving family members. Fortunately, a substantial and growing body of research has provided excellent descriptions of the experiences of these families.[1] These studies uniformly document the psychic and emotional devastation created by homicide and provide a record of "what murder leaves behind" (Magee 1983; for an especially thoughtful and detailed summary, see Rock 1998: 28–56). Although emotionally compelling, this research suffers from serious methodological shortcomings. Rynearson and Geoffrey state that "a systematic, prospective, controlled study of the effects of traumatic dying and its treatment has not been completed, leaving us with a very rudimentary understanding" (1999:109), further noting that "homicidal dying has received the least attention of all forms of traumatic death" (p. 112).

Background Issues

Some Questions of Scope and Definition

The central question is simple enough: *How does the death penalty affect the families of homicide victims?* A little thought, however, reveals that each of the terms in the question is complex and needs careful definition. To begin with, what is meant by family? It is possible, of course, to make a list of close relations by blood and marriage and then restrict research to those persons. But

---

1. For studies of the reactions of families to a relative's murder, see Amick-McMullan, Kilpatrick, Veronen, and Smith 1989; Amick-McMullan, Kilpatrick, and Veronen 1989; Armour 2003; Asaro 2001a; Burgess 1975; Johnson and Young 1992; Redmond 1996; Rynearson 1984; Rynearson and McCreery 1993; Sprang et al. 1989; Stevens-Guille 1999. The effects on different groups of survivors are considered by Burman and Allen-Meares 1994; Freeman et al. 1996; Hatton 2003; Horne 2003; Malmquist 1986; Murphy et al. 1999; Rinear 1988. Therapeutic interventions are described in Asaro 2001b; Getzel and Masters 1984; Jackson 1979; Lyon et al. 1992; Masters et al. 1988; Parkes 1993; Rynearson and Geoffrey 1999; Salloum et al. 2001; Temple 1997. A number of recent studies exploring grief and trauma reactions to homicide have improved significantly on the methods of earlier studies, using larger samples, comparison groups, and/or statistical analysis. See Amick-McMullan et al. 1991; Murphy et al. 1999; Sprang et al. 1992–3; Thompson et al. 1998; Vargas et al. 1989. For guides to assist the bereaved and those working with them, see Conrad 1998; Jenkins 2001; Redmond 1989; Spungen 1998. As of yet, there is little research specifically focused on victims' survivors who oppose the death penalty. See Cushing and Sheffer 2002; King, R. 2003.

the emotional content of those relationships obviously varies widely; cousins, for instance, can be as close as siblings, or may never have met. In some cases, a relationship unrecognized by law—for instance between gay couples—may be the victim's primary emotional affiliation. Whether close friends of the victim should be included in considering the effects of punishment is another question researchers must resolve.

Homicide is a broad term encompassing a wide range of behavior. Under modern American law, the death penalty is almost entirely reserved for first-degree murder, thus excluding most homicide defendants from any possibility of receiving a death sentence. Even among first-degree murders, most cases do not receive death (Bedau 1997:31–32). This means that the vast majority of victims' families will not see the offender sentenced to death, regardless of how much they may wish this outcome. The precise legal distinctions between degrees of homicide or between first-degree homicides with and without certain aggravating factors may not be entirely clear or compelling to grieving families. Any comprehensive assessment of the effects of capital punishment on victims' families must find a way to factor in the feelings of families who believed the penalty should be available to them by law, but discovered that it was not.

Even the term death penalty must be clarified. A study of the effects of executions on victims' families would exclude the vast majority of death sentences; there are 3,487 people on death row and fewer than seventy have been executed per year since 2001 (Death Penalty Information Center 2004a). Many victims' families experience the reversal of the offender's death sentence, resulting in a new sentencing hearing, another trial, or the reduction of the sentence to life. Families who experience the imposition and reduction of the death sentence should not be ignored by researchers.

Precise definition of terms will help to delineate the scope of the research topic. Questions of time and place also must be carefully considered, as the passage of time and the jurisdiction in which the homicide occurred may introduce variations in how the death penalty affects victims' families. Much of the discussion of families' sentencing preferences assumes that their wishes are stable over time, but research has not established whether this is actually the case. The mutability of opinion, as well as what is known about the stages of grief, points to the importance of incorporating time into research on victims' families. To assess the effects of the death penalty, researchers should study the reactions of families in the immediate aftermath of the crime, at trial, during the period of appeals, at the time of execution, and after execution.

Place is another essential element to consider. Twelve American states and the District of Columbia are abolitionist, and among death penalty jurisdictions the legal requirements for a crime to be prosecuted as a capital homicide vary (Bonczar and Snell 2003:2). The likelihood of a capital prosecution, death sentence, and execution after imposition of a death sentence, as well as the speed with which death sentences are executed varies widely among and even within death penalty states.

Finally, researchers must be sensitive to the fact that victims' survivors are not a monolithic group. Although they share the experience of losing a family member to homicide, their expectations of how society should respond to the homicide and their experiences with the criminal justice system can be vastly different. Some aspects of violence bereavement are probably universal; however, the social and cultural contexts of the survivors certainly influence their response to their loss. Understanding this should make researchers cautious about generalizing findings based on the study of homogeneous samples of victims.

There is overwhelming evidence that the system does not respond equally to victims; the racial and economic divisions of American society are tragically reflected in the processing of homicide cases (for a recent overview of the extensive literature on this issue, see Baldus and Woodworth 2003). Some victims are devalued, while others receive enormously disproportionate amounts of attention. Researchers hoping to learn the effect of the death penalty on victims' families must be sure that their samples reflect the racial and economic profile of victims. A sample of middle class white families will not be adequate to reflect the experiences and opinions of demographically diverse victims' families.

What Can the Criminal Justice System Do for Survivors?

Underlying much of the discussion of victims and capital punishment is the assumption that the criminal justice system can do something to help survivors. Marie Deans, founder of a group of murder victims' families opposed to executions, notes, "After a murder, victims' families face two things: a death and a crime" (quoted in *Schiro v. Summerlin, Brief of Amici Curiae* 2004:4; footnote 6). This insight can clarify researchers' thinking about the interactions of victims' survivors and the criminal justice system. It is reasonable to expect—or at least to hope—that the system should be able to deal effectively with the crime. But should victims' families expect that the criminal justice system can assist them in coping with the emotional effects of the violent death of a relative?

The American system of law is designed not only to prevent crime and to punish those guilty of committing crimes, but also to restrict the scope of the state's power against individuals who are suspected of committing crimes. The focus of the system is not to provide consolation or vindication to victims. In this sense, when victims complain of being ignored and left out of the system, they are correct.[2] But if the criminal justice system is primarily an arrangement between the state and the criminal offender, where do victims come into the picture? What rights do they have? What can the criminal justice system offer them?

In cases of nonviolent crimes, it is possible to provide some sort of restitution as part of the sentence imposed on the offender, making the sentence serve the double function of punishing the offender and restoring to the victim at least part of what was taken. How this can be done for violent crimes is less clear, and in the case of murder it is all too clear that what was taken can never be restored. (For a description of meetings between homicide survivors and offenders, see Umbreit et al., this volume; for further discussion of the role of restitution in capital cases, see Kay, this volume).

Susan Bandes notes that much of what survivors need is less likely to be provided by the criminal justice system than by "psychological, religious and social support systems ... [which] have greater ability to individuate among victims and to accommodate the shifting and complex needs of particular victims" (2000:1605–6). Indeed, preventing the criminal justice system from doing further harm to survivors may be a more realistic goal than expecting it to provide them with positive assistance. Research indicates that "repetitive confrontations with the criminal justice system" can disrupt the recovery of victims' families (Masters et al. 1988:116) and that the ways in which professionals treat the recently bereaved can have a lasting impact (Janzen et al. 2003–4). Treating the families of homicide victims with respect, scrupulously informing them of every development in the case, and providing them with an advocate—or at least a contact who can answer their questions—can go some way toward minimizing the damage that may be inflicted by contact with the criminal justice system.

---

2. It is worth considering for a moment what a criminal justice system run by the wishes of individual victims would be like. Victims' survivors differ widely on what they perceive as the best legal outcome of the case against the offender; it is an error to assume that "victims are a homogeneous group" (Hodgkinson 2004:338). If the outcome of prosecutions were dictated by the victims, there would be no consistency in treatment of offenders and few protections from capricious violations of rights. It is not clear even whether defendants would have rights under such an arrangement, as the state would serve merely as an instrument to carry out victims' punishment preferences. This scenario is a reductio ad absurdum, of course, and proponents of victims' rights do not propose such a system; but it illustrates the underlying problems of basing criminal justice decisions on victims' wishes.

Certainly many families of homicide victims want much more from the criminal justice system than simply the absence of further harm. Families may expect the system to restore some of their sense of security by ensuring that the murderer will never hurt them or anyone else again. They may hope that the trial can provide a forum for the expression of the value of the victim and the immeasurable depth of their loss. Many families want to be able to feel that murderers receive the punishment they deserve. Families may look forward to an end of their involvement with the criminal justice system as an important milestone.

The criminal justice system, unfortunately, is often unable to do any of these things for victims' families. If no one is caught for the crime, questions of punishment are moot—and it is worth remembering that about one-third of murders in the United States are not cleared by an arrest (Federal Bureau of Investigation 2003). Where there is a suspect, the strength of the evidence, particulars of the state's law, and other variables irrelevant to the pain suffered by the family may decide how the case will be charged, processed, and adjudicated. If the case goes to trial, the skills of the opposing attorneys and the decisions of the judge and jury may determine an outcome that is different from that desired by the victims' survivors. If a life sentence without the possibility of parole is imposed, the sentencing is likely to mark the end of the survivors' involvement with the criminal justice system; but if the offender is sentenced to death, the involvement of the victims' family with the courts will continue for many years.

Systematic research on how the death penalty affects victims' families needs to begin with close consideration of the issues outlined above. Careful definition of terms and attention to variations of time, location, and culture will focus the research questions and add to the reliability and validity of the results. Reflection on the limits of what the criminal justice system is able to do for victims' families will clarify underlying assumptions about the potential and actual role of the system in the aftermath of homicide.

Specific Areas for Research

The subject of this chapter is the death penalty as it is currently used in the United States. I am not asking the question of whether a hypothetical system of justice with a perfect death penalty might benefit victims' families. Such a question may provide grounds for speculation, but it is unanswerable by research. The system we have often seems to please neither supporters nor opponents of capital punishment, but it is this system that both defendants and victims encounter, and it is this system that researchers must study.

Convictions for first-degree murder are likely to result in one of three sentences: death, life without parole (LWOP), or life or a long term of years with the possibility of parole (LWP). How these sentences affect victims is an empirical question that research should be able to address. Does one of the sentences meet the needs of the families better than the others? Does the death sentence affect the families, either positively or negatively, in ways not done by the available alternate sentences?

Incapacitation and Families' Sense of Safety

One of the central concerns of victims' families is the incapacitation of the offender. This concern points to the empirical question of which sentence is most likely to make victims' families feel that they do not need to worry about their own or others' safety. In theory, a sentence of LWOP should mean that the family has no concerns about release—but does it? Do victims' families believe that LWOP means confinement until death?

Obviously the execution of the offender provides the victims' families with absolute assurance that he cannot offend again. But the reality of the modern death penalty in America is that condemned prisoners serve long prison terms before their executions, unless they choose to drop their appeals. The period of appeals can last as long as two or even three decades, and condemned inmates have a high probability of achieving a reversal of their sentence and/or conviction (Liebman et al. 2000). While most LWOP and LWP sentences can also be appealed, this is done less frequently and with a much lower rate of success. Thus, the death penalty may eventually provide perfect incapacitation, but only after a period of many years on the appellate roller coaster.

These considerations suggest several questions researchers might try to answer. Concerning sentences of life without parole: How do families interpret a sentence of LWOP? Does it give them a sense of security? Do they believe that the prisoner will be held until his death? Concerning the death penalty: Given the long gap between the imposition and the execution of a death sentence and the high probability of reversal on appeal, is the absolute incapacitation of death worth the price paid in uncertainty and waiting? Does prolonged engagement with the criminal justice system prior to execution harm victims' families?

Desiring the Most Severe Penalty vs. Desiring the Death Penalty

It is natural for families to feel that the most severe punishment best reflects the enormity of the crime against their relative and the depth of their sorrow and pain. Any sentence lighter than the maximum provided by law runs the risk of seeming to indicate that the criminal justice system, or society in general, did not properly value the victim's life or comprehend the magnitude of the family's loss.[3]

This raises the question of whether LWOP would be a more satisfactory punishment if it were the harshest punishment available. In other words, does the death penalty intrinsically offer something no other sentence can, or is it desired by many families simply as the most severe of the available options? A study contrasting the reactions of families to LWOP sentences in death penalty and non-death penalty jurisdictions could be a start to answering this question.

Influences on the Choice to Support a Particular Penalty

The adversarial nature of the American legal system leaves victims' families vulnerable to pressure from various sources. Research should investigate whether families feel any pressure to support one penalty versus another, from whom such pressure comes, and how families react to it. Related to this is the question of how homicide victims' families who oppose the death penalty are treated by victim advocates, police, and prosecutors. Research should further address whether and how religious affiliation, educational levels, and demographic variables influence survivors' preference for certain penalties.

Stability of Opinion over Time

Accounts by survivors indicate that some of those who oppose the death penalty for their family member's murderer came to that position after an initial period of desiring execution (e.g., Welch 2001). After the first shock, rage, and turmoil of the period immediately following the murder, people may reassess their opinion and decide against supporting the execution of the offender. (The opposite may also be true, but I have not seen any accounts of relatives who initially wanted a life sentence deciding later that they preferred death.)

Researchers should try to assess the stability of families' feelings about the proper sentence for the offender in their relatives' cases. Is it common for families who initially want the death sentence to change their minds over time?

---

3. Indeed, some victims' families find that even the harshest legal punishment is too mild and wish that the defendant could be made to suffer physically at least as much as their relative did (for examples, see Gross and Matheson 2003:495–97).

Does the opposite occur? If families want a death sentence, but the offender receives LWOP, do they continue to regret his not receiving death?

The Aftermath of Execution

Little is known about how offenders' executions actually affect families of victims. Media interviews with victims' family members immediately before and after executions provide a glimpse of their initial reactions to the execution. These interviews present the feelings of selected family members at moments of intense emotional strain, and should not be used as a basis to reach broad conclusions about the effects of executions.

Among the questions researchers need to explore in this area are the following: Does the emotional condition of survivors improve after the execution? If so, is this improvement due to the execution or due to the end of the survivors' involvement with the criminal justice system? Does any improvement in condition continue over the long term? Do survivors who supported the execution react differently than those who opposed it or were ambivalent? Is there a difference in response between those who did and those who did not witness the execution?

Especially Difficult Issues

The research questions suggested above are not simple. They make a number of simplifying assumptions, however, which often are not borne out in reality. In the following section, I consider several complex and difficult situations that tend to blur moral absolutes and defy simple answers.

Disagreement within Families
As to the Desired Sentence

Members of the same family often disagree as to the best outcome of the case against their relative's accused murderer. A related situation arises when a defendant has multiple victims; the various families are likely to have disagreements over punishment. These disagreements raise thorny issues for those who support the right of victims to have determinative input into sentencing. Should one family's opinion prevail over another's? How should opinions be weighed within families? Does a mother's preference outweigh a wife's? Is a child's opinion more important than a sibling's? Researchers should be aware of intrafamilial disagreement over sentencing, which can become a further source of stress, anger, and even estrangement within families.

Victim and Offender Are Members of the Same Family

Although most death sentences are imposed upon people convicted of killing strangers or acquaintances, rather than family members, there are cases in which the victim and defendant are members of the same family; a family member's testimony may even have helped to convict the defendant. The conflicts of loyalty in such situations are perhaps especially strong when victim and offender are related by blood rather than by marriage. Researchers should explore the reactions and sentencing preferences of survivors in various family situations to see if patterns emerge. The reactions of survivors related to both the victim and offender should be compared to reactions of survivors in cases where the murderer and victim were strangers.

Wrongful Convictions

In the past several years, a great deal of attention has been given to wrongfully convicted prisoners. As of September 2004, 116 innocent people have been released from death row (Death Penalty Information Center 2004b). The effects of the discovery of a wrongful conviction on the victim's family are rarely considered, but are likely to be profound. Imagine believing for years or even decades that the murderer of your relative was behind bars and then discovering that the wrong person had been convicted. That terrible discovery comes with an equally terrible corollary: the guilty person has not been punished for the crime, is probably free, and may have continued to commit crimes. With the exoneration of an innocent defendant, the victim's family members are returned to the position they were in immediately after the crime, searching for answers to the basic question of who killed their relative. It may be of interest to examine whether victims' families' experiences following the revelation of a wrongful conviction in a capital case differ from corresponding experiences in noncapital cases.

The Devalued Victim

The criminal justice system, the media, and society at large do not respond in the same way to all homicides. The deaths of victims whose activities placed them in vulnerable situations may not evoke the outrage and sympathy felt for victims who were attacked at random. Victims who were themselves suspected of involvement with gangs or criminal activity may even be blamed for the crime. The families of these victims are likely to find that the social response to their loss is heavily tinged with contempt and indifference.

Demographic characteristics contribute to different responses as well. Defendants convicted of killing members of a minority group are likely to receive more lenient treatment by the criminal justice system than those convicted of the homicide of white victims (Baldus and Woodworth 2003). Researchers must take into account the very different experiences survivors have with the system, based upon how highly their relative was valued.

The Effect of the Death Penalty on the Families of the Condemned

Special consideration must be given to one subset of families experiencing violence bereavement: the families of condemned inmates. As a small but growing body of research documents, the death penalty is unrelieved agony for this group.[4] Innocent of any offense, they pay a crushing price. If the death penalty benefits other families of homicide victims, it does so at the expense of these innocent people. No research on the effects of the death penalty on families can afford to ignore them.

Condemned prisoners come from families that are often ethnic or racial minorities and are almost always without financial resources (Haney 2003). A substantial number of these families have experienced the murder of a family member themselves, prior to the time that their relative is accused of capital murder. This means they know the trauma of the violent death of a relative and have encountered the criminal justice system as victims' families. Often their experiences have been very negative: their complaints may include indifference from criminal justice system personnel, lack of information, and a sense of helplessness about influencing the outcome (Vandiver 2003:619–20). In addition, they are likely to have experienced the imposition of a relatively light sentence for the offender who killed their family member.

When a relative is charged with a capital crime, these families face the criminal justice system again, but this time as the family of a capital offender. Again their experiences are intensely negative; they are once again likely to suffer

---

4. Beck et al. 2003; King, K. 2004; King, R. 2005; King, R. and Norgard 1999; Radelet et al. 1983; Sharp 2005; Smykla 1987; Vallejo 1995.

from the indifference or even hostility of personnel, from lack of information, and from a feeling of helplessness. They are, however, far more likely to experience the harshness of the criminal justice system, especially if their relative has been accused of murdering a white victim.

A Few Notes on Methods

I briefly outline below some of the principal issues researchers need to consider in designing studies on capital punishment and victims' families.[5] If research is to move beyond the anecdotal and provide solid evidence to support broad conclusions, researchers must first clarify definitions and pose precise research questions, as difficult as this may be in an area of such intense emotion. Bonanno (1999:38) notes that research in bereavement "has suffered from an absence of clear operational definitions," and this is certainly true of the subset of bereavement research dealing with homicide. The preceding discussion of background issues and specific areas for research is meant to provide a beginning to this process. In addition, researchers must deal with design issues—including samples, comparison groups, time, and baseline information. Finally, we must be aware of and open about the limitations of our work, being careful to acknowledge weaknesses in our designs and data.

Samples

Small, nonrandom samples that are not representative of the demographics of homicide victims are likely to yield misleading results. It might be tempting, for instance, to obtain a sample by using a list of executions in a state to identify victims' families. Such a sample would greatly over-represent white, middle class, and suburban victims. A sample drawn from families attending victims' support groups would add a further element of self selection.

A better strategy would be to start from a list of homicides and draw a sample that reflected the demographics of victims. A sample constructed in this

---

5. The methodological and ethical challenges facing researchers in this area are similar to those faced by researchers who focus on prisoners' families (see Hagan 1996; Vandiver and Berardo 2000; Parkes 1995).

way would have few cases resulting in death sentences and even fewer resulting in executions; it would, however, reflect the reality that only a very small number of homicide offenders receive death sentences.

Comparison Groups

Although true experimental designs are clearly impossible in this type of research, careful use of comparison groups would be a great advance. Study of comparison groups could illuminate the varying impact that sentences of death, LWOP, LWP, and less may have on victims' families. Comparison groups would make it possible to study what changes in survivors' condition are due to the response of the criminal justice system and what changes may occur simply with the passage of time. Comparison groups would allow researchers to explore whether families' attitudes about the death penalty, in combination with the sentence received, have an impact on their emotional condition.

Researchers could use comparison groups to examine differences that may exist between the impact of LWOP sentences on victims' families in death penalty jurisdictions and abolitionist jurisdictions. Such comparisons could explore the question of whether families interpret the meaning of LWOP differently where it is the most severe possible sentence versus where it is the less severe alternative to death.

Longitudinal Research

Studies of the effects of criminal sentences on victims' survivors must incorporate the effects of the passage of time on grieving. The extensive literature on bereavement has established that emotional reactions to loss change over time; while it is an oversimplification to expect grieving to progress in discrete stages, it is certainly true that the tenth year after a loss is different from the first. Researchers must incorporate measurements over a period of years, if not decades, in order to document these changes.

Baseline Measurements

With no baseline measurement of families' well-being before the crime, it is necessary to rely on people's retrospective self-reports of their feelings and emotional condition. Evaluations and memories of how one felt in the past, particularly before a traumatic event, are unlikely to be highly reliable. The lack of measures of well-being before the homicide is a problem that research design will not be able to remedy. Carefully designed longitudinal research may be able to provide reliable and comparable measurements of emotional and psychological responses at various stages after the homicide, allowing researchers to track changes for better or worse over time (for a description of instruments to measure grief reactions, see Stevens-Guille 1999). These considerations underline the perils of reaching conclusions based on one shot on-the-spot interviews at highly emotional moments (e.g., media interviews immediately after executions).

The Ideal Study and the Realities of Research

A study that incorporated the elements outlined above would be based on a demographically representative sample of homicide victims' families, randomly selected if possible, and drawn from at least two jurisdictions—one with and one without the death penalty. Such a study would include sufficient cases resulting in death sentences and executions for comparative purposes, perhaps through disproportionate sampling. It would continue for a long enough period of time to measure the effects of the progress of cases through the system and the effects of the passage of time on the families' feelings and opinions, incorporating some sort of systematic measurement of the emotional well-being of the families at each stage of the process. Is such a study realistic? The scope, expense, and time commitment are formidable from a researcher's point of view; the level of cooperation expected from bereaved families and the possible consequences of such repeated inquiries into their intimate emotional lives raise troubling ethical issues.

If the study outlined above is unrealistic, it still may be useful to consider it as a model. Incorporating as many of its features as possible will strengthen future research. Acknowledging the areas in which our research falls short of the ideal will help us avoid overstating our conclusions, particularly important in an area of such emotional and political volatility.

Conclusion

Few public policy issues generate stronger feelings than capital punishment, and no aspect of the death penalty creates more emotion than its presumed effects on victims' families. The feelings and opinions expressed, however, are based on almost no evidence. There is an urgent need for academic researchers to turn their attention to this area and to use their skills to learn as much as possible about how capital punishment affects the families of murder victims.

This research will be challenging methodologically, ethically, and emotionally, but a beginning must be made.

References

Amick-McMullan, Angelynne, Dean G. Kilpatrick, and Heidi S. Resnick. 1991. "Homicide as a Risk Factor for PTSD Among Surviving Family Members." *Behavior Modification* 15:545–59.

Amick-McMullan, Angelynne, Dean G. Kilpatrick, and Lois J. Veronen. 1989. "Family Survivors of Homicide Victims: A Behavioral Analysis." *The Behavior Therapist* 12:75–79.

Amick-McMullan, Angelynne, Dean G. Kilpatrick, Lois J. Veronen, and Susan Smith. 1989. "Family Survivors of Homicide Victims: Theoretical Perspectives and an Exploratory Study." *Journal of Traumatic Stress* 2:21–35.

Armour, Marilyn Peterson. 2003. "Meaning Making in the Aftermath of Homicide." *Death Studies* 27:519–40.

Asaro, M. Regina. 2001a. "Working with Adult Homicide Survivors, Part I: Impact and Sequelae of Murder." *Perspectives in Psychiatric Care* 37:95–101.

———. 2001b. "Working with Adult Homicide Survivors, Part II: Helping Family Members Cope with Murder." *Perspectives in Psychiatric Care* 37:115–24; 136.

Baldus, David C. and George Woodworth. 2003. "Race Discrimination and the Death Penalty: An Empirical and Legal Overview." Pp. 501–51 in *America's Experiment with Capital Punishment: Reflections on the Past, Present and Future of the Ultimate Penal Sanction*, 2d ed., edited by James R. Acker, Robert M. Bohm, and Charles S. Lanier. Durham, NC: Carolina Academic Press.

Bandes, Susan. 2000. "When Victims Seek Closure: Forgiveness, Vengeance and the Role of Government." *Fordham Urban Law Journal* 27:1599–619.

Beck, Elizabeth, Brenda Sims Blackwell, Pamela Blume Leonard, and Michael Mears. 2003. "Seeking Sanctuary: Interviews with Family Members of Capital Defendants." *Cornell Law Review* 88:382–418.

Bedau, Hugo Adam 1997. *The Death Penalty in America: Current Controversies*. New York: Oxford University Press.

Bonczar, Thomas P. and Tracy L. Snell. 2003. "Capital Punishment, 2002" (Washington, DC: Bureau of Justice Statistics). Available at http://www.ojp.usdoj.gov/bjs/ (accessed 16 September 2004).

Bonanno, George A. 1999. "Factors Associated with Effective Loss Accommodation." Pp. 37–51 in Charles R. Figley, *Traumatology of Grieving: Conceptual, Theoretical, and Treatment Foundations*. Philadelphia: Brunner/Mazel.

Burgess, Ann Wolbert. 1975. "Family Reaction to Homicide." *American Journal of Orthopsychiatry* 45:391–98.

Burman, Sondra and Paula Allen-Meares. 1994. "Neglected Victims of Murder: Children's Witness to Parental Homicide." *Social Work* 39:28–34.

Conrad, Bonnie Hunt. 1998. *When a Child Has Been Murdered: Ways You Can Help the Grieving Parents*. Amityville, NY: Baywood Publishing Company, Inc.

Cushing, Robert Renny and Susannah Sheffer. 2002. *Dignity Denied: The Experience of Murder Victims' Family Members Who Oppose the Death Penalty*. Cambridge, MA: Murder Victims' Families for Reconciliation. Available at: http://www.mvfr.org (accessed 16 September 2004).

Death Penalty Information Center. 2004a. "Executions by Year." Available at http://www.deathpenaltyinfo.org (accessed 16 September 2004).

————. 2004b. "Innocence and the Death Penalty." Available at http://www.death-penaltyinfo.org (accessed 16 September 2004).

Federal Bureau of Investigation. 2003. *Crime in the United States, 2002*. Available at: http://www.fbi.gov/ucr/02cius.htm (accessed 16 September 2004).

Freeman, Linda N., David Shaffer, and Helen Smith. 1996. "Neglected Victims of Homicide: The Needs of Young Siblings of Murder Victims." *American Journal of Orthopsychiatry* 66:337–45.

Getzel, George S. and Rosemary Masters. 1984. "Serving Families Who Survive Homicide Victims." *Social Casework*: 138–44.

Gross, Samuel R. and Daniel J. Matheson. 2003. "What They Say at the End: Capital Victims' Families and the Press." *Cornell Law Review* 88:486–516.

Hagan, John. 1996. "The Next Generation: Children of Prisoners." In Vera Institute of Justice, *The Unintended Consequences of Incarceration* (21–39). Available at: http://www.vera.org (accessed 16 September 2004).

Haney, Craig. 2003. "Mitigation and the Study of Lives: On the Roots of Violent Criminality and the Nature of Capital Justice." Pp. 469–500 in *America's Experiment with Capital Punishment: Reflections on the Past, Present and Future of the Ultimate Penal Sanction*, 2d ed., edited by James R. Acker, Robert M. Bohm, and Charles S. Lanier. Durham, NC: Carolina Academic Press.

Hatton, Rebecca. 2003. "Homicide Bereavement Counseling: A Survey of Providers." *Death Studies* 27:427–48.

Hodgkinson, Peter. 2004. "Capital Punishment: Meeting the Needs of the Families of the Homicide Victim and the Condemned." Pp. 332–58 in *Capital Punishment: Strategies for Abolition*, edited by Peter Hodgkinson and William A. Schabas. New York: Cambridge University Press.

Horne, Christopher. 2003. "Families of Homicide Victims: Service Utilization Patterns of Extra- and Intrafamilial Homicide Survivors." *Journal of Family Violence* 18:75–82.

Jackson, Anna Mitchell. 1979. "The Availability of Mental Health Services for Dependents of Homicide Victims." Pp. 91–100 in *Lethal Aspects of Urban Violence*, edited by Harold M. Rose. Lexington, MA: Lexington Books.

Janzen, Linda, Susan Cadell, and Anne Westhues. 2003–4. "From Death Notification through the Funeral: Bereaved Parents' Experiences and Their Advice to Professionals." *Omega* 48:149–64.

Jenkins, Bill. 2001. *What To Do When the Police Leave: A Guide to the First Days of Traumatic Loss*, 3d ed. Richmond, VA: WBJ Press.

Johnson, Norma C. and Saundrea D. Young. 1992. "Survivors' Response to Gang Violence." Pp. 136–46 in *Substance Abuse and Gang Violence*, edited by Richard C. Cervantes. Newbury Park: Sage Publications.

Kay, Judith W. This volume.

King, Kate. 2004. "It Hurts So Bad: Comparing Grieving Patterns of the Families of Murder Victims with Those of Families of Death Row Inmates." *Criminal Justice Policy Review* 15:193–211.

King, Rachel. 2005. *Capital Consequences: Families of the Condemned Tell Their Stories.* New Brunswick, NJ : Rutgers University Press.

————. 2003. *Don't Kill in Our Names: Families of Murder Victims Speak Out Against the Death Penalty.* New Brunswick, NJ: Rutgers University Press.

King, Rachel and Katherine Norgard. 1999. "What About Our Families? Using the Impact on Death Row Defendants' Family Members as a Mitigating Factor in Death Penalty Sentence Hearings." *Florida State University Law Review* 26:1119–73.

Liebman, James S., Jeffrey Fagan, and Valerie West. 2000. "A Broken System: Error Rates in Capital Cases, 1973–1995." Available at http://www2.law.columbia.edu/instructionalservices/liebman/ (accessed 16 September 2004).

Lyon, Eleanor, Nancy Moore, and Charles Lexius. 1992. "Group Work with Families of Homicide Victims." *Social Work with Groups* 15:19–33.

Magee, Doug 1983. *What Murder Leaves Behind: The Victim's Family.* New York: Dodd, Mead.

Malmquist, Carl P. 1986. "Children Who Witness Parental Murder: Posttraumatic Aspects." *Journal of American Academy of Child Psychiatry* 25:320–25.

Masters, Rosemary, Lucy N. Friedman, and George Getzel. 1988. "Helping Families of Homicide Victims: A Multidimensional Approach." *Journal of Traumatic Stress* 1:109–25.

Murphy, Shirley A., Tom Braun, Linda Tillery, Kevin C. Cain, L. Clark Johnson, and Randal D. Beaton. 1999. "PTSD Among Bereaved Parents Following the Violent Deaths of Their 12- to 28-Year-Old Children: A Longitudinal Prospective Analysis." *Journal of Traumatic Stress* 12:273–91.

Parkes, Colin M. 1995. "Guidelines for Conducting Ethical Bereavement Research." *Death Studies* 19:171–81.

————. 1993. "Psychiatric Problems Following Bereavement by Murder or Manslaughter." *British Journal of Psychiatry* 162:49–54.

Radelet, Michael L., Margaret Vandiver, and Felix M. Berardo. 1983. "Families, Prisons, and Men with Death Sentences: The Human Impact of Structured Uncertainty." *Journal of Family Issues* 4:593–612.

Redmond, Lula M. 1996. "Sudden Violent Death." Pp. 53–71 in *Living with Grief after Sudden Loss*, edited by Kenneth J. Doka. Washington, DC: Hospice Foundation of America.

————. 1989. *Surviving: When Someone You Love Was Murdered.* Clearwater, FL: Psychological Consultation and Educational Services, Inc.

Rinear, Eileen E. 1988. "Psychosocial Aspects of Parental Response Patterns to the Death of a Child by Homicide." *Journal of Traumatic Stress* 1:305–22.

Rock, Paul E. 1998. *After Homicide: Practical and Political Responses to Bereavement.* Oxford, New York: Oxford University Press.

Rynearson, Edward K. 1984. "Bereavement after Homicide: A Descriptive Study." *American Journal of Psychiatry* 141:1452–54.

Rynearson, Edward K. and Russell Geoffrey. 1999. "Bereavement after Homicide: Its Assessment and Treatment." Pp. 109–30 in Charles R. Figley, *Traumatology of*

Grieving: Conceptual, Theoretical, and Treatment Foundations. Philadelphia: Brunner/Mazel.

Rynearson, Edward K. and Joseph M. McCreery. 1993. "Bereavement After Homicide: A Synergism of Trauma and Loss." *American Journal of Psychiatry* 150:258–61.

Salloum, Alison, Lisa Avery, and Ronald P. McClain. 2001. "Group Psychotherapy for Adolescent Survivors of Homicide Victims: A Pilot Study." *Journal of the American Academy of Child and Adolescent Psychiatry* 40:1261–67.

Schiro v. Summerlin, Brief of Amici Curiae in the Supreme Court of the United States. (26 February 2004).

Sharp, Susan F. 2005. *Hidden Victims: Effects of the Death Penalty on Families of the Accused*. Brunswick, NJ: Rutgers University Press.

Smykla, John Ortiz. 1987. "The Human Impact of Capital Punishment: Interviews With Families of Persons on Death Row." *Journal of Criminal Justice* 15:331–47.

Sprang, M. Virginia, John S. McNeil, and Roosevelt Wright Jr. 1992–93. "Grief Among Surviving Family Members of Homicide Victims: A Causal Approach." *Omega* 26:145–60.

———. 1989. "Psychological Changes after the Murder of a Significant Other." *Social Casework: The Journal of Contemporary Social Work*: 159–64.

Spungen, Deborah 1998. *Homicide: The Hidden Victims*. Thousand Oaks, CA: Sage Publications.

Stevens-Guille, M. Elizabeth. 1999. "Intersections of Grief and Trauma: Family Members' Reactions to Homicide." Pp. 53–69 in Charles R. Figley, *Traumatology of Grieving: Conceptual, Theoretical, and Treatment Foundations*. Philadelphia: Brunner/Mazel.

Temple, Scott. 1997. "Treating Inner-City Families of Homicide Victims: A Contextually Oriented Approach." *Family Process* 36:133–49.

Thompson, Martie P., Fran H. Norris, and R. Barry Ruback. 1998. "Comparative Distress Levels of Inner-City Family Members of Homicide Victims." *Journal of Traumatic Stress* 11:223–42.

Umbreit, Mark S., Betty Vos, Robert B. Coates, and Katherine A. Brown. This volume.

Vallejo, Catherine Anne. 1995. "Death Sentence Experience: The Impact on Family Members of Condemned Inmates." Master's Thesis, California State University, San Bernardino.

Vandiver, Margaret. 2003. "The Impact of Capital Punishment on the Families of Homicide Victims and Condemned Prisoners." Pp. 613–45 in *America's Experiment with Capital Punishment: Reflections on the Past, Present and Future of the Ultimate Penal Sanction*, 2d ed., edited by James R. Acker, Robert M. Bohm, and Charles S. Lanier. Durham, NC: Carolina Academic Press.

Vandiver, Margaret. and Felix M. Berardo. 2000. " 'It's Like Dying Every Day': The Families of Condemned Prisoners." Pp. 339–58 in *Families, Crime and Criminal Justice*, edited by G. L. Fox and M. L. Benson. Amsterdam: JAI.

Vargas, Luis A., Fred Loya, and Janet Hodde-Vargas. 1989. "Exploring the Multidimensional Aspects of Grief Reactions." *American Journal of Psychiatry* 146:1484–88.

Welch, Bud. 2001. " 'I Don't Want the Death Penalty for Timothy McVeigh!': A Father's Struggle with the Death Penalty and the Oklahoma City Bombing." *Loyola Journal of Public Interest Law* 2:53–65.

CHAPTER 14

SECONDARY VICTIMIZATION AMONG FAMILIES OF HOMICIDE VICTIMS: THE IMPACT OF THE JUSTICE PROCESS ON CO-VICTIMS' PSYCHOLOGICAL ADJUSTMENT AND SERVICE UTILIZATION

Mark D. Reed and
Brenda Sims Blackwell

Introduction

This chapter describes the manner in which the families of homicide victims, or "co-victims,"[1] are often treated as their cases advance through the criminal justice system. In this review, we examine the impact of the justice process on co-victims' psychological adjustment and satisfaction with victim services. We also discuss the need for policy changes in how police investigations and court orientations are conducted in an effort to reduce the delete-

---

1. We use the term co-victim to refer to family members of homicide, believing that it best describes the effect of this crime on those left behind. Others have utilized somewhat different terminology to reference this same group, including "homicide survivor" and "survivor-victim," both of which are the preferred terminology of mental health professionals and victim advocates, as well as "indirect victim," which is the term generally utilized by researchers (Mawby and Walklate 1995).

rious effects of secondary victimization. We conclude by noting neglected areas of research and recommending directions for future study.

The treatment homicide co-victims receive from criminal justice personnel and as a result of the criminal justice processes often leaves them aggrieved and feeling alienated (Sherman 2000; Spungen 1998; Vandiver 1989, 2003). Researchers have coined the phrase "secondary victimization" (Williams 1984) to describe the trauma that victims of crime experience as a result of the system processes and/or interactions with criminal justice personnel (see Sherman 2000; Spungen 1998; Vandiver 1989, 2003). Specifically, secondary victimization is defined as the protraction and exacerbation of consequences related to crimes that are the product of negative, and generally judgmental, attitudes and behaviors directed at a victim. Rape is a prime example of a crime for which secondary victimization has received a great deal of attention (Campbell 1998; Madigan and Gamble 1991). For victims of this crime, secondary victimization includes having to detail the offense to strangers—often men—as they report the crime to police and unveil their personal lives in court sessions. Indeed, such secondary victimization in the processing of rape crimes propelled the development of rape shield laws, whose proponents asserted that such victims were being further victimized by a system that pointed the blame at the victim rather than the accused (Madigan and Gamble 1991).

The majority of research that describes secondary victimization primarily has focused on victims who have survived crimes (Erez and Belknap 1998; Orth 2002), with much less attention given to family members of those who have been victimized. This is particularly problematic in the context of homicide, as it is the family members, or co-victims, who are left behind and experience continued trauma beyond the event itself (Spungen 1998). Given the degree of trauma experienced by family members of homicide victims, and the fact that this trauma is likely exacerbated by their treatment during criminal justice processes related to the case (Redmond 1996; Rock 1998), a clear need exists to understand the sources and processes of secondary victimization affecting this population.

When family members of homicide victims are included among those who experience secondary victimization, the impact of system processes and interactions with personnel on the creation and exacerbation of trauma is astounding. Spungen (1998) estimated that homicide impacts up to 100,000 *immediate* family members annually in the United States.[2] This estimate is

---

2. Spungen (1998) produces these numbers by reviewing Uniform Crime Reports data to estimate the number of homicides that occur annually, then estimating that each homicide affects three family members on average.

conservative given the narrow focus of those considered intimates; Redmond (1989) had earlier projected that between 325,000 and 425,000 significant others are directly affected by homicide.[3] In another study by Amick-Mc-Mullan, Kilpatrick and Resnick (1991), estimates of homicide co-victims are even higher. These researchers asked a national sample of respondents if they had lost immediate family members, distant relatives, and/or close friends as the result of homicide.[4] Results indicated that 2.8 percent of those surveyed had lost an immediate family member, 3.7 percent had lost distant relatives, and 2.7 percent had lost close friends to homicide. These authors thus concluded that approximately 5 million adults are family members of homicide victims, 6.6 million have lost distant relatives to homicide, and 4.8 million have lost close friends to homicide, resulting in a total of 16.4 million homicide co-victims.

The impact of homicide on family members of the victim occurs not only in terms of the emotional trauma created by the loss of a loved one (Amick-McMullan et al. 1991; Freedy et al. 1994; Resnick et al. 1993), but also in the manner in which these family members are often treated by system personnel, as well as the media, as cases advance through the criminal justice system (Mawby and Walklate 1995; Rock 1998; Spungen 1998). Case studies and ethnographic research provide varying accounts of families' secondary victimization experiences involving interactions with the media, medical examiners, and criminal justice personnel (Bucholz 2002; Hammett 2000). For example, police and court personnel commonly keep the victim's personal property as evidence, withhold information about case status, and imply that the victim's behavior contributed to his/her own death (McGillis and Tomz 1997; Pasternack 1995). The link between such behaviors and secondary victimization is clear in the frequent descriptions of contacts with the criminal justice system as being frustrating and protracted (Redmond 1996). As Rock (1998:76) explains, families' alienation during the criminal justice process "constitutes one of the most potent symbolic assaults suffered by families in the wake of murder." It is, however, notable that the degree to which secondary victimization is exacerbated or ameliorated for co-victims when a homicide is prosecuted as a capital, rather than a noncapital, case has received little attention.

---

3. Redmond's (1989) estimate was based on seven to ten close relatives and other significant others—such as friends, neighbors, and co-workers—being affected by each homicide.

4. It should be noted that both criminal homicide and alcohol-related vehicular homicide were included in their definition and responses.

System and Community Responses
to Homicide Co-Victims

In their responses to homicide, both the system and community contribute to co-victims' experiences and recovery. The literature identifies four clear interactions highlighted by co-victims when they refer to the criminal justice system's responses, or lack thereof, as they negotiate the process of dealing with their loss. Specific issues include the death notification, requests and desire for information about the status of police investigations into the offense, navigating the court experience, and the ability to provide impact statements during the sentencing phase of a trial.

While these issues arise in all criminal cases and for victims of other crimes, the responses to co-victims of homicide traditionally were overlooked and undervalued, with even less attention paid to how capital cases further affect co-victims. However, the 1982 passage of the federal Victim and Witness Protection Act and the release of the Final Report of the President's Task Force on Victims of Crime (1982) were the catalysts for advancing victims' rights in general, as well as recognizing and responding to the needs of homicide co-victims. More than two decades later, it is necessary to recognize the strides that have been made as well as identify the gaps that remain.

To augment our review of the literature, we use data drawn from four focus groups and a single interview of homicide co-victims to illustrate the varying secondary victimization experiences and their impact on homicide co-victims. The sample consists of twenty-seven co-victims of twenty-four murder victims residing in a major metropolitan area in the southeastern United States. The study participants were recruited using contact information received from victim-witness assistance programs of the district attorneys' offices in five neighboring counties or selected from a local homicide survivor support group.

Notification

"One of the most defining events for a co-victim, other than the murder itself, is the death notification" (Spungen 1998:119). Indeed, it is widely recognized that death notification has a significant impact on co-victims, with the memory of the death notice often vivid and enduring (Byers 1996; Scott 1999). Unfortunately, those charged with delivering the notification of death often are not fully aware of the importance of this event and the ultimate consequences their methods may have for co-victims going through the healing process (Hendricks 1984; Spungen 1998; Stewart et al. 2001).

While most crisis theorists recognize that the normal grief process may last several months, the crisis experience of the notification itself is short (Byers 1996). However, Byers (1996; see also Clements and Burgess 2002) also notes that both the crisis experience and the grief process are affected by the particular circumstances confronting co-victims. This is particularly true in the case of homicide, which is traumatic by nature, as co-victims often re-live the experience, even the death notification itself, through numerous stages of criminal justice processing, including the investigation, arrest, trial, and sentencing (Clements and Burgess 2002). Hence, the normal grief process may be interrupted and/or prolonged. The process is further drawn out in capital cases, which are characterized by bifurcated trials (separate guilt and sentencing phases) and numerous appeals.

It is notable that those who deliver death notifications generally receive no formal training within the system (Byers 1991; Spungen 1998; Stewart et al. 2001). This is not to say that protocols for death notification are lacking, as a variety of models have been developed. For example, Mothers Against Drunk Driving (MADD) and the National Organization for Victim Assistance (NOVA) have developed such protocols, as well as training guidelines for death notification. These models generally reflect the following recommendations: 1) gather information; 2) deliver news; and 3) assess and provide follow-up. Specifically, the protocols highlight the necessity of gathering as much information as possible about the victim and the incident, as well as about the survivors, and verifying its correctness.

Developed protocols also emphasize the need to deliver the news in a contained environment, preferably inside the co-victim's home. The news should be provided in a caring, yet direct, manner (Scott 1999; Stewart 1999). Although notification of death inside the co-victim's home (not at the door) is preferable, Spungen (1998) recognizes that some notifications necessarily are performed in other settings, such as in a hospital. Because emergency-room and other medical personnel often lack formal training in death notification, problems can arise that may compound the traumatic experience. One mother in our study was notified of her son's death in a crowded hospital emergency waiting room, in the presence of people she did not know. She described the experience as follows: "You don't know what's going on ... it was so crowded. There were eleven people in that small area, and when I was told [my son] was dead, it's just like the air is being shut out and everyone is too close together and I had to find a way to get out." What made the situation worse for the mother was that the other service providers who accompanied the doctor during notification did not properly identify themselves. "I had the hospital administrator and the chaplain mixed up." Confused and embarrassed, she fled the waiting room, followed closely by her daughter. None of the hospital staff followed to check on her; in fact, only the police pursued the mother and daughter because they thought the daughter might have knowledge of the circumstances surrounding her brother's death.

Once the notification has been made, protocols emphasize the need to remain in the area for a time so that the survivor can process the news and ask for additional information. Notifiers additionally should assess the survivor's reactions and be present to provide emotional support if needed (Stewart 1999). The protocols suggest that ideally a third party, such as another family member or a clergy member, should be present to provide such support. If a third party is unavailable, the notifier should ask the survivor for the name of someone who can be called upon to provide support before leaving the premises (Byers 1996).

Finally, protocols stress the need for notifiers to provide as much information as possible to survivors (Byers 1996; Stewart 1999). Details should be offered incrementally during the notification. However, it is recommended that follow-up contact should be made with the survivors, both to assess their service needs and to provide additional information.

Although death notification protocols exist and can be adapted to serve co-victims of homicide, it is primarily victim advocates who seek out and receive such training. Those who are most likely to perform this task—police, emergency room and other medical personnel, medical examiners' or coroners' personnel—are among the least likely to be trained (Byers 1996; Stewart et al. 2001). Furthermore, it is necessary to recognize that death notification in homicide cases will have distinctive characteristics. Significantly, while it is important for the individual charged with death notification to gather information to share with co-victims, it is likely that there is little information to pass on in the case of a homicide, particularly at the stage of notification (Byers 1996). While it may be best for the co-victims' coping process to have a wide breadth of information, authorities may be reluctant to provide such information because disclosure often runs counter to the basic strategies of criminal investigation.

Information Requests

It is common for co-victims to seek out information about the homicide event and the offender. Spungen (1998) has detailed that this quest is a part of co-victims' recovery process, and has noted that denial of such information is likely to result in feelings of rage, uncertainty, frustration, helplessness, and confusion. This need for information increasingly has been recognized, and today many state laws include provisions that ensure victims and their families the right to be informed of advances in any investigation (Kilpatrick et al.

1998). Despite the adoption of such provisions as a legal right of co-victims, police agencies have maintained that the provision of crime-related information cannot occur to the detriment of the investigation itself. These competing positions may yield an uneasy, and often distrustful, relationship between police and co-victims.

The goal of police work in homicide investigations is to gather evidence that can lead to the identity and motive of the murderer and culminate in an arrest. However, co-victims often labor under the misunderstanding that a murder case inevitably will be solved and the murderer arrested. Although homicide has the highest clearance rate of any crime, over one-third of all homicides are never solved (Federal Bureau of Investigation 2003). These cold cases create a "chronic, never-ending disaster" for some survivors (Masters et al. 1988), resulting in frustration and anger toward the criminal justice system.

Recovery is especially difficult for co-victims as they observe or question the handling of police investigations. Co-victims often do not understand the problems associated with evidence-gathering and that not all evidence is considered "useful" or "good evidence." One mother in our study was greatly distraught over the fact that the police were unable to collect any useful fingerprints because of the amount of blood at the crime scene. The case stalled as the trail quickly became cold. Subsequently being ignored by the police only exacerbated her feelings of despair. In addition, it is not uncommon for co-victims to be considered as early suspects in the murder of a loved one during initial questioning by police. Although co-victims in these circumstances understand the importance of questioning family members as both witnesses and suspects, they nevertheless are frustrated with the process, and commonly perceive that valuable time is being lost in finding the real murderer.

Trial Process

The trial process is one of the most stressful experiences for co-victims, who often are surprised when they find that neither they nor the victim are represented by the prosecutor or district attorney at trial (Spungen 1998). Further, co-victims are often unfamiliar with how trials proceed, and capital cases—with their many appeals—can be particularly confusing. As previously noted, co-victims have been almost entirely excluded from the process, unless they also are victims. Commenting on a murder trial, a victim's father recalled that the district attorney's office did not readily provide him and his family with information. "It was like pulling teeth to get anything out of them. They just wouldn't tell us anything. Finally, we [said,] 'Tell us enough so that we can get by for a few days.'"

Co-victims also learn that homicides do not always result in convictions and that sentences do not necessarily match the severity of the crime. Perceptions of injustice and a lack of respect for their loved one often cause distress for homicide co-victims. This distress is reflected in one mother's remarks: "The district attorney told me that he was going for [a five-year sentence]. He said that was all he could go for. He thought that would be the best thing to do because, under the circumstances, there was no eyewitness, they had been life-long friends." After the convicted defendant was sentenced to five years in prison, the district attorney walked up to the mother and said, "Wow, she [the judge] gave him exactly what I asked for. I'm so sorry. I believe if I'd have asked for ten years, she would have given it to him." Recalling being shocked by the district attorney's comment, the mother went on to state that while a longer sentence "would not bring her son back," it should have been "more than a slap on the hand, because he [the defendant] got the same sentence for possession of cocaine."

In addition, it is notable that victims of homicide are seldom referred to by name, which can be viewed as insensitive by loved ones. Recollecting the hearing in her boyfriend's murder case, one co-victim describes how the prosecutor "never called him by his name. He always referred to [him] as 'the victim.' And I think it's really dehumanizing."

Finally, co-victims are often told to show little or no emotion in the courtroom so that they will not influence the jury. This is especially difficult to do when they face an alleged killer and hear painful details of their loved one's death. Contacts between the victim's and defendant's families are often strictly forbidden. Additionally, greater restrictions on dress and wearing items of remembrance, such as a button with the victim's picture on it, are placed on the victim's family in the courtroom, particularly in capital cases. One co-victim remarks, "The thing I don't understand is, the defendants can say whatever they want to the family members, they can sit over there, they can laugh, they can bring pictures, they can wear the shirts of their loved one being tried for murder, but the victims cannot." Perceptions of unequal treatment cause frustration and additional distress to co-victims. These sentiments can be exacerbated in capital cases, where pro-death penalty co-victims may perceive that the courts value the life of the defendant more than that of their loved one.

While numerous elements of courtroom processing affect co-victims, the process of plea-bargaining can be especially damaging, as some offenders enter guilty pleas in exchange for reduced charges and lesser sentences. Co-defendants may be given lesser punishments, despite their role in the murder, in order to obtain their cooperation. Insufficient evidence may lead to the dropping or reduction of charges. Many homicide co-victims are angered, troubled, and hurt by this process, feeling that the value of their loved one's life has been diminished. Angered at how accomplices turned over state's evidence in a plea-bargain agreement in his son's murder case, a father decries, "You don't feel that justice has been served. In this situation, for some reason, it's damn hard to get justice.... I always thought that if you were an accomplice, you're going to pay the cost just like the perpetrator. But these two guys are walking around free. Where is justice? I feel half-cocked. I feel like I want to put something on somebody. But that's the way the court leaves you."

With advances derived as a result of the recent victims' rights movement, the justice system—and courts in particular—has begun to acknowledge the feelings, needs, and, occasionally, the rights of co-victims in homicide cases. However, while the system and courts have made progress in their treatment of co-victims, as Spungen (1998:180) notes, "real change is slow to implement."

One advance that has occurred within the courts is the use of victims' advocates. These caregivers generally are associated with the district attorney's office and are charged with helping co-victims understand the criminal justice process (and its idiosyncrasies), providing support—particularly during the trial process—and assisting co-victims in attaining information about the status of their cases. Spungen (1998:181) describes the ultimate role of these advocates as decreasing "the impact of the second wound" that may be imposed on co-victims as a result of the criminal justice process. However, it should be noted that victims' advocates can also play a coercive role in the process. Specifically, when they are housed in district attorneys' offices they may attempt to steer co-victims in the direction desired by the prosecution. This is particularly problematic in cases where the co-victims oppose a strategy or outcome being pursued by the prosecutor, such as a death sentence. Not all co-victims support capital punishment, as the existence of such organizations as Murder Victim's Families for Reconciliation and Journey of Hope clearly demonstrates (King 2003; Pelke 2003).

Victim Impact Statements

Finally, and largely as a result of victims' rights legislation passed throughout the 1980s (Spungen 1998), co-victims increasingly have been allowed to provide statements regarding the impact the offense, and more specifically the loss of a loved one, has had on their lives. While there is some debate over the influence that such statements have on sentencing decisions (Erez and Roeger 1995), and over ethical considerations surrounding their use—particularly in capital cases (Arrigo and Williams 2003)—victims have increasing won the right to testify during the sentencing phase of trials. However, it should be noted that in cases where co-victims oppose a death sentence, they have been denied the right of presenting victim impact statements even in jurisdictions where such statements are generally allowed (Colb 2004; Cushing and Sheffer 2002).

Groups within communities are responding increasingly to the needs of homicide co-victims. Such responses have taken the form of crisis hotlines and interventions, self-help groups designed specifically to aid co-victims of homicide, and mediation. It is difficult to evaluate the effectiveness of these resources because co-victims self-select these services and may utilize more than one of them. Furthermore, some programs are designed to assist co-victims in long-term recovery from trauma, while others are aimed at addressing specific, short-term, crisis events. As such, it is difficult to assess the comparative value of these different interventions.

The Criminal Justice System and Its Impact on Co-Victims' Psychological Adjustment

A great deal of research has examined the impact of homicide victimization on co-victims' mental health. Grieving the traumatic loss of a loved one to homicide is one of the most difficult bereavement experiences, as widely documented by case studies and clinical reports (Amick-McMullan, Kilpatrick, and Veronen 1989; Asaro 2001; Hammett 2000; Rynearson 1984; Rynearson and McCreery 1993). Ethnographic research and clinical observations indicate that homicide co-victims experience greater horror, rage, desire for revenge, and fear than survivors experiencing bereavement when death results from other causes (Doyle 1980; Pasternack 1995). Survivors of loved ones murdered in stigmatizing circumstances, such as drug use or domestic violence, additionally may feel ashamed and isolated (Spungen 1998). Recent evidence confirms that families of homicide victims experience greater trauma and distress than direct crime victims and non-trauma control groups (Freedy et al. 1994; Freeman et al. 1996; Thompson et al. 1998), and in comparison to other forms of sudden loss (Murphy 1997; Smith et al. 1992). These findings have important implications for treatment and social service providers, as well as police and prosecutors who interact with co-victims.

Exposure to secondary victimization experiences and the resulting dissatisfaction with criminal justice personnel can exacerbate co-victims' adjustment problems. Co-victims have described secondary victimization as more severe than the psychological trauma of the murder itself (Redmond 1996). Surprisingly few studies assess the impact of families' experiences with the criminal justice system following the murder of a loved one. Studies that have been conducted emphasize co-victims' dissatisfaction with the criminal justice system. For example, Amick-McMullan, Kilpatrick, Veronen, and Smith (1989) reported that 42 percent of co-victims in their sample expressed general dissatisfaction with how the criminal justice system handled the homicide case. Families are particularly dissatisfied with the responses of law enforcement and court personnel (Getzel and Masters 1984), although perceptions of how different agencies and individuals treat homicide co-victims vary considerably. Thompson et al. (1996) found that the greatest dissatisfaction was with defense attorneys (71 percent), followed by the police (52 percent). Activities associated with the court, including poor treatment from the prosecutor or the defense attorney, were the most upsetting. Homicide co-victims also reported that reliving the murder during the court proceedings and failing to be provided information about the case were quite upsetting.

Although considerable research has documented the impact of the homicide on co-victims' grief and trauma, few studies have specifically examined factors outside the traumatic event that could increase the risk for additional problems. The findings from these studies are often conflicting. In a study of nineteen homicide co-victims recruited through victim-witness and victims' rights services, Amick-McMullan, Kilpatrick, Veronen, and Smith (1989) reported a striking relationship between psychological adjustment and satisfaction with how the criminal justice system handled the homicide cases. Specifically, the more satisfied co-victims were with the criminal justice system, the less likely they were to be depressed or anxious.

What accounts for the relationship between criminal justice satisfaction and psychological distress remains unclear. One possible explanation is offered by Thompson et al. (1996), who found that satisfaction with the police was a function of both the arrest status (e.g., whether an arrest had occurred) and whether the family member was kept informed about the progress of the case. Not surprisingly, co-victims were more satisfied with the police if an arrest was made and if a family member was kept informed about the progress of the case. The researchers further discovered that satisfaction with the police directly affected co-victims' beliefs about esteem, social support, control, and safety, and that more positive beliefs were related to less psychological distress.[5] Homicide co-victims' evaluations of the police are strongly related to

---

5. Contrary to Amick-McMullan, Kilpatrick, Veronen, and Smith (1989), Thompson et al. (1996) found that police satisfaction was unrelated to psychological distress. Additional research is needed to examine more fully the relationship between satisfaction with criminal justice services and psychological distress among homicide co-victims.

how much information police provide about the case, how frequently co-victims are contacted, and how considerate police are of their feelings. The more involved co-victims perceive themselves to be, the more satisfied they tend to be with police services.

Although the Thompson et al. study examined some aspects of co-victims' secondary victimization experiences, no quantitative studies have systematically measured exposure to secondary victimization or its influence on the trauma among homicide co-victims. Additional research is needed to identify and measure how criminal justice personnel and processes positively and negatively affect the lives of victims' family members.

Service Utilization Patterns among Homicide Co-Victims

Much of co-victims' dissatisfaction with the criminal justice system may stem from the discrepancy between the services they *expect* to receive and the support to which they actually have access. In a study of service utilization among crime victims and family members recently involved in the criminal justice system, Freedy et al. (1994) found that more than 90 percent believed the criminal justice system should provide a broad range of services, including psychological counseling, information about case status, personal protection, legal assistance, social service referral information, and assistance in dealing with the police or court. Yet, reported access to such services fell far below victims' expectations. For example, just 39 percent of victims described receiving adequate access to psychological counseling, and 60 percent (the highest percentage in this study) reported receiving adequate access to assistance in dealing with the police or court. A similar study, focusing only on homicide co-victims, reported that while 80 percent of homicide co-victims surveyed believed the justice system should provide them with legal assistance and information about the status of the case, only 33 percent received such services (Amick-McMullan, Kilpatrick, Veronen, and Smith 1989). Over 80 percent also believed the courts should provide an advocate and personal protection for family members, yet only 27 percent reported receiving an advocate and only 10 percent reported receiving protection for their family.

The criminal justice system historically has funneled most of its services to direct victims of crime. Compared to other victims of violent crime, homicide co-victims have received little social service outreach and few resources from formal organizations such as the criminal justice system (Moriarty et al.

1998; Spungen 1998). According to Freedy et al. (1994), overall, 27 percent of victims and co-victims received psychological counseling, with sexual assault victims the most likely recipients (63 percent), followed by victims of other violent crimes such as physical assault (22 percent), and family members of homicide victims (16 percent).

While homicide co-victims receive some assistance from police during the investigation stage, it is not typically until the beginning of the trial victim advocates are assigned to counsel co-victims (Horne 2003). Court advocacy services include providing information about the criminal justice process, court accompaniment, and interacting with others on behalf of and at the request of co-victims. As court advocates provide relevant expertise and knowledge about the case, co-victims' anxiety tends to decrease and their mastery of community resources increases (Lyon et al. 1992).

While the victims' rights movement has yielded numerous positive outcomes, such as increasingly recognizing and providing services and advocacy for co-victims of homicide, some results are mixed. For example, the placement of victims' advocates and advocacy services—such provision of information and financial assistance—in district attorneys' offices may prove to be most effective for co-victims who favor the death penalty. Cushing and Sheffer (2002) demonstrate through numerous stories that services and advocacy are frequently withdrawn from co-victims who actively oppose the death penalty.

Promoting Effective Interventions with Homicide Co-Victims

Little is known about what services best meet the needs and concerns of homicide co-victims. Although empirical evaluations are now beginning to appear, discussions about effective co-victim services typically have been prescriptive rather than evaluative. Early evidence suggests that services such as counseling, court advocacy, and case management are beneficial to homicide co-victims to meet psychological needs, and may help them navigate the rigid procedures and complex processes of the criminal justice system. Counseling services using psychodynamic and cognitive behavioral methods have also been utilized, and appear to be effective in treating post-traumatic stress disorder (PTSD), especially avoidance and intrusive symptoms that have been linked to co-victimization (Gerrity and Solomon 1996). Horne's (2003) study of service utilization patterns of 112 homicide victims' family members found that co-victims utilized counseling, court advocacy, and case management services more during the initial eight-week crisis period following the homicide than during the second eight weeks, with counseling services the most utilized. Similarly, a survey of 116 caregivers associated with clinics, self-help organizations, or victim/witness assistance programs (many of whom were co-victims themselves) reported strong endorsement of victim advocacy, crisis intervention, grief counseling, and family therapy (Hatton 2003).

Hatton (ibid.) also noted that the benefits of service delivery and treatment success were often negated or diminished as a result of negative experiences with the criminal justice system. Caregivers reported that the insensitive reactions of others (i.e., secondary victimization) along with the lack of social support were second only to severe mental illness in contributing to treatment failure. Caregivers collectively rated a poor criminal justice outcome as a very important contributor to treatment failure.

Though mental health services for homicide co-victims have greatly expanded in recent years, formal outcome evaluations have been limited to two treatment programs designed for co-victims by clinicians, one of which yielded negative results (Murphy et al. 1998; Redmond 1989). One of the earliest programs for homicide co-victims was the Homicide Survivors Group, Inc. of Pinellas County, Florida (Redmond 1989). The group treatment program consisted of three phases (three to four initial sessions of individual therapy, followed by a twelve-week group grief-therapy program, and ending with participation in a peer support group) and was administered to forty-three homicide survivors in four separate groups. Comparison of scores on the Grief Experience Inventory recorded at the beginning and end of the program indicated significant improvement in five of the nine grief symptoms, including reductions in despair, anger, guilt, depersonalization, and somatization.

Murphy et al. (1998) assessed the efficacy of a ten-week broad-spectrum intervention offered to bereaved parents about four months after the deaths of their children due to accidents, homicide, or suicide. Each two-hour session consisted of information-giving and skill-building support during the first hour, followed by emotion-focused support during the retelling of their experiences. Overall mental distress, PTSD, grief responses, physical health status, and marital satisfaction were assessed prior to the intervention, immediately following the intervention, and six months later. Results indicated that the outcomes at two follow-up points did not differ much between the intervention and control groups. There was support for the intervention among the highly distressed, but not among the less distressed mothers, and no apparent benefits were evident among fathers. Treatment effects did not depend on the manner of the children's deaths.

Future Policy and Research Directions

Research into the prevalence and correlates of service utilization among homicide co-victims is important from a policy standpoint. Communities must recognize that families of homicide victims have a legitimate claim to community resources. Over the past two decades, federal and state legislation has provided victim compensation and authorized mental health services for direct victims of crime. In the Office for Victims of Crime's (2003) *Report to the Nation*, the highest and second-highest number of claims paid were for assault (the majority of which are domestic violence-related) and child abuse, respectively. Homicide accounted for the third-highest number of paid claims, but was second only to assault in the absolute amount of payments made. Compensation to homicide co-victims included payments for crisis intervention and victim advocacy services, as well as funeral and burial costs.

Despite the passage of significant state and federal victims' rights legislation, there is a need for policy changes in how police and the courts approach surviving family members in homicide cases. Training and education of criminal justice and medical personnel are needed to reduce the deleterious effects of secondary victimization in general, but especially for homicide co-victims. Specifically, police officers should receive formal training in death notification and sensitivity training about the importance of briefing co-victims about the progress of homicide investigations. Homicide task forces should develop effective protocols to guide the police in dealing with co-victims in open, unsolved cases. Co-victims want the police to provide information about the status of homicide investigations. They also want to be called when the suspect is arrested and told whether the accused is in jail, released on bail, or is at large in the community. Finally, co-victims want more recognition from the legal system. Specifically, they want to be informed of deliberations and included in case developments. Protocols need to be developed that will determine what kinds of information about the case can be shared with family members, advise family members about what to expect during the investigation, and how co-victims should be kept informed as the case progresses.

The investigation of cold cases in particular causes a great deal of frustration and anger for co-victims, fueling a need for continued counseling services. Indeed, research indicates that survivors for whom the perpetrator remains unidentified were as or more likely to utilize counseling services as intrafamilial homicide survivors (Horne 2003). These findings suggest that service plans for homicide co-victims should prioritize ascertaining the survivors' relationship to the perpetrator during the initial assessment. In cases with no identified perpetrator, practitioners may need to be more proactive in relationship building to sustain a credible offering of counseling services (Horne 2003).

Victim advocacy through court orientations and court accompaniments is essential to help familiarize co-victims with how cases progress through the system. While the courts have been instrumental in bringing co-victims back into the justice process—through the use of victims' advocates—continued improvement is warranted. For example, it was clear in our sample that the quality and breadth of victim advocacy for co-victims varied widely depending on the court in which a case was being processed. Efforts should be made to provide more consistent advocacy across jurisdictions. Also problematic is the fact that advocacy generally does not occur until a case reaches the courts.

As previously noted, most victims' service programs are located at non-profit agencies or within prosecutors' offices, and services are thus offered only when a case reaches the courts. This clearly leaves a large population unserved, since only 21 percent of major crimes get to the prosecutor's office (Parker 2001). Additionally, while court-assigned victim advocates have been widely praised for their legal advocacy during the trial, it is clear that assistance also is needed earlier, such as during police investigations and pre-trial hearings. Significant problems emerge early in most homicide investigations, suggesting that co-victims would benefit from the earlier initiation of advocacy and counseling. Furthermore, advocacy should be provided to all co-victims, and the provision of these services and information should not depend on whether co-victims support or oppose the death penalty (Cushing and Sheffer 2002).

A new and innovative approach to addressing such problems is to establish victim services within law enforcement agencies. In Texas, the Austin Police Department is among a relatively small number of victim assistance divisions that conform to this model (Parker 2001). Here, division counselors meet with officers at a crime scene, confer about the investigation, and are able to respond more quickly to the needs of victims, families, and witnesses by providing crisis and trauma counseling. Victim advocates recommend establishing a victim services program within a law enforcement agency for several reasons. First, if victims and their families receive support from victim service counselors, they may be more likely to cooperate in an investigation, which may increase conviction rates. Second, victim services' work complements community policing, which emphasizes establishing relationships with members of a neighborhood. With a counselor on the scene, a police officer can go back into service while the counselor talks with the family. Finally, the counselor can act as a liaison for a child if a parent is being arrested and officers need to move to the next call.

Although our understanding of the harmful effects of secondary victimization among homicide co-victims has increased in recent years, additional research is needed to more fully examine the sources and nature of secondary victimization that co-victims face as homicide cases are processed, especially through the appeals process and executions. The types of secondary victimization experiences commonly associated with the different criminal justice and medical personnel and stages of the criminal justice processing should be identified. Ethnographical accounts have been useful in this regard (Bucholz 2002; Hammett 2000; Zehr 2001); however, it is not possible to determine the effects of secondary victimization on grief and trauma without the use of standardized measures. Research is needed to develop a self-rated, standardized instrument that has been validated. In a related vein, little is known about the psychological harm caused by secondary victimization experiences, relative to the murder itself. Longitudinal studies are needed to explore the relative contributions of pre-event, peri-event (i.e., murder circumstances), and post-event (i.e., exposure to secondary victimization) factors in predicting post-traumatic stress disorder and grief outcomes.

Very little is known about the impact of the death penalty on families of homicide victims (see Vandiver 2003 for a review). Research is needed to examine the differential impact of secondary victimization on co-victims' psychological adjustment in capital and noncapital cases. In particular, it is unclear if capital proceedings exacerbate, ameliorate, or perhaps have no influence on the secondary victimization of co-victims compared to noncapital cases. Further, empirical studies are needed to examine differences in secondary victimization experiences in capital proceedings where co-victims differ in their opinions about the death penalty. Anecdotal evidence suggests that some co-victims who oppose the death penalty are more likely to be denied information, assistance, and advocacy than those co-victims who support the death penalty (Cushing and Sheffer 2002).

Finally, research must be conducted to evaluate program services that are provided to homicide co-victims. This is particularly relevant given the patchwork quilt of services currently provided. Only through such evaluation research will the programs that work be separated from those that do not.

Concluding Remarks

"Victimization is about powerlessness; victims' rights are about the reclaiming of power" (Cushing and Sheffer 2002:8). A murder itself and the negative treatment of homicide co-victims at the hands of the criminal justice system touch many different lives, leaving individuals and families feeling alienated and without dignity. Although the U.S. Congress has passed the Victims of Crime Act and enacted additional laws urging states to treat crime victims with compassion, respect, and dignity throughout the criminal justice process, effective procedures and protocols to make these aspirations become a reality, and to provide adequate services to all victims, are still lacking. Surviving family members now have a voice in the aftermath of a murder, gained partly by their efforts to help shape new victims' rights legislation, and have made some progress in how they are treated by the justice system. Still, the efforts of all co-victims must be respected, independent of their gender, race, class, and stance toward the death penalty. As evidenced in some capital proceedings, silencing co-victims and denying the right to information and services to those who oppose the death penalty only serves to revictimize families and promote inequities in the justice system. "It is too easy for such families to be relegated to the status of second-class victims" (ibid.). All victims, including families of homicide victims, deserve the right to be informed about and to be present and heard at critical stages of the criminal justice process. Amendments to federal and state victims' rights laws and the adoption of "best practices" to support the rights of all victims remain necessary to allow this right to be fully realized (see Cushing and Sheffer 2002 for policy recommendations).

Ultimately, our understanding of the impact of the justice process on homicide co-victims rests upon continued research and policy work. Researchers, practitioners, policymakers, and, most importantly, homicide co-victims themselves must play an active role in the development of protocols and service plans to meet co-victims' psychological needs, as well as to reduce the deleterious effects of secondary victimization. It is through the coordinated efforts of criminal justice and medical personnel and mental health-care professionals that the "second wound" can be healed and recovery made possible.

References

Amick-McMullan, Angelynne, Dean G. Kilpatrick, and Heidi S. Resnick. 1991. "Homicide as a Risk Factor for PTSD Among Surviving Family Members." *Behavior Modification* 15:545–59.

Amick-McMullan, Angelynne, Dean G. Kilpatrick and Lois J. Veronen. 1989. "Family Survivors of Homicide Victims: A Behavioral Analysis." *Behavior Therapist* 12:75–79.

Amick-McMullan, Angelynne, Dean G. Kilpatrick, Lois J. Veronen, and Susan Smith. 1989. "Family Survivors of Homicide Victims: Theoretical Perspectives and an Exploratory Study." *Journal of Traumatic Stress* 2:21–35.

Arrigo, Bruce A. and Christopher R. Williams. 2003. "Victim Vices, Victim Voices, and Impact Statements: On the Place of Emotion and the Role of Restorative Justice in Capital Sentencing." *Crime and Delinquency* 49:603–26.

Asaro, M. Regina. 2001. "Working with Adult Homicide Survivors, Part I: Impact and Sequelae of Murder." *Perspectives in Psychiatric Care* 37:95–101.

Bucholz, Judie A. 2002. *Homicide Survivors: Misunderstood Grievers*. Amityville, NY: Baywood Publishing Company.

Byers, Bryan. 1996. "Death Notification: Theory and Practice." Pp. 287–319 in *Crisis Intervention in Criminal Justice/Social Service*, 2d ed., edited by James E. Hendricks and Bryan Byers. Springfield, IL: Charles C. Thomas.

————. 1991. "Death Notification." Pp. 179–211 in *Crisis Intervention in Criminal Justice/Social Service*, edited by James E. Hendricks. Springfield, IL: Charles C. Thomas.

Campbell, Rebecca. 1998. "The Community Response to Rape: Victims' Experiences with the Legal, Medical, and Mental Health Systems." *American Journal of Community Psychology* 26:355–79.

Clements, Paul T. and Ann W. Burgess. 2002. "Children's Responses to Family Member Homicide." *Family Community Health* 25:32–42.

Colb, Sherry F. 2004. "When Victims' Families Eschew Vengeance: Pro-Defendant Victim Impact Statements in Terry Nichols's Trial." http://writ.news.findlaw.com/colb/20040616.html.

Cushing, Robert Renny and Susannah Sheffer. 2002. *Dignity Denied: The Experience of Murder Victims' Family Members Who Oppose the Death Penalty*. Cambridge, MA: Murder Victims' Families for Reconciliation.

Doyle, Polly. 1980. *Grief Counseling and Sudden Death*. Springfield, IL: Charles C. Thomas.

Erez, Edna and Joanne Belknap. 1998. "In Their Own Words: Battered Women's Assessment of the Criminal Processing System's Responses." *Violence and Victims* 13:251–68.

Erez, Edna and Leigh Roeger. 1995. "The Effect of Victim Impact Statements on Sentencing Patterns and Outcomes: The Australian Experience." *Journal of Criminal Justice* 23:363–75.

Federal Bureau of Investigation. 2003. *Crime in the United States, 2003*. Washington, DC: U.S. Government Printing Office.

Freedy, John R., Heidi S. Resnick, Dean G. Kilpatrick, Bonnie S. Dansky, and Ritchie P. Tidwell. 1994. "The Psychological Adjustment of Recent Crime Victims to the Criminal Justice System." *Journal of Interpersonal Violence* 9:450–68.

Freeman, Linda N., David Shaffer, and Helen Smith. 1996. "Neglected Victims of Homicide: The Needs of Young Siblings of Murder Victims." *American Journal of Orthopsychiatry* 66:337–45.

Gerrity, Ellen T. and Susan D. Solomon. 1996. "The Treatment of PTSD and Related Stress Disorders: Current Research and Clinical Knowledge." Pp. 87–102 in *Ethnocultural Aspects of Posttraumatic Stress Disorder: Issues, Research, and Clinical Applications*, edited by Anthony J. Marsell, Matthew J. Friedman, Ellen T. Gerrity, and Raymond M. Scurfield. Washington, DC: American Psychological Association.

Getzel, George S. and Rosemary Masters. 1984. "Serving Families Who Survive Homicide Victims." *Social Casework* 65:138–44.

Hammett, Marcella. 2000. *Permanent Heartache: Portraits of Grief, Hope, Survival and Life After Homicide*. Huntington, NY: Kroshka Books.

Hatton, Rebecca. 2003. "Homicide Bereavement Counseling: A Survey of Providers." *Death Studies* 27:427–48.

Hendricks, James E. 1984. "Death Notification: The Theory and Practice of Informing Survivors." *Journal of Police Science and Administration* 12:109–16.

Horne, Christopher. 2003. "Families of Homicide Victims: Service Utilization Patterns of Extra- and Intrafamilial Homicide Survivors." *Journal of Family Violence* 18:75–82.

Kilpatrick, Dean G., David Beatty and Susan S. Howley. 1998. *The Rights of Crime Victims—Does Legal Protection Make a Difference?* Washington, DC: U.S. Department of Justice.

King, Rachel. 2003. *Don't Kill in Our Names: Families of Murder Victims Speak Out Against the Death Penalty.* New Brunswick, NJ: Rutgers University Press.

Lyon, Eleanor, Nancy Moore and Charles Lexius. 1992. "Group Work with Families of Homicide Victims." *Social Work Groups* 15:19–33.

Madigan, Lee and Nancy C. Gamble. 1991. *The Second Rape: Society's Continued Betrayal of Rape Victims.* New York: Lexington Books.

Masters, Rosemary, Lucy N. Friedman, and George Getzel. 1988. "Helping Families of Homicide Victims: A Multidimensional Approach." *Journal of Traumatic Stress* 1:109–25.

Mawby, R. I. and Sandra Walklate. 1995. *Critical Victimology.* Thousand Oaks, CA: Sage Publications.

McGillis, Daniel and Julie E. Tomz. 1997. *Serving Crime Victims and Witnesses*, 2d ed. Washington, DC: U.S. Department of Justice.

Moriarty, Laura J., Robert A. Jerin, and William V. Pelfry. 1998. "Evaluating Victim Services: A Comparative Analysis of North Carolina and Virginia Victim Witness Programs." Pp. 111–25 in *Current Issues in Victimology Research*, edited by Laura J. Moriarty and Robert A. Jerin. Durham, NC: Carolina Academic Press.

Murphy, Shirley A. 1997. "A Bereavement Intervention for Parents Following the Sudden, Violent Deaths of Their 12–28-Year-Old Children: Description and Applications to Clinical Practice." *Canadian Journal of Nursing Research* 29:51–72.

Murphy, Shirley A., Clark Johnson, Kevin C. Cain, Abhijit Das Gupta, Margaret Dimond, Janet Lohan, and Robert Baugher. 1998. "Broad-Spectrum Group Treatment for Parents Bereaved by the Violent Deaths of Their 12- to 28-Year-Old Children: A Randomized Controlled Trial." *Death Studies* 22:1–27.

Office of Justice Programs. 1982. *President's Task Force on Victims of Crime, Final Report.* Washington, DC: U.S. Government Printing Office.

Office for Victims of Crime. 2003. *Report to the Nation: Fiscal Years 2001 and 2002.* Washington, DC: U.S. Government Printing Office.

Orth, Uli. 2002. "Secondary Victimization of Crime Victims by Criminal Proceedings." *Social Justice Research* 15:313–25.

Parker, Susan G. 2001. *Establishing Victim Services Within a Law Enforcement Agency: The Austin Experience.* Washington, DC: Office for Victims of Crime.

Pasternack, Stefan A. 1995. "Homicide Bereavement: Diagnostic Assessment and Psychoanalytic Psychotherapy." *Psychoanalysis and Psychotherapy* 12:163–82.

Pelke, Bill. 2003. *Journey of Hope: From Violence to Healing.* Philadelphia, PA: Xlibris Corporation.

Redmond, Lula M. 1996. "Sudden Violent Death." Pp. 53–71 in *Living With Grief After Sudden Loss*, edited by Kenneth J. Doka. Washington, DC: Hospice Foundation of America.

_____. 1989. *Surviving: When Someone You Love Was Murdered.* Clearwater, FL: Psychological Consultation and Educational Services, Inc.

Resnick, Heidi S., Dean G. Kilpatrick, Bonnie S. Dansky, Benjamin E. Saunders, and Connie L. Best. 1993. "Prevalence of Civilian Trauma and Posttraumatic Stress Disorder in a Representative National Sample of Women." *Journal of Consulting and Clinical Psychology* 61:984–91.

Rock, Paul. 1998. *After Homicide: Practical and Political Responses to Bereavement.* New York: Oxford University Press.

Rynearson, Edward K. 1984. "Bereavement After Homicide: A Descriptive Study." *American Journal of Psychiatry* 141:1452–54.

Rynearson, Edward K. and Joseph M. McCreery. 1993. "Bereavement After Homicide: A Synergism of Trauma and Loss." *American Journal of Psychiatry* 150:258–61.

Scott, Brian J. 1999. "Preferred Protocol for Death Notification." *FBI Law Enforcement Bulletin* 68:11–16.

Sherman, Lawrence. 2000. "Evaluating Restorative Justice: What Works? Restorative Justice Approaches to Violence." Presented paper at the Reconciliation Symposium, Atlanta, GA: Emory University.

Smith, Peggy C., Lillian M. Range and Ann Ulmer. 1992. "Belief in Afterlife as a Buffer in Suicidal and Other Bereavement." *Omega* 24:217–25.

Spungen, Deborah. 1998. *Homicide: The Hidden Victims.* Thousand Oaks, CA: Sage Publications.

Stewart, Alan E. 1999. "Complicated Bereavement and Posttraumatic Stress Disorder Following Fatal Car Crashes: Recommendations for Death Notification Practice." *Death Studies* 23:289–321.

Stewart, Alan E., Janice Harris Lord, and Dorothy L. Mercer. 2001. "Death Notification Education: A Needs Assessment Study." *Journal of Traumatic Stress* 14:221–27.

Thompson, Martie P., Fran H. Norris, and R. Barry Ruback. 1998. "Comparative Distress Levels of Inner-City Family Members of Homicide Victims." *Journal of Traumatic Stress* 11:223–42.

———. 1996. "System Influences on Posthomicide Beliefs and Distress." *American Journal of Community Psychology* 24:785–809.

Vandiver, Margaret. 2003. "The Impact of the Death Penalty on the Families of Homicide Victims and of Condemned Prisoners." Pp. 613–45 in *America's Experiment with Capital Punishment: Reflections on the Past, Present, and Future of the Ultimate Penal Sanction*, 2d ed., edited by James R. Acker, Robert M. Bohm, and Charles S. Lanier. Durham, NC: Carolina Academic Press.

———. 1989. "Coping with Death: Families of the Terminally Ill, Homicide Victims, and Condemned Prisoners." Pp. 123–38 in *Facing the Death Penalty: Essays on a Cruel and Unusual Punishment*, edited by Michael L. Radelet. Philadelphia: Temple University Press.

Williams, Joyce E. 1984. "Secondary Victimization: Confronting Public Attitudes About Rape." *Victimology* 9:66–81.

Zehr, Howard. 2001. *Transcending: Reflections of Crime Victims.* Intercourse, PA: Good Books.

CHAPTER 15

THEIR DAY IN COURT: THE ROLE OF MURDER VICTIMS' FAMILIES IN CAPITAL JUROR DECISION MAKING

David R. Karp and
Jarrett B. Warshaw

What most influences your decision about the punishment? "I guess just the feeling for the family—or the victim's family."—Juror in a capital trial

Co-Victims in a Courtroom Context

The criminal justice process in death penalty cases is simultaneously re-strictive and burdensome to "co-victims"—the term we use for murder vic-tims' families.[1] The court system has marginalized the role of co-victims by providing very little means for them to actively participate in decision-mak-ing processes that influence how to justly respond to their traumatic loss. At the same time, prosecutors often place pressure on the victims' families, ex-pecting them to attend trials and appeals, sometimes testify, and follow closely a procedure with many potential reversals, delays, and emotional and moral challenges. Thus far the most crucial (and the most institutionalized) role for

---

1. We follow Spungen's (1998) use of the term co-victims to refer to family members of homicide victims. As she defines the term, "Family members and friends become co-victims when their loved ones are murdered" (p. 9).

co-victims is to provide testimony during the penalty phase of the trial. The legal community refers to this testimony as victim impact evidence (VIE), which is the only way for murder victims' families to give information about the victim and tell how the murder has affected them personally. The courts, however, do not allow family members to tell the jury what they would like the sentence to be.

No systematic studies have examined the impact of VIE on co-victims, and it is possible that this form of participation can facilitate healing in that it offers these families the opportunity to voice their grief in a public forum. On the other hand, it is possible that offering VIE is a form of secondary victimization; co-victim participation on this level may be hurtful because it may prolong the recovery process. While we cannot answer this question with our data, we do examine the impact of VIE on jurors in order to discover the influence it has on sentencing. Do victims' families, by testifying in capital trials, increase the likelihood that juries will vote for a death sentence? More generally, we explore the ways in which capital jurors tend to think about these families during their decision-making process.

In 1987 the U.S. Supreme Court ruled in *Booth v. Maryland* to prohibit co-victim participation in the trial because the justices feared that the emotionally driven testimony on behalf of the victim's family would distract jurors from considering the objective facts of the crime, thus rendering them unable to make a reasoned moral choice. The Supreme Court then overruled this decision in *Payne v. Tennessee*, on June 27, 1991. Here the Court deemed it permissible to have VIE presented during the penalty phase, essentially so that jurors can more carefully determine the overall wrongdoing of the defendant. Chief Justice William Rehnquist, expressing the opinion of the majority, stated that "a State may properly conclude that for the jury to assess meaningfully the defendant's moral culpability and blameworthiness, it should have before it at the sentencing phase victim impact evidence" (*Payne v. Tennessee* 1991: 4).

Theorists and legal scholars, predominantly Austin Sarat (1997) and Wayne Logan (1999, this volume), have pondered the significance of *Payne*, debating whether the use of VIE can increase the defendant's likelihood of receiving the death penalty; be instrumental in the healing process of co-victims; and simultaneously undermine the very justice system by bringing subjective, emotional evidence into a space (psychological and physical) that should only focus on reason, rational decision making, and objectivity. In other words, providing VIE may help co-victims recover by taking an active role in the justice system; however, doing so may unduly influence a jury to impose a death sentence. Such testimony, these scholars argue, may overwhelm jurors' ability to weigh equally mitigating evidence (factors relating to the defendant's background) or take seriously other factors that the law finds necessary in penalty phase deliberations.

Lives on the Line:
The Risks of Victim Impact Evidence

For Sarat (1997:164), the *Payne* ruling has prompted the "return of revenge [in that it] scrambles categories by allowing victims to use legal processes to express their grief and rage as they, or their surrogates, seek to enlist the loyalty of judges and juries in a quest for revenge." Here Sarat maintains several assumptions: victims' families and the victims' rights movement are only after vengeance, victim impact evidence is a legalized way of attaining such personal goals, and the *Payne* ruling subverts the justice system in that it easily permits all things irrational to infiltrate what should be perhaps the quintessential space of rational thought.

Given these assumptions Sarat suggests some possible implications of the *Payne* case on the future of the modern legal system. One implication is that *Payne* extends our legal conception of victimization to include victims' families: "*Payne* gave a voice to victims by expanding the legal recognition of victimhood to include the collateral suffering of those left behind, and insisting on vengeful justice for the survivors" (Sarat 1997:171). This suggests that family members of a victim, for example, now have a new identity under the law, and this identity, as Sarat implies, gives the co-victim a sense of entitlement to carry out revenge in the unjust, illogical way of revealing personal feelings during the course of a trial. Justice, from the Sarat perspective, thus becomes a euphemism for "blood-letting punishment" (p. 173). That is, co-victims can now fulfill a need for private justice (the dispelling of their suffering through capital punishment), instead of relying on public justice (the way the courts should operate according to reason without the use of victim impact evidence).

Citing the *Booth* ruling, Sarat comments that the Court at that time decided not to allow victim impact evidence because such emotionally charged testimony seemed to persuade a jury to sentence the defendant to death. Justice Powell, speaking on behalf of the majority, stated that the "formal presentation of this information by the State can serve no other purpose than to inflame the jury and divert it from deciding the case on the relevant evidence concerning the crime and the defendant.... The admission of these emotionally charged opinions as to what conclusions the jury should draw from the evidence clearly is inconsistent with the reasoned decision making we require in capital cases" (*Booth v. Maryland* 1987:12). Both Sarat and the Supreme Court believed that John Booth received the death penalty because of the co-victims' testimony, and this is why the Court reversed the sentence. However, neither Sarat nor the Court have clearly established that the testimony was, in fact, the cause of the jury's decision; and, more importantly, the Court has not made use of any empirical evidence supporting the claim that VIE produces the ill effects mentioned above. Furthermore, it is unclear if VIE is always used to advance the cause of the prosecution in that it is possible that co-victims have testified in the past in opposition to the death penalty.

Wayne Logan (1999; see also this volume) shares Sarat's concern about VIE, criticizing the Supreme Court for failing in *Payne* to define how VIE should be reintroduced in capital cases. "Highly prejudicial victim impact evidence is now routinely put before capital juries, with precious little in the way of substantive limits, procedural controls, or guidance in how it is to be used in assessing the 'deathworthiness' of defendants" (p. 2). Though there is not a universal code that all states follow in regard to how VIE should be restricted (how it is used, who can be a victim impact witness, how many witnesses there should be, jury instructions on how to use such information during deliberation, etc.), many states do have different takes on the *Payne* ruling. In terms of procedural controls, Logan reveals that New Jersey "imposes the strictest controls of all, requiring that defendants be notified of the State's desire to proffer impact evidence, and permitting testimony from only one family member.... Trial courts are required to admonish witnesses that they will not be permitted to testify if they cannot control their emotions, and minors typically are not permitted to testify" (p. 5). This suggests that New Jersey is sensitive perhaps to the concerns that Sarat, Logan, and the *Booth* Court discuss.

New Jersey does, however, seem to be the exception to the norm—to the extent that most other states do not have such stringent regulations on how prosecutors can present victim impact evidence. Logan finds that in the "vast majority of jurisdictions the prosecution enjoys virtual free rein over the method by which impact is conveyed" (ibid.). One case demonstrates this lax approach to the *Payne* ruling: a Missouri court, Logan notes, allowed "the mother and the sister of the victim [to convey] their emotional loss by means of pictures, letters, stories, diary entries, and a poem...." (ibid.). What Logan sees at stake here is the legality of allowing such a wide range of notably private documents, ones that give tangible evidence as to the sheer depth of the co-victims' loss and grief, to come before a jury. Whereas some jurisdictions impose minimal limitations on how VIE enters the courtroom, Logan presses for a judicial system that does whatever it can to effectively minimize the ultimate risk that VIE could arbitrarily lead to the death sentence. Some of Logan's more urgent recommendations for remedying the overarching problems of VIE include: only one witness should vouch for the impact of the murder; a judicial authority, after reviewing the written statement during the pre-trial, must read the testimony verbatim so that the co-victim does not take the stand; and impact witnesses need to give emotionally suppressed testimony, offering only factual commentary free of angry, vengeful remarks (pp. 13–14).

There are other states that despite having narrowly defined the word "victim," do not impose numerical limits on how many witnesses can testify. In Virginia, family, friends, co-workers, neighbors, and community members can all share their personal feelings with the court if they have felt the effects of the murder. "Some courts even permit impact evidence by proxy—allowing persons not immediately affected by the killing to testify on behalf of one who is so affected" (p. 6). The Florida Supreme Court has decided that impact evidence is in a category unto itself, ruling that it "is neither aggravating nor mitigating evidence. Rather, it is other evidence, which is not required to be weighed against, or offset, by statutory factors" (p. 11). As the Florida example suggests to Logan, victim impact evidence in certain jurisdictions—the ones in which the judge does not advise juries on how to use it—may cause VIE to become a bigger, more determining factor in juror decision making than other evidence that is of equal importance (i.e., mitigating factors).

The theoretical question of whether VIE will, as Logan, Sarat, and the *Booth* Court fear, prejudice juries to impose death sentences more frequently than juries who do not hear VIE is a query we seek to answer empirically in this chapter. Before doing so, we discuss prior empirical studies of capital juries to ascertain more generally what roles co-victims play in the penalty phase deliberations of capital jurors. Each of the studies discussed relies on preliminary data from the "Capital Jury Project" (CJP), a federally funded survey of jury members who served on capital cases. To understand the influence of VIE on capital juror decision making we examine a broad analysis of influential factors by William Bowers, the principal investigator of the CJP.

In a study by Ursula Bentele and William Bowers (2001), the researchers report on partial data from the CJP—a much smaller sample than the final data set. They examine interview transcripts with 240 jurors in a total of fifty-eight cases in six states. Part of the interview asked jurors to identify the topics they discussed most during the penalty phase deliberations. Of thirty-seven choices, the top five topics have to do with the strength of the evidence that led to the conviction, the nature of the killing, and the defendant's role and motive in the crime. Noticeably absent to Bentele and Bowers is juror discussion of mitigating evidence. What is most striking to us, however, is that jurors, based on Bentele and Bowers's findings, do not in any way talk about the families of murder victims or victim impact evidence. This suggests that VIE is not as decisive in penalty decisions as Logan, Sarat, and the *Booth* Court believed.

If, as Bentele and Bowers find, VIE is not central to juror decision making, is it relevant at all? Both Sundby (2003) and Eisenberg et al. (2003) provide a more direct assessment of how VIE affects juror decision making. Sundby, like his predecessors, makes use of preliminary CJP data, yet he relies solely on juror interviews from California. For this project Sundby gathers data from thirty-seven cases, with nineteen resulting in death sentences, seventeen cases ending with life without parole, and one case finishing in a hung jury. A total of 152 jurors took part in the study: seventy life jurors, seventy-eight death jurors, and four from the hung jury trial.

Sundby's two central concerns are how VIE provides information to jurors about the victim's characteristics and how the varying perceptions of victims may lead to different sentences. He hypothesizes that the more worthy the jury finds the murder victim, the more likely the defendant will receive the death penalty. For example, a child may be seen as a "worthy victim," one for whom a death sentence should be imposed; but a victim who had a criminal record may be seen as "unworthy" and, therefore, jurors would be less likely to reach a death verdict. Sundby's findings are especially significant because he finds that jurors do not seem to do as they say. For the most part, and with the exception of child victims, jurors said that the characteristics of the victim have no bearing on their decision making. But upon examining the data to find what jurors specifically discussed in their deliberations, he found that 43 percent discussed the victim's reputation or characteristics a great deal (11 percent) or a fair amount (32 percent). Furthermore, jurors who impose the death penalty are more likely to have viewed the victim as worthy than jurors who select life sentences. Sundby reveals that 61 percent of death jurors said that the community "admired or respected" the victim, while only 34 percent of life jurors did so. In addition, 51 percent of life jurors report that the victim was "too careless or reckless" in his or her behavior prior to the crime, compared with 11 percent of death jurors. As Sundby writes, "Jurors tend to value victims who played no role in the crime more than those who engaged in some type of risky or antisocial behavior" (p. 356).

The analysis Sundby offers does not speak directly to the influence of VIE on juror decision making. However, it is possible that VIE may alter jurors' views of the victims, increasing or decreasing the perceived worthiness of the deceased. Co-victims may not be the only means for jurors to gain an impression of victims, but the family members of victims may have the strongest ability to help shape impressions since they give a personal account of their loss and tell stories of the victims' death as well as their lives.

Eisenberg et al. (2003) turn to the South Carolina segment of the CJP data to see if the *Payne* decision from 1991, with its subsequent reintroduction of

VIE, affected the frequency of death sentences in capital cases. They examined data from 214 jurors and sixty-three cases, with 103 jurors serving in cases after the *Payne* decision. Of these jurors, a group of twenty-seven were asked additional VIE-related questions. Though a small sample, the researchers found that the "discussion of the loss or grief of the victim's family and the discussion of the victim's pain and suffering noticeably increased after 1991" (p. 315). That is, VIE seems to affect jurors' consideration of the harm to the victim and co-victims. But they further found that jurors generally did not think it was important to consider the punishment wishes of the victims' families.

Similar to Sundby, Eisenberg and his colleagues focus on the possibility that jurors' perceptions of the victim will affect sentencing—in their words, how "victim admirability" will lead to death sentences. They find that 59 percent of jurors personally admired or respected the victim, and 86 percent gave the victim the two highest community admiration scores. And, quite notably, such admirability of victims increases with "growing and improving use of VIE by prosecutors" (p. 325). Hence, the *Payne* ruling has affected capital murder cases in South Carolina in that it has caused greater discussion of and more respect for the victim. But Eisenberg and his colleagues did not find that VIE increases death sentences: "We find no significant relation between increased victim admirability and juror capital sentencing votes, nor do we find a significant relation between the introduction of VIE and sentencing outcomes" (p. 308).

In sum, preliminary studies of CJP data do *not* find that VIE affects sentencing outcomes in the way the Supreme Court in *Booth*, as well as some legal scholars, have argued. These studies, however, rely on rather limited samples and have other methodological restrictions.[2] Below we re-examine the impact of VIE on sentence decisions using the complete CJP data set. We additionally report descriptive findings on juror attitudes and experiences with the co-victims' role. After describing the data set in detail, we offer an analysis of our findings, which includes general conclusions about the role of co-victims in capital trials.

For this study we not only examine how co-victims participate in capital murder trials, but we also look at the overall impact that the participation or the lack of participation of co-victims has on juror decision making. More specifically, some of the questions we will consider are: How often do co-vic-

---

2. The Eisenberg et al. (2003) analysis, for example, uses the juror as the unit of analysis when testing case-level outcomes. Since the CJP has varying participation of jurors per case, this may bias results for cases with more participating jurors.

tims attend capital trials, and how often do they testify? Are there racial differences in such participation? Does VIE increase the defendant's chance for the death penalty? How does co-victim participation in the justice system affect juror penalty phase deliberations, and does this participation alter jurors' views of victims' families and their suffering? Taking our findings into consideration, we will then comment on what the role in the justice system should be for co-victims wanting to heal their unbinding wounds.

Methodology

The Capital Jury Project (CJP),[3] with support from the National Science Foundation, reports the experiences of jurors who have served in capital murder trials. Our study analyzes the complete CJP data, which includes 1,198 jurors from 353 different cases in fourteen states. In 1991 numerous scholars began interviewing jurors who served in trials between 1981 and 1996. An enormous undertaking, the CJP asks hundreds of questions to participating jurors, inquiries that probe all aspects of the trial experience. Researchers systematically structured the interview so that participants responded to both predetermined answers (such as "yes" or "no") as well as open-ended questions that allowed jurors to elaborate in a narrative way their trial experience as it pertained to specific sections of the instrument. Employing these data, the CJP enables scholars to use a combined qualitative and quantitative approach to capital juror decision making, simultaneously examining what jurors say and do. Our analysis here focuses exclusively on the available empirical data set; we do not examine or reflect upon the qualitative results from the CJP study.

We distinguish in our empirical analysis between juror- and case-level data. For the more attitudinal questions, like when jurors indicate their feelings toward a victim's family, it is more appropriate to examine all 1,198 juror responses because such answers are subjective, thus making them unreflective of the entire jury. Yet when we investigate the ways in which co-victims influence case outcomes, we must look at the data in a case-based manner. When we want to know, for example, if co-victims attended the trial or if their testimony influenced the sentencing outcome, we use a case-level analysis, using one juror for each case (353 in all) to represent the rest. This is neces-

---

3. See Bowers (1995) or the CJP website (http://www.cjp.neu.edu) for a detailed description of the CJP study.

sary because the CJP does not include every juror for each case, and since the number of jurors per case varies, those cases with more jurors would be over-represented, thereby skewing our results.

In order to create a case-level data file, we considered three important variables: the sentencing outcome, whether co-victims attended the trial, and whether co-victims testified for the prosecution. The rationale for focusing on these three items of the instrument is that each question should yield an objective result, meaning that whether or not a family attended the trial, for example, is not a subjective experience on behalf of the juror; rather it is a matter of fact. Since the CJP bases its data on jury members' memories, answers to the objective questions unfortunately differ sometimes between jurors in the same case. Hypothetically, if most of the jurors said a family attended, then we concluded that the family was in fact present during the trial. When we came across a tie for one specific category—say a disagreement on whether a family testified or not—we removed that case from our analysis since we could not resolve the discrepancy.

Findings

Co-Victim Participation

The CJP data reveal that co-victims nearly always participate in the trial by attending its proceedings. Jurors reported that close to 92 percent (304 of 331 cases)[4] of families attended the trial. Despite their presence, we see that by no means did all of the families testify. According to jurors, co-victims provided victim impact evidence in 38 percent of the cases (102 of 267 cases). Fortunately, the CJP provides data for cases during three relevant time periods—before the *Booth* decision when VIE was admissible; after *Booth* when it was prohibited; and after *Payne*, when it became admissible again. Ten percent of the cases come from the pre-*Booth* period, 65 percent from the *Booth* era, and 25 percent from the *Payne* era.[5] Not surprisingly, we find evidence that VIE has increased dramatically since the *Payne* decision, so that VIE was used in the majority (52 percent) of cases after the 1991 ruling. We were surprised,

---

4. While there are 353 cases in the data set, some cases have missing information, which explains why the total number in this instance is 331 and the number is 267 in the proceeding instance.

5. Unfortunately, the eighty-nine cases (25 percent) are missing trial dates and were excluded from this part of the analysis.

Figure 1. Race and Co-Victim Presentation of Testimony

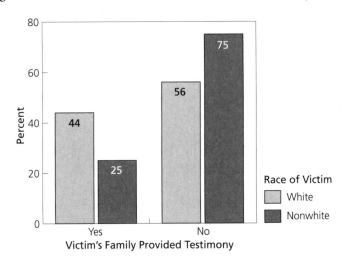

however, by the number of cases in which jurors reported that VIE was presented during the *Booth* period, when (according to the law) none should have appeared. Indeed, jurors claim that testimony was presented in thirty-seven of the 103 cases during this period. While we do not know the explanation for this, it is possible that practice was in violation of the law. Another reason may be that those jurors' memories of the testimony are faulty; for example, family members may have testified during the guilt phase of the trial as witnesses, which is permissible, but jurors remembered that testimony as part of the punishment phase.

When we cross-tabulated co-victims' testimony for the prosecution with the victim's race, we discovered a very significant finding: the co-victims of a white murder victim were more likely to offer testimony than the co-victims of a nonwhite victim. This is illustrated in Figure 1.[6] Whites are almost twice as likely to provide VIE as nonwhites (assuming victims and co-victims are of the same race). We do not know if this is because nonwhites choose not to testify at a greater rate or because prosecutors exclude them. Thus we find that co-victim attendance is high overall; but less than a majority provide VIE, with even fewer nonwhite-victim family members testifying.

---

6. These findings and all other bivariate analyses presented are statistically significant at the .05-level using a Chi Square test (unless explicitly stated otherwise).

Juror Attitudes Toward Co-Victims

Jurors generally appear to have positive attitudes toward the families of victims. Most (77 percent) believed that the victim was "raised in a loving family," and the majority (91 percent) perceived the victim as "someone who loved his/her own family." While jurors do not tend to personally identify with co-victims, their sympathy is apparent. Table 1 shows that most jurors could not imagine themselves as a member of the victim's family, nor did members of the victim's family remind the jurors of anyone they knew. This does not mean, however, that jurors felt detached from co-victims. More often than not jurors claimed they did *not* feel distant or remote from them, could imagine themselves in the family's situation, and had some sensitivity to their grief and sense of loss. Finally, jurors for the most part do not assign blame to the co-victims for the crime that occurred. Thus, many jurors were able to tunnel into the co-victim experience, both seeing themselves in the distraught state of the family and acknowledging their bereavement.

The Influence of Victim Impact Evidence on Juror Attitudes

Although we found jurors to be generally sympathetic toward co-victims, we wondered if co-victim testimony enhanced this emotional effect on jurors. Because most jurors are sensitive to victims' families even when they do not testify, we cannot expect large changes to occur. Nevertheless, we do find that VIE increases sympathy. For example, 85 percent of jurors who did not hear family members testify answered affirmatively that they felt the co-victims' "grief and sense of loss." Ninety percent of jurors who did hear VIE experienced the same subjective response. Similarly, jurors who heard VIE were not only more likely to believe the victim was someone who loved his or her family, but they were also better able to imagine themselves in the family's situation. Therefore we find evidence that by having co-victims testify, jurors understand the depth of bereavement, which then facilitates jurors being able to identify more closely with victims' families.

The Influence of Co-Victims' Grief and Loss on Trial Proceedings

In the last section, we found that most jurors had some feeling for the co-victims' loss and grief. Does this sympathy come directly from the trial pro-

Table 1. Juror Attitudes about Co-Victims

	N	Percent
Imagined Yourself as Member of Victim's Family		
Yes	340	29
No	831	70
Not Sure	11	1
Did Any Member of the Victim's Family Remind You of Anyone?		
Yes	147	13
No	855	76
Not Sure	120	11
Felt Distant or Remote from Victim's Family		
Yes	324	28
No	800	68
Not Sure	56	4
Imagined Yourself in Situation of Victim's Family		
Yes	752	63
No	421	36
Not Sure	15	1
Felt Family's Grief and Sense of Loss		
Yes	1016	86
No	158	13
Not Sure	11	1
Victim's Family Partly to Blame for Crime		
Yes	107	9
No	1047	89
Not Sure	26	2

ceedings? How much are families the focus of attention in the trial? And how much does such awareness of their grieving influence jurors' decision making? Table 2 reports our results on these issues. As it shows, in the majority of cases, the family's loss and grief was a prominent topic of discussion for prosecutors and jurors alike. In 68 percent of the cases, jurors believed that this factor—the severe loss and grief of the victims' families—influenced the sentencing decision.

While co-victims' suffering is a prominent topic in the trial proceedings, does victim impact evidence increase jurors' attention to the issue? Does co-victim testimony increase the likelihood that their bereavement will influence juror life and death decisions? We found that providing testimony did not in-

Table 2. Trial Focus on Co-Victims' Loss and Grief

	N	Percent
Prosecutor Focus on Loss and Grief of Co-Victims		
Great Deal	155	46
Fair Amount	111	33
Not Much	54	16
Not At All	18	5
Jurors' Focus on Loss and Grief of Co-Victims		
Great Deal	79	23
Fair Amount	108	31
Not Much	99	29
Not At All	58	17
Co-Victims Suffering of Severe Loss or Grief was an Influential Factor in the Case		
Yes	229	68
No	91	27
Not Sure	18	5

crease jurors' discussion of their loss and grief. However, it was associated with the likelihood of prosecutors' talking about it. This suggests that VIE may cause prosecutors to focus more intensively on the issue of co-victimization; or it is possible that such prosecutor focus may be a part of a pre-existing strategy that prioritizes the role of victims' families. Nonetheless, VIE did increase the likelihood that co-victims' suffering would become a factor in the decision-making process, as shown in Figure 2. What these statistics reveal is that the emotions of co-victims did permeate the courtroom, so much so that jurors took into consideration the family's situation when making a penalty decision. And this consideration increases when families provide VIE.

Since we found that testifying varies by race, we examined in a more in-depth way just how deeply race affects jurors' considerations of the grieving of co-victims. Victims' families appear to have *less* influence on jurors in cases with nonwhite victims. First, the idea that the victim had a "loving family" was not as important of a point to jurors in cases with nonwhite victims. Jurors believed this to be a factor in their decision making in 68 percent of cases with white victims, but in only 48 percent of cases with nonwhite victims. Second, the grief and loss that co-victims suffered was an important factor in 75 percent of the cases with white victims, but only in 63 percent of cases having nonwhite victims. These troubling findings indicate that for cases where the victim was white, jurors were more likely to give attention in the jury room

Figure 2. Co-Victims' Loss and Grief As Factor in Sentencing by Testimony of Co-Victims

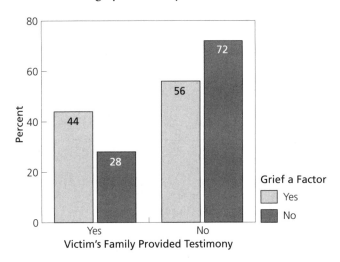

to the suffering of that victim's family. However, jurors are more likely to discount co-victims' suffering if the victims are nonwhite.

The Influence of Co-Victims' Punishment Wishes on Trial Proceedings

Though the *Payne* ruling mandated that victims' families should not make their punishment wishes known while giving VIE, evidence from the CJP data reveals that jurors often form opinions about what the families want. They may be doing this on mere speculation, from observations of family members seated in the court room, from innuendo or inference based on prosecutors' comments or family members who testify, or by direct statements that do indeed violate trial regulations. To what extent have juries honored the wishes of co-victims? How much are these wishes on the minds of jurors? Table 3 shows that, while prosecutors focus on co-victims' wishes to some extent, this does not lead many jurors to ponder them and believe they are an important factor in penalty decision making. Both prosecutors and jurors are most likely to ignore the punishment wishes of victims' families, with jurors seeing them as unimportant to their own individual votes for life or death.

Although the punishment wishes of co-victims do not seem of paramount importance, we must explore whether victim impact evidence increases the chances that jurors will consider the punishment that victims' families want.

Table 3. Influence of Co-Victims' Punishment Wishes

	N	Percent
Prosecutors' Focus on Punishment Wanted by Co-Victims		
Great Deal	37	11
Fair Amount	62	19
Not Much	87	26
Not At All	143	44
Jurors' Focus on Punishment Wanted by Co-Victims		
Great Deal	25	7
Fair Amount	28	8
Not Much	93	27
Not At All	197	58
Co-Victims Asking for the Death Penalty was an Influential Factor in the Case		
Yes	57	17
No	205	61
Not Sure	74	22

Here we do not find a direct link, but rather an important indirect effect.[7] When co-victims testify, they may either influence the jurors directly or be supporting a larger prosecutorial strategy to sway the jury. This latter path is more important in our findings. If family members testify, prosecutors are more likely to focus on the punishment wishes of the co-victims. We also find that when prosecutors discuss this, jurors are much more likely to view the families' wishes as an important factor in their decision making. Figure 3 illustrates how much prosecutors can enhance jurors' consideration of this issue.

Impact of Co-Victims on Sentencing

Thus far we have found that co-victims are often on the minds of jurors in that the participants report noticeable levels of sympathy for victims' families and also believe the suffering of co-victims matters in the penalty decision-making process. Important to a lesser extent are the specific punishment wishes of the family. But the central question in the debate about VIE is not whether it enhances consideration of co-victims' grief or their punishment

---

7. Our analysis shows that when co-victims testify, they do increase the likelihood that jurors will find their punishment wishes to be important. But this effect was only marginally significant statistically—p=.065.

Figure 3. Effect of Prosecutors on Juror Considerations of Co-Victims' Punishment Wishes

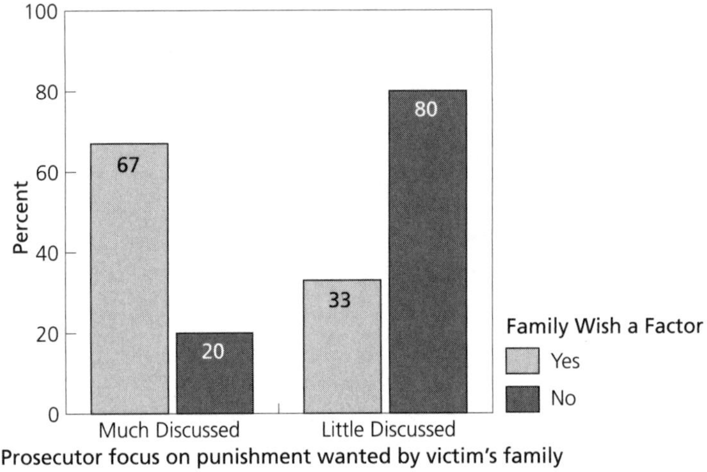

Prosecutor focus on punishment wanted by victim's family

wishes, but whether it increases the likelihood that the defendants will receive the death penalty. In previous analyses of the CJP, such an effect has not been found, yet those studies are more limited in their sample sizes. Here we are able to examine the sentences in 267 cases, comparing the 102 cases where co-victims testified to the 165 cases where they did not testify. As Figure 4 illustrates,[8] we do see a slight trend in which death sentences occur more often when co-victims testify than when they do not. This occurrence, however, is neither dramatic nor statistically significant. The fact that co-victim testimony is not statistically significant means that if we were to conduct another study, there is a very good chance that this trend would not reappear. Furthermore, the influence of families on sentencing, if there is any at all, is very small. The conclusion that we draw from this is that co-victim testimony does not have a notable influence on sentencing outcomes.

Conclusion

Our analysis of the data from the Capital Jury Project sheds light on the role of murder victims' families in capital trials. Below we review our key find-

---

8. This finding is not statistically significant, meaning that if repeated in future studies this outcome will not with any certainty be replicated.

Figure 4. The Effect of Co-Victim Testimony on Sentencing

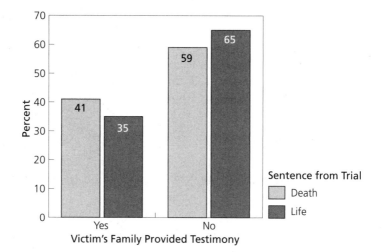

ings, note limitations of the available data, make suggestions for further research, and speculate on the present and future role of co-victims in death
penalty cases.

Participation

Co-victims are clearly interested in following the proceedings in capital
cases. Based on juror observations, they nearly always attend the trials. More
than half of the cases since the *Payne* decision included VIE, and we suspect
this percentage has only increased since the period of data collection of this
study. Presentation of VIE, however, is not bias-free. Families of white victims are more likely to testify than families of nonwhite victims. One reason
for this may be that nonwhites tend to be less supportive of capital punishment than whites (Bohm 2003). Further research is necessary to explore why
most co-victims choose to attend trials, what drives their decision to present
VIE, and what factors preclude them from having this opportunity. We found
evidence that participation rates differ by race, and we suspect that future research will find other differences, such as those between co-victims who support and oppose the death penalty. A corresponding survey of victims' families is necessary to uncover their perceptions of the role that they play in the
trial process. We especially need to know co-victim attitudes about their experiences attending trials and presenting testimony, and whether they would

like to see changes in their role that would either increase their influence in the decision-making process or better serve their recovery needs.

Juror Attitudes

We find jurors to be highly sympathetic to the plight of co-victims. While jurors do not identify with them to the point that they see victims' families as just like themselves, they can imagine having a similar trauma occurring in their own lives. As we have further discovered, jurors do not place blame upon families of the victims, and they tend to see victims as people who came from loving families. It seems that jurors have positive attitudes toward co-victims regardless of VIE, but presenting testimony does appear to increase juror sympathy and understanding even further.

The recent movement of justice systems toward victims' rights and restorative justice both in the United States and internationally confirms a new sensitivity of the courts toward meeting the needs of crime victims and their families. Restorative justice researchers have found that co-victims often seek and benefit from the opportunity to tell their story. This seems to help them make sense of the tragedy and feel less socially isolated (Umbreit 2003; Umbreit et al., this volume). Providing VIE is one opportunity for murder victims' families to tell others of their experiences, and our data show that co-victim testimony may achieve the simple goal shared by many victims' families of having those in the courtroom understand the trauma of enduring the loss of a loved one. Again, research on co-victims in capital cases is necessary to confirm if offering VIE is a valued goal. But co-victims may find some satisfaction in knowing that VIE can positively affect juror attitudes about them.

Co-Victims and Trial Proceedings

The CJP data reveal that co-victims are on the minds of capital jurors. A prominent topic of discourse for prosecutors is the loss and grief of victims' families, and these consequences of co-victimization figure into jury deliberations in about one half of cases, with most jurors believing that the families' bereavement was a factor in the sentencing decision. We find that VIE is associated with the likelihood that prosecutors will discuss co-victims' loss and grief. Family member participation in trials increases the chance that jurors will give their testimony weight in deliberations. Thus, VIE seems to be effective in highlighting during the trial the suffering of families.

Although jurors may be very aware of co-victim bereavement, they do not automatically embrace the punishment wishes of co-victims—an act that would undermine the *Payne* ruling. VIE could, however, cause some jurors to take the family's wishes, when illegally brought into the courtroom, seriously—or it may influence jurors to form their own opinions about what they think the victim's family wants. We found that VIE coincides with increased prosecutorial discussion of what co-victims would like to see as a sentence. When prosecutors focus on these wishes, jurors are more likely to weigh them as a factor in their decision making. Even so, we do not find evidence that jurors as a whole place much weight on this issue, even if co-victim punishment sentiments become a more prominent discussion topic.

Unfortunately, we find that jurors tend to be less concerned about the suffering of nonwhite-victim families than with white-victim families. With our small sample of cases with nonwhite victims and their families, we could not tell if providing VIE is an effective means to overcome this racial juror indifference. It is possible that since families of nonwhite victims testify much less often (perhaps as a result of institutionalized racism or their own feelings about capital punishment), their place in the minds of jurors is diminished. As a matter of policy, we would strongly encourage greater participation of family members of nonwhite victims in capital trials because their VIE may make their side of the story increasingly memorable to jurors. Although the findings we report do not show dramatic differences between whites and nonwhites in terms of participation, the evidence that jurors exhibit racially biased attitudes is statistically significant, and it is discouraging to see race bias plague yet another area of capital punishment.[9]

Victim Impact Evidence and Sentencing

The most important finding in our study is that co-victim testimony does not have a statistically significant effect on sentencing outcomes. We did find a small difference between cases with and without VIE, suggesting that it is certainly possible, under the right conditions, that a family member's testimony will sway a jury from giving a life sentence to imposing death. Such conditions seem to drive the Supreme Court's decision in *Booth v. Maryland*. However, we do not find it to be a structural flaw that produces bias in a consistent and problematic manner. In other words, the problem of juror bias as a result of VIE does not lie in the organization of the legal proceedings, but may still surface on a case-by-case basis.

---

9. See Baldus and Woodworth (2003) for a broader examination of race and the death penalty.

This chapter is an empirical examination of the role of co-victims in capital trials. Although our findings raise some red flags, they are also encouraging. The worst fears of VIE do not seem to have come to pass, and some distinctive benefits of VIE are apparent. Although the justice system is designed to be adversarial, it is our hope that the participation of co-victims in capital cases can be helpful to them in their recovery process (certainly not re-victimizing them, as is often the case)—but not harmful to defendants. Burr (2003) and Krause (this volume) describe scenarios where both co-victims' and defendants' needs can be met. Our findings suggest that VIE may be a valuable way to empower the families of murder victims, making their day in court free of the fear that this will bias jurors and thereby alter the course of justice.

References

Baldus, David C. and George Woodworth. 2003. "Race Discrimination and the Death Penalty: An Empirical and Legal Overview." Pp. 501–51 in *America's Experiment with Capital Punishment*, edited by James R. Acker, Robert M. Bohm, and Charles S. Lanier. Durham, NC: Carolina Academic Press.

Bentele, Ursula and William J. Bowers. 2001. "How Jurors Decided on Death: Guilt Is Overwhelming; Aggravation Requires Death; and Mitigation Is No Excuse." *Brooklyn Law Review* 66:1011–80.

Booth v. Maryland. 1987. 482 U.S. 496.

Bohm, Robert M. 2003. "American Death Penalty Opinion: Past, Present, and Future." Pp. 27–54 in *America's Experiment with Capital Punishment*, edited by James R. Acker, Robert M. Bohm, and Charles S. Lanier. Durham, NC: Carolina Academic Press.

Bowers, William J. 1995. "The Capital Jury Project: Rationale, Design, and Preview of Early Findings." *Indiana Law Journal* 70:1043–102.

Burr, Richard. 2003. "Litigating with Victim Impact Testimony: The Serendipity That Has Come from *Payne v. Tennessee*" *Cornell Law Review* 88 (LexisNexis Version).

Eisenberg, Theodore, Stephen P. Garvey, and Martin T. Wells. 2003. "Victim Characteristics and Victim Impact Evidence in South Carolina Capital Cases." *Cornell Law Review* 88:306–42.

Krause, Tammy. This volume.

Logan, Wayne. This volume.

_____. 1999. "Through the Past Darkly: A Survey of the Uses and Abuses of Victim Impact Evidence in Capital Trials." *Arizona Law Review* 41 (LexisNexis Version).

Payne v. Tennessee. 1991. 501 U.S. 808.

Sarat, Austin. 1997. "Vengeance, Victims and the Identities of Law." *Social and Legal Studies* 6:163–89.

Spungen, Deborah. 1998. *Homicide: The Hidden Victims*. Thousand Oaks, CA: Sage Publications.

Sundby, Scott E. 2003. "The Capital Jury and Empathy: The Problem of Worthy and Unworthy Victims." *Cornell Law Review* 88:343–81.

Umbreit, Mark S. 2003. *Facing Violence: The Path of Restorative Justice and Dialogue.* Monsey, NY: Criminal Justice Press.

Umbreit, Mark, Betty Vos, Robert B. Coates, and Katherine A. Brown. This volume.

CHAPTER 16

Victim Characteristics and Victim Impact Evidence in South Carolina Capital Cases[1]

Theodore Eisenberg, Stephen P. Garvey, and Martin T. Wells

Introduction

The use of victim impact evidence (VIE) has been a standard feature of capital trials since 1991, when the U.S. Supreme Court lifted the previously existing constitutional bar to such evidence (*Payne v. Tennessee* 1991). Legal scholars have almost universally condemned the use of VIE, criticizing it on a variety of grounds (e.g., Bandes 1996). Yet little empirical analysis exists of how VIE influences the course and outcome of capital trials. Valuable contributions have emerged from experimental studies, but such studies have often-rehearsed limitations, most of which are ultimately based on lack of verisimilitude. To begin to complement the experimental findings with real-case data, we analyze the influence of VIE based on interviews with over 200 jurors who sat on capital trials in South Carolina between 1985 and 2001.

---

1. Primary funding for the collection of data in South Carolina was provided by National Science Foundation Grant SES-90-13252. Supplementary funding was provided by the former South Carolina Death Penalty Resource Center and by Cornell Law School and the Cornell Death Penalty Project. Any opinions, findings, and conclusions or recommendations expressed are those of the authors and do not necessarily reflect the views of the National Science Foundation. We thank Ann M. Eisenberg and Bradford P. Maxwell for their research assistance. This chapter is based on Eisenberg et al. (2003).

We pursue three separable topics. First, we describe the VIE introduced at sentencing trials, using a subset of the interviews that posed questions directly focusing on VIE. Second, we analyze a factor closely related to, and influenced by, VIE—a factor we refer to as *victim admirability*. Third, we examine the connection between VIE and sentencing outcomes.

We find evidence of a strong association between victim admirability and VIE use. Victim admirability substantially increases as VIE has been increasingly used and refined. We also find some evidence of an association between victim admirability and jurors' perceived seriousness of the crime. Both increased victim admirability and increased crime seriousness might be expected to push jurors toward imposing death sentences. However, our data do not support these expectations. We find no significant relation between increased victim admirability and juror capital sentencing votes, nor do we find a significant relation between the introduction of VIE and sentencing outcomes.

Part I describes the data and changes in the law governing VIE's introduction in South Carolina. Part II reports how VIE is being used in South Carolina. Part III reviews the legal and empirical literature on VIE and formulates testable hypotheses about VIE's effects. We formulate these hypotheses based on empirical claims made in normative critiques of VIE, and on prior experimental studies. Parts IV and V report our empirical tests of the hypotheses set forth in Part III.

Data

Data Collection

The data analyzed here were gathered as part of the Capital Jury Project (CJP), a National Science Foundation-funded multi-state research effort (Bowers 1995). Prior to the CJP's efforts, empirical analyses of capital jury decision making were based primarily on mock jury studies. Data gathered from jurors who had actually served on a capital jury were unavailable. The CJP's research has started to fill the void (e.g., Blume et al. 2002).

Our analysis uses data gathered from jurors in South Carolina. Published research based on nationwide CJP data suggests that South Carolina jurors behave much like jurors in other states (Eisenberg et al. 1996). With one exception, our interviews cover cases brought from enactment of the South Carolina Omnibus Criminal Justice Improvements Act of 1986 through the summer of 2001.[2] Jurors who sat in sixty-three cases were randomly sampled,

---

2. The Omnibus Criminal Justice Improvements Act of 1986, No. 462, 1986 S.C. Acts 2955. The 1986 Act changed the standards of parole in capital cases and provided a natu-

with a goal of including four juror interviews per case.[3] The sample includes thirty-three cases resulting in a death verdict and thirty cases resulting in a life verdict. The total number of jurors interviewed was 214. Efforts were made to randomize the jurors interviewed for each defendant. Post-trial relocation of jurors to unknown addresses and declinations to be interviewed often limited randomization efforts. The results therefore should be understood to include only those jurors who were selected randomly, who were reachable, and who were willing to be interviewed.

The interview instrument (Justice Resource Center 1997) was designed and tested by the CJP and administered by trained interviewers. Several of the questions asked help analyze VIE. However, the original CJP survey instrument was designed after the Supreme Court's decisions in *Booth v. Maryland* (1987) and *South Carolina v. Gathers* (1989) prohibiting the use of VIE, and before the Court's turn-around in *Payne v. Tennessee* (1991) subsequently permitted such testimony to be offered in capital sentencing hearings. Consequently, although the survey instrument contained several questions relating to victims, it did not include any questions intended directly to probe the use of VIE in capital trials.

Beginning in the summer of 2000, the South Carolina segment of the CJP modified the instrument to include questions designed to assess VIE's operation in South Carolina. Jurors were asked, for example, how many, if any, of the victim's family or friends testified during the penalty phase, who testified, what generally they testified about, how they reacted emotionally to such testimony, and how important, if at all, such testimony was in their sentencing deliberations. These questions supplement victim-related questions asked prior to the introduction of the VIE questions. Since adding the VIE-specific questions, we have conducted twenty-seven additional interviews. Our analysis relies in part on these recent interviews, but much of it also uses the complete data set.

Limitations inherent in the data are discussed in greater detail elsewhere. They include possible lack of candor by some interviewees, erroneous recall,

---

ral starting point for the collection of data. The one exceptional case involved a trial conducted in 1985. A later amendment to the South Carolina death penalty statute provided that capital defendants not sentenced to death would be ineligible for parole for life. See Act of June 7, 1995, No. 83, 1995 S.C. Acts 545, 557. A few defendants in the cases sampled were resentenced as a result of errors in their initial sentencing trial. The data we use are based on the initial trials.

3. One juror was interviewed in five cases, two jurors were interviewed in six cases, three jurors were interviewed in twelve cases, four jurors were interviewed in thirty-nine cases, and five jurors were interviewed in one case. Our regression analyses account for the varying number of interviews per case.

and the fact that interviews are conducted after jurors have rendered their verdict (Eisenberg et al. 2001:281–82). A limitation worth emphasizing stems from this study's finding that little evidence exists of a relation between the use of VIE and sentencing outcomes. We explore VIE's influence on outcomes primarily by looking at case outcomes over time. To the extent that factors not accounted for in our models varied over time in a way that might mask VIE's effect, we could be understating VIE's influence on case outcomes.

Governing Law

The Supreme Court's first look at VIE in capital cases came in *Booth v. Maryland*, decided in June 1987. The prosecutor in *Booth* read a "victim impact statement" to the jury during the penalty phase of the trial. The information contained in the statement, which had been prepared by the state probation and parole department based on interviews with the victims' surviving family members, fell into three general categories: information "describ[ing] the personal characteristics of the victims," information about the "emotional impact of the crimes on the family," and information "set[ting] forth the family members' opinions and characterizations of the crimes and the defendant" (p. 502). The Court held that such "information is irrelevant to a capital sentencing decision, and that its admission creates a constitutionally unacceptable risk that the jury may impose the death penalty in an arbitrary and capricious manner" (p. 503).

Some South Carolina prosecutors construed *Booth* narrowly, reading it to bar them from introducing testimony about the victim from the victim's family members, but not from commenting themselves about the victim in closing argument. The South Carolina Supreme Court rejected this latter practice (*State v. Gathers* 1988), as did the U.S. Supreme Court. In *South Carolina v. Gathers* (1989), the U.S. Supreme Court held that "[w]hile in this case it was the prosecutor rather than the victim's survivors who characterized the victim's personal qualities, the statement [at issue here] is indistinguishable in any relevant respect from that in *Booth*" (p. 811).

Gathers was decided in June 1989. Two years later the Court reversed course completely and overruled both *Booth* and *Gathers*. The Court held in *Payne v. Tennessee* (1991) that "a State may properly conclude that for the jury to assess meaningfully the defendant's moral culpability and blameworthiness, it should have before it at the sentencing phase evidence of the specific harm caused by the defendant" (p. 808). Each state was therefore left to decide for itself whether it would follow *Booth* and *Gathers*, or *Payne*. The South Carolina Supreme Court gave its answer in October 1991, when it "adopted as state law the *Payne* decision" (*State v. Johnson* 1991). Of the 214 jurors we interviewed, 103 sat on cases tried after October 1991.

Of course, even before the Court lifted the constitutional ban on VIE in *Payne*, capital jurors would often hear basic biographical information about the victim during the guilt phase of the trial. Victims never remain completely faceless. After *Payne*, however, the prosecution was free to admit detailed information about the victim's life, as well as information about the impact of the victim's death on others.

VIE Use in South Carolina—An Overview

We asked several questions designed to give a general snapshot of how VIE is used in South Carolina capital trials. The resulting picture is more or less as we expected. VIE is indeed a routine part of capital trials in South Carolina in the post-*Payne* era. Of the twenty-seven jurors of whom we asked questions regarding VIE, all but two said that at least one member of the victim's family or one friend of the victim presented their views during the penalty phase. The two jurors not reporting such testimony are probably incorrect since a majority of jurors in each case indicated that such testimony occurred.

When we asked more specifically how the VIE witnesses were related to the victim, jurors reported that the victim's spouse, child, or parent were the most common witnesses, followed by siblings and friends, all of whom testified orally. Of the twenty-four jurors interviewed who reported that VIE was used, and who gave useable responses, ten indicated that the victim's spouse testified, ten indicated that a parent of the victim testified, ten indicated that a child of the victim testified, eight indicated that a sibling of the victim testified, and three indicated that a friend of the victim testified.

Interviewers asked the jurors about the general content of the victim impact testimony. Table 1 summarizes the responses. Two kinds of VIE—testimony about the personal qualities of the victim, and the impact of the victim's death on the witness—dominated. However, three (12 percent) of the jurors indicated that the witness or witnesses also testified about what kind of punishment the witness wanted the defendant to receive. The Court's decision in *Payne*, however, is reasonably construed to proscribe such testimony (pp. 830 n.2, 835 n.1).

Three questions probed the importance to the jurors of the VIE witnesses' actual or presumed wishes. The first question, which we used only from 2000 on, asked jurors how important it was "in determining the defendant's sentence to follow what you thought were the wishes of the victim's family and friends?" (Justice Resource Center 1997: Question X.A.13). Most jurors

Table 1. What Kinds of Things Did the VIS Witnesses Talk About?

(percent responding)

	Yes	No	n
How the crime affected them financially	4	96	24
How the crime affected them emotionally	92	8	24
How they needed professional help to cope	29	71	24
What kind of person the victim was	92	8	24
What the victim's future aspirations and plans were	67	33	24
How much they miss the victim	96	4	24
What punishment they wanted to see the defendant receive	12	88	24

Source—Juror interviews in South Carolina capital cases, 1996–2001.

(twenty-one of twenty-four responding) indicated that it was "not important at all" or "not very important" to follow what they believed were the wishes of the victim's friends and family in determining the defendant's sentence. Three jurors indicated the wishes were "somewhat important" and one indicated that it was "most important."

Before and after 2000, we asked all jurors the extent to which juror discussions focused on thirty-eight topics of possible relevance to the sentencing decision (Question III.D.2). Table 2 shows, on a 1-to-4 scale, the jurors' responses with respect to victim-related topics. The first numerical column shows the mean response for cases tried in 1988, 1989, 1990, and 1991. These years form the period when *Booth v. Maryland*'s prohibition on VIE should have led to its reduced use. The second numerical column shows the mean response for post-1991 cases, those tried after *Payne v. Tennessee* authorized use of VIE, and when continuous use of VIE might have changed jurors' focus to be more victim oriented.

Table 2's responses support exploring possible VIE effects on capital case processing. The direction of the change in jurors' responses is the same for six of the seven victim-related questions: the post-1991 mean is lower than the earlier period's mean. That downward shift in means signifies a shift towards increased discussion of victim admirability, victim-family loss, and increased victim suffering. Both the discussion of the loss or grief of the victim's family and the discussion of the victim's pain or suffering noticeably increased after 1991. The first increase is marginally statistically significant, with $p < 0.1$, and the second is statistically significant, with $p < 0.05$.

The only topic that was discussed, on average, less by jurors in the post-1991 period than in the earlier period is the "victim's role or responsibility in the crime." This change, reflecting reduced discussion of the victim's possible

Table 2. Focus of Juror Discussions Relating to the Victim in Capital Cases

How much did the discussion among the jurors focus on the following topics?
(1 = great deal 2 = fair amount 3 = not much 4 = not at all)
($n = 182$)

Discussion items relating to the victim	Mean 1988–1991 ($n = 86$)	Mean post-1991 ($n = 96$)	Significance of difference (p-value)
Reputation or character of the victim	2.52	2.34	0.230
Loss or grief of victim's family	2.14	1.94	0.088
Punishment wanted by victim's family	3.08	2.94	0.448
Victim's role or responsibility in the crime	2.69	2.81	0.463
Innocence or helplessness of the victim	1.81	1.70	0.307
Pain or suffering of the victim before death	1.91	1.69	0.048
Way in which the victim was killed	1.47	1.32	0.116

Source—Juror interviews in South Carolina capital cases, 1988–2001.

blameworthiness, is consistent with the pattern of change for the six other questions. This is the only question in which a numerical increase in the response corresponds to an improved image of the victim.

Table 2 also shows that, of the seven victim-related topics, juror discussion focused least on the punishment wanted by the victims' families. Jurors tended to discuss the victim's suffering, reputation, or other topics to a substantially greater degree than the punishment wanted by the victim's family in both time periods. The difference between reported discussion of the punishment wanted by the family and the next most discussed topic is highly statistically significant in each period ($p < 0.0001$).

Jurors' lack of focus on victims' families' wishes emerges again in response to a question about how important several considerations were in deciding punishment (Justice Resource Center 1997: Question IV.1). Using the same 1-to-4 scale and cases as in Table 2, the punishment the family wanted received a mean response of 3.10, with a slight but statistically insignificant decrease in importance after 1991. The importance of the victim's pain and suffering received a mean response of 1.62, with slightly more importance after 1991, but the difference between before and after 1991 is not statistically significant. The families' punishment wishes were said to be among the least important factors considered in sentencing.

This summary of juror responses to questions about VIE and discussion patterns is suggestive of what the analyses reported below reveal. The jurors' reported content of VIE and of their discussions suggest that VIE increased empathy for victims and their families. But VIE does not appear to have been directed to or to have had a direct and material effect on sentencing outcomes.

Hypotheses

This part reviews some of the empirical hypotheses formulated in the legal and empirical literature analyzing VIE's operation in capital cases. The hypotheses address VIE's effect both directly on the ultimate question of sentencing outcome, and on jurors' perceptions about victims' admirability, which might indirectly influence sentencing decisions.

From the Empirical Literature

Three published mock juror studies explore the effect that information about victim characteristics has on variables relevant to capital sentencing. The earliest study, Luginbuhl and Burkhead (1995), used undergraduate students, each of whom reviewed descriptions of two crimes (p. 7). One depicted a "moderately aggravated murder" in which the defendant was convicted of capital murder for shooting an innocent bystander during the course of a robbery. The other depicted a "severely aggravated murder" in which the defendant was convicted of capital murder based on repeatedly stabbing an elderly man, who the defendant had tied to a chair during the course of a robbery.

Luginbuhl and Burkhead's major hypothesis was that the "introduction of victim impact evidence would increase the number of subjects who voted for the death penalty" (p. 9). Their results supported that hypothesis. Overall, 51 percent of the students exposed to the victim impact statement voted for death, while only 20 percent of those not exposed voted for death. This effect was present for both the moderately and severely aggravated scenarios, but only among subjects who were neutral toward, or who moderately or strongly supported the death penalty (p. 10),[4] and who would therefore be eligible to serve on an actual capital jury.

The other two studies, one by Edith Greene (1999) and the other by Greene and her colleagues (1998), focused on VIE's relation to a variety of

---

4. This effect was significant only among those who moderately supported the death penalty.

intermediate variables. The first study found that jurors who heard VIE about highly respectable victims rated the victims as more likable, decent, and valuable; felt more compassion for the victims' family; believed that the emotional impact of the murders on survivors was greater; and rated the crime as more serious. Although subjects in the high-respectability condition tended to attach less weight to the mitigating evidence presented than those subjects in the low-respectability condition, they attached no greater weight to aggravating evidence.

The second study was designed to examine the effect not only of the personal characteristics of the victim, comparing high- and low-respectability, but also of the other two forms of VIE—i.e., evidence related to the impact of the crime on the victim's family, and testimony involving the opinions of the survivors about the crime and the appropriate sentence. Greene labeled these three forms of VIE 1) "victim qualities" evidence, 2) "impact" evidence, and 3) "opinion" evidence, respectively. In general, mock jurors who received all three forms of VIE had a more favorable view of the victim and the victim's survivors than did those who received only impact or opinion evidence, or no victim-related evidence at all. Moreover, consistent with the previous study, the reactions of the mock jurors to the defendant was uniform across the various conditions. Finally, and again consistent with the previous study, the subjects in the high-respectability condition tended to think more highly of the victim and to rate more highly the suffering of the victim's survivors than did subjects in the low-respectability condition.

From the Legal Literature

The legal literature addressing VIE in capital cases is almost uniformly negative (e.g., Bandes 1996). Some critics focus on the judicial process, arguing that the Supreme Court's overruling of *Booth* and *Gathers* reflected nothing more principled than a change in the Court's personnel (e.g., Dow 1992). Other critics argue that allowing jurors in capital cases to hear VIE is wrong because such evidence is irrelevant. In the eyes of the law, the life of one victim is or should be no different than the life of any other. Thus, VIE should be prohibited because, whatever its effect on jury decision making, it has no legitimate role to play in a capital trial. Other critics, however, focus on the effects of VIE on jury behavior and therefore bottom their claims on VIE's assumed consequences. These effects overlap with the effects explored in the experimental literature. We focus here on three asserted consequences.

VIE Causes Differential Valuation of Victims

First, some critics argue that allowing jurors to hear VIE is wrong because such evidence will prompt jurors to place greater value on the lives of some victims and less on the lives of others (e.g., Phillips 1997). In particular, these critics warn that jurors will place more value on the life of "respectable" victims and less on the lives of others. This differential valuation is inherently wrong, even if it does not influence jury's sentencing decision. This legal critique resonates with Greene's empirical evidence that VIE enhances victim admirability.

VIE Increases the Capriciousness of Capital Sentencing

Second, some critics argue that this differential valuation of victims will influence jury decision making. According to some, the impression a jury forms about the value or respectability of the victim depends on a variety of factors, none of which, they claim, is rationally related to the goals of capital sentencing. They fear, moreover, that jurors will rely on their valuation of the victim when they decide the defendant's sentence (Dubber 1993:86–87; Logan 1999:157). This legal critique corresponds to Luginbuhl and Burkhead's findings that VIE increases death sentences.

VIE Increases Estimates of the Seriousness of the Crime and Reduces the Influence of Mitigating Evidence

Third, some critics argue that VIE will focus the jury's attention on the victim, and that jurors who concentrate on the victim will not focus on the defendant (Bandes 1996; Engle 2000). Consequently, VIE will cause jurors to pay more attention and assign greater weight in their sentencing calculus to the harm the defendant has caused. Conversely, jurors also are likely to pay less attention and assign less weight in their sentencing calculus to any mitigating evidence the defendant presents. The concern about increased focus on harm to victims resonates with Greene's findings that VIE increases estimates of crime seriousness. The concern about VIE effects on mitigating evidence relates to Greene's finding that greater victim admirability leads decision-makers to attach less weight to mitigating evidence.

The empirical and legal literature thus generate the following hypotheses that we can explore: 1) VIE increases juror admiration or respect for victims; 2) VIE increases juror perceptions of crime seriousness; 3) VIE reduces the effect of mitigating evidence; and 4) VIE increases the likelihood of a death sentence.

Empirical Results: Victim Admirability and Its Influence on Crime Seriousness, Aggravating Factors, and Mitigating Factors

This part explores the first three hypotheses noted above. Part V explores the relation between VIE and sentencing outcomes.

What Influences the Degree of Admiration for Victims?

The idea that VIE improves jurors' views of victims, with possible consequences on sentencing outcomes, is a common theme of the experimental and legal literature on VIE. But there are limits on using real-case data to study this question. Since VIE is used in almost all post-1991 cases, one cannot explore whether VIE improves victim admirability by comparing cases with and without VIE in the same time period. Before 1991, however, VIE was forbidden for a few years. After 1991 prosecutors may have improved their use of VIE over time. Both of these considerations suggest the possibility of a time effect of VIE. That is, victim admirability should have increased once VIE was allowed and as prosecutors refined their use of it over time.

The juror interviews included two questions that directly address the victim's status. We use the answers to these questions as a proxy for victim admirability. One question focused on the jurors' perception of the victim's status in the community. It asked: "In your mind, how well do the following words describe the victim?" The words were "admired or respected in the community." The responses ranged from "very well," "fairly well," "not well," and "not at all." Those options were associated with numerical values ranging from 1 to 4, with 1 corresponding to "not at all" and 4 corresponding to "very well."[5] The second question focused on the juror's own reaction to the victim rather than the juror's perception of the community's attitude. It asked whether the juror "admired or respected" the victim and called for a "yes" or "no" response.

The jurors generally thought well of the victims. The mean response to the community-based question, 3.38 with 199 respondents, falls between the two highest admiration rankings. Roughly 86 percent of the jurors responded with

---

5. For convenience, this discussion reverses the interview instrument's actual numerical coding.

the two highest community admiration scores, 3 and 4. In addition, 59 percent of the 195 responding jurors replied affirmatively to the "yes-no" question about the juror's own admiration or respect for the victim.

Figure 1 explores the relation between the year-of-trial and juror reports of victim admirability by the community. For each year, we compute the mean of juror responses to the community admirability question. We also compute the number of juror interviews contributing to each year's admirability mean. The figure uses that annual count of interviews to identify the year's mean.

Figure 1. Victim Admirability over Time, South Carolina Capital Trials

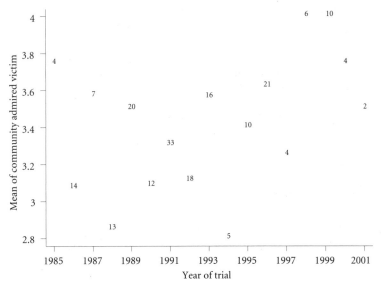

For example, for 1989, the data point indicated by the number "20" means that twenty juror interviews comprised that year's annual mean victim admiration rating. Those twenty interviews had a mean response on the 1-to-4 scale of victim admirability of a little over 3.5. Reporting the number of interviews comprising the mean suggests the relative weight that might be given to a year's observations. For example, the years 1985 and 1994 seem to depart most from the overall trend of the data. But both those years contain relatively few observations, four and five interviews, respectively.

The pattern over time is mixed until 1991, with a generally increasing trend in victim admirability since then. This result is consistent with VIE's uncertain status through 1991, and then its constitutional endorsement in that year. The figure suggests that over time, either defendants are murdering a more admirable group of victims; prosecutors are prosecuting cases involving a

Table 3. Descriptive Statistics of Variables Used to Model Victim Admirability

Variable	n	Mean	Std. dev.	Minimum	Maximum
Year of trial	214	1992	3.90	1985	2001
Victim age (years)	211	35.72	17.50	2	86
Victim sex (female = 1)	213	0.48	0.50	0	1
Victim race (black = 1)	212	0.12	0.32	0	1
Juror age (years)	212	44.38	11.69	22	75
Juror sex (female = 1)	213	0.54	0.50	0	1
Juror race (black = 1)	212	0.17	0.37	0	1

Source—Juror interviews in South Carolina capital cases, 1985–2001.

Table 4. Ordered Probit and Probit Models of Victim Admirability

	Model 1	Model 2	Model 3	Model 4	Model 5	Model 6
	Ordered probit			Probit		
	Dependent variable =			Dependent variable =		
	Community admired victim			Juror admired victim		
Year of trial	0.072**	0.071*	0.073*	0.081**	0.084**	0.092**
	(2.69)	(2.15)	(2.22)	(2.75)	(2.67)	(2.98)
Victim age		0.018**	0.018**		0.009	0.008
		(2.74)	(2.79)		(1.48)	(1.31)
Victim sex		-0.182	-0.174		-0.104	-0.136
(female = 1)		(0.81)	(0.79)		(0.42)	(0.55)
Victim race		-0.234	-0.246		-0.256	-0.314
(black = 1)		(0.80)	(0.82)		(0.54)	(0.67)
Juror sex			0.097			0.466*
(female = 1)			(0.48)			(2.13)
Constant				-161.381**	-167.152**	-182.562**
				(2.74)	(2.67)	(2.98)
Observations	199	195	194	195	190	189
Probability > F	0.0091	0.0062	0.0104	0.0079	0.0684	0.0086

Absolute value of robust t statistics in parentheses

+ significant at 10%; * significant at 5%; ** significant at 1%

Source—Juror interviews in South Carolina capital cases, 1985–2001.
Note—Models account for clustering at the case level.

more admirable group of victims; or prosecutors, assisted first by permission to use VIE and later by increasing experience in using VIE, recently have been able to convince jurors of greater victim admirability.

Figure 1's suggestion of a time trend in victim admirability can be tested further by controlling for other factors about the victim. Available information about the victim includes the victim's age, sex, and race. Table 3 summarizes the variables reported in Table 4's regression models of victim admirability. Two of the juror personal characteristic variables, age and race, are insufficiently helpful in explaining victim admirability to warrant inclusion in Table 4's regression models.

Table 4 combines the most salient variables in Table 3 into regression models of victim admirability. Models 1, 2, and 3 are of the community-based admiration variable, with its scale of 1 to 4. Models 4, 5, and 6 are of the dichotomous juror-admired-victim variable. The most consistent result across the models is the statistical significance of the "year of trial" variable. Victim admirability, at least in our sample, is increasing over time, a result consistent with jurors' discussion patterns reported in Part II. The trend is consistent with growing and improving use of VIE by prosecutors. Other results in Table 4 worth noting are the correlation between victim age and admirability for the community admiration models and the significance of female jurors in model 6.

Victim Respectability and the Seriousness of the Crime

The preceding section is consistent with VIE enhancing the victim's status in the eyes of jurors. Moreover, the victim's status can be a cause as well as an effect of certain case features. Greene reports a relation between the respectability of the victim and the subjects' rating of the seriousness of the crime. Crimes were perceived as more serious when victims were perceived as more respectable. Our juror interviews contained questions that serve as useful proxies for both the seriousness of the crime and the respectability of crime victims. We use the victim admirability variables discussed above as proxies for victim respectability.

We report elsewhere a summary of the interview variables relating to the seriousness of the crime (Eisenberg et al. 2001:287–89) and briefly summarize that discussion here. All murders are serious crimes, and capital murders are aggravated murders. Still, some capital murders are worse than others, and a juror is more apt to vote for death when she believes the crime is among the worst of the worst. To learn how each juror assessed the seriousness of the crime, we asked how well a particular word or phrase—for example, "vicious" or "bloody"—described the killing. The interviewed jurors were given twelve words or phrases to describe the killing. As reported elsewhere, several of the words or phrases used to describe the killing—"gory," "vicious," "depraved," "calculated," "cold-blooded," and "victim made to suffer"—bear a statistically significant correlation with whether jurors voted to sentence the offender to death. But only two words or phrases—"vicious" and "victim made to suffer"—retained their significance in models when we controlled for other key variables, such as the juror's race, the juror's support for the death penalty, and the defendant's remorse. Accordingly, we previously used the jurors' response to how "vicious" the crime was as a proxy for the seriousness of the defendant's crime (p. 289), and do so here as well.

Community Admiration and Crime Seriousness

Table 5 summarizes the responses to the viciousness and community admiration questions. Its "total" column suggests that jurors generally believed that the community admired the homicide victims. As reported above, the mean response to the community-based view, 3.38, is between the two highest admiration rankings. Table 5 also shows that most jurors thought "vicious" described the killing "very well," giving it the highest possible score of 4. The mean viciousness ranking is 3.70 on the 1-to-4 scale, with about 80 percent of jurors assigning the highest viciousness ranking.

Table 5. Relation between Victim Admirability and Crime Seriousness

Community admired victim	Crime Seriousness				
	1 least serious	2	3	4 most serious	Total
1 least admired	0 0.0%	0 0.0%	0 0.0%	7 100.0%	7 3.5%
2	1 0.0%	0 4.8%	5 23.8%	15 71.4%	21 10.6%
3	3 4.9%	1 1.6%	13 21.3%	44 72.1%	61 30.8%
4 most admired	2 1.8%	2 1.8%	13 11.9%	92 84.4%	109 55.1%
Total	5 2.5%	4 2.0%	31 15.7%	158 79.8%	198 100%

Source—Juror interviews in South Carolina capital cases, 1985–2001.

Table 5 also suggests that viciousness and victim admiration move together. For the most admired victims, over 84 percent of the jurors ranked the crime most serious. For the next-most admired victims (admiration variable equal to 3), 72 percent ranked the crime most serious. For the third-ranked score of victim admiration (equal to 2), 71 percent of the jurors rank the crime as most serious. For the least admired victims, however, the relationship changes. In general, therefore, the direction of the relation is as Greene's research suggests: more admired victims are viewed as the victims of more serious crimes. However, the relation between community admiration and crime seriousness is not statistically significant ($p = 0.156$).

Table 5's pattern of responses raises the question whether, for purposes of comparison with Greene's experimental results, the least-admired-victim category (the table's first row) causes the significance of the relation to be understated. All seven of the jurors who believed the community would least admire the victim ranked the crime as most serious. Given the small fraction of least-admired-victim responses, 3.5 percent of the responses, it is reasonable to test the relation between victim admiration and crime seriousness for those victims not regarded as belonging to the least admirable category. Excluding those seven responses does yield a statistically significant relationship between victim admirability and crime seriousness ($p = 0.045$). Although Greene varied the victims' respectability across two scenarios, in neither of her scenarios did the victim's admirability warrant ranking it at the lowest value of a four-point scale (Greene 1999:338). If one indulges in separate treatment of the least-admired victims, the significance of the relation between crime viciousness and victim admirability is reasonably robust, even surviving regression analysis that includes as an explanatory variable whether a death sentence was finally imposed.[6]

Juror Admiration and Crime Seriousness

The relation between crime seriousness and victim admirability weakens if one shifts from the juror's estimation of the community's assessment of the victim's admirability to the juror's own assessment. The direction of the relation is as expected. Jurors who admired the victim assigned the crime a mean viciousness rank of 3.73, while jurors who did not admire the victim assigned the crime a mean viciousness rank 3.66. But the relation is not statistically significant, and it remains insignificant after controlling for other factors, including sentencing outcome.

The real-case data generally support Greene's finding that victim respectability influences the level of perceived crime seriousness. But the relation is noticeably more significant for jurors' perceptions of community admiration of the victim than it is for reports of their own admiration.

---

6. The relation also remains statistically significant if one use the juror's first vote as an explanatory variable.

Victim Admirability and Aggravating and Mitigating Circumstances

Greene et al. found that mock jurors judging cases with more respectable victims tended to attach less weight to mitigating evidence presented than did mock jurors judging cases with less respectable victims (p. 153). In contrast, they found no evidence that mock jurors weighted aggravating evidence differentially. To explore the effect of victim status on juror receptivity to mitigating evidence, we used interview questions asking jurors about mitigating factors that, according to the jurors' self-reports, did influence their vote on the defendant's sentence, or might have influenced their vote if the factor in question had been present, though in fact it was not.

Table 6 lists a set of possibly mitigating factors extracted from the interviews (Justice Resource Center 1997: Question IV.B.1). If a juror reported that the presence of the ostensible mitigating factor made or would have made the juror more likely to vote for death, we coded the response as 1. If the juror reported that the presence of the potential mitigating factor made or would have made the juror "just as likely to vote for death," we coded the response as 2. If the juror reported that the factor made or would have made the juror less likely to vote for death, we coded the response as 3.

Table 6's first numerical column reports the jurors' mean responses. A mean of less than 2 indicates that, on average, the factor's presence would make a vote for death more likely. A mean of more than 2 indicates that, on average, the factor's presence would make a vote for life more likely. The pattern of means indicates that almost all the factors reported here would have some mitigating effect. For example, the mean of 2.72 when "defendant had a history of mental illness" suggests that this factor strongly influences jurors to vote for life.

The question here, however, is not the absolute level of the mitigating factors' influences. Rather, it is the relation between victim admirability and the jurors' reports of the mitigating factors' effect. If VIE's primary effect is on victim admirability, it is natural to ask whether admirability affects jurors' reactions to mitigating evidence. We can examine each mitigating factor and ask if its importance increases or decreases with increased victim admirability, and assess whether that increase or decrease is statistically significant.

Table 6's third numerical column shows that we cannot reject the hypothesis that victim admirability is unrelated to jurors' reactions to mitigating evidence. Nor can we confirm Greene et al.'s experimental finding that cases involving more respectable victims tended to diminish the weight of mitigating

Table 6. Relation between Victim Admirability and Mitigating Circumstances

Potential mitigating factor	Mean	*n*	Significance of relation between admirability and mitigating circumstance (*p*-value)
The killing was not premeditated but was committed during another crime, such as a robbery, when the victim tried to resist	1.98	150	0.922
The killing was committed while defendant was under the influence of an extreme mental or emotional disturbance	2.48	166	0.810
Victim was a known troublemaker	2.10	173	0.295
Victim had a criminal record	2.04	174	0.531
Victim was an alcoholic	2.03	172	0.255
Victim was a drug addict	2.04	171	0.486
Defendant had no previous criminal record	2.12	150	0.676
Defendant was mentally retarded	2.72	171	0.851
Defendant had a loving family	2.16	152	0.343
Defendant was under the age of 18 when crime occurred	2.36	173	0.756
Defendant had a history of mental illness	2.72	171	0.851
Defendant had a background of extreme poverty	2.15	162	0.223
Defendant had been seriously abused as a child	2.35	168	0.499
Defendant had been in institutions in the past but never given any real help or treatment for his problems	2.43	153	0.366

Source—Juror interviews in South Carolina capital cases, 1985–2001.
Note—The table reports the relation between juror reports of victim admirability and whether the presence of listed items of possibly mitigating evidence would make the juror more likely to vote for death. Mitigating factors range from 1 to 3, with 1 indicating more likely to vote for death and 3 indicating least likely.

evidence. Like Greene et al., we find, in results not reported here, no correlation between victim admirability and the weight accorded aggravating evidence.

Empirical Results of VIE's Effect on Case Outcomes

A central concern about VIE is that it can unjustly affect the sentencing outcome and influence jurors, who might otherwise vote for life imprisonment, to sentence an offender to death. The syllogism is that VIE enhances victim respectability or admirability, or the perceived seriousness of defendant misbehavior, which in turn increases the likelihood of a juror voting for a death sentence. This part explores the relation between victim status and juror votes as an *indirect* test of VIE's impact. If enhanced victim status does not increase the likelihood of a vote for death, VIE's effect on victim status might not translate into higher death sentence rates.

As described above, the admissibility of VIE was the subject of national constitutional developments. No constitutional limit on VIE at the Supreme Court level existed before 1987. In 1987 *Booth v. Maryland* held that introducing VIE at capital trials was unconstitutional. In 1991 the Court overruled *Booth* in *Payne v. Tennessee* and allowed each state to decide whether to admit VIE in capital cases. Most, if not all, states, including South Carolina, decided to allow VIE. Consequently, VIE could have been used freely before 1987, used less or not at all between 1987 and 1991, and then used again after 1991.

Our previous work with the South Carolina CJP data and the national VIE developments allows us to test the relation between VIE and juror sentencing votes. We have previously reported reasonably successful models of juror voting patterns in South Carolina capital cases (Eisenberg et al. 2001). We now add to these models variables to test whether victim admirability increases the likelihood of a juror voting for a death sentence.

Victim Admirability and Jurors' Sentencing Votes

Studying the influence of victim admirability requires accounting for other factors known to influence juror votes. In the extreme, if other factors completely determine the sentencing trial's outcome, no room would remain for victim admirability to affect outcomes.

Previous work using CJP South Carolina interview data develops models of jurors' sentencing decisions (Eisenberg et al. 2001; 1998). With respect to case characteristics, prior work shows that the viciousness of the crime, a defendant's remorse, and juror perceptions of defendant dangerousness all shape jurors' votes (Eisenberg et al. 2001:298–302). The more vicious the crime, the more likely it is that a juror will vote for death. The less remorseful the defendant, the more likely it is that a juror will vote for death. And the less time a juror believes a defendant will spend in prison if not sentenced to death, and therefore the more danger the juror believes the defendant will pose in the future, the more likely the juror is to vote for death.

The importance of crime-seriousness, as measured by the variable "vicious," in shaping juror votes poses a methodological problem. If crime seriousness and victim respectability were independent of one another, we could test for each factor's effect without concern for their effect on each other. But Table 5 suggests that increased victim respectability can lead to increased perception of crime seriousness. Therefore, using a case's seriousness as an explanatory factor may obscure the importance of the victim's admirability. We cannot completely avoid this problem, but we do offer a partial solution.[7] Some models reported below exclude the crime seriousness factor and replace it with a victim admirability variable. If victim admirability strongly overlaps with crime seriousness, the former should be nearly as important as the latter in explaining jurors' sentencing votes.

With respect to juror personal or demographic characteristics—such as race, sex, age, socioeconomic status, and religious affiliation—prior work shows that only race and religion substantially relate to a juror's first vote at sentencing. Holding several other juror characteristics constant, black jurors were more apt than white jurors to cast their first sentencing vote for life, while Southern Baptists were more apt than members of other religions to cast their first vote for death (Eisenberg et al. 2001:300–301).

In addition to collecting demographic information, interviewers asked jurors questions about the death penalty and the criminal justice system. Responses to a question about how strongly jurors supported the death penalty for convicted murders helped explain juror voting patterns. The five available responses ranged from death being the "only appropriate" punishment to death being an "unacceptable punishment." The question allowed each juror to rank herself on an ordinal scale reflecting the strength of the juror's support for the death penalty. The more a juror supported the death penalty the more likely she was to cast her first vote for death (ibid.). We use these variables to control for juror characteristics and the facts of the case while seeking to identify the effect of perceived victim respectability on a juror's voting behavior.[8]

---

7. A further refinement would be to model simultaneously crime seriousness and case outcomes in two equations.

8. Eisenberg et al. (2003:342) report descriptive statistics for each of these variables.

Table 7. Ordered Probit Models of Jurors' First Capital Sentencing Votes

Dependent variable = Juror's first vote
(1 = Life 2 = Undecided 3 = Death)

Black juror	-0.654*	-0.812**	-0.765**	-0.707*	-0.752*	-0.712*
(1=yes)	(2.38)	(2.86)	(2.78)	(2.55)	(2.63)	(2.57)
Southern	0.723*	0.540+	0.443	0.580*	0.655*	0.606+
Baptist juror	(2.45)	(1.89)	(1.58)	(2.07)	(2.17)	(1.99)
(1=yes)						
Support for	0.418**	0.422*	0.395*	0.407**	0.435*	0.433**
death penalty	(2.83)	(2.51)	(2.51)	(2.75)	(2.62)	(2.83)
(1–5 scale)						
Seriousness of	0.412*	0.525**	0.459*	0.495*	0.455*	0.393*
the crime	(2.35)	(2.89)	(2.32)	(2.60)	(2.62)	(2.09)
(1–4 scale)						
Defendant's	-0.279**	-0.304**	-0.250**	-0.302**	-0.256*	-0.212*
remorse	(2.90)	(3.01)	(2.81)	(3.41)	(2.43)	(2.14)
(1–4 scale)						
Expected	-0.022*	-0.010	-0.012	-0.011	-0.021*	-0.024*
prison term	(2.20)	(1.16)	(1.27)	(1.23)	(2.19)	(2.27)
(years)						
Community			0.136			0.047
admired victim			(1.05)			(0.37)
Juror admired		0.073			-0.042	
victim		(0.28)			(0.16)	
Post-1991		-0.301	-0.341	-0.306		
dummy		(1.18)	(1.44)	(1.30)		
Observations	202	185	188	202	185	188
Probability > F	0.0003	0.0001	0.0006	0.0001	0.0002	0.0029

Absolute value of t statistics in parentheses.

+ significant at 10%; * significant at 5%; ** significant at 1%

Source—Juror interviews in South Carolina capital cases, 1985–2001.
Note—All models include a dummy variable, not reported here, for whether the juror reported no expected prison term. Models 1, 5, and 6 include variables, not reported here, to account for the possible change in expected prison term after the U.S. Supreme Court's decision in *Simmons v. South Carolina* (1994). Models account for clustering at the case level.

Table 7 reports the regression results. Its first model is the model we report elsewhere (ibid.), but that we now supplement with data from juror interviews conducted following publication of these results. Models 5 and 6 explore whether adding variables about the victim's admirability improves this baseline model (Model 1). Model 5 adds the dichotomous variable representing whether or not the juror admired the victim. Model 6 adds the ordinal responses to the question whether the juror believed the community admired the victim. Neither variable has a large coefficient, nor does either come close to achieving statistical significance.

Models 2, 3, and 4 in Table 7 explore whether a time trend exists in jurors' first votes. The "post-1991 dummy" variable corresponds with the U.S. Supreme Court's decision in *Payne v. Tennessee* authorizing the use of VIE. If VIE increases the probability of obtaining death sentences, the coefficient for this variable should be positive and significant, i.e., post-1991 murders should be more likely than pre-1991 murders to lead to death sentences. We instead find a negative and insignificant coefficient. Thus, to the extent that the year dummy variable captures increased use of VIE, we find little evidence that VIE affected juror votes or sentencing outcomes in South Carolina cases.

Time Trend in Death Sentence Rates

The absence of evidence of a relation between victim status and sentencing votes and sentencing outcomes should be assessed in light of the substantial case selection effects that affect our capital trial sample. We only observe those cases in which prosecutors sought death and in which a trial is conducted. Focusing on a single decision, the jurors' sentencing vote, uses data that have been filtered by a highly discretionary selection process. Studying VIE's relation to sentencing outcomes using only trial data raises a problem of sample selection bias.

For example, allowance of VIE after *Payne* might have emboldened prosecutors to seek death sentences in more cases. If prosecutors did so, they might have sought death in a group of cases that were less "death-worthy," on average, than the capital cases brought before *Payne*. Adding the less death-worthy cases could lead to observation of a time trend towards life votes. But an increasing *percentage* of life votes at trial does not necessarily mean VIE had no effect. The *number* of death sentences might have increased despite the time trend observed at trial. That is, prosecutors would have been less likely to obtain death sentences at trial but more death sentences would be obtained because more murders were being pressed to capital trial. Thus, studying tried cases might show a declining trend in juror votes for death even though more death sentences were being imposed and *Payne*'s allowance of VIE had increased the death-obtaining rate by encouraging prosecutors to seek death more often. We are further limited by an incomplete sample of capital cases. Either case selection or sample limitations might mask a VIE effect in our data.

To study the absence of a post-1991 increase in death sentences, we explored a more "bottom-line" measure of death sentencing patterns over time, one not limited by our interview data. We examined the number of death sentences in South Carolina in each year and the number of murders out of which death sentences might emerge. A substantial pro-death VIE effect should lead to an increased percentage of murders that result in capital sentences. Prosecutors could be losing more at trial in the sense that juries impose death sentences at a lower rate. But if the number of cases in which prosecutors seek death substantially increased after *Payne*, then one should observe increased death-obtaining rates after 1991.

The murder and death sentence data, not reported here, indicate that failure to observe a time component in the CJP trial data, as shown in Table 7, is likely not an artifact of studying only tried cases. Within the tried-case sample, we found no VIE-related time trend. And in the broader sample of South Carolina murders and death sentences, not affected by case selection, we find no post-*Payne* time effect on death-obtaining rates. Thus, while we do have evidence that victim admirability increased over time, perhaps in response to VIE, we do not find evidence that VIE affected death sentence rates in South Carolina, either at the trial or aggregate level.[9]

Conclusion

Victim status is a part of a crime's effect writ large. Killing a more prominent or nobler victim might be viewed as inflicting greater harm on society, a society that believes deeply in retribution. So it might not be surprising to detect a strong VIE effect on sentencing outcomes. Failure to detect a relation between VIE and sentencing outcomes could of course be due to this study's data and other limitations.

But the absence of an effect in our far from trivial sample is also consistent with a substantial literature on the forces that shape case outcomes. Outcomes depend largely on facts (e.g., Guinther 1988:102; Lloyd-Bostock 1989:48), with secondary factors such as juror characteristics usually of little importance. In capital murder trials, unless the victim's behavior or status affects the nature or quality of the crime, VIE's modest effects are consistent with jurors' historic emphasis on salient facts. The absence of a VIE effect in our data and in the larger South Carolina murder and death row data sets is also consistent

---

9. Eisenberg et al. (2003:339–41) discuss the possible influence of jurors having been interviewed after they cast their votes and offering alternative explanations for how they voted.

with jurors' self-reporting of what they discussed during deliberations and what was important to them in deciding the sentence to impose.

References

Bandes, Susan. 1996 "Empathy, Narrative, and Victim Impact Statements." *University of Chicago Law Review* 63:361.

Blume, John H., Theodore Eisenberg, and Stephen P. Garvey. 2002. "Lessons from the Capital Jury Project." *Beyond Repair? America's Death Penalty*, edited by Stephen P. Garvey. Durham, NC: Duke University Press.

Booth v. Maryland. 1987. 482 U.S. 496.

Bowers, William J. 1995. "The Capital Jury Project: Rationale, Design, and Preview of Early Findings." *Indiana Law Journal* 70:1043.

Dow, David R. 1992. "When Law Bows to Politics: Explaining Payne v. Tennessee." *U.C. Davis Law Review* 26:157.

Dubber, Markus Dirk. 1993. "Regulating the Tender Heart When the Axe Is Ready to Strike." *Buffalo Law Review* 41:85.

Eisenberg, Theodore, Stephen P. Garvey, and Martin T. Wells. 2003. "Victim Characteristics and Victim Impact Evidence in South Carolina Capital Cases." *Cornell Law Review* 88:306–42.

_____. 2001. "Forecasting Life and Death: Juror Race, Religion, and Attitude Toward the Death Penalty." 30 *Journal of Legal Studies* 30:277.

_____. 1998. "But Was He Sorry? The Role of Remorse in Capital Sentencing." *Cornell Law Review* 83:1599.

_____. 1996. "Jury Responsibility in Capital Sentencing: An Empirical Study." *Buffalo Law Review* 44:339.

Engle, Matthew L. 2000. "Due Process Limitations on Victim Impact Evidence." *Capital Defense Journal* 13:55.

Greene, Edith. 1999. "The Many Guises of Victim Impact Evidence and Effects on Jurors' Judgments," *Psychology, Crime and Law* 5:331.

Greene, Edith, Heather Koehring, and Melinda Quiat. 1998. "Victim Impact Evidence in Capital Cases: Does the Victim's Character Matter?." *Journal of Applied Social Psychology* 28:145.

Guinther, John. 1988. *The Jury in America*. New York: Fact on File Publications.

Justice Resource Center, Northeastern University. 1997. Juror Interview Instrument, National Study of Juror Decision Making in Capital Cases.

Lloyd-Bostock, Sally M. A. 1989. *Law in Practice: Applications of Psychology to Legal Decision Making and Legal Skills*. Chicago: Lyceum Books.

Logan, Wayne A. 1999. "Through the Past Darkly: A Survey of the Uses and Abuses of Victim Impact Evidence in Capital Trials." *Arizona Law Review* 41:143.

Luginbuhl, James and Michael Burkhead. 1995. "Victim Impact Evidence in a Capital Trial: Encouraging Votes for Death." *American Journal of Criminal Justice* 20:1.

Phillips, Amy K. 1997. "Thou Shalt Not Kill Any Nice People: The Problem of Victim Impact Statutes in Capital Sentencing." *American Criminal Law Review* 35:93.

Payne v. Tennessee. 1991. 501 U.S. 808.

Simmons v. South Carolina. 1994. 512 U.S. 154.
South Carolina v. Gathers. 1989. 490 U.S. 805.
State v. Gathers. 1988. 369 S.E.2d 140; *aff'd* 1989, 490 U.S. 805.
State v. Johnson. 1991. 410 S.E.2d 547.

CHAPTER 17

Is Restitution Possible for Murder?—Surviving Family Members Speak

Judith W. Kay

In December 2003, Washington State sentenced Gary Ridgway, known as the "Green River" killer, to one term of life imprisonment and $10,000 in restitution for each of the forty-eight women he had confessed to murdering.[1] King County Prosecutor Norm Maleng had agreed not to seek the death penalty in exchange for additional confessions from Ridgway. The state may have decided on the sentence of life without parole (LWOP) plus restitution because Americans for the past twenty years have been saying they would accept just such a sentence in lieu of capital punishment.[2] When surveys have asked simply, "Do you support the death penalty?" upwards of sixty and even seventy percent of respondents endorse execution. However, when presented with a choice between the death penalty and LWOP, or the death penalty and LWOP plus restitution to victims' families, a majority of respondents prefer alternatives to capital punishment. Indeed, as many as two-thirds of those surveyed prefer LWOP *and* restitution to families over the death penalty as punishment for murder.[3] Research indicates that this preference has remained consistent over

---

1. Thanks to Jeanette Star Howard, Ronnie Friedman-Barone, David Karp, and James Acker for helpful comments on earlier drafts of this paper.

2. "In Arkansas, California, Wisconsin, Idaho, and Oregon, restitution to the victim's family can already be required of the offender in homicide cases" (Dieter 2003).

3. In a March 1993 poll, 77 percent of those surveyed supported the death penalty in the abstract. Support for capital punishment dropped to 49 percent when respondents were offered simply the alternative sanction of life imprisonment without any chance of parole (LWOP). Support for capital punishment dropped to 44 percent when respondents were

time and is unrelated to political party, religious affiliation, gender, race, or region of the country (Doble 2004; Bowers 1993).

Death penalty abolitionists have advocated legislation that would replace capital punishment with LWOP and restitution to victims' families, hopeful that legislators, backed by a majority of their constituents, would support such bills. However, to secure the passage of this kind of statute, legislators would need murder victims' families to speak in its favor. The two studies discussed in this paper were conducted with murder victims' families in order to ascertain if they would support, in principle, restitution as part of a sentence to replace the death penalty. The studies asked surviving family members what restitution might mean to them as hypothetical beneficiaries.

Before these studies could be conducted, three questions needed to be addressed: 1) What is restitution? 2) Is restitution for murder a new idea? 3) Why do so many Americans support restitution to victims for a broad range of crimes, including murder? After presenting the results of the two studies, this paper relates the subjects' concerns about restitution to moral objections raised in Biblical texts that have informed American life through Judaism and Christianity.

A Definition

Restitution is defined as a payment—or other benefit—extended by an offender to a victim who has suffered losses as a result of the offender's actions (Holmgren 1983). At least two different methods exist to help make good a crime victim's loss. First, offenders should restore victims to the same level of well-being they occupied before the crime. Second, if such restoration is not possible, then offenders should compensate victims for their losses. For example, in the case of assaults, the offender might pay the victim's medical bills or lost wages. For a homicide victim's relative, the murderer might be responsible for funeral expenses and fees associated with closing the victim's es-

---

offered the options of LWOP or twenty-five years imprisonment plus restitution to the victim's family. Only 41 percent of those surveyed continued to choose the death penalty over the option of LWOP coupled with restitution (Dieter 2003). In surveys conducted between 1985 and 1991, when offered the alternative sentence of LWOP and restitution, support for the death penalty plummeted "by 62 percentage points in Florida; 32 points in Georgia; 40 points in New York; and 54 points in California. Among our own samples, it dropped 52, 49, and 56 points, respectively, in New York State, New York City, and in Nebraska" (Bowers 1993:163).

tate. Originally, restitution did not take into account nonfinancial loss such as emotional suffering, but now in some jurisdictions restitution statutes cover psychological injuries and associated care (Harland 1980).

Criminal restitution—justified as a form of redress—is different from state compensation to victims. Compensation is provided either as a state duty arising from its failure "to protect" or as a form of "welfare" (Wright 1991:27–8). Unlike criminal restitution, compensation programs operate independently of the criminal justice system and dispense funds even when offenders are not apprehended or convicted. In contrast, restitution flows directly from the offender to his or her victim.

Is Restitution for Murder a New Idea?

What does justice require when murder has occurred? For much of human history the answer to this question has been revenge. Although its specific rules vary with culture and context, revenge typically granted authority to victims or their representatives to exact death for a killing or other grievous injury. The obligation was framed as an economic metaphor—a moral debt—but the currency was nonmonetary: suffering or death. The retaliatory injury inflicted by the avenger was morally permissible as a form of payback. The victim's family was permitted to derive pleasure from seeing the murderer humiliated and destroyed. Restitution for murder within a code that demanded revenge was often perceived as a less honorable resolution than killing the offender. Avengers who lacked the means to perpetrate violence had to settle for "blood money" (Blumenthal 2002).

Revenge, however, did not always secure justice. The killer's family might resist, or the killing could be seen as a new offense, igniting more retaliatory violence and leading to a blood feud that could last for generations. Blood feuds were evident in the ancient Near East, as suggested by the Torah stories of Lamech (Gen. 4:23–24) and the rape of Dinah (Gen. 34), but could be ended by the involved parties' migration to new land. When the option to flee faded as nomadic tribes became settled, blood feuds became more intense (Hanks 2002). However, as the wealth of clans increased, they had both the incentive and means to negotiate peaceful pacts, sealed with restitution.

Restitution for noncapital wrongs was used in ancient practices that today are characterized as restorative. Within ancient Israel, "the earliest payments intended to make good a wrong took the form of a composition, the amount being fixed by the offended party" (Falk 1964:83). Restorative justice primarily relied on a relationship-based model of harm rather than an economic-oriented one. More than a debt payable in pain or money, the malefactor left a trail of broken relationships that required mending. Restorative justice, concerned with identifying responsible parties and holding them accountable, simultaneously concentrated on meeting needs. Victims of noncapital crimes ideally found satisfaction, not in the vindictiveness of seeing rapscallions brought low, but in having harms repaired and needs addressed.

Ancient cultures varied in whether they permitted restitution for murder. Early Hebrew law restricted restitution to cases involving the accidental death of victims of low status, such as fetuses or slaves.[4] Some of Israel's neighbors, such as the Hittites, permitted the punishment of a substitute for the actual murderer or allowed a ransom to be paid for the murderer's life. The Code of Hammurabi (c. 2250 B.C.E.) made no general rule prohibiting composition for premeditated murder.[5]

The Hebraic Covenant Code, the early legal structure established before the monarchy in Jerusalem, effected a change in these earlier laws. This Code ended the practice of allowing limited composition by prohibiting restitution for murder (Jackson 1973:25). It instead provided that "you shall accept no ransom for the life of a murderer who is guilty of death, but he shall be put to death" (Num. 35:31). The Covenant Code also explicitly forbade substituting another person's life for the life of the killer, whether the slaying involved premeditated murder or manslaughter. These prohibitions applied, presumably, regardless of the economic status of the victims.

Biblical scholar Hanks (2002) views the Hebraic prohibition of restitution for murder as a move toward "equality in punishment" and away from the "status-defining purpose of feuding" (pp. 69–70). Equality before the law pointed in several directions. First, no one should be condemned to death because he was too poor to defend himself. Second, the wealthy should not be permitted to evade death through payment.[6] Hebrew justice would not be compromised by economic inequalities. And third, no one was to be executed for property crimes, which clearly established the value of humans beyond

---

4. The following Biblical passages permit payment in the case of accidental killing of slaves or fetuses. "If the ox gore a man-servant or a maid-servant, he shall give unto their master thirty shekels of silver, and the ox shall be stoned" (Exod. 21:32), and in Exod. 21:22, composition must be paid for a pregnant women's miscarriage caused by men engaged in a fight.

5. Section 207 of the Code reads: "If a man die of his wounds, he shall likewise swear [that it was not intentional], and if he [the victim] be a free-born man, he shall pay one-half mina of silver" (Davies 1905:88).

6. See Blecker (2003): "Abolishing the blood price, and thus *extending* the death penalty to the wealthy who deserve it, advanced Western Civilization" (p. 181).

their economic merit. This concern for equality stood in contrast to the Code of Hammurabi, in which the value of the victim was correlated with the severity of the punishment: individuals who harmed "less valuable" people could get away with a payment (Hanks 2002). Hebrew law pointed in the direction of valuing all victims of capital crimes equally by prohibiting restitution for murder.

Various factors explain the Bible's eventual prohibition of restitution for murder. Because humans were created in the image of God, their worth was not reducible to monetary compensation. Although in ancient societies (as in ours) a death meant the loss of an actual or potential worker, the deceased had human worth beyond social utility. The ancient Israelites perceived murder as an outrage not only against the image of God (Yahweh) but also as a pollution of Yahweh's land (Num. 35:33). The idea of blood pollution involves "the voice of the dead crying out in anger and anguish as his killer, living free, pollutes the land" (Blecker 2003:193). This notion appeared prior to the seventh century B.C.E. and existed alongside other perspectives. But after the seventh century, the idea of blood pollution became dominant and prompted communities to conclude that a murder affected the collectivity, requiring them to take action (Jacoby 1983:67). Maimonides in the twelfth century C.E. summarized this heritage succinctly when he warned against the payment of ransom for murder, even if all parties agreed to it. Jacoby (1983) translates: "'For the life of the murdered person is not the property of the avenger of blood but the *property of God*'" (p. 77, emphasis in original). As such, murder could never be settled financially between two families; the community must deal with homicides nonmonetarily. Perhaps because restitution for homicide was particularly vulnerable to distortion by the relative wealth of victims and offenders, later Roman law also prohibited payment for homicide. When Christianity became the dominant religion within the Roman Empire, it would seem that Western Europeans, in particular, might have been opposed morally to restitution for murder.

Yet, despite both Roman and Biblical opposition, the practice of restitution for murder survived until the late Middle Ages in Europe. Jacoby (1983) writes, "Restitution, or tribal *Wergild*, was a commonplace of many cultures— a stage between vendetta and the elevation of murder, through the new religious doctrine of pollution, to the status of an offense against society as a whole" (pp. 70–71). In many cultures, composition settled among kin lost favor to restitution exacted by courts. Yet even when the law, and not the families, determined the amount, payment still went to the survivors, revealing perhaps the durability of families' claims upon offenders for redress.

Legal retribution eventually began to replace both revenge and restitution. This process of outlawing community composition had both economic and ideal motivations. Sovereigns began to categorize formerly private offenses as crimes against the king's peace. Under Anglo-Saxon law, in addition to paying the victim's family the *wergild*, the murderer had to pay a fine, called a *wite*, to the lord or king (Jacob 1970). Legal scholar Laster (1970) observes, "The victim was necessarily reluctant to give up his previously favored position to the state, but he was forced into compliance by a slowly evolving carrot and stick philosophy" (p. 76). The common law withheld restitution until "a victim did everything in his power to get the wrongdoers to justice" (ibid.). Schlosser (1997) writes, "By the twelfth century the wite had grown so much larger than the wergild that the nobility took the murderer's entire payment, usurping the monetary claims of the victim's family. The ancient relationship between the murderer's clan and the victim's clan was erased" (p. 45), while the nobility's coffers swelled. European communities may not have abandoned restitution for murder on moral grounds, but due to pressure from ruling elites.

The transition to state retribution had ideal motivations of greater objectivity, impartiality, and consistency in sentencing. But with this shift came several costs. Eventually the crown (and nation-state) succeeded in defining itself as the victim. The crown's designates (state prosecutors) became the only authorized avengers. A painful penalty was imposed to discharge criminals' debt. In the name of justice, the state monopolized punitive power and institutionalized state killing. Legal retribution shifted attention away from the murderer's obligations to make amends and redress the surviving family's needs to the offender's blameworthiness. This transition blocked informal resolutions of a less punitive nature, forcing families into demanding capital punishment as an abstract measure of their "satisfaction." Retributive justice banished victims from the criminal justice system; a homicide victim's family was welcome only in so far as it could help the prosecution win its case. Victims, surviving families, and restitution thus were marginalized.

Although pushed aside, restitution did not entirely disappear. Restitution was advocated in the eighteenth century by utilitarian reformers such as Jeremy Bentham (1843). These reformers argued that restitution produced more good than harm. Utilitarians also believed that rehabilitation would be realized and recidivism reduced by forcing criminals to appreciate the harms they had caused. But restitution as a method of offender rehabilitation never gained ground. In order to be resurrected as a sentencing option for murder in the United States, advocates of restitution would need to deal with the power of the state's retributive practices, the public's support of the death penalty, and the moral objections to restitution for murder in Judaism and Christianity.

Restitution Embraced by Much of the American Public

Restitution languished in the United States for the first fifty years of the twentieth century. Victims of serious crimes received little attention from the justice system, leaving them to seek restitution outside the criminal process. Civil suits were so expensive and delayed payments so seriously that many victims' needs remained unmet. English penal reformer Fry (1951) resurrected the argument for the rehabilitative value of restitution. Meanwhile, abroad, interest in restorative justice prompted countries such as New Zealand and Great Britain to aid crime victims by sponsoring programs that included offender restitution.

Early academic proponents of restitution in the United States, such as Barnett (1977) and Holmgren (1983), argued that the principles underlying civil law should replace those of criminal law. They advocated a shift to what they call pure restitution. Restorative justice theorists favored pure restitution, which they viewed as requiring repair of both material and emotional harm. When coupled with mediation or conferencing, restitution served to restore dignity to victims and perpetrators, make concrete the offender's expressed desire to make amends, and rekindle a sense of civic trust (Strang 2002).

Others cautioned that restitution ought never to replace retributive punishment (Ellin 2000; Dagger 1991; Pilon 1978). For instance, Mackenzie (1981) argued that offenders must be forced to see their punishment as more than payment for their crimes. Using pure restitution, some criminals might be tempted to see financial payment as "fair wages" for their criminal activity. Ellin (2000) contended that restitution should leave offenders worse off than if they had not committed their crimes.

By the late 1970s, this country's criminal justice system turned away from rehabilitation and became decidedly retributive. Punitive restitution as part of retributive sentencing received significant support from burgeoning demands to recognize victims' rights. Schlosser (1997) observes, "Outrage at the mistreatment of rape victims soon led to a reappraisal of how the criminal-justice system treated all crime victims. A grassroots movement in behalf of victims' rights attracted support from unlikely allies: women's groups and law-and-order Republicans" (p. 46). In 1982, a Task Force on Victims of Crime appointed by President Ronald Reagan "called for mandatory restitution in all criminal cases, unless the presiding judge could offer compelling reasons to the contrary" (National Center for Victims of Crime 2002). In the 1990s, the Christian Coalition's *Contract with the American Family* called for the use of "federal funds to encourage states to require prisoners to study and work, and require restitution to victims subsequent to release" (Wilcox 1996:113). Today, eighteen of thirty-two state "crime victims' rights" constitutional amendments give victims the right to restitution, and efforts have been underway since 1996 to secure a National Victims' Rights Constitutional Amendment (2004). Every state now gives its courts authority to mandate restitution, and as of 2002, twenty-nine states required their courts to impose restitution or to provide a reason if not ordered (National Center for Victims of Crime 2002).

Within the victims' rights movement, restitution has been couched in retributive, if not vengeful, terms. Americans' commitment to due process has always sat uneasily alongside their allegiance to vigilante justice, which is a quintessential form of revenge. Vigilante justice persisted into the 1930s in the form of lynching and is reflected currently, legal scholar Zimring (2003) argues, in the conviction that executions bring closure to victims' families. By viewing the state as a deliverer of "therapeutic benefit," the "vigilante tradition," he says, "neutralizes one powerful argument against allowing the state to kill its enemies: the fear of unlimited government power" (p. 99). By portraying the state as caring for families and offering them the mythical blessing called "closure," advocates can hide their appetite for revenge.

Other scholars similarly view some victims' demands for restitution as motivated by revenge. Political scientist Sarat (2001) observes that the victims' rights movement seems to demand considerably more from restitution than compensation for loss. He suggests:

> It seeks participation and power by making the victim the symbolic heart of modern legality.... [B]ubbling just beneath the surface [is a] growing pressure for the return of revenge.... [It allows] victims to use legal processes to express their grief and rage as they ... seek to enlist the loyalty of judges and juries in a quest for revenge.... The demand for victims' rights and the insistence that we hear the voices of the victims are just the latest 'style' in which vengeance has disguised itself (pp. 35, 43).

Rather than skill at dueling, "verbal acumen would become the tool for exacting revenge" (p. 48). Zimring (2003) notes that the penalty phase of capital trials has been:

> remade into what sociologists call a 'status competition' between the offender ... and those who were directly or derivatively injured by the crime.... The symbolic transformation of the death penalty trial into a private competition ... [suggests that] the greater the suffering to

be inflicted on the offender, the better the victim's loved ones should feel (p. 55).

Appeals to victims' needs and the use of victim impact statements can emotionalize the courtroom, as these authors suggest. Sessar (1990) concludes that when restitution becomes imbued with punitive and vengeful agendas, it becomes part of a "rearmament of the criminal justice system that uses the victim's alleged needs and interests in tough law enforcement against the offender" (p. 43). For these reasons, Murder Victims' Families for Reconciliation (MVFR), a national organization devoted to abolition of the death penalty, is opposed to victim impact statements by the relatives of the deceased in a capital case (Cushing and Sheffer 2002). When restitution is tied to victim impact statements and other ways of fanning vengeful feelings in juries and judges, some MVFR members may prefer to forego restitution. Thus, the criminal justice system can use restitution to further its retributive goals without regard to the genuine needs of victims. Murder victims' family members within this retributive context remain far short of having their needs met.

In sum, restitution is an ancient form of justice that in the modern era has been framed within competing paradigms. Advocates of restorative justice embrace restitution because it avoids the state monopoly on justice seeking and can repair harm and heal broken relationships among perpetrators, victims, and their communities (Zehr 2001; Braithwaite and Pettit 1992). Utilitarians argue for restitution as a method of reforming criminals. Retributivists seek punitive restitution as an effective mechanism to make offenders pay for their crimes (Schafer 1965). Revenge-based models view restitution as a means of satisfying angry victims. Depending on the advocate, restitution can be an opportunity for offenders to make amends and redress harms, a carrot to encourage prisoner accountability, a bludgeon to make prisoners suffer, or a stick to express the vindictive feelings of survivors.

Given this conjoining of motivations and rationales, most crime victims favor restitution. Shapland (1986) found that victims view restitution as integral to the criminal sentence for both material and emotional restoration. Erez and Tontodonato (1992) found that restitution increased victim satisfaction with the criminal justice system. When Sessar (1990) segregated victims by type of victimization, he found that victims of violent crime favored the following sentencing proposals that involved restitution: "35.3% restitution; 6.1% restitution and labor; 13.1% restitution and punishment" (p. 42).[7]

---

7. Of the remaining respondents (all victims of violent crime), 41.4 percent favored punishment and/or labor and 4 percent favored discharge (Sessar 1990, p. 42).

Restitution's re-emergence in criminal punishment in the twentieth century is due to its ability to garner support through an unlikely coalition of proponents of restorative justice, rehabilitation, retribution, and vigilante values. Shapiro (1990) compares restitution to a "chameleon," since it can assume different colors depending on how it is used (p. 79).

But proponents have not attended to the tensions between these various aims of justice. As a federal report concluded in 1981:

> The current popularity of restitution rests largely on an intuitive sense of its rationality, rather than on a balanced research consideration of the conditions under which it might be an effective and appropriate way of dealing with certain criminal defendants *and* provide a meaningful benefit to the victim (Harland 1980:vii).

In light of restitution's rhetorical uses within incompatible projects of punishment, and how strongly Americans feel about victims' rights, it is not surprising that so many bystanders support restitution without asking what it means with regard to murder.

Surprisingly, the findings presented in this paper suggest that murder victims' families might constitute a group with views distinctive from victims of other forms of crime. Although the total sample size in the two studies analyzed in this paper is small, the respondents are remarkably consistent in their views. Their common ground suggests that murder victims' families might be a significant voice of dissent on the matter of restitution for murder.

Methodology

The results of two studies are the basis of the analysis in this paper; Friedman-Barone (2000) conducted the first study, and I did the second. In both studies, subjects were sought who: a) had lost a close family member to murder; b) were willing to consider legislative alternatives to the death penalty; and c) were available for in-person interviews or were willing to correspond in writing. Both Friedman-Barone and I contacted murder victims' family members we had met through our respective work against the death penalty; interviewees suggested additional names of people who might be willing to participate. Thirteen people were interviewed. Friedman-Barone's final study (2000) includes "comments by and references to family members" she worked with over the years, bringing the total number of subjects in both studies to twenty-five. All twenty-five persons were opposed to the death penalty.

It was not a requirement of participation that the killers had been sentenced to death. In one case, the murderer had not been captured or even identified. In the majority of cases, there had been an arrest and conviction, but a sentence of less than death. Such defendants were either juveniles charged with second-degree murder, recipients of a plea bargain, or individuals who had secured a lesser sentence due to compelling mitigating evidence. One defendant was found not guilty by reason of insanity. Several cases had been tried in states without the death penalty. In none of the cases had a death sentence been imposed.

Friedman-Barone restricted her interviews to those who had lost immediate family members to murder; her additional contacts included people who had lost extended family members (one aunt and one niece). My interviews included only one subject who had lost an extended family member to murder (one granddaughter); the others had lost immediate family members. Respondents hailed from four regions of the country and ranged in age from late-20s to 60s. The in-person interviews lasted from thirty minutes to four hours.

All interviews were conducted in a similar format. Each subject was informed that several states were considering the possibility of legislation that would replace the death penalty with a sentence of LWOP coupled with restitution to victims' families. Each subject was told that while a majority of Americans appeared willing to consider such an alternate sentence for murder, no one had asked murder victims' family members about the meaning of restitution in this context. Subjects were then asked about the meaning of restitution coupled with LWOP as a punishment for murder.

Murder Victims' Families' Reactions to Restitution

Life imprisonment without the possibility of parole is a harsh, retributive penalty. Restitution to the victim's family would not be a substitute punishment for murder, but one that supplements LWOP. Nevertheless, subjects reacted indifferently or negatively to the idea of restitution in this context, pointing out its inapplicability to murder. First, subjects rejected restitution as payment of a personal debt. Second, they resisted restitution as direct redress by the killer to the family. And third, they denied that restitution would bring either satisfaction or closure.

Restitution as Payment of a Personal Debt

The economy of revenge is a moral debt between offender and victim, whereas in retribution the debt lies between the offender and society. LWOP arguably satisfies the public debt, while restitution is directed toward satisfying the private one.[8] Proponents of restorative justice also argue that restitution redresses private harm. Subjects shared this same concept of restitution as repayment of a personal debt, but opposed it as being offensive with respect to murder. "More often than not, 'restitution' is seen as equivalent to 'blood money,' an attempt by the persons who took the lives of one's loved one to pay them for losses that cannot be replaced" (Friedman-Barone 2000:5). One person declared:

> There is nothing that that man can do that can ever repay me for what he took from me. And I don't want him to try. I don't want there to be any sense in anyone's mind that he can, in any way, come close to compensating anybody in my family for what he did (Friedman-Barone 2000:7).

One grandmother, whose thirteen-year-old granddaughter was raped and murdered, said she was "put off by [groups] lobbying for restitution.... Although some may want it," she did not want to give the impression that her "primary interest rests on income." She insisted that "No restitution is possible for the ongoing physical and emotional ramifications of my family's loss." Throughout the interview she lamented that what she wanted could not be captured by any existing terms. She desired neither revenge nor retribution. The subjects' wariness if not downright opposition to "restitution for private harm" included the strong belief that no amount of money would be enough to compensate for a death. "Family members refer to it as 'blood money,' 'cheap grace,' 'insulting,' 'extraordinarily distasteful,' an attempt to '[monetize] the value of a human life' and to imply that, somehow, family members can 'benefit' from the death of their loved ones" (Friedman-Barone 2000:8). Subjects found it degrading to have life reduced to a dollar amount, since they

---

8. Although none of the interviewees thought of LWOP as a form of restitution, Holmgren (1983) makes an interesting argument that life imprisonment could be seen as restitution. Society experiences "secondary harm" from violent crime since communities are forced to take steps to protect themselves. She suggests that legal punishment can be a form of restitution to society for this secondary harm, if such punishment actually reduces the need of people to protect themselves and restores them to their "baseline position" of safety and security (p. 40).

loved their deceased family members for their inherent worth, not as exchange items in the marketplace.

Even proponents of restitution acknowledge that its meaning with respect to homicide is not self-evident (Wolfgang 1965). Ellin (2000), for example, argues that "under tort theory compensation erases the effects of the crime, restoring the victim to his or her previous condition, as if the crime had not occurred. Technically a victim should be indifferent between a crime never occurring, and obtaining restitution after a crime has occurred" (p. 301). These assumptions clearly do not apply to homicide.

Restitution as an extension of tort law shares with criminal law the notion that an action in the present can mitigate or even right a wrong. Murder, perhaps more than any other crime, creates a sharp and clear line between past and present. The murder is committed and nothing can undo it, fix it, or make it right. The past is determined. The future has the potential to be bright and beautiful, an empty page waiting to be filled. But the future will never include the deceased, so every new page brings its share of loss and rage.

In rejecting the notion of restitution as personal debt repayment, one subject, whose mother was murdered when he was seven, said, " 'Restitution' is a dirty word. It's an insult to compare it to an economic problem. We need a spiritual term. We don't need a concept that recommends a pay-off. We do need something that recognizes our pain."

Not only did the subjects find the concept of payment repugnant, but many reacted sharply against the idea of receiving something directly from the murderer.

Restitution As Redress by the Killer to the Victim's Family

The subjects interviewed by Friedman-Barone and in the second study recoiled at the prospect of a direct "payee" relationship.

> One family member describes her stomach as 'flip-flopping' when she thinks about taking money from the person who murdered her sister, as an arrangement of this kind would, for her, imply a lifelong relationship with that person when she credits her healing with her ability to sever her connection to him. Others echo her response by saying it forces the victims to be linked to a person to whom they have no desire or need to be linked, or implies an expectation that they take something from somebody from whom they claim to want nothing (Friedman-Barone 2000:7–8).

When the murderer is a nonfamily member, the evil deed creates an unwanted relationship with a stranger who caused enormous pain.

In contrast, many victims of violent crime support the idea of offenders being required to make restitution directly to them (National Center for Victims of Crime 2002). Crime victims generally show a strong preference to be paid directly by the offender (Shapland 1984); about 70 percent of respondents in Umbreit et al.'s (1994) study felt that receiving restitution from the offender was a gesture indicating that the offender had accepted responsibility for the harms committed. A director of a state compensation fund reported that many victims—and some homicide family members—continued to call the office years after the crime to make sure that the offender was still paying. The director explained that the callers want to know that the convict was being reminded forcibly every month of what he or she had done (Personal Communication 2002).

However, in the subjects' eyes, restitution was not only offensive, but also inapplicable to murder. Subjects rightly argued that the murder victim would neither receive nor benefit from the offender's payment—a reality that violates a base premise of restitution.[9] Although they felt victimized by the crime, they did not believe that the definition of restitution could or should be stretched to mean direct payment to the deceased's family.[10]

---

9. Ellin (2000) cites philosopher Jan Narveson's attempts to meet this objection: Does [dead victim] A have any values for which he would be willing to live a shorter life, if necessary? Interestingly enough, the answer in virtually all cases is in the affirmative. A might have been willing to sacrifice his life in the interests of achieving political freedom for some group, say. If so, then if there is some way of effectively harnessing [A's killer] B to that particular cart, A might have regarded this shortening of his life as adequately compensated (p. 308).

Narveson assumes that most people are willing to die for their ideals—that is, they are saint-like—and that if the murderer adopts his victim's ideals and carries on the victim's cause, then the victim might be compensated posthumously. Narveson is naive on three grounds. First, although people might theoretically be willing to die for their ideals, they are rarely put to the test in daily life. Second, being willing to die for one's principles is not the same as being murdered. Third, many murderers are not capable of dedication to such ideals, and even if they did subscribe to a particular cause, they would be prohibited from acting for it by prison. Murder victims' families would almost certainly find this proposition far-fetched.

10. Two subjects had experienced intrafamilial murder, e.g., a husband killed his wife. Restitution may become more complicated when the victim is a relative of the murderer. For example, in Washington State most people on death row do not have any source of funds except from their families. Thus, if the son were to mail twenty dollars to his father on death row, to help him buy personal care products, 25 percent would be taken by the state and returned to the son as restitution. Essentially the son would be providing the funds for his own restitution. When perpetrators are financially dependent on their own

Speaking against restitution as repayment and as direct redress, the subjects also repudiated the frequent rationale that restitution brings closure.

Restitution as Satisfaction or Closure

The criminal justice system often justifies stiff punishments with the promise of making victims feel better (Kaminer 1995). As a result of increasingly frequent rhetoric since the 1980s about victims' need for closure, Zimring (2003) cites a study in which 60 percent of those Americans surveyed in 2003 "agreed either strongly or somewhat" that capital punishment brought closure to homicide families (p. 61). But "for survivors, *healing*, like *closure*, is a word abhorred, implying as it does 'getting over it'" (Kay 2005:150). At a recent conference on the impact of the death penalty on murder victims' families,[11] one survivor in the audience said that the word "closure" should be included in a book on things never to utter in survivors' presence.

For all those interviewed, there was a visceral, angry reaction to the concept of restitution as providing satisfaction or closure. The very idea of closure was considered wholly misplaced. According to one respondent, "Restitution would mean giving the life of my loved one back. That is impossible" (Friedman-Barone 2000:7). The woman who lost her granddaughter said, "There is no redress, the murderer could not make amends, there is no way he or anyone could ever make things right."

One man who lost his father said he "understands the motivations" of those who seek legislative alternatives to the death penalty. "But," he said, "as restitution implies the ability to 'be made whole,' it is, for him, a baseless expectation." An interviewee who lost his son similarly maintained: "'Conviction might bring closure to the law enforcement and judicial communities who bring and hear the cases. But where the family is concerned, that kind of psychological and emotional resolution is only a mirage'" (Friedman-Barone 2000:7–8).

Hershenov (1999) suggests that restitution received from criminals provides victims a "judicial vindictiveness" that comes from getting even. Revenge and restitution go hand in hand, he says, since they satisfy the need to be "psy-

---

families, survivors thus may pay for their own restitution, which is not a benefit. Of course, perpetrators who have extrafamilial sources of income would be able to pay restitution without using their families' money.

11. Audience member at "The Impact of the Death Penalty on Murder Victims' Families," sponsored by Skidmore College, University at Albany School of Criminal Justice, and Justice Solutions; Skidmore College, Saratoga Springs, NY; 11–13 September 2003.

chologically compensated" or "emotionally replenished" (pp. 90, 88). An interviewee explained that she often encountered such views:

> It's almost like … restitution.… [If] the sentence is okay, and you get enough restitution, your mom gets to come back.… And people … get so caught up in, 'Oh yeah, then I'll feel better.' [But] only you can make yourself feel better by what you do, and the actions you take (Friedman-Barone 2000:19).

Only one subject, while opposing the death penalty, exhibited feelings of pleasure about the degradation the offender would experience in prison.[12]

In sum, restitution construed within vengeance or restorative justice seems inadequate to capture what these murder victims' families demand by way of justice. They perceived the idea of payback as blood money, rejected the notion that the murderer should or could redress the family directly, and found false the idea that restitution could satisfy or bring closure. So what do they want?

Murder victims' families' constructive observations, in both studies, abandoned restitution in favor of a needs-based compensation system that fostered prisoner responsibility.

Murder Victims' Families Prefer to Focus on Needs

Repayment of a Social Debt

Subjects expressed the belief that offenders should pay back society. Families of homicide victims know better than others, perhaps, the importance of the interpersonal connectedness that sustains life. Some took a strongly communitarian position, suggesting that society is harmed directly by murder. Others used a weaker notion, namely that murder produces secondary harm for society, which creates a debt. If murderers paid into a fund as a form of reparation to the community rather than to the victim, then subjects found morally acceptable the prospect of accepting money. One said:

---

12. Interviewees' views are both similar to and different from Blecker (2003), who calls support of LWOP and restitution "retrograde and wrong" (p. 181). He argues that the feeling that "the victim's blood morally pollutes us" until the killer is punished as deserved arises from a "deep-seeded retributive urge" (p. 189). The interviewees did not express any blood lust even while rejecting the idea of a blood price.

But the notion that he has also committed a horrible crime against society and that he can, therefore, in some way, help to repay society for what he did, I do believe in. To me, that's what the difference is. That's the difference between money going into a pool that helps some poor kid in the inner city go to college or to me.... The notion that people who harm society try to pay it back by doing something productive for it, I think is a wonderful idea (Friedman-Barone 2000:12).

The U.S. criminal justice system often has combined these two strands—reparation to victims and reparation to the community—"in one project" (Wright 1991:32). Subjects, however, made a distinction between payment of an incalculable personal debt and payment of a social debt.

Social Debt Paid through Prisoner Labor

Retribution aims to ensure that the perpetrator is not left better off than the one directly harmed by the crime. Within a retributive system, the only just outcome appears to be lose-lose, making the offender's loss comparable to the victim's. Restitution for noncapital crimes couched within a framework of victims' rights uses this retributive premise by seeking to secure a win for the victim at the expense of the offender. It is a zero-sum game in which "any right or benefit given to offenders will be at the expense of the rights or interests of victims" (Strang 2002:155–56). Kaminer (1995) observes that some victims resentfully feel that "every show of compassion for offenders (and their families), every effort to humanize prison life, is an insult to the victims of crime and their families" (p. 71). In order to satisfy this retributive aim with respect to murder, the only acceptable punishment would be death. The topic of the two studies in this paper, the acceptability of an alternative to the death penalty, fails to satisfy this retributive aim.

All of the interviewees opposed the death penalty and therefore did not regard justice as a zero-sum game, life for a life. But they still struggled with the retributive impulse to see the perpetrator suffer some loss. However, since LWOP meant that the murderer would live, they instead compared the losses the perpetrator would suffer in prison to those faced by the surviving relatives.[13] Many interviewees felt that the criminal justice system had so disrespected their rights and needs that they had "lost" while the offender "won."

---

13. Some subjects opposed LWOP as harshly retributive without any "positive return"; others were relieved that the killer would never be free.

They believed that while prisoners have it on "easy street," survivors struggle with the challenges of living with their trauma in a society that naively presumes that murder is "gotten over" in about six months. The families decried that their taxes supported murderers while they have to "fend for themselves." Friedman-Barone (2000) observed:

> Even the family member who claims to not care whether the prisoner is 'watching soap operas all day, writing poetry, painting, running, doing computer science, making number plates or breaking rocks,' because he does not care about offenders, expresses great consternation about benefits that accrue to prisoners but not to those who committed no crimes (p. 9).

Although the interviewees erred in depicting the conditions in prison as easy, their concern reveals a strong aversion to freeloaders. Murderers ought to be made to work at "meaningful labor" that could "benefit society." Locking prisoners in concrete cells and feeding them at taxpayers' (including homicide families') expense violated interviewees' belief in merit-based justice. In the United States, personal merit (how hard one has worked, the value of one's contribution) is related to an individual's worthiness to have his or her needs met. Within capitalism, people are valued for their ability to produce goods through their labor. People who do not work deserve their sorry state. One man insisted:

> Life should be the same as for those on the outside.... The prisoner should get up every morning, go to work and receive fair compensation for that work. But if you did not perform, you would not get compensated. And if you don't get compensated, that reflects the quality of life you have in there (Friedman-Barone 2000:11).

LWOP with labor was thus felt to address the concern that the perpetrator at least should not be better off than the survivors, even if the perpetrator is not reduced to the same state as the murder victim.

For other subjects, prisoner labor was justified on different grounds. Underlying this desire to see prisoners work was a broader concern about one of the core values that criminal justice is supposed to protect and embody—responsibility. Prison life enforces irresponsibility. One subject said:

> The way the system is right now, everything is taken away from you, even your responsibility to yourself. Well, I think that's wrong.... You ... still must be responsible for providing for yourself.... So the system needs to give you the opportunity to do that (Friedman-Barone 2000:10).

These subjects desired prisoner responsibility, perhaps stemming from a needs-based concept of justice. That is, violent perpetrators have a basic human need to take responsibility for their past actions and future livelihoods. Surviving relatives also have a human need for perpetrators to take responsibility for the harms they caused, which includes acknowledging the humanity of the victim. Justice means honoring the shared need of both survivors and murderers to have perpetrators assume responsibility for their lives. The interviewees were willing to consider alternatives to the death penalty from a commitment to affirm the killer's need to become a responsible human. Unlike Kant, they did not believe that respecting the offender's human dignity necessitated the death penalty, but rather that perpetrators do something constructive with their lives.

For other subjects, prisoners repaid society best if they "influenced the world positively" by becoming a model of service, work, and integrity. Honoring the victim meant the perpetrator should "become the best person he can be." For instance, murderers could help make amends through "self-rehabilitation" and service, rather than through financial restitution (Wright 1991:35).

Thus, for a variety of reasons—but not restitution per se—having offenders pay a social debt through responsible work begins to capture these subjects' sense of justice.

Needs-Based Compensation

Every state now provides compensation to families of homicide victims. States vary in how much support is available, how the funds can be used, and how difficult compensation is to acquire. No state provides the aid that most families need. One mother recounted that she and the other primary caregiver of her murdered daughter were each allotted $50,000 for counseling. "We went through that like water," she said. Friedman Barone (2000) found "unanimity in support of a compensation system that would help out those in need, and ensure that family members who have lost the 'breadwinner' to murder do not have to go on welfare" (p. 13). Most subjects felt that family need was the best basis on which to distribute scarce compensatory funds, although practical and theoretical objections have been made to evaluating survivors' financial hardship (Galaway and Rutman 1975:426). Wolfgang (1965) points out that such compensation in cases of murder should be considered only as a "gesture of assistance," since "the victim cannot be compensated, and no state can really compensate a victim's family by trying to transfer compensation from the victim to others" (p. 240). State compensation funds have nothing to do with restitution, but instead are justified on the rationale that the state has a duty to assist citizens it failed to protect (Wolfgang 1965) or as a form of social welfare (Schultz 1965).

Most subjects linked prisoner labor with contributions to a general survivor compensation fund. One said that having "'a prisoner work in order to generate some fund or resources that would help to subsidize or to support the family who has been victimized ... [is] a step in the right direction'" (Friedman-Barone 2000:11). Even though they wanted proceeds from prisoners' labor to benefit victims' families, they did not view this as restitution. They wanted earnings to go into a general fund so that a single offender's contribution would not be paired to the family he or she had harmed. This difference avoided the taint of taking "blood money" in a direct payee relationship. In addition, subjects realized that prison labor would never generate enough money to meet families' needs; the fund would therefore need subsidy from the government. Rather than viewing payments by offenders into a general fund as direct restitution, they framed the prisoners' contributions as a debt to society or as promoting rehabilitation.

The subjects did not appeal to victims' rights, which has been the main language used in the United States to draw attention to victims' needs. In Europe the victims' movement has not focused on rights within a retributive framework but rather on advocacy and support. Its objectives are "primarily to alleviate suffering, and only secondarily to lobby for better treatment and more legal rights" (Strang 2002:32). Community groups that are unconnected to criminal justice proceedings, rather than offenders or the government, provide victims with charitable support. However, the interviewees do not fall neatly into the European support and advocacy model. They expressed a desire to get their needs met by the state through funds supplemented by offenders' labor—not through charity. This difference could reflect the relatively atomistic nature of U.S. society, where there is more reliance on legal remedies than on citizen mutual assistance.

Among the major concerns raised by interviewees were families' needs over a long period. Many discussed the continuing effects of the tragedy. One woman recounted: "'My father had a heart attack a year to the day of the murder.... I entered therapy, my marriage dissolved, my brother ... developed into a full-blown alcoholic, [and] I dropped out of school for two years'" (Friedman-Barone 2000:14). Family members also recognized the special needs of child survivors, who live with the trauma the longest and often receive the least attention. In the absence of healing, children may opt for suicide, drugs, or silence, as evidenced by the desperate paths taken by one subject's siblings. Another interviewee proposed a summer camp where "children who have lost family members to violence can share the special circumstances of their grief" (ibid.). A question raised but not answered was the duration of the period for assessing and compensating families' needs, such as whether college tuition should be paid for small children whose parent was murdered. It is difficult to quantify long-term needs, yet these homicide survivors "are insistent that governments, with or without restitution by the perpetrator, provide more financial and institutional help, with fewer bureaucratic impediments, to families than is made available today" (ibid.).

Meeting Needs Includes Prevention

When subjects brought up prevention of violence, they departed from both rights-based and support-advocacy frameworks, as well as from restitution or compensatory programs. Survivors endure ongoing repercussions from violence. Not surprisingly, subjects expressed an urgent desire to prevent other families from experiencing the trauma of murder. The following quotes reveal the depth of this concern:

- What we don't have as a society ... are processes that direct our impulses in ways that deter violence in our society.
- We need to help people who are in trouble as soon as we see the signs of trouble, so we don't allow them to degenerate to the point where they end up killing someone.
- A state unwilling to put money into programs that will make its citizens less violent is less concerned with the plight of the victims than it claims.
- A society unwilling to rescue children living in poverty, end racism and dedicate itself to healing the rifts that bring one person to murder another endorses a criminal justice system [that] will bring neither justice nor peace.
- Politicians [who focus] on punishment to the exclusion of transformation ensure that others will end up experiencing the same tragedies and unspeakable pain experienced by those who have already lost loved ones to murder (Friedman-Barone 2000:16–17).

Preventing violence takes the concept of "need" to a level beyond that envisioned by state compensation systems.

In sum, subjects found inapplicable vengeful, retributive, or restorative[14] frameworks of restitution. Their moral justification for receiving funds *indi-*

---

14. The interviewees were cautious about the concept of restorative justice. "Not one person interviewed [was] willing to engage in [it] without a heartfelt admission of guilt and apology from the person responsible for the murder of the loved one." For example, statements to this effect included: "In order for me to begin to even explore [those] concepts, I need to see some movement on the other side;" and, " I can't say what it would mean to me if [the murderer] apologized to me, but I can tell you that I wouldn't travel

rectly from offenders is not grounded in payback, a desire to punish the offender further, personal redress for direct harm, or an assertion of victims' rights. Rather, it is grounded in the desire to meet needs. For a variety of reasons subjects believed that murderers had a social debt that should be paid partially through their own labor. Offenders' contributions would go into a general state compensation fund designated for surviving families, including support for significant violence prevention programs.

For these reasons, in proposed legislation offered as an alternative to the death penalty, the word "restitution" should be avoided. "General fund for relief and prevention" would be an improvement (cf. Friedman-Barone 2000:22). One subject believed that homicide survivors should serve on the board that administers such a fund.

Proponents of legislation to replace death penalty statutes with LWOP and restitution to victims' families face a dilemma. The public and its civil servants will most likely respond positively to the idea of including restitution in such legislation, because Americans' support for restitution is generic, that is, they have not stopped to think about its inapplicability to murder. However, proponents of legislative alternatives to the death penalty will very likely fail to garner the support of victims' families if the word "restitution" is used (cf. Friedman-Barone 2000:6). And without the backing of victims' families, such legislation is likely to fail. If proponents of such legislation wish to secure surviving relatives' endorsement, they would be wise to drop the word "restitution," at least until they have studied more families of murder victims.

Enduring Moral Concerns

When interviewees called restitution "blood money," they drew on ancient language and moral sentiments. In the United States, the Bible continues to provide texts and traditions that inform American moral sensibilities.

The ancient Biblical opposition to restitution for murder was based on human equality grounded in the shared image of God, a belief that a harm to one injured the whole, and principles of justice that condemned convictions and punishments imposed unevenly on the rich and poor. These moral concerns have not abated. Restitution for a human life continues to smack of disregard for the inherent worth of the individual. This country's pursuit of retributive justice without regard to economic justice means that prisoners receive benefits

---

five minutes to hear it.… [But] maybe if it happened it would change my mind about it completely" (Friedman-Barone 2000:16).

from the state that may exceed those available to honest citizens. Homicides, convictions, and maximum sentences continue to fall heavily on the vulnerable. Restitution ignores the poverty that too often is a source of lethal crime, the classism and racism that frequently result in stiffer sentences for those who kill people of higher social worth, and the economic burden that restitution places on the offender's family. The use of economic metaphors obscures the importance to murder victims' families of tending to broken hearts and mending severed relationships within families and with the community that failed to protect them. Bystanders, eager to feel that they have met the needs of survivors, have not listened carefully to them, and as a consequence may voice support for restitution. Without recognizing the many different paradigms in which restitution can be framed, bystanders do not understand why restitution is inapplicable to murder and offensive to at least some survivors. Within such a context, murder victims' families risk being ignored or injured by legislation that has been ill-conceived and poorly designed to meet their needs.

References

Audience member. "The Impact of the Death Penalty on Murder Victims' Families." Sponsored by Skidmore College, University at Albany School of Criminal Justice, and Justice Solutions. Skidmore College, Saratoga Springs, NY. 11–13 September 2003.

Barnett, Randy E. 1977. "Restitution: A New paradigm of Criminal Justice." *Ethics* 87:279–301.

Bentham, Jeremy. 1843. "Political Remedies for the Evil of Offenses." Vol. 11 of *The Works of Jeremy Bentham*, edited by his executor John Bowring. London: Simpkin, Marshall.

Blecker, Robert. 2003. "Roots." Pp. (169–231) in *America's Experiment with Capital Punishment: Reflections on the Past, Present, and Future of the Ultimate Penal Sanction*, 2d ed., edited by James R. Acker, Robert M. Bohm, and Charles S. Lanier. Durham, NC: Carolina Academic Press.

Blumenthal, Laura. 2002. *Revenge: A Story of Hope.* New York: Washington Square Press.

Bowers, William. 1993. "Capital Punishment and Contemporary Values: People's Misgivings and the Court's Misperceptions." *Law & Society Review* 27:157–75.

Braithwaite, John and Philip Pettit. 1992. *Not Just Deserts: A Republican Theory of Criminal Justice.* Oxford, England: Clarendon Press.

Cushing, Renny and Susannah Sheffer. 2002. *Dignity Denied: The Experience of Murder Victims' Family Members Who Oppose the Death Penalty.* Cambridge, MA: Murder Victims' Families for Reconciliation.

Dagger, Richard. 1991. "Restitution: Pure or Punitive?" *Criminal Justice Ethics*: 18:29–39.

Davies, W. W. (ed.). 1905. *The Code of Hammurabi and Moses.* Cincinnati: Jennings and Graham.

Dieter, Richard C. 1993. "Sentencing for Life: Americans Embrace Alternatives to the Death Penalty." Death Penalty Information Center. http://www.deathpenalty-info.org/article.php?scid=45&did=481 (17 December 2003).

Doble Research Associates. May 2004. "Death Penalty in North Carolina: The Public Considers the Options." Englewood Cliffs, NJ: Doble Research Associates.

Ellin, Joseph. 2000. "Restitutionism Defended." *The Journal of Value Inquiry* 34:299–317.

Erez, Edna and Pamela Tontodonato. 1992. "The Effects of Victim Participation in Sentencing on Sentencing Outcome." *Criminology* 28:451–74.

Falk, Ze'ev. 1964. *Hebrew Law in Biblical Times*. Jerusalem: Wahrmann Books.

Friedman-Barone, Ronnie. 2000. Unpublished paper, "Responses of Members of Murder Victims' Families to the Concept of Restitution: Implications & Suggestions for Legislation in Lieu of Capital Punishment." Cambridge, MA: Urban Ministry Fellowship Program, Harvard Divinity School.

Fry, Margery. 1951. *Arms of the Law*. London: Victor Gollancz.

Galaway, Burt and Leonard Rutman. 1975. "Victim Compensation: An Analysis of Substantive Issues." Pp. 421–36 in *Considering the Victim: Readings in Restitution and Victim Compensation,* edited by Joe Hudson and Burt Galaway. Springfield, IL: Charles C. Thomas.

Hanks, Gardner C. 2002. *Capital Punishment and the Bible*. Scottdale, PA: Herald Press.

Harland, Alan T. 1980. *Restitution to Victims of Personal and Household Crimes: Analytic Report VAD-9*. Washington, DC: Criminal Justice Research Center.

Hershenov, David B. 1999. "Restitution and Revenge." *The Journal of Philosophy* 96:79–94.

Holmgren, Margaret. 1983. "Punishment as Restitution: The Rights of the Community," *Criminal Justice Ethics* 2:36–49.

Jackson, Bernard S. 1973. "Reflections on Biblical Criminal Law." *Journal of Jewish Studies* 24:8–38.

Jacob, Bruce R. 1970. "Reparation or Restitution by the Criminal Offender to His Victim: Applicability of an Ancient Concept in the Modern Correctional Process." *The Journal of Criminal Law, Criminology and Police Science* 61:152–167.

Jacoby, Susan. 1983. *Wild Justice: The Evolution of Revenge*. New York: Harper and Row.

Kaminer, Wendy. 1995. *It's All the Rage: Crime and Culture*. New York: Addison-Wesley.

Kay, Judith W. 2005. *Murdering Myths: The Story Behind the Death Penalty*. Lantham, MD: Rowman and Littlefield.

Laster, Richard E. 1970. "Criminal Restitution: A Survey of its Past History and an Analysis of its Present Usefulness." *University of Richmond Law Review* 5:71–98.

Mackenzie, Margaret. 1981. *Plato on Punishment*. Berkeley: University of California Press.

National Center for Victims of Crime. 2002. "The Right to Restitution from Offenders." Section 11, *Victims' Rights Sourcebook*, 1. www.ncvc.org/law/sbook/ch11.html (12 April 2002).

National Victims' Constitutional Amendment Passage. 2004. "Victims' Rights Amendment (VRA) text." www.nvcap.org (6 July 2004).

Personal Communication. Director of a state compensation fund for victims of crime. 17 April 2002.

Pilon, Roger. 1978. "Criminal Remedies: Restitution, Punishment, or Both? *Ethics* 88:348–57.

Sarat, Austin. 2001. *When the State Kills: Capital Punishment and the American Condition*. Princeton, NJ: Princeton University Press.

Schafer, Stephen. 1965. "Restitution to Victims of Crime—An Old Correctional Aim Modernized." *Minnesota Law Review* 50:243–54.

————. 1960. *Restitution to Victims of Crime.* Chicago: Quadrangle Books.

Schlosser, Eric. 1997. "A Grief Like No Other." *The Atlantic Monthly* 280:37–76.

Schultz, LeRoy G. 1965. "The Violated: A Proposal to Compensate Victims of Violent Crime." *Saint Louis University Law Journal* 10:238–50.

Sessar, Klaus. 1990. "Tertiary Victimization: A Case of the Politically Abused Crime Victim." Pp. 37–45 in *Criminal Justice, Restitution and Reconciliation,* edited by Burt Galaway and Joe Hudson. Monsey, NY: Criminal Justice Press.

Shapiro, Carol. 1990. Pp. 73–80 in *Considering the Victim: Readings in Restitution and Victim Compensation,* edited by Joe Hudson and Burt Galaway. Monsey, NY: Criminal Justice Press.

Shapland, J. 1986. "Victim Assistance and the Criminal Justice System." Pp. 218–33 in *From Crime Policy to Victim Policy: Reorienting the Justice System,* edited by Ezzat A. Fattah. New York: St. Martin's Press.

————. 1984. "Victims, the Criminal Justice System and Compensation." *British Journal of Criminology* 24:131–49.

Strang, Heather. 2002. *Repair or Revenge: Victims and Restorative Justice.* Oxford, England: Clarendon Press.

Umbreit, Mark S., Robert B. Coates, and Boris Kalanj. 1994. *Victim Meets Offender: The Impact of Restorative Justice and Mediation.* Monsey, NY: Criminal Justice Press.

Wilcox, Clyde. 1996. *Onward Christian Soldiers? The Religious Right in American Politics.* Boulder, CO: Westview Press.

Wolfgang, Marvin E. 1965. "Victim Compensation in Crimes of Personal Violence." *Minnesota Law Review* 50:223–41.

Wright, Marvin. 1991. *Justice for Victims and Offenders: A Restorative Response to Crime.* Philadelphia: Open University Press.

Zehr, Howard. 2001. *Transcending: Reflections of Crime Victims.* Intercourse, PA: Good Books.

Zimring, Franklin E. 2003. *The Contradictions of Capital Punishment.* Oxford, England: Oxford University Press.

CHAPTER 18

FACILITATED DIALOGUE ON DEATH ROW: FAMILY MEMBERS OF MURDER VICTIMS AND INMATES SHARE THEIR EXPERIENCES

Mark S. Umbreit, Betty Vos,
Robert B. Coates and Katherine A. Brown

Introduction

The practice of victim offender mediation or dialogue is but one of many emerging developments in what is called "restorative justice." Conceptually, the restorative justice paradigm begins with the notion that crime is an act against people and a violation of relationships as well as a breaking of the law. Zehr (2002) offers a fuller definition of restorative justice: "Restorative justice is a process to involve, to the extent possible, those who have a stake in a specific offense and to collectively identify and address harms, needs, and obligations, in order to heal and put things as right as possible" (p. 37).

The Western criminal justice system is focused chiefly on the questions of what laws have been broken, who broke them, and what punishment they deserve. Restorative justice views this focus as not sufficient to address the very real harms, needs, and obligations of persons directly involved in any particular crime. Instead, it attempts to focus on repairing the harm caused to victims through holding offenders directly accountable for their behavior. Offender accountability includes both an understanding of the harm caused by the crime, and an effort to repair the harm to the extent possible. It is hoped that through such processes both the victim and the offender will gain an increased sense of closure.

Victim Offender Mediation/Dialogue

The practice of bringing offenders and the persons they have harmed together in facilitated dialogue was begun by a pair of creative probation officials working with juveniles in Kitchener, Ontario, in 1974 (Peachey 1989). Initially called victim offender reconciliation programs because of the largely Mennonite underpinnings of the pioneering programs, the practice quickly expanded across both Canada and the United States. Other names that have come to be used for the process include victim offender mediation, victim offender dialogue, and victim offender conferencing. The process is now widely practiced, with many variations, in over 300 programs in the United States, and over 1,100 additional programs throughout North America, Europe, and the South Pacific, as well as initiatives in Japan, South Africa, and South America (Umbreit, Greenwood, Umbreit, and Fercello 2003). The great majority of these programs focus chiefly on property crimes and minor assault (both misdemeanor and felony level), and often with an emphasis on juvenile offenders.

In the three decades since the practice of victim offender mediation/dialogue was begun, there have been over sixty empirical studies of its process and outcomes in five different countries. The research on VOM/D programs demonstrates that both victims and offenders are typically satisfied with the process, believe it is fair, are satisfied with the outcome, and would recommend it to others in similar situations (Umbreit et al. 2002). Among those studies that have examined more quantitative outcomes, there is evidence that offenders who have participated in dialogue are more likely to complete restitution agreements and have a lower recidivism rate than offenders who have not. When participating offenders do recidivate, they do so less frequently and tend to commit less serious offenses than their counterparts who have not participated (Nugent et al. 1999; Latimer et al. 2001).

The Texas Victim Offender Mediation/Dialogue Program

The use of victim offender dialogue in serious and violent crime arose from a very different starting point. Rather than developing out of a focus on offender rehabilitation, it has been entirely initiated by victims. Some violent crime victims had heard of the mediation/dialogue process in other contexts and sought to receive the service themselves. Others had never heard of any such program but simply felt a burning desire to have a human encounter with the person who had harmed them or their loved one.

In 1993, largely due to the efforts of Texans who had been victimized by violent crime, Texas became the first U.S. state to establish a state-supported mediated dialogue service for victims of serious and violent crime who wished to meet with the offender who had harmed them or their loved ones. The Texas VOM/D Program, which conducted its first violent crime victim offender dialogue in 1995, is a component of the Victim Services Division of the Texas Department of Criminal Justice.

Through the use of both paid staff and community volunteers who have received extensive training in facilitating dialogue in cases of severe and violent crimes, the VOM/D program responds to victims who have requested to meet with their offenders, reaches out to invite offenders to participate, and provides several months of careful and thorough preparation for both victims and offenders before bringing them together for facilitated dialogue. The meetings are typically held in the correctional facility where the offender is housed, and they usually last for several hours. If participants consent, whenever possible the meetings are videotaped. After the meetings there is considerable follow-up with both victim and offender, including review of the videotaped dialogue meeting as well as periodic check-ins.

The VOM/D service is entirely victim-initiated. Offenders who express interest in meeting victims who have not requested a meeting are invited to write a letter to be placed on file in case there is future contact from a victim. This is done to protect persons who have already been victimized by the crime from potential re-victimization through experiencing pressure to meet offenders or through perceiving that they are expected to help the offenders in any way. Additionally, it is important to point out that offenders receive no justice system benefit from their participation. Meeting with victims in no way has any impact on parole decisions, sentence length, or within-prison status for offenders. The proceedings of the preparation meetings as well as of the actual dialogue meetings are confidential and cannot be used in court.

Overview of the Research Study

While the early programs that pioneered in offering the service to these victims rested on the sound research base undergirding victim offender dialogue in general, very little was known about how the process might work or what its impact might be in this specialized application. Largely for these reasons, in 1997 the Center for Restorative Justice and Peacemaking undertook the largest study to date of victim offender dialogue in serious and violent crime.

Working with Texas and Ohio, the first two states to offer such services at a statewide level, the study invited all of the early participants in each state to participate in research interviews and through this process developed a total sample of forty victims and thirty-nine offenders, roughly half from each state.

Our study did not set out to examine death-row issues, but it happened that four of the victim participants in the early years of the Texas VOM/D Program were relatives of family members whose killers had been convicted of capital murder. The program had only been in operation for two years when it was approached in the fall of 1997 by the mother of a murder victim who sought to meet with her daughter's death-row killer before his execution. No such meeting had ever previously been attempted with a death-row inmate, and though no one knew whether it could be arranged, the program staff advocated for the victim's needs and received a green light to proceed, just five months before the scheduled execution. This first death-row mediation was followed by requests from three additional family members of capital murder victims during the data-gathering period of our study. Thus, our final Texas research interview sample of twenty victims/family members and nineteen convicted offenders included four family members who met with three death-row offenders. All three offenders were executed by the state of Texas not long after their mediation/dialogue sessions and their research interviews.

There is inherent controversy in the choice to offer mediated dialogue in capital cases, and not all states that authorize the death penalty have elected to do so. Of all the consequences an offender may incur for criminal behavior, capital punishment is clearly the most extreme. Some would argue that "restorative justice" programs have no place in such a context because the only truly restorative response would be to eliminate the death penalty. Radelet and Borg (2000), responding to an earlier report on two of the present cases, pointed out that there is no potential for offender rehabilitation in such a context, and that the enormity of retributive execution cancels out any potentially restorative benefit. Umbreit (2000) offered the following rejoinder:

> I agree with Radelet and Borg that capital punishment is abhorrent, and it is also contradictory to my understanding of the principles of restorative justice. However, to advocate the ban of victim-offender mediation and dialogue in cases with inmates on death row who are awaiting execution is to strip those most directly affected by the horror of the crime of the opportunity to find some degree of meaning, healing, and closure: a fundamental pillar of restorative justice (p. 94).

The Texas VOM/D Program chose to act upon the requests of the four crime victims and obtained permission from the Texas Department of Criminal Justice for the dialogues to take place. The following analysis of what these seven participants had to say about their experiences is offered, in part, so that readers can reach their own conclusions about the impact of these meetings and the advisability of offering such a service in capital cases.

In the case summaries and discussion presented here, identifying information and some details have been changed to protect the privacy of the participants. The present chapter draws from two earlier reports on this specialized data set: Umbreit and Vos (2000), and Umbreit, Vos, Coates, and Brown (2003). All information about participant perceptions and experiences reported here is drawn from the extensive open-ended research interviews held individually with these seven participants in 1998 and 1999.

Case Narratives

The three participating death-row offenders were convicted of a total of six counts of murder and two counts of attempted murder. Michael Henderson had been incarcerated for a previous violent crime and had been released early for good behavior. Not long after his release, he committed a series of violent crimes that resulted in his conviction and death sentence for three murders, two of which also included abduction and rape, as well as an additional abduction, rape, and attempted murder. Benjamin Graves had no previous history of arrest for violent crime, though he had served a one-year sentence for theft by check. He broke into a private home before dawn, stabbed two of its occupants to death, and attempted to murder the third, leading to his conviction and death sentence for two murders and one conviction for attempted murder. Paul Marshall was convicted and sentenced to die for a single murder. With the aid of an accomplice, he entered a private home and killed the man who owned it with a medieval sword, dismembering the body.

All four family members who participated in the mediation/dialogue sessions with these three offenders were women, as were 85 percent of our Texas victim/family member sample. The first, Kelly Cartwright, was the granddaughter of an elderly woman who was abducted, raped, and murdered by Michael Henderson. The second, Rachel Hollister, was the sister of another of Michael Henderson's victims, a young mother whom he murdered when she struggled during his attempted abduction. The third participant, Ellen Smithson, was the mother of one of the young women murdered by Benjamin Graves, and the fourth, Edwina Holmes, was the mother of the man murdered by Paul Marshall.

The participants' accounts of what they experienced at the time of the crime, its impact on them, and how they journeyed toward meeting in dialogue are offered in the case narratives below. Much of the material that participants shared with the research interviewers was also shared in their mediation sessions with one another. The narratives will be followed by discussion of some of the common themes and differences that emerged.

Case Narrative 1

Kelly Cartwright was a high-school senior at the time of her grandmother's murder. She was pulled from her classroom and told that her grandmother hadn't returned from her usual morning walk. The family drove two hundred miles to the small town where her grandmother lived. There they waited together at the search headquarters that had been established in the church parking lot where her grandmother usually parked her car for her daily walk. Already there was a sense of dread; Kelly Cartwright commented, "I think we all assumed the worst." But it was the evening of the second day before policemen on patrol some fourteen miles away from town noticed fresh car tracks on a remote dirt road, investigated, and found her grandmother's body. Michael Henderson was apprehended in relation to a different crime; it was some two years before he confessed and stood trial for her grandmother's murder.

Rachel Hollister had a much shorter wait than Cartwright to learn what had happened to her sister Allison, another of Michael Henderson's victims. Rachel had spent the day with Allison and her daughter Katie. She had just gotten home when Allison's husband called and asked her to meet him at the sheriff's station. There he told Rachel that Allison was dead. "That's really when the nightmare started, because Katie was there, and she was just covered in blood." Rachel assumed there had been some kind of car accident. She was horrified to learn instead that Allison had been murdered at a gas station while five-year-old Katie watched.

In describing events leading up to his crimes, Michael Henderson stated in his research interview that from as far back as he could remember, he had developed a habit of burying emotions of any sort. "And of course this is a very explosive thing." He offered no further detail about what these emotions were or what events had led him to harbor such explosive feelings. He reported that he did not use drugs or alcohol because his teenage experimentation had been unpleasant. All four of the crimes for which he was convicted followed a similar pattern. In each instance, he "happened on" a woman alone; he accosted her and abducted or attempted to abduct her. If successful, he drove to a secluded area, raped her, and murdered or attempted to murder her. He reported that initially he found it difficult to remember the specifics of the crimes. "I would suppress it so bad that even by the next day, I would almost have no memory." He was unable to offer any further explanation for his actions: "My trouble is I have never been able to come up with a satisfactory explanation for myself."

In the research interview, Michael Henderson described his murder of Kelly Cartwright's grandmother in vague, general terms. He gave somewhat more detail about his murder at the unattended gas station of Rachel Hollister's sister Allison. He stated that he was filling his truck when he noticed a woman and her daughter filling their car at another pump island. He attempted to abduct the woman but she struggled. He remembered that he stabbed her multiple times and fled when it appeared other persons were approaching the gas station.

Though Kelly Cartwright was away at college during Michael Henderson's trial and thus was unable to attend, she was in close touch with her family members who were present. She was distressed about the way in which the proceedings seemed more focused on protecting the offender than on protecting or supporting her grandmother's family members. She felt the justice system caused separation and disconnection where there should be connection. Early on, she decided she wanted to find a way to meet with her grandmother's killer; but she was still in college, and in her words, "nobody takes a blond twenty-one-year-old seriously." Years later, when his execution date was set and the family began to discuss who among them would wish to attend, she met with corrections staff for preparation and happened to mention that she really wanted to meet with him. Staff put her in touch with the VOM/D program.

A primary reason she sought to meet Michael Henderson was to let him know "how far reaching the impact is, and how time consuming, and how long it lasts, and what it does." She also sought detailed information about the actual crime, wanting to know such things as how her grandmother had been selected, whether she said anything, whether she was scared, and how he got her in his truck. And, she added, "I really needed to see this guy face-to-face."

Rachel Hollister attended Michael Henderson's trial and was active in asserting her rights as a victim from the very beginning: "I told them I wanted to be notified and called up on … every move Michael made." Initially she wanted to meet with him to rule out her suspicion that her sister's ex-husband might have had some involvement in the murder. Additionally, she hoped to find out why it happened and whether the offender knew her sister. She wanted him to know the impact of his action on her own life and on the life of Allison's daughter Katie, she wanted to hear him take responsibility, and she wanted "to look him in the eye, just to see him, just to hear what he had to say."

Michael Henderson spent nearly a decade in prison, much of it on death row. In the intervening years he had become a Christian and participated in twelve-step groups in the prison system. In response to the question of why he agreed to meet with his victims' family members, he stated that he had come to wish he could contact his victims' families to say he was sorry and ask for forgiveness. Some two years after this realization, a VOM/D staff member informed him that a family member wished to meet with him. "When he first contacted me, it was an answer to a prayer," Henderson said. He decided to participate in spite of any possible risk to his case. "It got to the point where I really didn't care about that part of it."

Case Narrative 2

Ellen Smithson, the mother of Benjamin Graves's victim Gayle, had awakened at about 4:00 the morning of Gayle's birthday with a strong feeling that she should call her daughter. But she felt it was an unreasonable hour and waited until 7:00. By then Gayle's phone was busy, so Smithson left for work, where a truck backed into a telephone pole and knocked out all phone communication to and from work for the rest of the day. She did not learn of Gayle's death until late that evening, when her ex-husband's wife called her at home with the news. "The impact was just so devastating, I just literally died inside." Smithson later learned that her daughter's murder had occurred about the time she had awakened, and that when she had attempted her call later, the phone lines were busy with police making phone calls from Gayle's apartment.

Benjamin Graves was fairly explicit about the links between his early history and his crimes. He reported that his childhood experience included flagrant physical and sexual abuse and early drug use. By the time of his crimes, he was a regular user of several drugs as well as a producer and dealer of amphetamines. Despondent over a failed marriage, he developed an idea that even he recognized as bizarre by the time of his research interview: "I decided I would rape and make women love me, and if I could practice this and get real good at it, I could do it to my wife and then my personal life would be great again."

The two counts of murder for which Graves was sentenced to die as well as an attempted murder were the result of a single incident in which he reported that his intent was to carry out such a rape. But two factors intervened. By his own account, he was high on more drugs and alcohol than he had ever previously consumed. And, warned by her barking dog, his intended victim put up a struggle and screamed. He reported that he blacked out and flashed back to his early abuse, and that when he regained consciousness his victim was

lying on the bed bleeding from multiple stab wounds. He heard more screaming and followed the sounds to encounter her roommate—Ellen Smithson's
daughter Gayle. Again, he reported blacking out during the actual murder.
The second woman's boyfriend awoke and attempted to pull the offender off
his victim. In the struggle that ensued, the boyfriend also sustained multiple
stab wounds, but ultimately survived. Benjamin Graves escaped and reported
having no memory of how he got home. He was apprehended within a week.

Smithson attended all of Graves's pretrial hearings as well as the actual trial,
a sixteen-month long process, and resolved before the trial ended that she
would find a way to meet with him. "The man I saw in the courtroom was not
human, he had no life in his eyes. For thirteen months I looked at his eyes
and I saw absolutely nothing." The day after he was sentenced she went to the
jail to try to meet with him but was unsuccessful. For the next fourteen years
she organized her work life so that she could always be immediately available
to attend any new developments to try to prevent Graves's release, or to meet
with him if he would consent. Her reasons for wishing to meet were vague at
the time. She did not seek information, nor did she wish to know why Graves
had killed her daughter. But she did wish to hold him accountable, and she
felt she "had to see his eyes, that he was a real person."

During the intervening years, Ellen Smithson experienced a powerful event
in which she came to forgive Benjamin Graves, though not his actions. "After
I was finally able to separate him from what he did, I was able to forgive him,
but I could never forgive what he did." By the time it became possible for her
to meet with him, she viewed sharing her forgiveness as a potentially important part of her own healing. "I just knew this was something I needed for me
to be able to go on with my life. And it was really important to me to let him
know that he had been forgiven."

Benjamin Graves also had converted to Christianity while in prison, and
had become a member of a religious order. As part of this process he developed a desire to offer to meet with family members of his victims if it would
help them heal in any way. He contacted reporters and lawyers to try to find
a way to reach out to his victims, and finally was put in touch with the VOM/D
staff, who clarified that such a meeting would occur only if victims spontaneously sought it. It was only a few months later that VOM/D staff were back
in touch with him to let him know a victim's mother, Ellen Smithson, wished
to meet. In his research interview he said his reasons for agreeing to meet with
her were to try to help her heal and to offer something back for the wrong he
had done.

He reported that in the courtroom at the end of his trial, he had looked at
Ellen Smithson and mouthed the words "I'm sorry," and she had responded,

"It's not enough." He wanted to answer any questions she might have and to help her healing in any way possible, even if this meant experiencing her rage. He also looked to his own history to explain what he hoped he could accomplish: "Because of my childhood, I understood that hate was a cancer." He hoped family members would be able to release some of their negative feelings and diminish the power of such intense feelings in their lives. And he felt it was a religious necessity: "I owed it to her and myself and God to do this."

Case Narrative 3

Edwina Holmes, the mother of Paul Marshall's victim, Richard, was home washing dishes with her husband, Richard's stepfather, when the phone call came. Her husband answered because Edwina's hands were wet and soapy. "When he got off the telephone he stood to face me with his hands on my shoulder and told me that my son had just been killed. I did not understand one word he said, it was like some kind of a garbled foreign language. I was in total denial." Edwina Holmes's denial only began to abate when they arrived at the funeral home. "Folks were upset, I had to believe something."

In describing the events leading up to his crime, Paul Marshall reported that he was picked on in elementary school to the point of becoming a "punching bag." In his account, his feelings simply came boiling over in the seventh grade and he lashed out. "From that day forward I was made a complete new person. I wasn't taking it no more." He was vague about the intervening years, on the one hand reporting that he was not involved in "the criminal element," yet on the other hand mentioning previous personal and property offenses. Finally, out of work, out of money, and living in his car with his girlfriend, he reported that he agreed to her plan that they "knock somebody in the head and take their money."

Paul Marshall drove his girlfriend to a bar where she met the victim—Edwina Holmes' son Richard—and persuaded him to take her to his home; Paul Marshall followed in his car. Growing tired of waiting, he approached the house to see what was happening and became enraged when he saw his girlfriend attempting to seduce their intended victim. "Picked a bad weapon for trying to knock him in the head. But it turned out a part of me really wanted to go in there and kill him ... and that's what happened. And I mutilated the guy with a sword." Immediately he was nauseated by what he had done. "I wished I could have been able to pick him up and get him to a hospital and say, 'Here, put this man back together,' but he was beyond putting back together."

Edwina Holmes did not comment on how far back she had decided to try to meet with Paul Marshall. She simply stated that when she decided she wanted to do so, she spoke with the victim services workers who were already involved with her, and they put her in touch with the Texas VOM/D Program. Her reasons were similar to Ellen Smithson's: "The main thing was that I wanted to look him in the eye and tell him I had forgiven him." She also wished to ask him about several details, including what her son's last words were and what Paul Marshall had done with some of the things he stole from her son's house. Her only worry was whether meeting with him or having forgiven him could in any way reduce his sentence; she was relieved to learn there was no way this could happen.

Paul Marshall, too, experienced conversion while in prison and came to understand that he had been forgiven by God: "I know that God forgave me of my sin, cleansed me, and I know the people that know me have moved past what I did and still love and support me." He told the research interviewer that he had always wanted to meet with the mother of his victim and tell her that he was sorry, but hadn't known how to go about it. He reported that when he was approached by the mediator, "I was all for it as soon as he opened his mouth." The only risk he considered was whether she might rage at him. He felt that if she did, he deserved it, and that it might help her to release her anger.

Common Themes across the Narratives

All seven of these participants shared in common with our larger sample the enormity of the impact of serious and violent crime. Three of the four family members identified early on that they wished to meet with their respective offenders. In our broader sample there was wide variation in how quickly victims and family members reached a decision to try to meet their offenders, and some family members had quite negative responses to the idea the first time they heard about it. It was characteristic of our entire sample that several years elapsed between the occurrence of the crime and the actual dialogue meeting, and these four family members were typical.

In our larger sample, there was a wide range of reasons that family members sought to meet with offenders, and our small death-row sample is no different. The only reason shared in common by the four family member participants was the wish to have some form of human encounter with the person who had taken their loved one's life. Three family members sought information, but only two of them wanted to know anything about why it happened. Two specifically sought to share their forgiveness. Two wanted to let the offenders know the impact of their actions. One of these, and one who didn't, sought to hear the offender take responsibility. It should be noted that many of these themes turned up frequently in the benefits family members said they reaped from the experience, regardless of whether they had listed the theme as a specific reason initially. The wide range of reasons for seeking to meet underscores that there is no one way to heal, and no single "correct" goal for victim-offender dialogue in serious and violent crime.

The one commonality across the three offenders in their account of their crimes was that they connected their crimes in some way to their early history, which included abuse, violence, explosive emotions, and no skills for handling emotions. Beyond this, their accounts of their crimes had little in common; one was involved in drug and alcohol abuse, two were not. Two reported memory loss about the events of the crime, one did not. Two reported no premeditation, one was less clear. Where the three offender experiences begin to converge, however, is in their use of their time while in prison. All three offenders had become active in religious organizations, and two also reported active involvement in twelve-step groups. And, all three of these death-row offenders told the research interviewer that they had hoped to be able to meet with the family members of their victims before they were approached by the VOM/D staff.

All three of the participating offenders referred to their personal religious faith in discussing their decision to participate; across our wider Texas sample, only 30 percent of the offenders spontaneously mentioned religious or spiritual reasons. Across our larger sample, when offenders were asked to share the reasons they agreed to meet with their victims or victim family members, they typically answered the question with victim-focused reasons, and these three offenders shared that characteristic. Apart from these characteristics, no specific reasons were common to all three death-row offenders. Helping the family members heal and being accountable were named by two of the three; the other reasons were each offered by only a single offender: to answer the family member's questions, to apologize, to ask for forgiveness, to relieve a burden, to feel better, because he owed it to the family member, and because he felt he owed it to God.

Preparation for Mediation/Dialogue

The Texas VOM/D Program has developed extensive protocols for preparing victims and offenders to meet with one another. Once a victim has initiated a request to meet, a mediator contacts the offender to explain the program and learn whether the offender is willing to meet. Offenders are accepted into the VOM/D program if they wish to meet, if they have admitted guilt for the crimes against the participating victim or family member, and if their attitude and participation is not likely to cause harm or further victimization.

There follows an intensive period of meetings between the mediator and each of the participants. Mediators use a thick packet of questionnaires and reading materials to help participants explore their experience of the crime, their feelings, their path toward healing, and their goals for meeting one another. The packet includes inventories on such domains as grief, forgiveness, and core beliefs; reading materials on thinking errors, trauma, and the twelve steps; and exercises for exploring feelings and journaling. As part of their preparation process, participants are encouraged to write out a statement of the things they wish to say when they meet together, and to bring it to the dialogue meeting.

The purpose of this rigorous preparation is to promote healing for both the victim/family member and the offender, to explore participants' hopes for their encounter, and to thoroughly cover the content that is likely to surface during the meeting. VOM/D staff commented that they try to avoid having negative surprises in the sessions. The emotionally loaded content of the meetings will naturally push some buttons for participants. Staff hopes that all these buttons have been pushed during preparation so that both the mediator and the participants are prepared to deal with them constructively.

During the time period of our study, the preparation period across the entire VOM/D program averaged fifteen months and typically included several meetings with each participant. Because of the dates of the scheduled executions, five of the death-row participants experienced a much shorter time frame for preparation than was usual for the Texas program, all at less than six months. Only one victim (Ellen Smithson) and one offender (Paul Marshall, who had murdered her daughter) had a more typical time frame; they were afforded nearly two years to prepare to meet.

All seven participants rated their preparation for the mediation/dialogue very highly. All were very impressed with the questionnaires and written materials they were given to work with. One family member and one offender expressed surprise that such an elaborate set of materials was already prepared for them. Michael Henderson (offender) commented, "I was really surprised because he had a little preparation sheet and everything to work through, to really look at some of your thoughts and feelings … it is actually kinda a healing process that once you get started on … gave me a little more insight into some of the things I'd gone through."

All four family members felt that the preparation materials were helpful in their healing process. Kelly Cartwright was also grateful for the way the questions helped her organize her thoughts and plan what she wanted to say. Rachel Hollister worked through the questions with another of her sisters. She found the process very difficult but was impressed with how helpful it was for both of them. She later requested extra copies of the materials to share with her brothers, and reported that this shared experience helped open up family communication about her sister's death in a way that had never happened since the murder. Ellen Smithson also commented that the preparation work was difficult, yet "totally necessary." She was also the only participant who referred to any type of conflict with the mediator during the preparation phase. "Even when I'd get mad at him and he'd push my buttons, it was still a very positive, positive experience, and it's one I wouldn't trade anything for."

Two of the offenders likened the preparation process to the twelve-step programs in which they participated. Michael Henderson additionally felt that the preparation helped him open up and gave him tools to express his feelings, and he used the materials to help him talk with his own family members about his pending execution. "I think it helped open up some doors, having more visits with them, more heartfelt discussion. It's really helped them face it."

Benjamin Graves felt the preparation materials actually pushed beyond the twelve-step program by helping him identify and understand both the cycle of abuse that had victimized him, and his own cycle of abuse and offending that had victimized others. Paul Marshall did not refer to twelve-step work but reported that the preparation helped teach him "how to talk to somebody you wronged ... without bringing more pain to her."

All seven participants had high praise for the way in which their mediator conducted the preparation. Kelly Cartwright and Michael Henderson were particularly moved by how much the mediator cared. Edwina Holmes and Paul Marshall were each grateful to learn that the mediator shared their religion.

Feelings Immediately before the Session

There was some variation in the feelings participants reported immediately prior to the sessions. Among family members, Kelly Cartwright (granddaughter) was basically calm and reported that she experienced only momentary nervousness when the offender entered the room. Rachel Hollister (sister) was both excited and somewhat nervous, and Edwina Holmes (mother) reported feeling nervous and shaking. Ellen Smithson (mother) reported the highest degree of anxiety: "I was scared to death. It was a long walk, believe me!" She also was the only family member who specified a particular fear: she worried whether the anger and rage others had told her to anticipate might surface during the session and overwhelm her.

The three offenders were more uniformly apprehensive than were the family members. All three anticipated being on the receiving end of substantial rage; in Michael Henderson's words, "I really expected a lot more anger.... This is something I could not blame them for if this was to take place." Benjamin Graves had similar expectations but tried to focus on staying calm and unexpressive in order not to revictimize his victim's mother. He added, "At the same time of knowing that I owed that to them, I didn't want to do it, I was scared. It's very fearful having to sit in front of somebody, I mean, what do you say? I killed your daughter? What else goes with that? I expected to be yelled at and cussed at and everything else." Paul Marshall described a mix of sadness and fear, and added, "I felt like I was fixing to meet the most awful judgment I've ever faced."

The Mediation/Dialogue Process

All three mediation/dialogue sessions were held in the visiting room of the penal institution housing the death-row offenders. The sessions were similar in several ways: each lasted approximately five to six hours, the mediator sat with the offender on the inmates' side of the glass partition, and the family member(s), with any support persons, sat on the other. The session with Michael Henderson departed in one important way from the usual Texas format. Due to the time constraints deriving from his scheduled execution date, he met simultaneously with the participating family members of his two different victims. Both this session and the mediation between Benjamin Graves and his victim's mother, Ellen Smithson, were videotaped, a routine practice in the Texas VOM/D Program; no recording was made of the third mediation/dialogue.

In general, the three sessions followed the usual format of the Texas VOM/D Program. The mediator always opens the session by welcoming participants and going back over the ground rules that govern the dialogue. Victims are given choices about how they wish to begin the session and whether they wish to read their statements. Opening moments are often nerve-wracking and awkward, but once participants have begun, the meetings typically have the flow of a conversation. The mediator usually remains largely in a background role, available if trouble arises and helping to keep the dialogue focused if need be, but largely leaving the content and direction of the conversation up to the participants.

Two of the four participating family members were in such an intense emotional state during the actual mediation session that they initially had very little memory of the details, a not uncommon component of reactions to traumatic events. Rachel Hollister (sister) was especially grateful for the video recording: "There was so much that I do not remember took place until I sat back and watched the video. It was like I was there, but I wasn't there." Ellen Smithson's experience was similar. "I couldn't remember anything that we talked about, a fraction of what I said, or how I behaved." Much of the detail these two women gave in their research interviews was drawn from their review of their videotapes. No such recording was made of the third session. However, Edwina Holmes reported that in the days immediately following the session she wrote a ten-page description of what happened so that she could share her experience more easily with her remaining children. Kelly Cartwright did not report any difficulty remembering her session.

In general, the themes of the material shared by family members in all three sessions were very similar. They described their own experiences of the day or days surrounding the murder, they talked about how it affected them personally, and they shared its impact on other family members of the murder victims. In our research interviews we asked about total "talk time" during the dialogue meeting and found that in these three meetings participants had the floor for roughly equal amounts of time. In the session with two family members and a single offender, Kelly Cartwright worried that this distribution might have created unfairness for Michael Henderson: "Because there were two victims and only one offender, I would say probably overall the victims had more talk time than the offender."

Michael Henderson had elected not to prepare a specific statement, so Kelly Cartwright and Rachel Hollister chose to begin by asking him to tell them about his life. They had come with a list of questions about his history and the actions leading up to the crimes, and they had anticipated that it would be hard to get him to open up. But Kelly Cartwright commented, "Actually, we didn't even ask him a question because he just went off and basically went from the very beginning of his life all the way up through the murders. It was very nice, actually." When he was finished, Kelly Cartwright and Rachel Hollister traded off reading portions of their statements, using one another to take a break when emotions became overwhelming.

By all accounts, sessions one and two proceeded fairly calmly. Both Michael Henderson and Benjamin Graves reported that listening to the family members' statements made a powerful impact. Each had anticipated that the family members would be openly angry and attacking, and each was grateful that such reactions did not occur.

Edwina Holmes had come to her session seeking detailed information about her son's murder, but found herself shocked and enraged when Paul Marshall answered her questions and described what he had done. Paul Marshall recounted the beginning of this exchange: "She covered a lot of areas that she wanted to know about.... A lot of them were traumatic. She didn't ever see the body of her son, and when I talked to her about it, I could see the ripping inside of her." Edwina Holmes's description continues: "I found that I had some anger left inside of me that I didn't realize was there. I raised my voice to him, I began to cry, I was pretty much sobbing." She tried to stop herself because she's not normally "a person who screams and yells and raises my voice." But the mediator encouraged her to continue, "so that I could vent every bit of my anger. I believe that was really beneficial."

Both Kelly Cartwright and Rachel Hollister had developed a list of questions about the crimes for which they hoped to receive answers. As their session with Michael Henderson unfolded, they found that they did not in fact request many details. They became more interested in piecing together some kind of explanation through obtaining information about his life and history. And, as reported earlier, Ellen Smithson did not seek any details about either the events or the reasons surrounding her daughter's murder.

As described previously, both of the mothers involved in these mediation/dialogue sessions reported that they had forgiven their offenders prior to seeking to meet with them. Both were able to share their forgiveness during the mediations. Ellen Smithson felt that this experience changed her perspective on her choice to witness Benjamin Graves's execution. "When I first decided I was going to witness, it's because I wanted my face to be the last thing that he saw, to be aware that he's where he is because of what he did to my daughter. And now I want him to see his victim's mother who has forgiven him." Benjamin Graves was deeply moved by this aspect of their encounter. When asked what had surprised him most about the session, he responded, "Her compassion, her deep feeling for me. I met another face of God that night. The God I know is a God of mercy, a God of love, a God of forgiveness, and that night I met all those things in her."

Edwina Holmes reported, "The most important thing was that I could tell him that I had forgiven him." She and Paul Marshall also spoke about his pending execution, but with a different flavor. Edwina Holmes had never wavered in her belief that he ought to be executed for the murder of her son, even though she had forgiven him. As they discussed her views, she asked Paul Marshall whether, if he were set free, he would commit murder again. "And he tossed this question around a bit.... Then he said, 'No, I'm sure, quite sure that I would.'" Paul Marshall confirmed this self-portrait in his statement to the research interviewer: "If I was on the street I'd still be taken in.... I would definitely kill again. Something would come on me where I would be placed in a high risk factor and I would kill somebody again. Once you kill once it's not hard to do it again."

The offenders did not give much detail in their research interviews about the types of information they shared with family members during the mediation. Some differences in focus among the three were apparent, but these variations may have been more a consequence of the questions the family members chose to ask than of the offender's plan or intention. Michael Henderson shared his history: "I basically started with my childhood ... and the things that led up to the crimes." Benjamin Graves tried to focus chiefly on understanding and responding to whatever his victim's mother shared. He reported that he tried hard to understand the feelings she had gone through but was also aware of his limited ability to do so. He was surprised to learn that she had additional children. He reported that he had been deeply concerned that he had robbed her of any chance for grandchildren. He was relieved to learn this was not the case, but also stunned to realize how much devastation he had caused these additional two persons. Paul Marshall mostly focused on the details of the events, and on trying to reassure his victim's mother that he was sorry and didn't wish to add to her pain.

Role of the Mediator

All seven participants were unanimous in their praise for the process and for their mediator. With one exception, to be discussed below, they concurred in their descriptions of the mediator's role during the session: after his introductory remarks setting the stage, he was relatively silent, and simply let the sessions flow freely. As Ellen Smithson noted, "He had tutored us both well, and he really didn't have to [talk] very much." Benjamin Graves, who met with Ellen Smithson, found the mediator's respect for silence especially significant: "Those moments of silence were very precious at times because it was just a time to sit back and reflect momentarily on what we had said."

The exception to the mediator's typically silent, background role occurred during the mediation between Paul Marshall and Edwina Holmes after she asked for and received details about her son's murder. Her comments about the mediator's role in helping her keep in touch with her intense feelings have been referred to earlier. In response to the interviewer's question "did the mediator talk much," Paul Marshall gave a more extensive account of this departure from the more typical background role:

> He helped us see inside of emotion that was happening at that moment. She was having one emotion where it was angry and it turned into rage and then it turned into a void. And he walked her through it. And at the bottom of the void she was able to fill it with God. So he really guided her and me through the process. Without him it

wouldn't have turned out near as well as it did with him.... He really was a tool in helping the process come to an understanding where me and her could actually make a meaning of our hearts instead of just the flesh that was devastated.

All seven participants described the mediator's few interventions in similar terms. Clearly, much of the mediator's role in these capital cases was not dissimilar to the role in other serious and violent crime mediations. The mediator occasionally helped remind participants of topics they had wanted to bring up, and consistently helped all participants stay in touch with their feelings. There was less mention of redirecting the conversation or of keeping things going than in the noncapital mediations, suggesting that there may have been even more space for silence and reflection in these death-row cases than was typical in other mediations.

The family members commented on the mediator's sense of balance and his capacity to be fully present for both themselves and the offenders, a process they presumed was very difficult. Ellen Smithson commented, "It's hard to be fair in something like this.... It would be hard, I think, to be fair to a murderer." Kelly Cartwright felt that without the mediator's intense preparation and his capacity to be present in his relationship with the offenders, Michael Henderson would never have participated so openly. "Michael had probably opened up more to the mediator than he had to anyone else, probably ever, about these crimes and about his life. I felt like he probably saw the mediator not just as a friend, but as someone he could go to and lean on a little."

Outcome and Evaluation

The language used by all seven of these interviewees to describe how they felt immediately after finishing the meetings is remarkably similar: they reported that the experience was powerful and healing, and they felt relieved and renewed.

When I walked out, it was like this load, some type of negative energy kind of was lifted out of me, and I was also exhausted.—Kelly Cartwright, granddaughter

I felt a sense of relief.—Rachel Hollister, sister

There just aren't any words that would adequately express what I feel. I feel human for the first time in twelve years.—Ellen Smithson, mother
I was pretty much numb. I felt more relief the next day. It was so healing.—Edwina Holmes, mother

I think I'm more alive now than I ever have been at any one point in time. I'm actually living life now, instead of just existing.—Michael Henderson, offender

Very much at peace. I told the mediator I felt cleansed. I felt a great burden had been lifted off my shoulders. I felt joy.—Benjamin Graves, offender

Like a burden had been lifted off me, like something had been removed that was a thorn in my side for years.—Paul Marshall, offender

All seven participants thus experienced the mediation/dialogue as very healing, even though not all of them explicitly named this as a goal initially, and not all of their reasons for seeking mediation were satisfied.

Family Member Perspective

For all four family members, an important component was hearing the offender take responsibility. Kelly Cartwright reported it this way: "I had heard that he had confessed—it was gratifying to hear it out of his mouth and not out of a reporter's mouth." Edwina Holmes echoed these sentiments: "He was extremely accountable for everything he did. He wanted me to understand that he was totally responsible for the murder of my son."

All four family members reported that their negative feelings had greatly diminished, and all four mentioned a decrease in anger specifically. In the words of Rachel Hollister, "I'm not angry like I used to be." She also reported a decrease in her bitterness and fearfulness.

Three family members felt their respective offenders were sincere. Rachel Hollister had more doubts. During the session she told Michael Henderson that she didn't want him out on the street, and he assured her that he wouldn't do this again, but would admit himself to a hospital instead. She remained unimpressed: "I'd say that too, if I was on death row."

When asked if their opinions of their offenders had changed, all four family members responded affirmatively, in similar language that made clear their encounters had humanized the offender:

Before, he was just a murderer.... After, he was a human being.—Kelly Cartwright, granddaughter

I pictured him as just an animal, but after meeting with him it was just so hard to.—Rachel Hollister, sister

I saw a person and not just the man who murdered my daughter.—
Ellen Smithson, mother

I think I may have more compassion for him. I think I have more of
an understanding.—Edwina Holmes, mother

In no way did this shift toward perceiving the offender as more human
make the offender any less accountable. For Kelly Cartwright, it paradoxically
made him even more accountable. "It's very easy in a crime as horrible as that
one to not really be able to place blame anywhere.... So for me it was important to establish some level or balance of accountability among everyone, and
not no-one and nothing." Rachel Hollister added, "After sitting and talking
with him, he is a person, but he's not a person who needs to be returned to
society."

Three of the family members further underscored the salience of such humanizing in their comments about the importance of having met face-to-face
and looked eye-to-eye. In Ellen Smithson's words, "Just being able to look at
somebody and see that they smile with their eyes.... It was very intimate, very
spiritual and very personal." Kelly Cartwright felt that just doing this much
would have been sufficient: "Even if I had only gotten in the room and sat and
done that for five minutes, I would have been happy."

As described above, receiving answers to her questions was a most powerful experience for Edwina Holmes. She attributed much of her healing to the
opportunity this experience gave her to fully express and release her rage. The
other two family members who had initially sought information about the
crime as part of their motivation for participating in fact received very few answers. Yet both of them found that receiving such details mattered less than
they had anticipated. Kelly Cartwright commented, "It's funny how when you
go through a process like that, the unknowns become much less important."

All four family members reported that their mediation experience enriched
their spirituality. Ellen Smithson commented, "What I felt leave me that night,
that was a gift that God gave me, He took that heaviness out of my heart." Edwina Holmes reported that Paul Marshall had been writing sermons and posting them on the Internet, and that he asked her if she would help disseminate
them after he was gone. "Since I have committed to doing that, it is just unbelievable the way God is opening doors.... The lives that I can reach out to [to]
try and do what he asked me to, it's almost like a burning desire within me now."

At the time of the family-member research interviews, the executions of
Michael Henderson and Benjamin Graves were still pending. Paul Marshall
had already been executed, and Edwina Holmes had attended. She reported
what for her was a very moving experience: the offender made eye contact

with her, nodded, and began to cry. "I personally felt like his tears were his last statement, and that he was saying to me again 'Oh, how sorry I am that I have hurt you.' I believe that he had repented for the sin, and I believe that Christ has forgiven him, and I think he's in heaven today."

The other three family members, all of whom were making plans to witness the executions, reported some shift in their feelings about the death sentence and the respective offenders' pending executions. Both of the family members who met with Michael Henderson had initially been so enraged they wanted to kill him: "For a very long time I would have put the needle in his arm" (Kelly Cartwright). "Before, I wanted to execute him myself. I think a lot of us did" (Rachel Hollister). Both Kelly Cartwright and Rachel Hollister softened their positions after meeting with him, though they still experienced mixed feelings. Kelly Cartwright added, "People have asked me if I want him to die ... and that is something I can't decide. I'm gonna leave that up to God." As reported above, Ellen Smithson had changed her perspective from wishing to attend as a punishment for Benjamin Graves, to being present as someone who had forgiven him.

Offender Perspective

All three offenders spontaneously described the healing that they felt had come to them through the mediation. Words in common to all three included relief, release, and the lifting of a burden. Benjamin Graves and Paul Marshall also described themselves as more at peace, and Graves added that he felt joy.

Restitution themes dominated their explanations of how such healing evolved. For all three, the most salient factor appeared to be the experience of doing something, however small, to try to make better what they had done.

> That you've done something positive, that at least something positive will come out of this. — Michael Henderson

> To take whatever darkness I could out of this world. I had already brought too much darkness into it. — Benjamin Graves

> It felt good to be able to mend that broken spot in her life, though I can't ever replace what was lost. — Paul Marshall

First and foremost was the impact of being able to offer something directly to the family members who participated with them in the mediation/dialogue sessions. All three offenders reported that they were grateful to have been able to help these family members begin to heal. Benjamin Graves commented, "For years I've prayed for Ellen's peace, and I saw her possessing peace that night. That helped."

For all three, this impetus to "make it better" reached beyond the family members with whom they had met to include others in some way. Michael Henderson had left an open letter to be made available to any other family members of his victims. Both he and Graves hoped that their participation and the videotapes of their sessions could help make it possible for more people to access the healing process of mediation. They felt this was as important for other offenders as it was for victims and their family members. Henderson spoke further about his own efforts to reach out to other inmates on death row: "I can touch this person and say, 'Hey, I've done this, this is what I've learned, let me share this with you.'" Paul Marshall did not comment in his interview about his wish to reach out to others, but as described above, Edwina Holmes reported that he had been writing sermons and posting them on the Internet: "And he asked me if I would do everything I could to try to get those out, especially to young people who might be persuaded to avoid the road that he took and try to deter some of the violent crime that's going on. And I told him that I would do everything I could."

An additional factor in the offenders' positive response to the mediation derived from the humanizing nature of the encounter, as similarly reported by the family members. When asked if they thought family members' perceptions of them had changed as a result of the mediation, all three offenders responded positively, and it is clear that they were quite moved by the compassion and understanding they felt they received. In their comments, two of the offenders conveyed a more personalized understanding of the relationship than was described by the family members. "I realized that all of a sudden, if I had met these people in other circumstances I probably could have been friends" (Michael Henderson). "Had I not killed her daughter, I think Ellen and I would have been best friends. I do see a lot of parallels to our problems" (Benjamin Graves). None of the three family members who met with Henderson and Graves used the term "friend" in any of their descriptions of their own perceptions or relationship with the offenders.

All three offenders placed their positive responses to the mediation/dialogue sessions in the context of their upcoming executions. Each felt that having participated in the mediation made it easier to face his impending death. Michael Henderson described it this way: "And it actually makes it a lot easier to face the execution ... that you've done something positive, that at least something positive will come out of this." Even though one of his reasons for participating had been his hope to ask for forgiveness, he did not mention either asking for or receiving forgiveness in his discussion of the mediation process. But it is clear that for him, the actions of meeting with his victims' family members, facing what he had done, accepting responsibility and offering what he could to help, all played a part in his own healing and readiness to face death.

For Benjamin Graves, Ellen Smithson's forgiveness was central: "She doesn't hate me, she hasn't forgiven the crime, but she's forgiven me. Now I know that when I'll be on that gurney, that a great burden has been taken away from me." Paul Marshall's comment was in response to the interviewer's question about whether he had any regrets regarding his participation: "I would have regrets if I couldn't have done it and I was executed next Wednesday. That would be my regret, if I wasn't able to do it." He later commented on the difference between his victim's death and his own: "I took something from her, that she didn't get to say goodbye to him like my mama's doing now."

Advice for Others

All seven participants recommended that others in similar circumstances participate in mediation/dialogue. The family members clarified that they know this process is not for everyone, but they still felt strongly that family members should consider participating. Ellen Smithson was the most enthusiastic: "I think that if I could convince people to go through this program, not because they just need to sit with the offender, but just to do something for themselves, I would, because it's that good."

Edwina Holmes cautioned that mediation is difficult and advised, "Don't try it without God. It's a very stressful thing if you don't have something really solid to hold on to." Rachel Hollister felt that the state should be more assertive in letting victims and family members know that the service is available. And Kelly Cartwright felt that mediation was as much needed by offenders as by family members, to improve offender accountability.

As discussed above, two of the offenders hoped mediation would become more generally available for both victims and offenders. Michael Henderson was particularly concerned about the potential impact for offenders: "Maybe it can open up a lot more awareness as far as opening up and learning ... that there actually can be attempts made at rehabilitation instead of just holding prisoners until their time is served." Benjamin Graves was more focused on helping victims heal, and offered the use of both his research interview and his videotaped session in any way "that you think would intensify the healing process." Both Henderson and Graves also wished there was some way to alert family members if their specific offender wished to meet, without somehow implying that the family member ought to do so or in any way owed anything to the offender.

Conclusion

All seven participants in these groundbreaking sessions reported positive gains. Both the family members and the death-row offenders who participated in these meetings were grateful they had the opportunity to do so, and none of them had any regrets. All of the participants were moved beyond their expectations, all were relieved, and all reported significant impact on their healing. Still, the extent of the actual healing and transformation that took place for the offenders can never be documented beyond their self-reports in these interviews, which occurred a matter of weeks or days before their executions.

All seven participants pointed to the same set of components to account for their response: careful and compassionate preparation; gentle and unobtrusive guidance during the session; and above all, the opportunity for genuine, human, face-to-face encounters—which increased, rather than decreased, offender accountability and responsibility. They were unanimous in their hope that this potentially healing process can be made more generally available for both victims and offenders in cases of violent crime.

In our recent book (Umbreit, Vos, Coates, and Brown 2003) we detailed the more general conclusions arising out of our study about the advisability of offering a mediated dialogue service for victims in cases of serious and violent crime. Our policy recommendations included that departments of corrections develop specific procedures for responding to such requests, that public funding be appropriated to provide the service, and that crime-victim compensation laws be expanded to provide reimbursement to victims for the costs they incur in participating. In our practice-focused recommendations, we urged extensive training for mediators, a minimum of two preparation sessions for each participant, strong adherence to the principles of victim initiation of the service and voluntary participation by offenders, the active involvement of victim-services providers and correctional staff in the planning and delivery of the service, maximum flexibility in responding to the great range of needs of the participants, and continuing attention to assessing the impact on offenders within the framework of the victim-focused program delivery.

Our strong recommendation that such services be made available for all victims who wish to meet in no way implies any judgment about whether victims *should* wish to meet their offender. Many victims embark on a journey of healing from the harm they have suffered with no thought or wish ever to meet the offender who harmed them, and we deeply respect that choice. But we believe that the positive benefits reported by all seventy-nine participants in our larger study support our recommendation that all victims of serious and violent crime should be entitled to meet their respective offenders if they so wish.

We see no inherent reason for refusing to extend such services to victims and offenders who desire them in capital cases. There may be obstacles presented by state policies and correctional institution regulations, but the Texas VOM/D Program was successful in advocating for its victims' needs and negotiating solutions to such obstacles in a timely manner. We are aware of death-row cases in other jurisdictions in which executions have been carried out before victims who wished to meet the offenders could do so. We encourage providers of services to victims and correctional departments to engage in dialogue toward making this potentially healing service routinely available for all who seek it.

In summary, we return to the characteristics of restorative justice with which we opened this chapter. Victims of violent crime often find themselves and their needs passed over or minimized in the formal criminal justice process. Even with the relief that may come when the offender is apprehended, tried, found guilty, and sentenced, many victims and survivors of victims find that something is missing.

The nature of what is missing varies greatly, as corroborated in the wide range of reasons the four individuals cited here gave for wishing to meet the death-row offenders who murdered their family members. Clearly, nothing can replace the person who was murdered, and there is no sense in which such vast harm can be repaired. But each of our four participating family members identified some need that could only be met through direct encounter with the person who had committed the crime, and each came away feeling that the encounter had a powerful, positive impact on her healing journey—a core value of restorative justice.

Was participation restorative for the offenders? Execution can never be restorative for the person executed. Given that the executions could not be halted by any of the participants in these groundbreaking dialogues, did the offenders experience anything they would have labeled "restorative"? We believe their responses to our interview questions demonstrate that they did. They, too, used language of healing, peace, and even joy to convey the impact of their experience. Each felt better prepared to face his upcoming execution, and each was grateful for the opportunity to participate.

Within the constraints of the three offenders' impending deaths, the dialogues addressed the "harms, needs, and obligations" of all seven participants, and moved toward the goal identified by Zehr (2002): "to heal and put things as right as possible" (p. 37).

References

Latimer, Jeff, Craig Dowden, and Danielle Muise (2001). *The Effectiveness of Restorative Practices: A Meta-Analysis.* Ottawa, CAN: Department of Justice, Research and Statistics Division Methodological Series.

Nugent, William R., Mark S. Umbreit, Lizabeth Wiinamaki and J. Paddock (1999). "Participation in Victim-Offender Mediation and Severity of Subsequent Delinquent Behavior: Successful Replications?" *Journal of Research in Social Work Practice* 11(1):5–23

Peachey, Dean E. (1989). "The Kitchener Experiment," in Martin Wright and Burt Galaway (eds.), *Mediation and Criminal Justice.* London, UK: Sage, pp. 14–26.

Radelet, Michael L., and Marian Borg (2000). "Comment on Umbreit and Vos." *Homicide Studies* 4(1):88–92.

Umbreit, Mark S. (2000). "Reply to Radelet and Borg." *Homicide Studies* 4(1):93–97.

Umbreit, Mark S., Robert B. Coates, and Betty Vos (2002). "The Impact of Restorative Justice Conferencing: A Multi-national Perspective." *British Journal of Community Justice* 1(2):21–48.

Umbreit, Mark S., Jean Greenwood, Robert, Schug, Jenni Umbreit, and Claudia Fercello (2003). *Directory of Victim Offender Programs in the U.S.* St. Paul, MN: Center for Restorative Justice & Peacemaking.

Umbreit, Mark S., and Betty Vos (2000). "Homicide Survivors Meet the Offender Prior to Execution: Restorative Justice Through Dialogue." *Homicide Studies* 4(1):63–87.

Umbreit, Mark S., Betty Vos, Robert B. Coates, and Katherine A. Brown (2003). *Facing Violence: The Path of Restorative Justice and Dialogue.* Monsey, NY: Criminal Justice Press.

Zehr, Howard (2002). *The Little Book of Restorative Justice.* Intercourse, PA: Good Books.

PART IV

POLICY IMPLICATIONS: CAPITAL PUNISHMENT, CRIMINAL JUSTICE PRACTICES, AND VICTIM SERVICES

CHAPTER 19

REACHING OUT TO THE OTHER SIDE: DEFENSE-BASED VICTIM OUTREACH IN CAPITAL CASES[1]

Tammy Krause

My last memory of Lori is her waving at me as I backed out of her driveway to return to Lexington, Kentucky. I spent the weekend with Lori and her nine-month old daughter, Alexis, while her husband was on a business trip. We did all of our favorite things—shop and spend time with the baby. I remember thinking, "Lori is so happy being a mother. It's what she has always wanted to be."

It's a seven-hour drive from Springfield, Illinois. The phone was ringing as I walked in the door at Lexington later that day. It was a police officer from Springfield saying, "Your daughter is missing. We have your granddaughter." I knew that Lori would never abandon her baby. I said to the police officer, "You keep that baby. I will be right there to get her." My husband, daughter, and I got in the car and went back to Illinois. By the time we got there, the police had handed Alexis over to Child Protective Services. It took us three days to be able to get her from them.

By some miracle, Lori's body was discovered the following evening. Her body had been dumped in a cornfield. Several days later the police made an arrest of a local man based on DNA that linked him to other

---

1. Debbie Espinosa helped with the research of articles for this paper. Kim Smith-Stout provided research and editorial assistance that were of enormous help.

rapes committed in the community. The hardest part about Lori's mur-
der, besides losing her, was the fact that Lori's murder could have been
avoided. If the police had listened to the rape victims who said that they
could identify the man who raped them, Lori would still be alive, rais-
ing Alexis.[2]

Tragic stories like this are a reality for many people in the United States. In capital cases, victims[3] are assumed by the prosecutor, the courts, and even the defense team to be in favor of a death sentence. This misconception is perpetuated when options are not explored with the family of the victim. The prosecution's argument for the death penalty implies that this punishment is what the family needs for justice to be done. Prosecutors speak about the victim's family as a stakeholder in the outcome, yet define justice in capital cases only by the ultimate sanction. This assertion sets the stage for two outcomes: it discourages the defendant from accepting responsibility for his/her actions when appropriate because many courts will not allow a defendant to plead guilty when facing the possibility of the death penalty, and it primes the victim's family to think that anything less than the death penalty would be an injustice to their loved one's memory.

In one case, for example, the prosecution said in its closing argument, "He ought to get his dues, and I ask you ladies and gentlemen to go out there and convict this man of capital murder as charged in this indictment in the interest of justice ..." (*Henderson v. State* 1988:856). In another case, the prosecutor argued to the jurors that "they would be cooperating with evil and would themselves be involved in evil just like" the defendant if they recommended a life sentence (*King v. State* 1993:488).[4] These prosecutors reasoned that if the juries were going to vote for justice, they would need to sentence the accused to death. Clearly, there was no other option.

---

2. I want to thank Bob, Connie, Sarah and Greg Kotzbauer for allowing me to share with readers their experiences of the judicial system after the death of their daughter and sister, Lori. Throughout the chapter, it is their voice in italics. It is a humble honor and a difficult task to represent another person's story. But more importantly, it is a gift to know them and to call them friends.

3. Throughout this chapter, I use the term "victim" and "victim's family" interchangeably, because the family of the deceased are victims. When referring to the person who was killed, I use that specific terminology in order to eliminate confusion about the term "victim."

4. For further examples of cases in which the prosecution contends that a defendant's capital punishment must be chosen in order for justice to be served, see *People v. Floyd* 1970:81 and *People v. Montiel* 1993:1310.

Victims' families need to be given the opportunity to discern choices—choices of punishment, of ways the defendant can take responsibility, of what happens to the person that caused their loss, and more importantly, of what can be done to recognize their pain and uphold their right for attention and judicial closure. This chapter will examine the historical roles of the victim, the prosecution, the defense attorneys, and the accused in death penalty cases and recommend how legal professionals can produce meaningful solutions to justice for those most affected by the crime—the victim's family and the defendant.

Pattern of Justice

We were told right away by the district attorney that we were not the victims in this case; that this was a crime against the state. The prosecutor argued that because of the horrendous nature of the crime, justice demanded the death penalty for Dale Lash. We continued to ask the prosecutors to plead the case out. Each time we were told by the prosecutors we had no voice in the process. Our role was to sit by, wait and support what they were doing in court.

Few victims choose the death penalty. For many like the Kotzbauer family, it is the only option given to them. While there are victims who do support the death penalty and the government's pursuit of it, as it stands now, when the government makes the decision to seek the death penalty, that alone defines justice. After the grievous loss that murder causes, loved ones have an overwhelming need for justice that few in our society ever come to know. Rather than work to gain clarity about what justice means to the bereaved, the government typically argues that it knows what is required. This presumption eliminates the potential for greater healing for the victim's family because the focus of justice becomes what can happen *to* the accused, rather than what the accused can *do* in the name of justice—or, more importantly, what the victims can do for their empowerment. Families learn that their "choice" is to support the government's position.

Historically, victims do not have a role in the case against the accused. When a crime is committed, the government presents itself as the victim—it is the *United States v. John Smith* or the *State of California v. John Smith*, essentially arguing that the crime happened to the state, not to a person. From the first stages of the crime, the family of the victim had little choice: they did not choose to have their loved one murdered, and they were not consulted in how to move forward with this devastating loss. They were told to let the professionals do their job. Prosecutors may truly care about victims, but their energy is focused on the charges against the defendant. In their zeal to prove the guilt of the accused, prosecutors may be unaware of or choose to ignore the impact of their actions on the victims. Once the decision is made to seek the death penalty, the prosecution's two objectives are to prove the defendant's guilt and to convince jurors that the aggravating circumstances accompanying the murder justify sentencing the defendant to death. As one juror in the case against Washington, D.C., sniper John Muhammad said:

> During the six weeks of the trial, I became very angry at the prosecution, because in trying to recreate the horror, they bombarded us with the most gruesome and painful photographs. The prosecutors were careful to point out where the brain matter had splattered on the ground. To have them suggest we look at the brain matter was a little bit much. I still wake up with nightmares (Marhalik and Williams 2003).

The words of this juror give a glimpse into the profound impact that evidence has on those close to the crime. One can only imagine how a family experiences the legal system while attorneys dispute and diminish the facts of the death of the family's loved one. Regardless of the nature of the crime, legal teams on both sides use the raw circumstances of the death to bolster their case. The prosecution commonly places an emphasis on the horrific facts of the crime and the emotional response it provokes. Defense attorneys, on the other hand, look for ways that could diminish their client's culpability and implicate the victim into having responsibility for his or her own death. Mary Achilles, the Victim Advocate for the State of Pennsylvania, states plainly, "You have no rights when you are dead" (1998). Without integrating the needs, concerns, and interests of the victim's family, and with the prosecution deciding what outcome will be sought, is it honest to say that the family's needs for justice are being met?

As victims' experiences with the judicial system received more attention, Congress passed the Victim and Witness Act of 1982, which was enacted "to ensure that the Federal Government does all that is possible within limits of available resources to assist victims and witnesses of crime without infringing on the constitutional rights of defendants" (96 US Statutes 1982:1249). But in subsequent rulings, the courts argued that victims could not testify about how the crime affected their lives because such evidence violated the defendant's Eighth Amendment rights. The argument was that victim impact evidence introduced arbitrariness into the sentencing process based in part on the emotional nature of the victim's testimony. In 1991 *Payne v. Tennessee* overruled previous decisions and held that victims are allowed to give a victim impact statement explaining how the crime had affected their lives (Burr 2003). *Payne v. Tennessee* has come to be perceived as a significant victory for victims who wish to have more of a voice in the judicial proceedings.

Over the last twenty years, more statutes and state constitutional amendments have been passed that increase victims' judicial involvement in the crimes against them and their loved ones. While the various legislative acts were enacted with the right intention, they do not engage victims in the process, for two reasons: 1) the mandates of the laws are prescriptive, narrowly defining the role of the victim; and 2) the legislation includes only the prosecution as the voice for the victims.

Identifying the prosecution as the only source of information and support for victims and their families exacerbates the trauma and hostility experienced by victims who are trying to navigate the judicial system. Dick Burr, a respected defense attorney who has worked on capital cases for twenty-five years, argues that having the prosecution represent the victim's family's interests perpetuates the contentious attitude that defense attorneys have toward victims.

> The effort to constrain the outpouring of emotion in victim impact testimony can distort defense counsel's view of the individuals providing the testimony. Rather than seeing them as completely innocent and profoundly hurt, defense counsel are inclined to see them in an adversarial light—as impassioned and embittered adjuncts to the prosecution team (Burr 2003:526).

Because victims are discouraged, and in some states defense attorneys are actually barred[5] from contacting victims, both parties view one another with skepticism and fear. This limitation has not only defined a standard of what roles are expected in court, it has also created perceptions and attitudes that are difficult to change. Defense attorneys want to isolate the court (and themselves) from the victims' pain; prosecutors want to control the victim; and victims view defense attorneys as morally repugnant individuals who work to acquit their client and discourage the accused from accepting responsibility for his/her actions.

In death penalty cases, both legal teams have incredibly hard tasks before them. The high stakes of the possible outcome do not foster creative think-

---

5. In the state of Arizona, unless the victim approaches the defense team and requests to talk with them, the defense is not allowed to make any attempt to contact the victims without the consent of the prosecution. Arizona Constitution Article 2, Section 2.1 (added 1990), as supplemented by Ariz. Rev. Stat. Section 13-4433.

ing. That is, rather than looking for innovative ways to improve the process for the victim and the accused, the legal teams remain intransigent in the adversarial nature of the system. Both sides fight for control over facts and dispute what is argued as the truth. It is important to protect the innocent and the rights of the accused. But by making these issues the main focus, our system loses the opportunity to transform the way the accused and the victim's family could participate within the system and, more importantly, confront the shattering experience of a murder.

A New Idea

We went to the prosecuting attorneys and told them, "We don't want to go to court. We don't want to go to trial; plead this case out." We did not want to go to court because we had to raise a granddaughter. We were still experiencing the pain of losing our daughter and we didn't want the details of what happened to Lori being played in court. We also knew that this man, Dale Lash, did not begin raping and murdering women at the age of 37. He had to have a past of doing this. We thought it would give the victims' families more peace of mind as part of a plea agreement if he was told to name all the women he had raped or murdered and where.

The victim's family and the accused have needs specific to the crime that could be addressed within the legal system. The system's emphasis is on the rights of the accused, which are guaranteed by the U.S. Constitution. These guarantees include the right to a fair trial and the right to court-appointed counsel if the accused cannot afford one. If convicted, defendants also have a right to a review process that allows an appeal of their conviction and sentence. Because the underpinning of our judicial system has focused solely on these rights, the organic relationship in this situation between the victim and the defendant is overlooked. *They* are the parties that are most affected by the crime and concerned about what happened.

The Kotzbauers were clear about what they wanted and asked the district attorneys to address their need for a conviction and full, truthful disclosure. The family did not want to experience the appeals process and possible execution while their granddaughter was in the height of adolescence. Their reasons were personal and involved the defendant in two ways: they sought his confession to crimes against other women and his acceptance of responsibility for the rape and death of Lori so that they no longer had to interact with the legal system and could move forward in their healing. The

Kotzbauers wanted the prosecution to plead out the case and not go to trial, and they wanted an agreement for Lash to serve a life sentence without the possibility of release. Unfortunately, the district attorneys were not willing to address the Kotzbauers' needs. To have pursued the family's interests would have meant that the prosecution had to work with the defense team and defendant in a way that is not familiar to most legal professionals. In this situation, the victim's family was clear in what they wanted from the defendant and the legal system, but the prosecution was not prepared to hear an answer that was different from their own. If a victim's family expresses an interest in justice that is viewed as counter to the prosecution's pursuit of justice, it is too often assumed that they are at odds with one another. But the family's and societal view of justice are often the same—both need public admonishment of the offender for what happened and a conviction, to feel safe, and both hope that achieving these objectives will give them a sense of vindication.

The adversarial approach discourages the victim and the accused from stating what they need out of the process. By denying the victim a formal venue to consider what these needs may be and to express them to both legal teams, the family's only recourse for justice is the outcome deemed appropriate by the prosecution and jury. When the death penalty is sought, the defendant is discouraged from accepting responsibility for his/her actions or providing others with an understanding of what happened at the time of the crime. Due to these and other hurdles, the legal system denies the opportunity for reasonable judicial finality and fails to address the interests of both parties. Marc Mauer of The Sentencing Project observes:

> For far too long, we have created artificial barriers between victims and offender.... By pitting "victims' rights" against "prisoners' rights," we have done a disservice to all. A healthy society should do all it can to provide healing to those who have been harmed by crime while providing decent conditions to those who are imprisoned (1999:192).

Mauer's vision sets forth an idea that is within our grasp. Working within the judicial structure, the legal teams can incorporate an ethic that addresses the concerns of both the victim and the defendant. Some may argue that the defendant has given up all rights and that his/her concerns are irrelevant. While this perspective is understandable, if the accused sees that societal justice is not about revenge, he/she may be more apt to recognize and honor the victim's family's needs. Both legal teams are given the charge to reconcile the laws that have been broken and address the ramifications for the accused. This mandate is the very link needed to seek meaningful solutions to justice.

Victims need a sense of justice and the opportunity to be included in the process. Trauma is disempowering because victims feel little sense of control over what has happened. The judicial system exacerbates this sense by offering them no place to participate actively and meaningfully. For example, New Mexico corrections officer Ralph Garcia was stabbed to death in 1999 when he tried to stop a prison riot. His wife, Rachel, has waited over five years for a trial. In winter 2005 she learned about plea bargains that some of the prisoners had made to become witnesses against other inmates. She learned at the same time about financial settlements that the government had made, although not with her family. Ms. Garcia decided to write a letter to the editor of her local newspaper in hopes that her needs would be validated and addressed. She wrote, in part:

> I have had the opportunity to read all the reports and plea bargains to which I have a right. I was never informed about the plea bargains that actually took place—bargains that were offered in exchange for shorter sentences to witnesses for the district attorney. If I had known this, I would have detested it.
>
> I was also never told of sentencing or dates of release of these prisoners. And I was never told why restitution was not made to me but to the Department of Corrections instead. We are the ones at loss here, not the department. My rights as a victim have not been protected. I shouldn't have to go asking for information or ask that restitution be made.
>
> There are so many other things about which I also feel as if I was totally left in the dark. For instance, no one ever told me about the reparations program for victims. Five years later, I learned it was available to me. To this day I have not received my husband's belongings. I would especially like to have his wedding ring back ... (*Albuquerque Tribune* 2005).

In her letter to the editor, Ms. Garcia wrote that she no longer supported the death penalty and that she would rather have the money that would be spent on the trials to go toward reparations for victims' families. She learned that the prosecution had decided to seek the death penalty against three inmates, but those trials are still pending.

Although each person is different, it has been my experience in working with families that victims commonly have three needs: safety, justice, and the truth. Victims believe that safety and justice are achieved through a conviction in court. Unfortunately, they are led to believe the truth will be revealed by going to trial. Families often do not understand that the defendant rarely takes the stand and that it is the job of the defense team to attempt to suppress any evidence that may harm their client's interests. The responsibility the defense team has to its client directly contradicts the needs of the family of the victim.

Defendants have concerns as well. They need to know that their attorneys take their case seriously, will listen to what they think is important, and will defend their rights. They want to make sure that they are given a fair trial. In order for defense attorneys to truly counsel their clients, the defendants need to trust their lawyers. This takes time, due to the nature of the situation and the defendant-attorney relationship. Defendants typically do not want their families to hear testimony that dishonors their family; most would like to avoid the death penalty and want to emerge from the trial with some dignity intact (Olive 2005).

Prosecutors and defense attorneys can work toward a resolution of the case and maintain the integrity of the judicial process by engaging both the victim and the defendant with the same two questions: What is most important to you? What do you need from the judicial process?

Each party has a critical stake in the outcome, but due to the protracted adversarial approach, the system must help the victim and the accused determine their needs. The legal system cannot assume what is best for the victim; victims' families may want a range of issues addressed. Emily Lyons, a nurse who was severely injured at an abortion clinic bombing in Birmingham, Alabama, voiced her need for answers—about what happened and why—from both the government and Eric Rudolph, the man convicted of the bombing. "I have no concept of what a bomb does except for what happened to me. I want to know what happened. I want them to piece the day together for me" (Associated Press 2005).

Victims often want to know about their loved one's last moments. They want to know if the defendant is remorseful. They want to know that their family is safe from further harm. They want to make sure that the defendant will not be able to harm another family. Some families want the opportunity to meet with the defendant in a professionally facilitated and controlled setting, to have the defendant answer their questions directly. Others never want to see or hear the defendant again and think that without further judicial proceedings the accused will fade into media obscurity. Fallon Stubbs was injured and lost her mother due to the bombing of the Centennial Olympic Park to which Eric Rudolph pleaded guilty in April 2005. She wanted to see Rudolph in person and ended up feeling pity for him. "I was looking for a man this morning and I found a monster. He was taught to hate," she said after Rudolph's hearing (Markiewicz and Seymour 2005).

One reason family members want their questions answered is that it is an attempt to contain the pain. The experience of having a family member murdered is disorienting beyond explanation. What once made sense in daily living no longer has meaning. As people move forward in their healing, one aspect of the journey is to try to make sense of the senselessness (Bloom 1997). It is a time when people want to address the "how, why, where, and when" sorts of questions. Well-meaning people also have a natural tendency to want to shield people from this sort of information. We want to block victims from further pain; we want to surround families with support rather than the cold harshness of their loved one's death.

But what we may not understand is that by blocking families from this information or trying to answer their questions based on speculation rather than information coming directly from the offender, we inhibit the healing they seek. When doubt lingers because a trial did not answer victims' questions with the fullness they had hoped, families may struggle to accept explanations given by experts, jailhouse snitches, or the prosecution. Getting answers from the accused regarding the death of a family member is one way to stop the invisible tape of trauma that continually runs through victims' minds. And it is the legal system—both the prosecution and the defense attorneys—that can work toward aiding a family in this process.

Slight Shift, Significant Impact

It's difficult to explain the process victims feel when they are forced to go to trial in order to achieve justice. Our son, Greg, was trying to get married in Europe to a woman he had met just before Lori was killed. They had to postpone their wedding two times because of the continuances. For two years Sarah postponed getting a professional job because she felt that she couldn't leave a job to go to the trial. Did the court ever ask us about our lives? We never knew when we could do anything because times were constantly being changed in deference to the defense team's requests. We lived two states away and we knew no one in the area where the trial was going to be held. We had to set up babysitting for six weeks for Alexis so that we could attend the trial. It was an enormous process. I had to buy plane tickets for two kids from across the country. They had to drop everything they were doing to come to the trial, only to be given days' notice that, "No, the trial is not going to happen this time." Is that justice?

Up to this point, I have described how the legal teams ignore or stymie the process of meeting victims' family's needs in capital cases. However, as I have alluded, there are ways to work within the judicial system; slightly altering the way legal professionals regard the victims' families can produce significant outcomes—in terms of saving money and time, securing victim and societal safety, providing greater victim satisfaction, and increasing the possibility of reaching a settlement in the case. The work is loosely called "defense-based victim outreach" within the defense community, but it is a bit of a misnomer. It is a *values*-based approach that requires both the prosecution and the defense teams to have experts actively engage victims' families in conversation about what is most important to them and what they need from the judicial process. For years, prosecution teams have employed victim advocates to notify victims of their rights and of court dates related to their case. Some victim advocate offices, such as those in Pennsylvania and Illinois, are well established and able to provide victims with a broad array of services. The reason victim outreach cannot be done solely by the prosecution—as it historically has been rendered—is that defense teams too have information that is helpful to the victim.

If we look at the relationships produced by the crime, it brings us back to the one not formally addressed, between the victim and the accused. To follow the thread from this relationship, we can see how both legal teams need to recognize and create professional work relationships with the victim. Since capital crimes almost inevitably involve murder, the only person who can knowledgeably discuss the details and circumstances of the crime is the defendant. The victim's family may want this information; but the defendant's interests are protected by the defense team (they act as the gatekeeper for their client), and the prosecution does not have access to the defendant. Therefore, the prosecution needs to rely on the defense team to work both with their client and with the victim's family to understand what the family's interests are and how the defendant can attend to these issues. The prosecution can work with the family to understand what can and cannot happen due to possible legal constraints and can ensure that the outreach is in the family's best interests. Both legal teams need to understand that they can play a role in aiding the victims while proceeding with their duties. This shift requires each team to carry new responsibilities; but overall, if done from the beginning— in the pretrial period—and carried out with integrity, the approach can prevent further harm to the victim's family and may result in less of an investment of resources than the traditional legal approach.

Many challenges could prevent attorneys from adopting this type of approach. One is that the prosecution has an obligation to ensure that the process meets the requirements of the law, that it satisfies society's need for justice, and that the outcome protects others from further harm. The defense team, meanwhile, has an obligation to ensure that the government has not wrongly accused their client of the crime, that their client receives a vigorous defense, and that the defendant receives a fair sentence. The obligations of both legal teams are tremendously time consuming. And as compassionate as both sides are for those they represent, the adversarial nature of their work fosters selective compassion (Branham 2004).

In order for this approach to be successful, the work must be done by individuals who are professionally trained in a values-based approach to working with victims. Assuming the family favors this approach, the work cannot be done by someone with an agenda other than to seek ways to more fully engage the victim's family in the legal process. The victim outreach specialist's job is to work with the victims to flesh out decisions in order to create a menu of options that are possible within the legal framework and more directly affect the family than a traditional trial may offer. This process honors the family because it is about what can be done *for* them rather than *to* someone else (i.e., the defendant).

The most effective outcome for victims' families often can be a plea agreement, because it is a legally binding document that can effectively address the family's needs and because it ends the judicial process—both the trial and appeals—against the defendant. A plea agreement requires the defendant to accept responsibility; it ensures a conviction and a sentence respectful of the crime; and the defendant must recognize and abide by the family's interests that are included in the contract.[6] In these situations, the prosecution and the defense work with professional victim outreach specialists, the victims, and the defendant. The approach works regardless of whether a family is in favor of the death penalty or not because it broadens the dialogue from what can happen to the defendant to how the judicial system—and the defendant—can address issues that affect the family.

When a family works with a victim outreach specialist and wants the case to go to trial, the family has the opportunity to be heard and to make a reasoned decision. The effort of victim outreach does not stop at this point—it is the job of the specialist to continue to support the family throughout the legal process. One responsibility of victim outreach work is to inform attorneys of victims' concerns about how the trial proceeds. With this awareness, attorneys are able to address issues such as informing a family about delays; being careful not to schedule court dates around the murder victim's birth-

---

6. For examples of plea agreements that included the families' interests and ended the defendants' legal proceedings, including the appeals process, see *United States v. Dean* 1998 and *United States v. Stayner* 1999.

day, wedding anniversary, or the anniversary of the death; allowing the family to have input about the trial date, because family members will want to be present for the trial and will have to adjust their schedules accordingly; using the deceased's name rather than referring to him/her as "the victim"; and not desecrating the memory of the deceased victim. The effort of defense-based victim outreach is to broaden the defense team's scope of compassion to include the victim's family and to show both legal teams that while the system may need to be adversarial to protect the rights of the accused, it does not have to be adversarial toward the victims. Victims obviously did not choose to be a part of the proceedings of a capital case—they would rather have their loved one still alive. Accordingly, it is imperative that both legal teams remember that victims should be given every consideration throughout the process.

The shift seems counterintuitive within the legal community, but where defense-based victim outreach has been used over the course of the last eight years, more opportunities have been provided to victims' families to have greater involvement in the legal proceedings—both at trial and in plea agreements. Both legal teams have had a role in the development of this work, and many have made great strides to include victim outreach in their practice while still litigating the case. It is important to look at the barriers both sides face and how they have begun to transform the historical mode of representation.

Defense Attorneys

It was difficult to lose Lori to such a senseless murder. What added to the difficulty was to have our lives be put on hold for a trial. The court granted the defense team's requests for continuances on Dale Lash's case, which pushed our pain deeper. One year went by, two, three. On Alexis' fourth birthday, jury selection began.

Defense attorneys have earned a reputation for being cold-hearted. Many would scoff at the idea of introducing themselves to the victim's family, much less offering their condolences for the family's loss. Defense attorneys fear that such a remark is an admission of their client's guilt. Attorneys are also afraid of the raw pain that victims feel and know that some of their anger can be transferred to them as representatives of persons accused of killing their loved one. They would rather pretend that they do not see the victims in the court hallway or bathroom because they are not prepared to be humane in the enormity of such loss and litigation. The standards of the adversarial nature of capital cases, of the victim being the "property" of the prosecution, and of the defense zealously representing its client have perpetuated the isolation the defense team maintains from the victim's family. But over the last eight years, defense attorneys have begun to learn that being simultaneously compassionate for their client and for the victim's family does not detract from their work.

It would be inaccurate to say that defense attorneys do not have an agenda; their job is to save their client's life. The charges and possible sentence against their client are so great that defense attorneys can become myopic and focus only on what may help their client avoid the death penalty. Attorneys may view the victim's family as collateral in helping with this pursuit. And when victims see the agenda is about saving the defendant's life, with little regard to what their own needs are, the family may well feel further violated and end any communication with the defense. Some defense attorneys relish the idea of going to trial and fighting for their client's acquittal. These attorneys most likely would not consider using a values-based approach in reaching out to the victim's family. In light of these realities, it is imperative that the defense community continue to educate attorneys about victim sensitivity and the value and ethics of using a victim outreach specialist, and to have attorneys who have used this approach in their cases share their experiences.

The work of a victim outreach specialist can have a profound impact on defendants, the victim's family, and defense attorneys themselves. Attorneys are able to appreciate that the results can maintain integrity for both their client and the victim's family. In *United States v. Lentz* (2001), the defense team developed a relationship with the victim's family over the course of time before the trial. The case had a heightened emotional element in that Lentz was accused of kidnapping and murdering his ex-wife; both families wanted custody of the Lentzes' young daughter. Although members of Doris Lentz's family wanted the government to seek the death penalty, the sister of Doris Lentz agreed to testify on behalf of the defense team during the penalty phase of the trial. She had no interest in protecting Lentz's life, but she was concerned about how losing both parents would affect her niece. During the testimony, defense attorney Judy Clarke asked what hopes the aunt had for her niece. She replied that she hoped that when her niece was a mature adult, she would be able to confront her father and ask him what happened to her mother (*United States v. Lentz* 2001). In this situation, the defense was able to honor the victim's family by asking about their interest for their niece while pursuing the defense of the client. The jury sentenced Jay Lentz to life without the possibility of release, thus giving him and his daughter the opportunity to continue to have a relationship.

Defense teams that integrate victim outreach into their practice see tangible results for their clients, not only benefits to the victim's family. By creating a professional relationship with the family, the defense attorneys simultaneously present a model of compassion for the victim's family and the defendant. Leading by example has the potential to convey what attorneys want citizens—the jury pool—to remember: that we can do justice without hate, and justice does not mean revenge. Also, if victim outreach efforts develop so that the family wants to explore the defendant's willingness to agree to help satisfy their judicial needs and concerns, the work can produce a plea agreement. A plea agreement shortens the judicial process, which saves tax dollars and the legal community's time, not to mention the defendant's life. Victim outreach also can assist the defense team in working with their client. This approach offers the defendant options, including making decisions about the process, reducing the shame that a trial would bring to his or her family, and accepting responsibility for what happened. The challenge for defense attorneys in using the values-based approach is to move from a position of considering only what is best for their client to considering what is best for all parties.

Prosecution

One struggle that I still cannot explain is my reaction to Lash's trial. When we were told that our only choice was to support the death penalty, we ended up doing just that. It is this mindset that happens once you are forced into this system; it becomes competitive. It's competitive in that you want the most for your child. You want the jury to give the maximum sentence possible. Somehow in your mind if the jury doesn't give the maximum sentence possible, it's a way of the jury saying to you, "Your child was not that important. Your child's death wasn't important enough to get the death sentence." And it messes with you as a family who didn't even want to go to trial to all of a sudden be so locked in to make sure this man gets the death penalty. Families should never have to go through that type of thinking.

It may be possible to imagine what it would be like to be responsible for deciding whether to seek the death penalty against an accused person, but I do not think one can fully understand the pressure that prosecutors must experience when they reach this decision. The struggle to discern the facts and aggravating circumstances of the case, the societal outcry for justice, the victim's family's pain, and the political pressure are enormous facts to consider. But in the end, the prosecution must make the decision and then pursue the sentence with as much focus as the defense team puts into trying to prevent it.

With the state taking on the role of the victim, the prosecution often becomes so focused on the outcome that it may lose sight of what the best interests may be for the state and the victim's family. Prosecuting attorneys who personalize a crime can create a dynamic that makes it appear that they are seeking revenge, not justice. Another shortcoming of acting as the victim is that the prosecution may not discuss the reality of a capital case with the victim's family. Victims often do not understand the amount of time that will pass before a trial, or that if the defendant is sentenced to death, he/she has the right to appeal the conviction and sentence. The average length of time before an execution is almost eleven years while the defendant challenges conviction and sentence through the legal process (Bonczar and Snell 2004). As one family member wrote, the death sentence locked the family into a seventeen-year relationship with the defendant and his family (Brill 2001). This is not what families expect when they begin the legal process.

Another difficulty that presents itself in capital cases is similar to what happened with the Kotzbauers. When a case moves toward trial, the family can be further traumatized if the jury convicts the defendant and sentences him/her to a sentence less than death. Families feel affronted by the idea that somehow their loved one was not important enough for the death penalty. How could the jury sit through all the facts and testimony of so many people and decide that the defendant was worth saving but their loved one was not? A capital case escalates the expectation by narrowly defining justice.

Prosecutors who pursue a conviction of the accused *and* honor the family's needs do a great service for both society and the family, regardless of whether the outcome results from a plea or a trial. They are ensuring public safety and meting out justice. In Florida, a man named David Nolan was accused of murdering Michael Sessions. Mr. Nolan wanted the court to sentence him to death for his crime. On the other hand, Mr. Sessions' mother, Janie Shivers, wanted judicial finality in the case and thought that Nolan should have to consider his actions and the consequences as he spent the rest of his life in prison (Angier 2004). The prosecution reached a settlement with the defense team, which had to work to get their client to agree not to seek the death penalty based on the wishes of the victim's family.

Finding the Way

After Lash was sentenced to death, the state's victim advocate walked us out of the courtroom. She was still holding the door into the courtroom open when she pumped her arm in the air saying, "Yes! Yes!" I looked at her and said, "There is no joy in this—there is nothing to celebrate. Nobody won here."

Historically, the judicial system embedded deep suspicion, hostility, fear, and trauma into legal proceedings. The checks and balances of the adversarial process that are designed to protect the rights of the accused led to ignoring the needs of the victims. The legal system became so focused on the rule of law that it forgot that crime deeply affects people. In attempting to ameliorate this state of affairs, victim rights groups and politicians pushed for more victim involvement within the system, gaining formal rights to notification and participation. While these successes are important, the involvement of victims has become so politicized that we do a disservice to the very people the laws are intended to help. Victims should never be put in the middle of the adversarial process. They should never have to choose between talking with the prosecution and the defense in order to ensure that their needs are being met. The legal teams should accommodate the victim's family so that the adversarial nature of the legal proceedings continue to protect the accused but do not adversely affect the family. And finally, the rights that have been created for victims exclude the very link that can aid the family's healing—formal access to the defendant.

The prosecution has become so zealous in the protection of the victim that attorneys miss the opportunity to help discern the best interests of justice for society and the family. Without dialogue involving what the defendant can do for the victim's family, what seems like a victory to others may not be a victory for the family. State attorneys need to keep a skeptical eye on defense-based victim outreach, to help ensure that the defense attorney does not harm the victim's family. Defense attorneys need to embrace an ethical values-based approach of reaching out to the victim's family and work within the parameters that guide victim outreach specialists. It will take years to undo the hostility and fear that have become the norm in capital cases. No outreach to victims' families can undo the trauma that they have experienced with the death of their loved one. But the legal teams need to understand that while their job is to focus on the laws that have been violated, there is great potential to incorporate the needs of those who have been most affected by the violation. And it can begin when both teams reach out to the other side.

References

Achilles, Mary. 1998. Personal Communication.

Angier, David. 2004. "Victim's Mother: Killer Need Time to 'Consider His Act.'" *The News Herald*. 29 June 2004. Available at http://66.21.108.67/interconnect/browser/intercon.dll.

Arizona Constitution. 1990. Article 2, Section 2.1.

Arizona Revised Statute, Section 13-4433.

Associated Press. 2005. "Rudolph's Lawyer an Expert at Deals." Cable News Network. Available at http://cnn.com/2005/LAW/04/09/rudolph.attorney.ap/index.html.

Bloom, Sandra. 1997. *Creating Sanctuary*. New York: Routledge, p. 225.

Bonczar, Thomas P. and Snell, Tracy L. 2004. "Capital Punishment 2003." *Bureau of Justice Statistics Bulletin*, November 2004, NCJ206627;, available at www.ojp.usdoj.gov/bjs/pub/pdf/cp03.pdf.

Branham, Kelly. 2004. "Defense-based Victim Outreach: Engaging in Peace-making." *First National Seminar on the Development and Integration of Mitigation Evidence*, New Orleans, LA; 17 April 2004.

Brill, William. 2001. "Finality? Not for Us, and It's 17 Years Later." *Washington Post*, 29 April 2001 (editorial page).

Burr, Richard. 2003. "Litigating with Victim Impact Testimony: The Serendipity that Has Come from *Payne v. Tennessee*." *Cornell Law Review* 88:517–29.

Garcia, Rachel. 2005. "Don't Kill the Killers." *Albuquerque Tribune*, 15 March 2005 (editorial page).

Henderson v. State. 1988. 584 So. 2d 841 (Ala. Crim. App.).

King v. State. 1993. 623 So. 2d 486 (Fla.).

Marhalik and Williams, "The Trial After the Trial." 2003. *New York Times*, 21 December 2003 (Back Page of *New York Times Sunday Magazine*).

Markiewicz, David and Add Seymour Jr. 2005. "Victims Find Closure on Own Terms." *Atlanta Journal-Constitution*, 14 April 2005. Available at www.ajc.com/metro/content/metro/atlanta/0405/14ervictims.html.

Mauer, Marc. 1999. *Race to Incarcerate*. New York: The New Press.

Olive, Mark. 2005. Personal Communication.

People v. Floyd. 1970. 464 P.2d 64 (Cal.).

People v. Montiel. 1993. 855 P.2d 1277 (Cal.).

United States v. Dean. 1998. (D. VT) (2:98-CR-63-01).

United States v. Lentz. 2001. (E.D. VA) (CR-01-CR-150).

United States v. Stayner. 1999. (E.D. CA) (CR-F-99-5217 AWI).

Victim and Witness Protection Act of 1982. Public Law No 97-291, 96 Stat. 1248 (1982), codified in various sections of Title 18, U.S.C.

CHAPTER 20

LEARNING FROM HOMICIDE CO-VICTIMS: A UNIVERSITY-BASED PROJECT

Michael L. Radelet and
Dawn Stanley

Introduction

Supporters and opponents of the death penalty share many areas of agreement. Both groups voice equal levels of outrage about the criminal violence that plagues our communities. Both believe that our communities and political leaders need to do more to reduce our high rates of criminal victimization. Both groups believe that those convicted of murder deserve harsh punishments. This chapter focuses on yet another area of accord: we all agree that we need to learn more about how to help families of homicide victims and act in ways that implement those ideas.

While disagreement remains about the ultimate wisdom of capital punishment, arguments supporting the death penalty have undergone significant shifts in the past twenty-five years. A generation ago, by far the most widely used pro-death penalty argument was deterrence: we need to execute murderers to send a discouraging message to potential killers and thereby reduce the homicide rate. A second important argument from this era focused on cost savings: Why should our tax money pay for the survival of brutal murderers? A third popular justification was Biblical, voiced with frequent citations to Old Testament verses in which the death penalty was used or justified.

As those arguments declined in popularity among students of the death penalty and the general public, retribution has emerged today as the most frequently cited justification for capital punishment (Radelet and Borg 2000).

More specifically, today more than ever before, the purported needs of families of homicide victims are being used as a way to justify the death penalty. This rationale maintains that murderers need to be punished severely, and that life imprisonment without parole provides insufficient punishment for the unimaginable pains that the killer caused.[1] In this line of reasoning, the death penalty gives the families of homicide victims (also referred to as "co-victims") a sense that justice has been done—that the killer has "paid" for his or her crime—and a sense of safety that comes along with the assurance that the person who killed their loved one will never again harm another person. As one woman said, watching the hearse that carried the executed killer of her husband, "The ordeal is over. It's been a long time coming.... It was a relief to know that he is no more—that he's not sitting up there with those evil, evil thoughts of his" (Vandiver 2003:623). Although insufficient data have been collected to study whether executions actually provide long-term relief to co-victims, and some evidence suggests the opposite (e.g., Goldberg 2003[2]), the notion that capital punishment serves this goal has clearly struck a chord with some segments of the American public.

In this chapter, we describe efforts we have made to learn more about the needs of families of homicide victims, and university-based initiatives we have undertaken to begin addressing some of those needs. After describing our informal work with family members of homicide victims, we describe how and why we focused our efforts on those families dealing with a murder that has not been solved. Finally, we describe work we are doing with our students to help organize these families into a group where common interests and concerns can be pursued. We believe that universities are ideal settings for such work, that the work benefits both families and students, and hope this essay will lead to the development of similar programs and experiments elsewhere. In our view, investing resources in programs of this general nature is far more responsive to the real needs of murder victims' families than pursuing the uncertain promises of capital punishment.

---

1. Today the death penalty is available in thirty-eight states. In thirty-six of those (all but New Mexico and Texas), offenders convicted of capital crimes can be sentenced to life imprisonment without parole. See Death Penalty Information Center 2004.

2. According to Goldberg, "No psychological study has ever concluded that the death penalty brings 'closure' to anyone except the person who dies, and there's circumstantial evidence that it can prolong the suffering of families." She argues that those who have "actually been through the tortuously long emotional and legal process from one death to another" rarely find the experience one that brings long-lasting relief.

Listening to Families of Homicide Victims

The senior author of this paper has been dealing with death-row inmates and their families for twenty-five years. Michael Radelet's experiences include giving testimony in seventy-five death penalty cases throughout the United States, several hundred visits to various death rows, going through last visits with approximately fifty death-row inmates and their families, and researching a wide array of death penalty issues, including matters of concern to families of death-row inmates (Radelet et al. 1983).

Initially, this work did not involve any contact with families of homicide victims.[3] Then, in the early 1990s, Radelet was invited to participate in a death penalty debate at the University of Florida Law School.[4] He opposed executions; the person speaking in support was Pat Cadena, head of the Gainesville chapter of Parents of Murdered Children (POMC). During the debate, Radelet tried to make the point that lots of anti-death penalty people supported families of homicide victims, pointing to religious leaders as examples. He argued (by hunch rather than experience) that one of the chief sources of support for families of homicide victims has always been from religious communities. After the debate, Cadena pulled Radelet aside and began to explain that religious leaders rarely give needed support to the families, and, in fact, often say and do things that contribute to their anguish.

That interaction began a close friendship that ended only with Cadena's death in 2002. She was an extraordinary teacher. She invited Radelet to POMC meetings (initially to learn about the lack of involvement or even re-victimization of family members of murder victims by the religious community). Radelet became very active with the group and eventually won two "Special Service" Awards from them. In 1994 POMC, the sociology department at the University of Florida, and a local anti-death penalty group (Gainesville Citizens Against the Death Penalty) co-sponsored a daylong seminar for religious leaders to learn how to better address the needs of families of homicide victims (Pulley 1994). Cadena and many members of POMC still supported the death penalty, and Radelet still opposes it, but everyone found they had much more in common than they initially thought. In their interactions, opinions on the death penalty became a bit like political or religious preferences — we

---

3. A similar history of first working with death-row inmates and then with families of homicide victims has been recounted by Sister Helen Prejean, a New Orleans nun whose ministry has attracted widespread attention (Prejean 1993).

4. Radelet was on the faculty of the University of Florida, 1979–2001.

assumed that those in the group had diverse positions, but we rarely (if ever) talked about them.

Shortly before Radelet joined the faculty at the University of Colorado in 2001, the 17-year-old daughter of a university sociology professor was murdered. Radelet attended part of the trial with this friend, who in turn invited Radelet to speak on the topic of capital punishment at a meeting of the Front Range (Denver) chapter of POMC. At first glance this may not seem to be an audience that was interested in listening to an anti-death penalty speaker. However, it turned into a wonderful night.

As is the custom at POMC meetings, the evening began with the members (about fifty) sitting in a circle, sharing the details of the murder of their loved ones (see Schlosser 1997). Given the speaker's topic, they were also invited to share their feelings about the death penalty. The first few co-victims were strongly in favor. The next few opposed the death penalty because they thought that life imprisonment would be a more retributive sentence. Some spoke in opposition because of religious beliefs or a feeling that the death penalty was racist. Then, Howard Morton spoke.

Howard and Virginia Morton's oldest son, Guy, was murdered in Arizona in 1975 (because of misidentification of the remains by the medical examiner, Guy was classified as "missing" for a dozen years before his body and cause of death were properly identified). To this day, the killer has still not been identified or apprehended. Morton spoke about the monetary costs of the death penalty, with each execution costing millions of dollars more than life imprisonment. He noted that Colorado had carried out only one execution since 1967 and had only three people on death row, making the death penalty irrelevant to over 99 percent of the families of homicide victims. He argued that if communities really wanted to help families of homicide victims, financial and other resources could be better used. His suggestion: focus more efforts on solving the crime and arresting the offender. The severity of punishment, he argued, is less important than identifying the perpetrator and making sure that at least *some* punishment is meted out.

A fortnight later, Morton spoke to 100 students enrolled in Radelet's senior-level criminology course at the University of Colorado. With him was a woman whose son was murdered in 1984 while attending the University of Colorado. Both guests talked about a group that Morton was forming called "Families of Homicide Victims and Missing Persons," or FOHVAMP.[5] At the end of their lecture, a dozen students encircled the podium, asking the speak-

---

5. See www.unresolvedhomicides.org.

ers how they could help. Dawn Stanley, a graduate student then interested in studying the needs of families of homicide victims, soon joined the group.

The Problem of Unresolved Homicides

Before the death penalty can have any relevance, the crime must be solved. Nationally, the proportion of homicides cleared by arrest dropped from 79 percent in 1976 to 63 percent in 2000 (Bureau of Justice Statistics 2002). In other words, some 37 percent of those who committed a murder in 2000 were not apprehended for their crime. In 2002, 64 percent of American homicides were cleared by arrest (Federal Bureau of Investigation 2003:222). In 2003 in Colorado, there were 168 homicide offenses (Colorado Bureau of Investigation 2003a) and 112 arrests for homicide (Colorado Bureau of Investigation 2003b), a clearance rate of 66.7 percent.

Charles Wellford and James Cronin designed a multi-state study of 798 homicides from 1994–95 in four large cities, to learn what factors affected the clearance rate (Wellford and Cronin 2000; 1999). They identified three principal factors. First, the type of homicide helps determine how readily the crime will be solved. For example, domestic homicides regularly result in arrests, while drug-related murders are the most difficult to solve. Similarly, increasing numbers of stranger-on-stranger killings in recent decades have made solving homicides more complicated. A second factor related to the success of solving homicides is the reaction of bystanders. If members of the community fear the police, they are less likely to assist with investigations or prosecutions. A final factor is police resources. Do law enforcement authorities have the personnel needed to do a competent homicide investigation? Do they have the training in proper evidence collection and access to decent forensic laboratories?

Wellford and Cronin identified fifteen significant factors associated with higher clearance rates. One explicit message from their work is that homicide investigators need more resources. Their data indicated that with better training and more homicide detectives, the rate of solving homicides would be significantly increased. It is particularly important, according to Wellford and Cronin's research, to assign at least three or four officers to a homicide case immediately upon discovery of the crime (assigning five or more officers had no significant effect on the clearance rate unless at least eleven officers were assigned to the case). This number of investigators allows for a twenty-four-hour-a-day opportunity to work on the homicide and maximizes the ability of the police to collect the information needed to solve the crime. Other factors associated with high clearance rates include having the medical examiner prepare a body chart of the victim; running computer checks on various suspects, guns, and witnesses; and interviewing witnesses, friends, and acquaintances of the victim.

Another factor associated with a better clearance rate is simply keeping track of those crimes that remain unsolved. We were amazed to learn that there is not a national tracking system for unsolved homicides, and no state (to our knowledge) has developed a tracking system or even a simple list of homicides that remain unsolved. While some individual police departments have developed "cold-case squads" and their own tracking systems for unsolved homicides, anecdotal evidence from families of homicide victims suggests that once a murder is over three months old, it typically moves to the police department's "back burner" as newer cases are given higher priority.

FOHVAMP

Families of Homicide Victims and Missing Persons (FOHVAMP) is an organization in Colorado comprised primarily of families who are dealing with the lifelong challenges of 1) experiencing the murder of a loved one, and 2) living with the knowledge that the murderer has not been identified or brought to justice. Other members include those with a longtime missing relative who usually believe that the loved one was murdered (but for various reasons have failed in their attempts to get the police to agree). The organization was founded in 2001 by Howard Morton and Mark Reichert. It now has over 150 active members in fourteen states, representing slightly more than 100 murder victims.

The group is not intended to be a support group (although members often do find support from others experiencing the same frustrations). Instead, this is an activist group with a primary mission to work with police departments to increase the attention paid to unresolved homicides. To that end, FOHVAMP raises money for rewards for information relating to the murders (working with CrimeStoppers and independently), funds billboards that seek new leads (when funding from outside sources allows), and attempts to educate police departments about how they can improve their work (and relations with families of homicide victims). Members also work on "consciousness-raising" activities in the community by speaking with local media, maintaining a website (see FOHVAMP 2005), and speaking on college campuses.[6]

---

6. In early 2004 an hourlong interview about FOVAMP was aired on several Colorado public radio stations. It is available at http://www.cpr.org/co_matters/ (enter "Howard Morton" in their search engine).

FOHVAMP's work with law enforcement also includes passing on leads to the police about unresolved homicides. Occasional leads on homicides are made available through the FOHVAMP website. In addition, family members of homicide victims (whether or not they are formal members of FOHVAMP) occasionally provide leads on the case that are passed on to law enforcement through FOHVAMP. These leads may surface because the family member feels more comfortable talking with FOHVAMP members than with the police, or because so much time has passed since the homicide that the family member decides to reveal new facts that (for a wide array of reasons) he or she decided not to disclose at the time of the homicide. In addition, members (and students) have many conversations with law enforcement officials that heighten awareness of each other's concerns and constraints, generally paving the way for better communication to occur in the future.

One of the biggest challenges faced by FOHVAMP is identifying families who have a loved one who has either been missing for an extended period (usually around two years) or was victimized by an unresolved homicide. As an organization with no funding sources other than a few small grants and member contributions and unpaid staff, it is extraordinarily difficult to find the time and resources necessary to identify all the unsolved homicides in Colorado and then to track down the family members of the victims. This process becomes even more challenging when family members have left the state.

The Homicide Victimization Course

After Howard Morton spoke to Radelet's criminology course in October 2002, so many student volunteers came forward that Morton and Radelet decided to structure the group into a formal course, where students would enroll and receive college credit (rather than a paycheck) for their services. Much like standard internship courses, this experience was offered as a special topics course in spring 2003. A dozen students matriculated (eleven females and one male). The class met once a week for three hours, and students were expected to complete at least six hours of work each week outside of the classroom. Howard Morton drove fifty-five miles from his home to Boulder each week to attend the class. Approximately half of the students continued with the work after the semester's end (some for independent-study credit, some as volunteers).

In addition to meeting with families of homicide victims and learning from them, the class had two distinct goals: to identify unsolved homicide cases in Colorado and to locate family members of each victim. In order to identify all the unsolved homicide cases in Colorado, each student was assigned responsibility for designated counties (one large county or several smaller counties). The student proceeded to contact the municipal police departments and sheriff's offices in each county. In most cases, both local police departments and a sheriff's office exist within a given county. (For example, Boulder County has a sheriff's office as well as police departments in the cities of Boulder, Longmont, Lafayette, Westminster, and others.) In order to locate family members of each homicide victim, the students became, in essence, amateur private investigators. They searched newspapers for articles related to the homicide (including funeral notices and obituaries) and, if a survivor could be identified, used Internet resources to find current addresses and phone numbers for those family members. The students did not directly contact the family members of victims. Instead, members of FOHVAMP who (unlike the students) had a loved one whose homicide was unresolved made the initial phone call to the survivors.

From the beginning, there were complications and unanticipated challenges. Not one of the several dozen police or sheriff's departments maintained a list of unsolved homicides from their jurisdiction. Initially, few were eager to check their files and send us the information, even after being reminded that unsolved homicides are a matter of public record. The students were bombarded with excuses: no one tracked that information, the records were kept on paper (not electronically) and no one had the time to search through all of them, the student could not have the information until the county attorney had approved its release, or the students were informed (falsely) that there simply were not any unsolved homicides in the relevant jurisdiction. Occasionally, the student was directed to the person who worked at the station the longest (e.g., a secretary) and relied on that person's recollection to identify the unsolved homicides.

A handful of departments fell at one of the ends of the spectrum: extremely helpful or doggedly uncooperative. Those that were uncooperative received letters from Radelet on University of Colorado letterhead requesting the same information the student had sought. In some cases, it took several letters and a dozen or more phone calls and faxes before a response was received. One sheriff did not respond until Radelet contacted the local newspaper and encouraged reporters to write an article about how the sheriff was snubbing families of homicide victims (the sheriff thereafter provided us with a list of the unresolved murders within forty-eight hours).

As soon as a student received a list of unsolved homicides from a police department, he or she began the process of learning more about the crime and identifying family members of the victim. We did not request names of the homicide victims' next of kin from the police departments because many departments claimed that those names were confidential, and we wanted to focus our initial efforts simply on obtaining names of victims. But once the name of a victim was known, the student would typically begin the search for surviving relatives by gathering newspaper articles about the homicide (including obituaries and funeral notices). Search engines at the university library, such as Lexus/Nexus, ProQuest, and Dialog@Carl, were used for these searches. Unfortunately, the students could not find newspaper coverage or published obituaries for many of the cases. When a student was able to learn the name of a surviving family member, he or she began searching for a current address and phone number for that person. Typically, the students used Internet sources for this task, such as WhitePages.com, Google.com, People-Search.net, and www.reversephonedirectory.com.

Students were able to find the homicide victim's relatives and current contact information for the relative(s) in only about 10 percent of the unresolved homicide cases. They then provided the following information to FOHVAMP: the name of the victim, the circumstances of the homicide, the investigating officer's name and contact information, and the name(s) and contact information for the family member(s) of the victim. FOHVAMP then contacted the family member(s) and offered them information about the organization. The victim's story and the investigating officer's name and contact information were added to the FOHVAMP website, so that anyone with information about the homicide could contact the appropriate police department. In addition, the information collected by students was collated and later used to create a database of all known unsolved homicides in Colorado.

One problem confronted in the class was keeping students motivated. The students regularly faced uncooperative law enforcement officials and frequently were unable to collect information about family members, and these experiences were frustrating. Although the students usually took uncooperative law enforcement officials more or less in stride, they became overwhelmed at what they perceived as their failure to collect enough information on family members of the homicide victims. Even though they were forewarned that they could expect a success rate of roughly one in ten (that is, finding information on any family members of one victim for every ten victims on the unsolved homicide list), there was frustration when this prediction became a reality. Meeting weekly as a group and especially meeting members of FOHVAMP helped rekindle and bolster their motivation, and hearing that other students faced the same problems helped build their persistence. However, any course that follows this model would be advised to include ways to encourage students when they discover that it is very hard to locate family members of victims of unresolved homicides. Meeting families of homicide victims and learning about their experiences is key to sustaining the interest and effort.

A second problem we encountered in the course was developing research techniques. It would not be an understatement to say that none of us knew what we were doing when we started. However, all of us agreed that if we waited until we knew what we were doing, we would never do anything. We started with what we had and learned from our mistakes. The students who continued their research for a second semester were assisted by a private investigator who volunteered his services to FOHVAMP. When the students reached a dead end, they could give what research they had completed to the investigator, who sometimes was able to locate family members using search techniques not available to the students. Enlisting the assistance of journalists or journalism students sometimes proved beneficial, because of their having access to nonpublic newspaper databases.

Finally, FOHVAMP and the student volunteers struggled with database management. Students were collecting large amounts of data, and it was imperative to create a database that could be used by FOHVAMP. At the time, FOHVAMP had a volunteer who created and maintained the organization's website, but lacked other volunteers with extensive computer experience. The majority of the data initially was kept in an Excel file (which several FOHVAMP members could use), and also was recorded on paper. Eventually, new volunteers with computer experience joined FOHVAMP and a new database was developed. We strongly recommend that any group that wishes to follow this model have at least one student/volunteer who is capable with database management programs and can train others to use the database.

The students were successful on several fronts. Because of their work, for the first time there exists at least a partial database of unsolved homicides in Colorado. No law enforcement agency had previously collected this information nor, mysteriously, has any law enforcement agency requested the list created by the students. The students also were able to identify several dozen family members of the victims of unsolved homicides, many of whom formally joined FOHVAMP. As a learning experience, the students gained a firsthand understanding of why so many families of victims of unresolved homicides have very negative feelings about the investigating police department.

Currently, a half-dozen undergraduate students each semester continue this work, either as volunteers or as part of independent studies or internships directed by Radelet (who is now a member of FOHVAMP's board of directors). Our list of unresolved Colorado homicides now numbers more than 400, but it is far from complete, so we plan to continue our work on developing the list for the foreseeable future. Students also help with a wide array of miscellaneous tasks for FOHVAMP (e.g., in September 2004 they administered a questionnaire to all FOHVAMP members to get feedback about future directions the group might take). Each semester Howard Morton and other FOHVAMP members speak in criminology courses at the University of Colorado, helping educate students about the experiences of crime victims. The unique insights that students gain are very different from the type of knowledge available in textbooks.

Conclusion

We believe that the students get much more out of their work with FOHVAMP than they are able to give to that organization in return. The vast majority of the students enrolled in the class indicated that it was the best class they had taken in their undergraduate careers, and the students who have followed up through independent studies or noncredit volunteer work voice widespread agreement. Many students report being deeply moved by hearing the stories of the families, and most leave the experience with a new and lifelong commitment to working with victim-related issues.

Through this experiences we have come to perceive the death penalty as being akin to winning a lottery. The best way to help one poor person might be to give that person $1 million, but if the goal is to help poor people *as a group*, the funds would do more good for more people if they were more equitably distributed. The cost of the death penalty is astronomical: a typical capital case costs several times more than a prosecution seeking and resulting in a sentence of life imprisonment, with estimates in the neighborhood of at least two to three million dollars per execution.[7] Considering that less than one percent of murders in the United States result in a sentence of death for the perpetrator(s) and most of those sentenced to death are never executed (Liptak 2004), at best only a miniscule proportion of families of homicide victims are ever able to find out if the execution of the offender actually brings them any long-lasting relief.

This chapter focuses on an alternative way of using resources that, we believe, better addresses the needs of families of homicide victims as a whole. We believe that one of the best ways to help such families is to strengthen efforts made to find the person responsible for causing the death of their loved one.

---

7. For more information, see the "costs" section of the website of Death Penalty Information Center (2004).

This goal can be achieved only if we allocate more resources to the police, and better train individual police departments in ways to improve their communication with affected families. In our experience, the energy of students and the resources of universities are ideally situated to help achieve these goals.

References

Bureau of Justice Statistics. 2002. "Homicide Trends in the U.S.: Clearances." Available at http://www.ojp.usdoj.gov/bjs/homicide/cleared.htm (site visited 1 February 2005).

Colorado Bureau of Investigation. 2003a. "Crime in Colorado: Colorado 2003 Statewide Major Offenses." Available at http://cbi.state.co.us/dr/cic2k3/state_totals/statewide_offense.htm (site visited 1 February 2005).

Colorado Bureau of Investigation. 2003b. "Crime in Colorado: Colorado 2003 Statewide Major Offense Arrests." Available at http://cbi.state.co.us/dr/cic2k3/state_totals/statewide_offense_arrest.htm (site visited 1 February 2005).

Death Penalty Information Center. 2004. See www.deathpenaltyinfo.org (site visited 1 February 2005).

Federal Bureau of Investigation. 2003. "Crime in the U.S.: 2002" (Uniform Crime Reports). Washington, DC: U.S. Government Printing Office (also available at http://www.fbi.gov/ucr/cius_02/html/web/, site visited 1 February 2005).

FOHVAMP (Families of Homicide Victims and Missing Persons). 2004. See www.unresolvedhomicides.org (site visited 1 February 2005).

Goldberg, Michele. 2003. "The Closure Myth." Available at http://www.salon.com/news/feature/2003/01/21/closure/index_np.html (21 January 2003;site visited 1 February 2005).

Liptak, Adam. 2004. "Fewer Death Sentences Being Imposed in U.S." *New York Times*, 15 April 2004, 16.

Prejean, Helen. 1993. *Dead Man Walking*. New York: Random House.

Pulley, Bob. "Seminar Focuses on Ministry to Victims' Families." *Gainesville Sun*, 26 February 1994, 5D.

Radelet, Michael L. and Marian J. Borg. 2000. "The Changing Nature of Death Penalty Debates." *Annual Reviews of Sociology* 26:43–61.

Radelet, Michael L., Margaret Vandiver, and Felix Berardo. 1983. "Families, Prisons, and Death Row Inmates: The Human Impact of Structured Uncertainty." *Journal of Family Issues* 4:593–612.

Schlosser, Eric. 1997. "A Grief Like No Other." *Atlantic Monthly* 280 (September): 37–76.

Vandiver, Margaret. 2003. "The Impact of the Death Penalty on the Families of Homicide Victims and of Condemned Prisoners." Pp. 613–45 in *America's Experiment with Capital Punishment*, edited by James R. Acker, Robert Bohm, and Charles Lanier. Durham, NC: Carolina Academic Press.

Wellford, Charles and James Cronin. 2000. "Clearing Up Homicide Clearance Rates." *National Institute of Justice Journal* (April): 3–7. Available at http://ncjrs.org/pdf-files1/jr000243b.pdf (site visited 1 February 2005).

Wellford, Charles and James Cronin. 1999. "An Analysis of Variables Affecting the Clearance of Homicides: A Multistate Study." Unpublished manuscript available at http://www.jrsa.org/pubs/reports/Clearance_of_Homicide.html (site visited 1 February 2005).

CHAPTER 21

THE PROCESS OF HEALING AND THE TRIAL AS PRODUCT: INCOMPATIBILITY, COURTS, AND MURDER VICTIM FAMILY MEMBERS

Peter Loge[1]

In the fall of 1999 I was hired to direct an new organization that became The Justice Project and the related Campaign for Criminal Justice Reform and Criminal Justice Reform Education Fund. Those groups led the effort for the passage of an Innocence Protection Act[2] and helped advance criminal justice reform efforts in a number of states. It was in that capacity that I was asked to join a small group of scholars, victim advocates, and murder victim family members for a weekend at Skidmore College to discuss the impact of capital punishment on victim family members. Between my time at The Justice Project and my current work with advocacy groups around the country, I have spent the past half-dozen years working with murder victims' family members, the wrongfully convicted, activists, and academics.[3]

---

1. The author is a Senior Vice President at the public affairs and political consulting firm M+R Strategic Services and a Lecturer at The George Washington University. He would like to thank Marcus Trombetta of GWU for his invaluable assistance, and the editors for their commitment to the conference, the book, the authors, and most importantly to the subject.

2. Signed into law by President George W. Bush as part of the Justice For All Act of 2005. Public Law No: 108-405.

3. It is important to note that I oppose capital punishment. I believe that the end of intentionally taking the life of another outside of war or for reasons other than in self-de-

The capital punishment system in the United States is deeply flawed and often fails the victims' family members. In this chapter I speculate about why this may be, and make some policy recommendations that can help the criminal justice system do a better job of meeting the needs of victims and strengthening the system as a whole.

The Failing Capital Punishment System

Very few people think the justice system handles capital punishment well. Those who support the death penalty grow frustrated with what they see as undue focus on process, viewing it as "offender focused,"[4] and believe executions will bring "closure" to victim families (Justice For All 2004).[5] Those who oppose capital punishment are equally frustrated with the system. They claim the process disproportionately punishes those accused of killing white victims, insisting that verdicts have more to do with race and class than justice; and they note that more than two-thirds of all trials are reversed, the result being that 80 percent of individuals initially sentenced to death are either found innocent or given lesser sentences (National Coalition to Abolish the Death Penalty 2004).

---

fense is wrong. Apart from the morality of the ends, there is no way that we can construct a capital punishment system that is fair and doesn't execute the innocent; and efforts spent trying to "fix" the system, even if successful, would draw scarce resources from other critical needs, such as victim services, law enforcement, and courts. It is also important to note that I am not a victim family member, attorney, or full-time researcher. I'm a political consultant who works with a number of criminal justice reform and anti-death penalty groups.

4. The phrase "offender focused" is deeply troubling, but is commonly used by prosecutors and those in the victim community. The point of a trial, of course, is to determine if the defendant is in fact the "offender." The system isn't *offender* focused, it is *defender* focused. The law bends over backward to protect the defendant, because it's supposed to; that's how the system was designed. Giving more leeway to victims and others may be a good idea, and rights are certainly not a zero-sum game; a good system can protect and respect everyone.

5. The notion of "closure" for victims' families through punishment is rarely advanced by the families themselves. Leah Popp, whose niece Wendy was murdered in 1997, told a joint hearing of the New Mexico House and Senate Judiciary Committees, "We hear a lot about 'closure' and would like to comment briefly on that—there is [no such] thing. There are things that help, such as the capture of the murderer and conviction.... The event, the trial, the murderer and all of the memories remain but somehow become incorporated into our forever-changing lives" (Popp 2005). At the same hearing Pat Songer, whose son Jeffrey was murdered in 1983 said, "If and when Mr. Smith's [Derrik Smith, on death row in Florida for the crime] execution date comes, his death will not ease our pain nor will it honor our son. And it certainly will not make our world a safer and more just place" (2005).

A growing public understanding of these problems and others has led to a significant decline in death sentences over the past several years (Liptak 2004). Some death penalty supporters have given up completely and called for outright abolition of capital punishment (Editorial, *Arizona Republic* 2002).

Flaws in the justice process and death penalty rulings make victims' family members suffer the most. Those who "survive" homicide are often dragged by the prosecution into trials as props, put under the glare of the media, blamed as terrible parents (or siblings, or spouses) by defense attorneys and the public, and used by all sorts of interest groups to advance all sorts of claims. Just as family members lose a loved one, they can also lose their identity in becoming tools to advance others' agendas.

Unlike non-death penalty trials, capital trials are really two events: the guilt/innocence phase and the punishment phase. In addition to this extension of the process, all death penalties are subject to an automatic appeal, which drags it out even further. Studies demonstrate that many of those trials and appeals are flawed, leading to yet more appeals and more trials (Liebman 2002, 2000a).[6] Families must endure proceedings over years and through a series of iterations, forcing them to keep reliving the crime. Regardless of the outcome—guilt or innocence, prison sentence or death—the family is always punished.

While many attempts have been made to limit appeals and streamline the process, the system continues to fail. In some cases the attempted solutions make it worse—stricter *habeas* rules, for example, may actually increase the amount of time someone spends on death row rather than shorten it as the law intended (Liebman 2002, 2000b).

Victims' Experience of the Criminal Justice System

One success in the criminal justice system has been the official recognition of the role and importance of victims.[7] For example, thirty-two states have

---

6. These appeals are not, by and large, driven by minor technicalities. Instead, cases are appealed because the defense attorney slept, was drunk, had no idea what he or she was doing, was having an affair with the prosecutor, used racial epithets to describe his or her own client, and in one case apologized to the jury for representing the defendant. Prosecutors withhold evidence and lie, arbitrary rules prohibit some kinds of evidence, and countless other events that have real bearing on the outcome of the trial lead to most appeals. See, for example, Liebman 2002, 2000b; Center for Public Integrity 2003; Southern Center for Human Rights 2004.

7. This is true for murder victims' family members, and for victims of other violent crimes.

amendments to their constitutions, codifying the importance of victims (National Center for Victims of Crime 2004). But this success has not delivered all that victims want or need.

Murder victim family members don't start that way. They do not choose, and cannot prepare for, their role. They learn about the criminal justice system the same way the rest of us do: by watching television, talking to their friends, and trying to get out of jury duty. For most of us, most of the time, the criminal justice system is like the Olympics—we watch it when it's on TV, get caught up in the drama, and forget about it when the games are over. But when the non-negotiable moment of murder happens, families are suddenly in the system in irrevocable and complicated ways.

Following a murder, families get a forced, limited and incomplete crash course in the criminal justice system and what distinguishes its realities from television programs. During a capital trial there is no time to learn about the broader criminal justice system and the roles of the participants. Family members want explanation, comprehension, retribution, resolution, solace, and a host of other intangible, conflicting, and rapidly changing outcomes. That is not what the criminal justice system wants or provides. As Orth wrote, "If crime victims expect the criminal proceedings to be psychologically beneficial, this will often prove to be an illusion" (2002:323).

The justice system does not, and was not designed to, provide understanding. Defense attorneys and prosecutors want victories. Judges want to keep an orderly court that efficiently moves cases through the docket. Jurors just want to go home. Too often, victims turn into tools used by the other participants in the process; like fingerprints and witnesses, they are a tactic that can be employed and then put aside when no longer needed.

The courts are primarily interested in outcomes. Being a victim is a process that starts with loss and then lurches, with more or less success, toward understanding and healing.[8] Accurate and appropriate verdicts can happen, and

---

8. Gillis and Hart (2003:117) write, "As the events of September 11 so compellingly demonstrated, the impact of violent crime is not just physical or financial, it tears at the souls and psyches of its victims, co-victims, and society at large. The events of September 11 helped to advance the understanding of the spiritual and emotional struggles that attend incidents of mass violence, but many people are just beginning to acknowledge and understand the trauma and sense of tragedy and loss experienced by the thousands of women, men, and children who are violently victimized every day. Many victims, including survivors of prolonged, repeated trauma, such as abused children and battered women, need specialized mental health services to help them begin and continue the healing process. The consequences of domestic violence do not end when the victim leaves the abusive relationship. The impact of homicide does not abate with the killer's apprehension.

families of murder victims can achieve a level of emotional healing—but the two are not necessarily connected. This almost epistemic incompatibility inevitably leads to tension and frustration between the process of being a victim and the production of verdicts.

Popular Understanding of the Criminal Justice and Death Penalty Systems

Most of us, most of the time, have nothing to do with the criminal justice system—and like it that way. We try to avoid jury duty, don't think of a fun day out as sitting in the gallery at a trial, and we don't read legal journals. Law has its own private language to which we do not generally have access; and while we may want our children to go to law school, we disparage lawyers. One result of this detachment is that our understanding of the legal system tends to be informed by popular culture.

Television series, for example, often portray defense lawyers as either highly paid flacks for the clearly guilty, hardworking but naive and overwhelmed, or feel-good lefties more concerned with getting the bad guys off on technicalities than in finding true justice and punishing heartless criminals. Prosecutors, on the other hand, are often portrayed as dedicated public servants drawn to the field to avenge a wrong while fighting for justice. They eschew power and glory to promote the common good. If they break the rules, it is for the larger cause of achieving a just result.

But reality is a bit more complicated and nuanced than what we see on television. Fictitious (even "reality-based") TV series connect events and systems to people and stories—a family is wronged, the court intervenes, justice is sought, and a resolution for that family is found. In real life, the criminal justice system is set up to help society at large, not the individual. And rather than providing resolution, it is designed to provide verdicts that are in the aggregate fair and accurate.

Our familiarity with the steps involved in a trial is far more likely to come from popular television series like *Law & Order* and *CSI* than a text on criminal procedure (Carlson 1985).[9] The incompleteness of this understanding has

---

The trauma of sexual assault does not dissipate with the pronouncement of guilty. On the contrary, it has barely begun. With the help of mental health professionals, society is beginning to recognize that the treatment of psychological injury is as important as the binding of a wound or the setting of a broken bone."

9. For a more complete discussion of law and popular culture, see, for example, the *Journal of Criminal Justice and Popular Culture*.

a variety of consequences—on one hand there is the "*CSI* effect," in which juries are reluctant to convict accused criminals without complete and apparently foolproof DNA or other evidence (Rosinski and Weber 2004). On the other hand, there is also widespread support for assigned counsel and *Miranda* rights (Loge 2003; Wood 2001). Both sentiments are a staple of the legal system that we see on television cop shows. They are not, of course, a complete and accurate representation of what goes on in court.

The Justice System As Product Generator

The judicial system is set up to increase the chances of convicting the guilty while protecting the innocent in the aggregate. Because mistakes are often difficult to catch, and if caught are remedied many years after the trial, those responsible for the errors are rarely punished. Consequently there is little professional incentive to be accurate, while there is significant incentive to be productive. This is especially true in capital cases, which tend to be considerably longer and more complex than noncapital trials (Liebman 2002).

The error rate in death penalty trials is staggering; the most comprehensive study ever conducted on the subject found that 69 percent of capital convictions or sentences are vacated, with 80 percent of these reversals resulting in a sentence less than death and 7 percent resulting in complete exoneration (Liebman 2000a). One reason for this error rate is the delayed feedback mechanism: the time between making a mistake and finding that mistake can be years, sometimes decades. By the time the courts attempt to correct the mistake, it is unlikely the responsible parties will still be around to discipline: many will have left criminal trial work, and others will have left the practice of law entirely. There is simply no incentive to refrain from "over producing" death sentences (Liebman 2002).[10]

Another way to view the criminal justice system is as a series of "games." The game is played by teams, with the prosecution on one side and the defense on the other. In a contest of state vs. defendant, the judge is the referee, ruling what's a legitimate tactic or approach. An illegal motion by the defense attorney brings a reprimand and threat of a fine for contempt; illegal motion in the backfield results in a flag. The final score is determined by the jury, which only learns the rules at the start of the game and renders a verdict at the end.

---

10. The incentive structure is changing, but not because of better feedback or a change in the way the system works. Rather, the politics of the death penalty have changed and there is not as much political gain to be made by seeking death sentences (Liptak 2004).

A crime triggers each game. The game has a beginning with opening statements from both sides. There is a middle, during which the players take turns advancing their arguments and positions, and an end, in which each side wraps up its position. When they have finished their moves, the players wait for the jury to issue a verdict and determine a winner. Following the announcement, the players move on to the next game. Like good athletes, successful lawyers do not carry the last win or loss into the next game—they put it behind them and begin anew. Lawyers often play more than one game at a time, further decreasing their personal involvement in any one game.

In such an environment the players are motivated by the outcome of the game, not by any one play. It is not the particular crime, defendant, or victim that matters, but rather crimes, criminals, and victims in general. This is not to suggest that attorneys are heartless participants who view individual cases as chips to be accumulated. Being a defense attorney or prosecutor is difficult work that generally pays less, demands more, and requires longer hours than many other areas of law. To be successful, lawyers must focus on the big picture. Just as doctors concentrate on the practice of medicine rather than on the health of any one patient, lawyers give their attention to the practice of law rather than on the details of any one defendant, victim, or case.

Given the limitations of the legal system, it is fortunate that victim family members have access to other resources, many of which are better geared toward supporting them on a more personal level. Thanks to the victims' rights movement and the individual work of advocates—many of whom have written their stories in this volume—there are more and more support mechanisms in place for those who need it most. Unlike the legal system, however, these support elements have as their reason for existence the helping of those who need it. And unlike the criminal justice system, for which crime serves as the starting gun for a race to a verdict, those other support mechanisms are not designed to produce a "win" for anyone. The primary "product" offered by nonlegal resources—e.g., churches, therapists, social workers, and support groups—is aid and support during the never-complete process of healing.

Victims As Process

Courts and court participants deal with a lot of victims' families because they deal with a lot of crimes. Murder victim family members, mercifully, usually only have one crime. Their experience is unique and cannot be generalized. Capital lawyers have experience with the death penalty—courses and rules, cases and colleagues. For them a murder is often simply one murder in a line of many. Murder victims' families on the other hand have no experience on which to draw, no special training or preparation. Capital attorneys choose murder; victims families don't.[11]

Being a victim family member isn't about producing an outcome. There is no one point at which the rules say it's over and the next bit starts or everyone moves on to the next event. Victims' family members go through a process of learning to live, more or less, with their loss. They experience periods of anger, sadness, denial, confusion, resolution, acceptance, forgiveness, and a host of other emotions. These emotions do not happen in sequence; they repeat themselves in predictable and unpredictable ways and vary from crime to crime and person to person. Some family members find ways to forgive, others want to forget, others refuse to do either, most do all of those things and more. There is no point at which one stops being a murder victim family member. Being a murder victim family member is a process of continually becoming that which one is.

Just as the process varies so do participants and resources. Some victim family members turn to faith communities and church for understanding and comfort; others turn away, losing their belief in a divinity that would allow the killing to happen. Some turn to professional help, others do not. Some have the means to continue paying for home and education following the sudden loss of a breadwinner, while others must rely on the state, friends or other support. In the ongoing process of being a victim, individuals encounter a number of intersecting systems, only one of which administers the law. The legal system is only a stop on a longer journey, a hut along the trail.

The other areas of support (church, family, therapy, books, arts, advocacy) are also stops on the trail, but they are visited again and again; they are not laid out in a line. These other supports are designed to be visited by those who need the help, when the time is right. Over the course of a lifetime, family members can turn to and away from and back to, the church, for example, in the struggle to find meaning and understanding in their loss. Or, a survivor may seek professional counseling on and off for years.

Healing from the trauma of murder is about the process of living. Trials, on the other hand, are about concluding. As Herman writes, "The mental

---

11. This is obviously not always the case. There are victims who choose murder, there are multiple-victim murders, and families who lose more than one loved one to the same— or even different—crimes. Likewise there are attorneys, usually on the defense side, who have no experience with capital prosecutions. The death penalty can be as jarring to a specific system or jurisdiction in its own way as it is to a family. This lack of experience and ability to effectively deal with the death penalty is, for some opponents of the practice, a reason to abolish it.

health needs of crime victims are often diametrically opposed to the requirements of legal proceedings" (2003:159).

Good prosecutors, and there are a lot of them, work with the victim's family to talk about the crime and legal options. Among the most important topics of discussion between the prosecution and family is whether or not to seek a death sentence. Unfortunately, some prosecutors assume the family wants a death sentence, without asking. The consequences of this assumption can cause even more pain. As Leah Popp, whose niece was murdered in 1987, told a joint State House and Senate Judiciary Committee hearing in New Mexico, "We [Leah and her husband] had always been ambivalent about the death penalty prior to our niece's murder. During preparation for the trial, the District Attorney explained to us apologetically why Wendy's case didn't qualify for the death penalty, and to our surprise we felt a tremendous sense of relief. At another time the D.A. suggested that a man as small as the murderer wouldn't last long in prison. This was seemingly said as a consolation of sorts. Instead, we found it truly painful. The thought of the loss of another life over this tragedy was just too much to bear" (2005).[12]

Once a decision is made, regardless of what the family wants, a murder trial stops being about the victim and becomes the property of the prosecutor. If a death sentence is sought, the rules of the law "game" take over. There is the appointment of attorneys, jury selection, the guilt trial, the punishment trial, the legally mandated appeal, and potentially other appeals. These events do not happen when it is convenient, easy, or desired by the victim's family. A trial proceeds whether they want it to or not. Further, if a survivor changes his or her mind about seeking the death penalty, there is little to be done. The game has begun and can only end with a final verdict; it will not end sometime during the second half because the person who started the game decided it ought not to be played. A trial is not something victims' family members visit on a journey as they feel the need; a trial visits a family, whether they want it to or not.

Intersection and Consequences

The criminal justice system and the process of learning to live as a murder victim family member inevitably intersect. All victims have questions and concerns they want the courts to address. Thanks to the work of advocates over the past several decades, many of those needs are being met. Still, unfortu-

---

12. See also Cushing and Sheffer 2002.

nately, many needs remain. Not all victims know their rights, too many families are left without financial support, victim reparation funds do not always go to victims, too many victims are not led through the process as participants (instead being tossed in as prosecutorial tactic), too many defense lawyers try to use or abuse victims, and ultimately too few victims create the needed space to heal.[13]

While prosecutors and victims' families clearly have a shared interest in the trial, there is a differentiation to be made: A family wants the person who committed the heinous act to be punished, and the prosecutor wants to ensure that the person *arrested* for the crime is punished. This seemingly minor distinction is further evidence of the delineation between the process nature of being a victim's family member and the product nature of the justice system (even here needs can vary; see Orth 2002).

The former is about removing the guilty from being a threat. The latter is about securing the win, which may well mean the guy in cuffs gets a verdict of death regardless of guilt or the level of culpability. The incentive system, the rules of the game, don't allow for anything else. Wins, not justice, are rewarded. Prosecutors are prohibited from saying, "We think this is the killer, but aren't positive," nor are they allowed to change their minds and tell the jury, "Sorry, wrong guy, come back next week and we'll try again." Defense attorneys are punished for telling a jury their clients are guilty and should hang—indeed, such an action would not only void the game being played (in the form of a mistrial) but ensure the game would be played again with a more willing team and the offending attorney would be barred from the sport. At no time are the defense, prosecution, and judge allowed to confer about what they think *really* happened. The logic and process of law also attract professionals who are competitive; even if compromise was acceptable partway through a trial, it is unlikely that lawyers for both sides would do it. People are drawn to law in part because they like to win, and winning is rewarded. The crime is the reason to compete. The only hope is that equal adversaries will do a good enough job of presenting their sides that the jury makes the right call.[14]

---

13. See, for example, State Bar of New Mexico Task Force 2004 for a discussion of this problem, and Garcia 2005 for the personal impact this conflation can have.

14. Some might assert that prosecutors know exactly what they are doing and in fact exploit crushing pain for their own shallow political gain. I am unwilling to make this accusation. The prosecutor's job is to win and lock up the bad guy, the victim wants to heal and lock up the bad guy. That's enough of an incentive for each to reach out to the other. No prosecutor wants to send an innocent person to death, and no defense attorney wants

Because of their initial shared interest, victims' family members and prosecutors find each other. One result of this intersection of victim advocacy and prosecutorial enlightened self-interest has been the integration of victim services with prosecutors' offices. This co-location (and funding stream, staffing, and so forth) further solidifies the ties between the two groups. And, because prosecutors' offices often have political clout, the fortunes of victims get tied to the fortunes of prosecutors. Prosecutors begin to speak for victims and their families. The relationship has become codified—victims are now part of the prosecutors' courtroom arsenal, one more tool in the guilt box.

This seemingly subtle and logical shift has profound consequences. It takes victims out of their own journey, and places them in the trial game. There are several implications resulting from a change in "ownership" of the murder. Once placed in the hands of the prosecutors, the crime belongs to the lawyers. In a sense, the family no longer owns their own tragedy, the state does.

One result is that the victim is transformed from an outsider searching for a variety of answers (spiritual, emotional, financial, and legal) to an integral part of an adversarial process. As a tool of the prosecution, a victim is positioned in opposition to the defense. The defense attorney, who might otherwise offer helpful insight into case, is perceived as playing for the other team and must be beaten. Healing and understanding take a back seat to winning. Someone interested in healing might talk to the defense team to try to understand why murderers act the way they do or why the attorney thinks it's important (or even acceptable) to defend this particular person. Once victims and defense counsel are placed on opposing teams, however, such conversations do not take place—it would be like joining the other side's huddle to gain a better understanding of the essence of football.

Another result is that victim family members are virtually prohibited from changing their minds. Having started the game playing for one team, it is nearly impossible to switch teams or take back the support for the prosecution and become a disinterested observer. Those who attempt such conversions face intense pressure and scrutiny from the criminal justice system, and often from the victim's community as a whole.

Inevitably the system will fail to meet the needs of the victim's loved ones. A "win" is not resolution or understanding. A verdict plays a role, but is not itself healing. Death penalty trials are long, complicated, messy, and emo-

---

to set loose a killer on the community. But the rules of the game prevent informed dissent. Most attorneys are good people trying to do the right thing, but once a trial gets going— once the indictments are handed down and the game has begun—it is nearly impossible to stop.

tionally difficult. The result is a tentative verdict that takes, on average, more than a decade to resolve.[15] Some scholars suggest that trials themselves constitute "secondary victimization" (Herman 2003; Orth 2002). Facing this frustration, some victims' family members lean in harder to the only place that seemed to offer help: prosecutors' offices and the courts. No one else, and no other organization, is saying "come here, we'll fix it."

Victims want answers and healing, which prosecutors promise, and so victims talk to prosecutors. Answers and healing aren't forthcoming; prosecutors say they can help only if a ban on victim impact statements is lifted, changes are made to *habeas* laws, restrictions are eased on admissibility of evidence, and other limitations are removed. Victims, in turn, lobby for removal of the barriers. Answers and healing still aren't forthcoming, so prosecutors say the problem is more barriers. Victims lobby more, and continue to be let down. The problem is that finding solace is a process, not a solution. Healing can never be found in a statute. The hope that healing is an event or a phrase is a false one—a "hollow victory" in the words of Queens District Attorney Richard Brown (Capital Defense Weekly 2002). Andrea Vigil, whose husband Carlos was murdered in 2000, told lawmakers in New Mexico, "Our system tries to tell murder victims' family members that once they get to the courtroom or the execution chamber they will be okay—that they will experience closure and that everything will be okay. But this is not necessarily true—it certainly wasn't for me" (2005).[16]

The criminal justice system *cannot* provide healing. It can only provide verdicts. Verdicts can be an important part of a journey, but they are not the journey itself.

Solutions

There's an old saying that the definition of insanity is repeating the same behavior and expecting a different result every time. If the above analysis is correct, an over-reliance on prosecutors to provide solutions is a dead end that takes the crime from the victim and gives it to lawyers, confuses process with product, and in the end leaves victims' families feeling abandoned.

---

15. Even after an execution, increasing questions of the reliability of the system can leave lingering doubt. Efforts to speed up the time between trial and execution not only slow the process, but also can lead to more mistakes and thus further decrease the reliability of the outcome (Liebman 2002).

16. The Vigil case was not a capital one, but the logic remains the same.

Below are several initial steps that can be taken to improve the quality of the process for murder victim family members; most come down to guarantees of independence.

Keep Victim Services Independent of Prosecutor's Offices

The first and most important step that can be taken—and is already, in a number of areas—is to remove victim services from prosecutors' offices. One effect of such a move is clear—victims' families are not part of the adversarial system and thus cannot be co-opted onto a "side." Their fortunes are not tied to the fortunes of prosecutors, but rather to their own specific and unique needs.

In addition, the separation helps ensure that victims are not punished for not cooperating with a prosecutor's wishes. The State Bar of New Mexico noted, for example, that there have been "instances ... in which survivors' views as to whether the death penalty was appropriate affected the services that they received from the prosecuting attorney's office" (2004:22). The report suggests, "The legal case, from the perspective of the prosecution or defense, should not dictate the approach of the survivor's advocate" (ibid). The only way to ensure that there is neither the perception nor the reality of prosecutors punishing families is to remove victim services from prosecutors' offices entirely.

Allow Victims' Family Members to Veto a Capital Sentence

One way to check the prosecutor's hijacking of the family members needs is to provide as much information as possible to the family in regard to proceeding with a capital trial—before the prosecutor's office has made a decision. Once a decision is made, a prosecutor's office ought not be allowed to override a victim's family's wishes to not seek death.

Prior to seeking a capital conviction a prosecutor should meet with the victim's family on neutral ground (out of the prosecutor's office) to discuss the sentencing options and probable outcomes. This conversation should include the number of capital cases over the past ten years that have led to death sentences, the capital reversal rate in the state over the past ten years (including the number of capital exonerations and average number of trials and appeals), and the average length of time between sentencing and execution in the state. The family should also be provided with the same information for other sentencing options, such as life without parole.

Two obvious objections to this arise. First, what if family members do not agree among themselves? And second, why not also let a family veto a decision *not* to seek death? In the first instance, the law ought to follow existing laws about family participation in estate and other similar decisions; or if the immediate family is split, the decision should fall to the prosecutor (or the decision should be to seek life in prison without parole). The second objection seems strong on the surface, but given that capital cases are profoundly stressful on prosecutors' offices,[17] and that capital cases are legally extremely difficult, it is not practical for the family to dictate if a prosecutor should extend his or her reach but rather only to limit it.

Remove Barriers between Victims and Other Participants in the Process

There are too many artificial barriers between victim family members and other participants in the process. In some jurisdictions, defense attorneys are prevented from speaking to victim family members. In many instances victim family members aren't fully informed about all the proceedings, and even when the law allows access and information, the law is often ignored in practice.[18] These obstacles isolate victims from the process, setting them up in an adversarial relationship to it. Family members want to know what's going on and why—the system should be set up to meet this most basic need. Family members cannot own the legal system or change the adversarial premise of the courts, but they can own the process. This adds a layer of bureaucracy and may slow down the criminal proceedings; but given all that is at stake, it seems a minor price to pay.

Offer Independent Explanations and Ongoing Counseling

An independent entity should invite prosecutors, defense attorneys, former jurors, and judges—none affiliated with the case at hand—to talk about

---

17. See, for example, Baicker 2001, who writes, "The trials are quite costly relative to county budgets, and the costs are borne primarily by increasing taxes. The results highlight the vulnerability of county budgets to fiscal shocks: each trial causes an increase in county spending of more than $2 million, implying an increase of more than $5 billion in both expenditures and revenues between 1982 and 1999." See also Washington Death Penalty Assistance Center 2004.

18. See for example, Garcia 2005.

the trial process, the roles of the participants, what to expect, and how the case will proceed. Such briefings will help victims' family members better understand the court proceedings, allow for informed interaction, and result in outcomes that are more satisfying to family members. Rather than going to the courts or lawyers, victims can make the courts come to them. Outside of the game, the players—judges, prosecutors, defense attorneys, even jurors who have previously served on capital trials—can discuss what happens in court and why. As Orth found, "secondary victimization can be reduced by offering victims more legal and psychological counseling during the criminal proceeding. Legal counseling issues address information about the course of the proceedings, about the victim's rights throughout the proceedings, about support available in case of threats by the perpetrator, and about confusing legal language" (2002:324).

Promote Joint Participation by Victim Family Members, Prosecutors, Defense Attorneys, Judges, and Legislators in Each Others' Meetings, Conferences, and Publications

A look at the programs for state, regional, and national meetings of various legal organizations rarely turns up mention of victims. Their presence is also absent from conferences and professional publications addressing issues related to capital punishment. Including victims' family members in these settings would result in a better understanding of their unique needs. Lawyers, judges, and advocates would have a richer understanding of how the trial affects those directly hurt by the crime. It would also help loosen the grip too many prosecutors have on victims by making victim families part of every element of the trial.

Keep Internet Sites Independent

Just as some prosecutors claim to speak for all victim family members, many pro-death penalty web pages devote tremendous resources to victims. They provide links to victim services, advocating for victim rights and otherwise purporting to speak for victims. For example, ProDeathPenalty.com named Virginians United Against Crime (www.vuac.org)[19] as their "featured

---

19. See Stanley and Phyllis Rosenbluth, this volume.

site" in March 2005. These sites are often accessed by those hoping to learn about the logistics of the law, the public policy arguments around capital punishment, and what it means to be a murder victim family member. By purporting to speak for all victims, these web sites give the mistaken impression that all victims want and will benefit from a death penalty trial. As this chapter demonstrates, neither the process nor the product of capital cases is in the best interest of all victims—and critically, the assertion that an execution will lead to healing can actually further damage families.

Similarly, VUAC's site says the organization's goal is "To provide a support system for crime victims and the loved ones of homicide victims as they struggle to cope with the emotional and spiritual devastation which accompanies victimization" and later, "Our organization believes that the death penalty should be available as a punishment for aggravated homicides." Conversely, with the exception of Murder Victims Families for Reconciliation (www.mvfr.org) and the newer Murder Victims Families for Human Rights (www.murdervictimsfamilies.org), few anti-death penalty or pro-reform sites list any victim support services By conflating healing with trials, pro-death penalty support sites further entrench the connections between prosecutors and victims' family members. While many families want the accused to be executed, many do not, and by asserting universality of opinion these sites may actually impede the healing journey of those they are attempting to help.

This is not to suggest that victims' family members ought not work for the extension or abolition of capital punishment—they should, a rich and informed discourse is critical to the functioning of our democratic system. But they ought not confuse healing with law, and ought not perpetuate that confusion among those who want to learn about both.

Use Helping Victims As the Premise for Action, Not the By-Product

Michelle Geiger, a member of the national Board of Directors of Murder Victims Families for Reconciliation, told New Mexico legislators, "We don't need false hopes about closure—we need crisis intervention and assistance with crime scene cleanup. We don't need revenge—we need grief counseling, so we can begin healing and rebuilding our lives. We don't [need] years of protracted trials and hearings and court appearances—we need financial assistance so we can cope with the sudden loss of income and funeral expenses that follow a murder" (2005).

As discussed above, one outcome of co-locating victim services in prosecutors' offices is that victims' needs are determined by prosecutors' needs.

Prosecutors and victims do share some needs—but not all. Creating independent victim offices will help steer scarce resources to victims' families first; the needs of the families will help determine when (and if) to bring in capital prosecutors, not the reverse.

Conclusion

These steps are by no means comprehensive (indeed, many of the ideas offered in this chapter as well as many others have been or already are being adopted by various jurisdictions). They are meant to provide a starting point, a different way of conceptualizing the role of murder victims' family members in capital cases. The new conceptualization is one that respects the victim while seeking justice, and it does not conflate the two needs.

Neither are these proposed reforms uncontroversial. Those with the most at stake, particularly prosecutors whose offices frequently house victims' services or who otherwise have a legal or suasive monopoly on access to victim family members, might be expected to argue the hardest against them. One can imagine two lines of opposition: first, that victims are best served by prosecutors, and second, that implementing such reforms will result in cuts to funding. Both arguments serve to advance my position. Victims are not best served by prosecutors because prosecutors and victims want different things. For the prosecutor, the trial is the point; for the victim, the trial is one step on a very long journey. And, as noted throughout this chapter, such close alignment with prosecutors actually cuts off victims' access to healing and understanding. Similarly, if prosecutors want to defend their funding by holding up victims, it is obviously not the victim the prosecutor wants to protect.

No law, no punishment, no support structure, no political campaign or public relations effort can ever give families what they want and need most. Nothing can turn back the clock and offer time for a final moment of warning before a crime is committed. There is no closure, no rewind or cap on the past. There is only trying to live today and tomorrow. The question for advocates and policymakers is how to best achieve the related but separate goals of healing and justice.

The one non-negotiable moment of murder starts a long and painful journey, one part of which is a trial. In an effort to be heard and respected in the process, and to make some sense of what's happening, many victims have turned to the criminal justice system for solutions. Unfortunately, that system, and in particular the over-reliance on prosecutors' offices too often lets victims' families down. The solution is not greater investment in prosecutors but rather less. Victims need to help create and increase community-based programs that bring advocates from all sides to them. Only by controlling and owning their journey can victims hope to heal.

References

Baicker, Kathleen. 2001. "The Budgetary Repercussions of Capital Convictions." National Bureau of Economic Research. Available at www.azdeathpenalty.org/BaickerCapital.pdf.

Capital Defense Weekly. 2002. "Other Resources." Available at http://capitaldefense-weekly.com/archives/021223.htm.

Carlson, James M. 1985. *Prime Time Law Enforcement*. New York: Praeger.

Center for Public Integrity. 2003. *Harmful Errors: Investigating America's Local Prosecutors*. Special report (26 June 2003). Available at http://www.publicintegrity.org/pm/default.aspx?sID=main.

Cushing, Renny and Susannah Sheffer. 2002. *Dignity Denied: The Experience of Murder Victims' Family Members Who Oppose the Death Penalty*. Cambridge, MA: Murder Victims' Families for Reconciliation.

Death Penalty Information Center. "Innocence." 12 October 2004. Available at http://www.deathpenaltyinfo.org/article.php?did=412&scid=6).

Editorial. 2002. "Call for Abolition" *Arizona Republic*, 28 July 2002.

Garcia, Rachel. 2005. "Don't Kill the Killers." *Albuquerque Tribune*, 15 March 2003. Available at www.abqtrib.com/albq/op_commentaries/article/0,2565,ALBQ_19866_3622816,00.html.

Geiger, Michelle. 2005. Prepared testimony before the New Mexico House and Senate Judiciary Committees, 23 February 2005.

Gillis, John W. and Sarah V. Hart. 2003. "Guest Editorial: A Message from the Directors of the Office for Victims of Crime and the National Institute of Justice." *Journal of Traumatic Stress* 16:117.

Herman, Judith Lewis. 2003. "The Mental Health of Crime Victims: Impact of Legal Intervention." *Journal of Traumatic Stress* 16:159–66.

Journal of Criminal Justice and Popular Culture, School of Criminal Justice, University at Albany. Available at http://www.albany.edu/scj/jcjpc/.

Justice For All. 13 October 2004. See www.prodeathpenalty.com.

Liebman, James. 2002. *A Broken System II: Why There Is So Much In Capital Cases and What Can Be Done About It*. Available at http://ccjr.policy.net/proactive/newsroom/release.vtml?id=26641

———. 2000a. *A Broken System: Error Rates in Capital Cases 1973–1995*. Available at http://ccjr.policy.net/proactive/newsroom/release.vtml?id=18200.

———. 2000b. "Overproduction of Death." *Columbia Law Review*: 100: 2030–2157.

Liptak, Adam. 2004. "Fewer Death Sentences Being Imposed in U.S." *New York Times*, 15 September 2004, p. 16.

Loge, Peter. 2003. "We Support Gideon Because It Is Fair." *The Champion*. January/February 2003, p. 47.

Murder Victim Families for Reconciliation. 2002. *Dignity Denied*. See www.mvfr.org.

National Center for Victims of Crime. 2004. See http://www.ncvc.org/ncvc/Main.aspx.

National Coalition to Abolish the Death Penalty. 13 October 2004. See www.ncadp.org.

Orth, Uli. 2002. "Secondary Victimization of Crime Victims by Criminal Proceedings." *Social Justice Research* 15:313–25.

Popp, Leah. 2005. Prepared testimony before the New Mexico House and Senate Judiciary Committees, 23 February 2005.

Rosinski, Jennifer and David Weber. 2004. "DAs: 'CSI' Effect Spoiling Jurors." *Boston Herald*, 12 November 2004, p. 2.

Songer, Pat. 2005. Prepared testimony before the New Mexico House and Senate Judiciary Committees, 23 February 2005.

Southern Center for Human Rights. 13 October 2004. See www.schr.org.

State Bar of New Mexico Task Force to Study the Administration of the Death Penalty in New Mexico Final Report. 23 January 2004.

Vigil, Andrea. 2005. Prepared testimony before the New Mexico House and Senate Judiciary Committees, 23 February 2005.

Virginians United Against Crime. 13 October 2004. See http://www.vuac.org/capital.

Washington Death Penalty Assistance Center. 2004. "Washington's Death Penalty System: A Review of the Costs, Length and Results of Capital Trials in Washington State."

Wood, Jennifer K. 2001. "The Rhetorical Transformation of *Miranda v. Arizona*." *Qualitative Research Reports in Communication* 48:42–48.

CHAPTER 22

THE IMPACT OF THE DEATH PENALTY ON CRIME VICTIMS AND THOSE WHO SERVE THEM

Carroll Ann Ellis, Karin Ho
and Anne Seymour

Introduction

In the field of crime victims' rights and services, few issues are more controversial and divisive than capital punishment. The death penalty raises volatile issues that evoke passion and perseverance based upon religious, cultural, political, ethical, and moral beliefs. Yet the death penalty is highly *personal* for co-victims—the surviving family members and loved ones of homicide victims.

This chapter will examine the death penalty from the perspective of co-victims and victim service providers, who journey together through the often long and always painful journey of capital cases. For co-victims of crime, their feelings about the crime itself, the efficacy of capital punishment, and the lengthy process involved in capital cases combine to form individual responses that are extremely varied, complex, and highly personal. For victim service providers, many of whom are called to advocate for victims and provide support throughout the capital punishment process, these cases can be extremely challenging, difficult, and frustrating, and sometimes lead to vicarious trauma that is a direct result of feeling the co-victims' chronic pain and anguish. For victim service providers, the nature and impact of capital crimes also become highly personal. Similar to our societal conflict, there is little consensus about feelings surrounding the death penalty among victim service providers. The *only* consensus emerges within the context of the response to crime victims, which must attempt to *identify and address their most salient needs.* The needs of co-victims are often varied based upon a multitude of issues that this chapter addresses. Responses must therefore be tailored to meet those needs, and victim service providers must be prepared to address any issues that arise due to co-victims' potentially conflicting feelings about the death penalty and the criminal justice process.

What is clear about the role of victim service providers is just how vital their responsibilities and services are to co-victims in capital cases. This role requires an ethical commitment to serve the co-victims in a manner that is sensitive and supportive, and that respects their diverse feelings. At times, this commitment may require victim service providers to put aside their personal feelings about the death penalty (or, when they cannot effectively fulfill this role because of personal or moral conflicts, refrain from taking on such cases). It is critical that the case and related services have *little* to do with the victim advocate and *everything* to do with the co-victims as well as the deceased victim, whom the victim service provider will get to know in a very personal way through the surviving family members.

At the first national conference addressing the impact of the death penalty on victims' families, conducted in September 2003 in Saratoga Springs, New York, we gathered a group of family members to discuss their experiences. We draw on that discussion to present select perspectives of the participants.

Shane Wagner, whose father Dale was murdered during the 1997 robbery of his pawnshop (see Wagner, this volume), observed, "This is a delicate research area that we are embarking upon." Bud Welch, whose daughter Julie was killed in the bombing of the Murrah Federal Building in Oklahoma City in 1995, noted, "There are a number of inequities about the death penalty." Elizabeth Scholz, director of the Illinois Attorney General's Crime Victim Services Division, echoed the sentiments of several family members when she said, "If we care about this issue, we need to be concerned about the legal status of victims...." All of the co-victim and service provider discussants recognized the pioneering nature of their on-record discussion; the potentially volatile nature of discussion about the death penalty among parties whose opinions vary considerably; and finally, that regardless of their personal feelings about the death penalty, co-victims need and deserve rights and services throughout the extended legal process and beyond.

The Homicide Differential

We have come to recognize that family members and others who had special ties of kinship with murder victims experience a complex range of reactions to the deplorable act of homicide. While the term "survivor" describes the role that family and friends enter following the murder of a loved one, the term generally used to reflect the level and intensity of their reactions is "co-victims" of homicide (Ellis and Lord 2002). These reactions include shock, trauma, denial, disbelief, and anger at the sudden, unexpected, and devastating loss. For homicide co-victims who do not receive support or mental health counseling, these reactions do not go away and often intensify over time.

In order to understand the breadth and depth of criminal homicide, it is necessary to recognize that 1) homicide differs from other types of death; and 2) cultural attitudes toward death and spirituality influence societal perceptions of homicide. These special qualities represent the "homicide differential." Just as there are unique physical, mental, emotional, social, and financial components to every sudden death, there are spiritual ramifications as well. Individuals who have never thought much about God before will often do so after a loved one has died under traumatic circumstances. Even persons of faith, who assume that what happens to them is "God's will," are forced to reshape their faith positions to incorporate the fact that bad things do indeed happen to good people (Lord 1996).

Specific elements of criminal homicide distinguish the impact of such deaths upon the surviving family members from other forms of dying. They include:

The Intent to Harm

One of the most important factors distinguishing death caused by criminal means from other forms of dying is the *intent* of the murderer to harm the victim. Co-victims must deal with the anger, rage, and violence that have been inflicted upon someone they love.

Stigmatization

Society sometimes places blame on murder victims for their own death, which imputes blame to the victim's family when it is believed that they should have helped control behavior that led to the death. As a result, homicide co-victims often feel ashamed, vulnerable, powerless, and abandoned (Redmond 1989).

Media and Public View

Co-victims are quickly thrust into public view, and media stories involving them become fair game for public consumption. While some journalists exercise consideration and objectivity in their reporting of homicide cases, the degree of intrusion into the lives of co-victims constitutes a major difference between criminal homicide and deaths resulting from accidents or other causes.

Criminal Justice System

Unlike family members of individuals who die natural deaths, co-victims of homicide are thrust into a complex system of legal players and jargon. Co-victims must quickly become acquainted with a world of crime scenes, evidence, and autopsies. They have much to learn about the investigative, prosecutorial, and judiciary branches of the criminal or juvenile justice system in a very short time and are often expected to quickly comprehend a system that in some instances may be insensitive and specifically designed to protect the rights of the accused, with little regard for the victim.

Bereavement

As early as 1983, Dr. E. K. Rynearson determined that intense bereavement after homicide is so prevalent that it deserves clinical attention. His clinical studies revealed that the psychological reactions of the family members of murder victims differed significantly from previously experienced forms of bereavement following the natural death of a relative. Rynearson's research forms the basis of the shift from viewing co-victims' grief issues separately from the impact of trauma associated with the death of a family member (Ellis and Lord 2002).

Traumatic Grief

Traumatic grief following a homicide is distinctive from other forms of grief because of the problematic overlap of symptoms created by the co-victims' inability to move through the grief process, owing to a preoccupation with the trauma itself. Homicidal deaths are sudden, unexplainable, unjust, involve violence, and therefore inflict trauma. Co-victims struggle with two distinct processes: 1) the grief associated with the loss of a loved one; and 2) the wounding of the spirit created by the trauma. Both processes impose a tremendous psychological burden.

In capital murder cases, the homicide differential can be exacerbated by issues related to personal feelings about the death penalty. Co-victims often feel that they must consider the deceased victim's feelings about the death penalty (if such feelings are known—if they are not, family members' perspectives of what those feelings were may differ), as well as their own feelings (which often differ among family members). Yet such considerations are not always accepted by courts. Sharon English, whose mother, Chloe, was murdered by a parolee she had met through a prison ministry, believes, "Most often, we never think about what the victim would want." However, English knew that her mother opposed the death penalty. She observed, "We wouldn't want to put doubt in the jury's mind about what the victim wants."

The relationship between the murder victim and the alleged or convicted perpetrator can raise additional vexing issues. Many capital cases involve victims and offenders who are related to each other by birth, marriage, partnership, and/or friendship, which inspires additional personal, moral, and interfamilial conflicts about death as the ultimate penalty. Ellen Halbert, director of victim/witness services for the Travis County, Texas, district attorney, believes that, "It's very important how victims feel about it—those victims who support [the death penalty], and those victims who oppose [it]." The co-victims' perspective should *always* be presented to the prosecutor and court."

Bud Welch said simply, "When your child dies, you bury them in your heart." In addressing the long-term impact of homicide, Renny Cushing, executive director of Murder Victims Families for Human Rights, whose father, Robert, was murdered in 1988, said, "It affects us forever. My dad is always going to be dead."

Because of their experiences with criminal homicide and their collective wisdom, co-victims of homicide have much to teach us about the impact of the death penalty, but they are not always called on to share their viewpoints. Co-victims invariably become caught up in the dynamics of the issue. The death penalty—whether imposed or not—is a major component of the co-victims' acquired culture, a culture so clearly defined that it has its own logic, institutions, values, and language.

The Language of Trauma and Victimization

Victim trauma is not generally understood and frequently causes confusion for individuals who find themselves face-to-face with victims who are coping with trauma. Even family members and friends have difficulty comprehending the magnitude of the victim experience, and this situation sometimes compounds the victim's reaction to the traumatizing experience.

When individuals and communities frame trauma within their own perspectives—as they often do—and attempt to put traumatic grief on a timetable, the implicit pressures not only re-traumatize the victim, but also can have unfortunate policy implications as well. For example, employers might expect grieving employees to "get over it" and get back to work too quickly, within a few weeks. Insurance companies may only cover mental-health assistance and treatment for physical ailments associated with trauma for a limited time or fixed number of treatment sessions (e.g., ten).

The words used to offer "comfort" to victims often do the opposite. When terms such as "closure" and "forgiveness" and "healing" are brought up, many co-victims have strong, adverse visceral reactions because they view them as conveying implicit judgments or expectations about them. "Closure" falsely implies a finality that, for many co-victims, is just not possible because victimization produces life-altering changes. A mother of a man killed in the bombing of the Murrah Federal Building said simply, "You close on a house; you don't close on your son's life." Phyllis Rosenbluth's (see this volume) son Richard and daughter-in-law Becky were murdered in 1993, and their murderer subsequently was executed. She says, "I don't know why the powers that be have come up with the word 'closure.' There is no closure, and there never, never will be. You have 'acceptance,' which should be substituted for the word 'closure.'"

The concept of forgiveness is highly personal, and it seldom addresses the concurrent issues of offender accountability and earned redemption. Forgiveness should never be encouraged nor expected from co-victims, because it is a personal decision based on one's values, mores, and spirituality—in other words, it is nobody else's business. To pressure someone in any way to forgive illustrates the expectations of the person applying the pressure, not the victim's perspective and values. And when co-victims do not feel "healed" long after the crime has occurred, others' expectations of "healing" can make them feel like failures. Renny Cushing notes that "closure and forgiveness impose a further burden upon the victim." Roberta Roper (see this volume), whose daughter Stephanie was raped and murdered in Maryland in 1982, says simply, "There will be closure when *my* casket is closed."

Victim Advocacy and Services in Capital Cases: A Historical Overview

Although the field of victim services began in 1972 in the United States, not until the late 1980s did the important discipline of "corrections-based victim services" emerge, which recognized that victims and survivors have myriad needs in the post-sentencing phases of their cases. The unique and diverse needs of victims in capital cases became evident through the process of developing the initial policies and programs that addressed victims' rights and services, offender accountability, and related issues. The second curriculum text developed with support from the U.S. Department of Justice's Office for Victims of Crime, in 1991, included, for the first time, specific protocols for assisting victims through the death penalty process (Office for Victims of Crime 1991). Its recommendations included the implementation of victims' rights throughout the appellate process; identifying and respecting co-victims' wishes regarding executions and their possible attendance; and providing supportive services to co-victims before, during, and after executions—including crisis intervention, counseling, coping with the vigils outside prisons prior to and following executions, media advocacy, and ongoing family support. All these services require careful coordination among justice professionals and victim advocates from the prosecution, court, department of corrections, office of the attorney general, and office of the governor.

The authors and editors of this first protocol were somewhat overwhelmed by the magnitude of their task: addressing a highly controversial and divisive issue, strictly within the context of victims' rights, and providing quality victim services. The finished product provided the first simple, sensitive, and vital guidance to victim service providers about their role and responsibilities with respect to co-victims of death penalty crimes. Since then, protocols have been refined and improved, based upon years of experience. A training videotape developed by the Office of the Victim Advocate of the Commonwealth of Pennsylvania in 2000 now offers practical, step-by-step guidance to victim assistance and correctional professionals whose duties involve victim assistance in capital cases.

The Criminal Justice System and Capital Cases

Thirty-six states currently authorize capital punishment (at this writing, death penalty legislation in two other states—Kansas and New York—has recently been declared unconstitutional). It is important to note that the prosecution formally represents "the state" and, within this context, the interests of society and public safety when seeking the death penalty. From this perspective, "success" is often defined by securing a capital sentence. A core tenet of the victims' rights movement since its inception is to recognize that while the prosecution represents the state, the interests, needs, and concerns of victims have a rightful place within our system of justice. Nowhere is this principle more relevant than in death penalty cases, which are often complex and usually involve what many victims perceive to be endless appeals.

It is critical that the victim's and surviving family members' views on the death penalty are considered by the justice system. There have been prosecutions resulting in death sentences that the victims' families openly opposed.

Victims' families have even become witnesses for the defense throughout the appeals process in some cases, in an attempt to reverse what the prosecution had accomplished. Family members often feel revictimized when they are not included in the process. The criminal justice system also has an inherent responsibility—one that is not always articulated within state laws and codes—to inform and involve victims at every stage of the criminal justice process.

Crime victims' rights in capital cases involve the "traditional" justice agencies—law enforcement, prosecution, courts, and institutional corrections—but also involve the state attorney general and governor. A study conducted by the National Association of Attorneys General in July 2004 found that direct assistance to victims while cases are on appeal is provided by a designated victim assistance unit in twenty-seven states and, in eight states, by another unit within the office of the attorney general. Twenty-eight states provide victims' rights assistance through a designated unit, with seven offices providing victims' rights by another unit (Seymour and Derene 2004).

Most state governors have the authority to commute a death sentence through their clemency powers. Accompanying this executive power is a moral authority that should result in co-victims of a case being engaged in the decision-making process, and informed of its outcome. The frustration and anger of the co-victims in the cases involving the blanket commutation of the sentences of death-row inmates by Illinois Governor George Ryan in 2003—who were *not* engaged in any meaningful way in his ultimate decision—were an inevitable outcome because victims' needs and voices were neither addressed nor heard.

In addition, death penalty verdicts are subject to intense scrutiny by a series of higher courts, including the U.S. Supreme Court. As noted earlier, many victims express frustration with the "endless appeal" process, but even more so when they are not kept informed of and involved in key hearings and decisions. Coordination among the prosecutor, the original sentencing court, and higher courts is critical to ensure that victims' rights are implemented. Sharon English emphasizes the notification challenges that co-victims face:

> Few survivors of homicide victims understand the appeals process, and [survivors] are seldom routinely informed of the case status. Often, only self-initiated calls to the victim services coordinator may reveal the information. Years can go by before any action is taken on these cases, and often survivors learn about decisions about appeals through the media.

Six key rights are relevant to co-victims in capital cases:

Information and Notification

Co-victims in capital cases need basic information about their rights, what those rights mean, and how they can best exercise them. They need to be informed about the status of their case and any rights that allow them to attend and participate in key proceedings. They need to be made aware of the unique processes involved in capital cases and provided with guidance about their personal options and opportunities related to the cases. They need—at all times—to be kept apprised of the status and location of the accused or convicted offender. And they need to be informed about the outcome of their case and related activities, including the sentence, any appellate hearings, and the execution process itself.

Victim Compensation

All fifty states, the District of Columbia, the Virgin Islands, and Puerto Rico sponsor victim compensation programs that help remunerate victims for losses resulting from criminal victimization. In capital cases these losses include, but are not limited to, expenses related to funerals, crisis intervention, and counseling for co-victims, and financial support from the murder victim. Victims in capital cases—at all junctures of the criminal justice process—should be provided with information about and assistance in completing applications for victim compensation (a summary of state programs and application requirements can be found at www.nacvcb.org).

Victim Protection

Even in murder cases, where the victim is deceased, surviving family members sometimes are threatened, intimidated, or harassed—by the alleged or convicted offender, his or her colleagues, and even by people who oppose the death penalty. Co-victims should *always* be asked if they have any concerns about their safety or security, no matter how minor or insignificant they might seem. Victim advocates and justice professionals can assist co-victims by helping secure protective orders, helping them develop safety plans, and validating their concerns.

Victim Participation

From the time of an alleged offender's arrest through the execution, victims should be provided the opportunity to attend and participate in all hearings at which the alleged or convicted offender has such rights. For many co-victims, the process of seeking justice honors the memory of their loved one, and they feel it is the one thing they must do to stand up for the rights of a victim who can no longer stand up for his or her own rights. Yet as Roberta Roper explains, "While victims' concerns *should* be relevant and *should* be considered, victim involvement is going to be limited at best. It isn't within our control." (This volume.)

It is very important that criminal justice agencies involved in the post-conviction process include opportunities for the victims' families to participate, if they want. Throughout the judicial appeals and governor's clemency process, families should be informed and kept up to date. One creative approach that Ohio has taken to welcome victims' families into the process is to periodically conduct post-conviction death penalty symposia for anyone interested. Families as well as victim advocates have participated in these day-long events, discussing literally every aspect of the process. Topics include state and federal appeals; the role of defense attorneys; what life is like on death row; experiences of survivors whose offenders have been executed; the role of victim advocates; the parole board's and governor's office's role in clemency; and the execution process and related victims' rights. Families have reported feeling more connected to the process following their participation in such symposia and not being afraid or reluctant to ask questions in the future.

Informational services of this nature make it much easier for families to understand what is happening when they confront an execution date in their cases. With the advance and ongoing provision of information, family members gain a deeper appreciation of their rights and options and can make more meaningful decisions about them.

Victim advocacy throughout the execution process is usually handled by a corrections-based victim services office. These advocates understand the process and, in some states, are considered an extended member of the execution team. Their role is to ensure that the needs of the victims' families are identified and met to the extent possible, given legislative and policy constraints. Whether or not surviving family members support the death penalty or want to actually witness the execution, victim advocacy must adapt to each individual family and its respective members. In addition, special considerations are required when the victim's family and the offender's family are one and the same. Being adaptive and allowing each family member to identify his or her needs become even more critical in such cases.

Services to family members should span the entire process, including follow-up after an execution occurs. While they no longer require notification or information about the offender, co-victims might need emotional support and referrals to community-based agencies for needs as they develop.

It is also critical that victim advocates involved in capital cases be given specialized training and opportunities to debrief. Death penalty cases are very different from other cases. As such, they require additional training and considerations for the advocates' personal well-being.

Victim Impact Statements

Issues involving a co-victim's right to submit a victim impact statement in capital cases have been reviewed three times by the U.S. Supreme Court. In the first two cases (*Booth v. Maryland* in 1982 and *South Carolina v. Gathers* in 1989), the high court disallowed the use of victim impact statements in the sentencing phase of capital trials. However, in *Payne v. Tennessee* (1991), the Supreme Court overruled *Booth* and *Gathers*, and held that victim impact statements are admissible in capital sentencing proceedings (see Logan, this volume).

The victim impact statement provides an opportunity for co-victims to tell the sentencing jury about how the crime affected them physically, emotionally, financially, and spiritually, and to reflect on the ultimate loss they have endured as a result of a heinous crime. The victim impact statement validates the voice of the victim as an essential element of justice, and allows co-victims to pay homage to their murdered family member one final time within our system of justice. As Tina Chery, whose 15-year old son Louis D. Brown was murdered in 1993, explains, "The victim survivor needs to know that [his or her] input is going to really be heard, applied and taken seriously."

Despite the high court decisions, some states still preclude victim impact statements in capital cases. This is a public policy issue that requires further attention from *all* key participants in death penalty cases.

Victim Information and Referrals

Co-victims may have a number of issues and concerns related to their physical, emotional, financial, and spiritual needs in the aftermath of a capital crime. Victim assistance programs that can help identify and meet the needs of victims exist in nearly every jurisdiction. Criminal justice system-based programs provide victims with information, notification about the status of their cases, and advocacy throughout the justice process to promote greater understanding and meaningful involvement. Community-based programs—such as those offered by the National Organization of Parents of Murdered Children—sponsor homicide support groups for co-victims, and generate public awareness about the devastating impact of murder in American society.

Other Critical Needs

If a capital case results in a change of venue, a burden is placed on co-victims in terms of costs, time, and victim assistance resources. Efforts should be made to coordinate services between the two jurisdictions, as well as to provide remuneration to victims for out-of-pocket expenses related to attending hearings and the trial. Three examples of remarkable coordination efforts include:

1) When the venue of the trial of Timothy McVeigh for the 1995 Oklahoma City bombing of the Murrah Federal Building was changed to Denver, a community-based group was established by Oklahoma and Colorado federal, state, and local victim service providers to offer support and services to victims in both jurisdictions. The goal of the Colorado/Oklahoma Resource Council was to minimize retraumatization of victims from Oklahoma City who had to leave home during the trial process. With strong support from the Denver community, victims were provided with shelter and food, counseling, media advocacy, and support through the conclusion of the trial.

2) The multiple trials of deadly snipers John Allen Muhammad and Lee Boyd Malvo in 2004 required coordination among jurisdictions in Maryland, Washington, D.C., and Virginia. Using lessons learned from the Oklahoma bombing case's change of venue, victim advocates acting with law enforcement, prosecutors, supporting agencies, the news media, and the communities of Virginia Beach and Chesapeake, Virginia, established a network to address the needs of victim survivors throughout trial preparation as well as the lengthy, grueling trials. The primary consideration and focus of the supporting cast of players were the provision of care, support, and service to victims during what a mother of one victim described as "the daily painful reminder of the evil, destructive legacy of the snipers."

3) Physical space limitations might prevent co-victims from personally witnessing executions in cases where an offender committed multiple murders. For example, in Ohio, Alton Coleman was known to have killed seven victims and received three death sentences in three different states. In order to honor each family involved, the department of corrections opted to permit witnesses to view the execution via closed-circuit television, as well as include families whose cases were held in abatement (i.e., held to be prosecuted if necessary at a later point, as certified by a prosecutor). Ohio was the first state to make

such accommodations by allowing a total of eighteen victims/witnesses, setting a precedent for other states.

Conclusion

The complexity, controversy, and conflict that surround most death penalty cases can have a profound impact on co-victims, our system of justice, and society as a whole. The many facets of capital cases *all* have the potential to contribute to increased trauma, frustration, and fear among co-victims.

This chapter has sought to describe the devastating impact of homicide on co-victims, how responses from others (including criminal justice officials) can increase or mitigate such trauma, and how the implementation of victims' rights and the provision of victim services can make a positive difference in victims' lives. In capital cases, the actual or direct victim is deceased, but the wake of tragedy and trauma can consume the co-victims left behind. A greater understanding of co-victims' needs and statutory rights can help ensure that an already painful process is aided by compassion, dignity, and recognition of their most salient concerns.

Homicide co-victim Cheryl Ward Kaiser of California eloquently noted that, "Victims remember two things: those who *help*, and those who *hurt*." This simple yet powerful statement should be the guiding theme behind the efforts of *all* who seek to help co-victims in the aftermath of a capital crime.

References

Booth v. Maryland. 1987. 482 U.S. 496.

Ellis, Carroll Ann and Janice H. Lord. 2002. "Homicide." In Office for Victims of Crime, *National Victim Assistance Academy* textbook. Washington, DC: Office for Victims of Crime, U.S. Department of Justice, available at http://purl.access. gpo.gov/GPO/LPS27722.

Lord, Janice Harris 1996. "American's Number One Killer: Vehicular Crashes." Pp. 25–39, in Kenneth J. Doka, ed., *Living With Grief After Sudden Loss: Suicide, Homicide, Accident, Heart Attack, Stroke*. Bristol, PA: Taylor & Francis.

Office for Victims of Crime. 1991. *Promising Practices and Strategies for Victims Services in Corrections*. Washington, DC: Office for Victims of Crime, U.S. Department of Justice.

Payne v. Tennessee. 1991. 501 U.S. 808.

Redmond, Lula M. 1989. *Surviving—When Someone You Loved Was Murdered: A Professional's Guide to Group Grief Therapy for Families and Friends of Murder Victims*. Clearwater, FL: Psychological Consultation and Education Services.

Seymour, Anne and Steve Derene. 2004. *National Survey of Attorneys General Offices: The Scope of Victim Services.* Washington, DC: National Association of Attorneys General.

South Carolina v. Gathers. 1989. 490 U.S. 805.

INDEX

Note: t = table, f = footnote